Reinventing Germany

German Political Development Since 1945

Anthony Glees

D0223582

BERG

Oxford · Washington, D.C.

First published in 1996 by
Berg
Editorial offices:
150 Cowley Road, Oxford, OX4 1JJ, UK
22883 Quicksilver Drive, Dulles, VA 20166, USA

Berg is an imprint of Oxford International Publishers Ltd.

Library of Congress Cataloging-in-Publication Data

A catalogue record for this book is available from the Library of Congress.

British Library Cataloguing-in-Publication Data

A catalogue record for this book is available from the British Library.

ISBN 1 85973 190 2 (Cloth)
1 85973 185 6 (Paper)

Typeset by JS Typesetting, Wellingborough, Northants.
Printed in the United Kingdom by WBC Book Manufacturers, Bridgend,
Mid Glamorgan.

This book has been written for Linda, and for Amy, Laurie and Geoffrey Glees.

Contents

Contents

Contents

Contents

Acknowledgements

The material has been arranged in ten chapters (plus an introduction and bibliography). It is based on primary and secondary sources, many of them written in German and published in the last ten years, as well as on formal interviews and conversations, sometimes in a seminar setting, with individuals whose assistance I record with gratitude:

Carlo Schmid, Lord Annan, Sir Frank Roberts, Peter Pulzer, A. J. Nicholls, Adolf Birke, Susanne Miller, Anneliese Poppinga, Fritz Heine, Marianne Heine, Nevil Johnson, Thomas Kielinger, Barbara Marshall, K. G. von Hase, Gerhard Hirschfeld, Kai-Uwe von Hassel, George Foggon, Clare Baines, Ludger Eling, Norman Reddaway, Carl Anders, Horst Ehmke, Ferdinand Friedensburg, Hans von Herwarth, Frau Clarita von Trott, Christabel Bielenberg, Hans Mommsen, Wolfgang Mommsen, Sir Alec Cairncross, Ian Turner, Professor Kurt Biedenkopf, Senator Peter Radunski, Willie Paterson, Giles Radice, Gordon Smith, Baroness Thatcher, Colin Munro, Alyson Bailes, Theda Ehmke, Rosemary Spencer, Sir Julian Bullard, Maureen MacGlashan, Air Cmdr Bob Martin, Sir Reg Hibbert, Dr Helmut Kohl, Lord Dahrendorf, Norman Reddaway, Richard von Weizsäcker, Geoffrey Denton, Connie Martin, Alan Watson, Reinhard Stuth, Ralf Bierett, Christoph Liedtke, Frau von Isenberg, Dr Renate Kremer, Thomas Habicht, Robert Lochner, David Rose, Richard Davy, Maxine and Pieter Vlieland, Gerhard Kunz, Sir Christopher Mallaby, Dr Peter Hartmann, Dr Klaus Kinkel, Andreas von Below, Bernhard Wilhelm, Hermann Kreutzer, Jorg Drieselmann, Dick de Mildt, Brigitte Seebacher-Brandt, Donald Cameron Watt, Cora and Werner Creutzfeldt, C. C. Schweitzer, Elke Berger, Jonathan Wright, Anne Deighton, Michael Hughes, Mathew Clayton, Guenter Gillessen, Gerhard Kunz, F.-W. Witt, Simon Kenyon and my German politics students at Brunel.

My thanks must also go to the following institutions who enabled my research to be undertaken with funding, or by providing an opportunity of discussing with others some of the material in this book:

The BBC: BBC Radio Four/Continuing Education and Gordon Hutchings for making some of these interviews possible (of which several were broadcast in the 'German Renascence' in 1989); St Antony's College, Oxford; the Deutsch-Englische Gesellschaft; the

Friedrich-Ebert, Konrad-Adenauer and Koerber Foundations; the Evangelische Akademie Loccum; the British Council; the German Academic Exchange Service; Inter Nationes; the Federal German Press Office; the German Embassy in London; the Anglo-German Foundation; the BBC's German Service; the Deutschland Radio, the Saarländischer Rundfunk, the Deutsche Welle and the Süddeutscher Rundfunk.

Special thanks to Berg's Editorial Director, Kathryn Earle, and to David Phelps.

Preface

Most books about German politics emphasize that they have now become predictable, reliable, Western and ordinary. This account seeks to explain how, and why, this happened. It suggests that what we may today regard as normal about Germany is actually quite remarkable, and abnormal, judged by the standards of German politics before 1945. We see that this was the product of a very particular reinvention of Germany after 1945.

This book also attempts to address the question whether German politics will continue to be like this, now that Germany, after fifty years, is once more a single nation. Its answer is unsettling and, perhaps, surprising. We shall see that what the new Germany will become will rely as much on the policies of other nations as on the German people themselves, who almost certainly still do not want the new role as the motor of European political change, now being created for them by contemporary realities. This book has been written to interest the general reader who wants to understand the new Germany and its place in Europe and in the world today, as well as students of German contemporary history, politics and literature.

Map 1

German Federal Election Results, 1949–94

Date	Votes (mi.)	Turnout (%)	CDU/CSU	SPD	FDP	Greens	PDS	REP	Others
14.8.49	31.2	78.5	31.0	29.2	11.9	–	–	–	27.8
6.9.53	33.2	85.8	45.2	28.8	9.5	–	–	–	16.4
15.9.57	35.4	87.8	50.2	31.8	7.7	–	–	–	10.3
17.9.61	37.4	87.7	45.3	36.2	12.8	–	–	–	5.7
19.9.65	38.5	86.8	47.6	39.3	9.5	–	–	–	3.6
28.9.69	38.6	86.7	46.1	42.7	5.8	–	–	–	5.5
19.11.72	41.4	91.1	44.9	45.8	8.4	–	–	–	0.9
3.10.76	42.0	90.7	48.6	42.6	7.9	–	–	–	0.9
5.10.80	43.2	88.6	44.5	42.9	10.6	1.5	–	–	0.5
6.3.83	44.0	89.1	48.8	38.2	7.0	5.6	–	–	0.5
25.1.87	45.3	84.3	44.3	37.0	9.1	8.3	–	–	1.4
2.12.90	60.4	77.8	43.8	33.5	11.0	5.1	2.4	2.1	2.1

of which

-old FRG	48.1	78.6	44.3	35.7	10.6	4.8	0.3	2.3	2.0
-old GDR	12.3	74.5	41.8	24.3	12.9	6.1	11.1	1.3	2.5
16.10.94	60.4	79.0	41.4	36.4	6.9	7.3	4.4	1.9	1.7

of which

-old FRG	48.4	80.5	42.1	37.5	7.7	7.9	1.0	2.0	1.9
-old GDR	11.9	72.6	38.5	31.5	3.5	4.3	19.8	1.3	1.2

(source: Federal German Press Office)

Key:

CDU	Christian Democratic Union (die Christlich Demokratische Union Deutschlands)
CSU	Christian Social Union (die Christlich-Soziale Union)
SPD	Social Democratic Party (die Sozialdemokratische Partei Deutschlands)
FDP	Free Democratic Party (die Freie Demokratische Partei)
Greens	(Die Grünen)
PDS	Party of Democratic Socialism (die Partei des Demokratischen Sozialismus)
Reps	Republicans (die Republikaner)

Introduction: Reinventing Germany

On 8 May 1945, at twenty-three hundred hours Central European Time, the German armed forces capitulated unconditionally to the British and American armies at Rheims in France, and to the Red Army at Karlshorst, outside Berlin. What happened to, and in, German politics in the western part of Germany after that – from capitulation to unity in 1990 and beyond – is the subject of this book.

It is obvious that in many senses, a history of German political development *up to and including* unity in 1990 has to be the history of a remarkable political, economic and social success. Out of Germany's material and moral destruction at the war's end in 1945, a German state was reinvented, based on part of the former German nation. Slowly, but surely, it won for itself a striking position in modern Europe and the world. Forty years after its formal inauguration, a deeply democratic West Germany had become so strong – economically, politically and internationally – that it could quite literally take over the other, undemocratic and Communist, East German state. This was an *Anschluss*, but unlike its precursor in 1938, it did not add to the power of a totalitarian Germany but increased the strength of a liberal one. Since unity, not least through its leader, Helmut Kohl, Germany has exuded a sense of confidence and purpose that has increased since unification with each passing year. We need only compare the present position of Germany with the rubble that was the Third Reich in 1945 to realize the extent to which major advances had taken place in the way the Germans practised their politics.

To provide an account of German political development during this period is, however, also to invite a different, if related, question about the *future* condition of German politics and Germany's place in the world. After 1945, a new kind of German state was reinvented in the West (*re*invented because, naturally enough, there was old alongside the new). But what, exactly, *had* been reinvented after 1945? What was new? What was old?

Now, following unification, Germany is once again the subject of reinvention. Reinventing itself, it should be added, is something of a German speciality, a veritable theme of continuity in German history if ever there was one. Once again, then, we are forced to ask what, precisely, *is* being reinvented? Will the reinvention of 1990 benefit Germany and the world? Or will it, like every other previous reinvention before 1945, end in disaster?

Germany has experienced many fresh starts: in 1815, in 1848–9, in 1866 and in 1871; then again in 1918, in 1933 and in 1945–9 and, finally, of course, in 1990. The very act of nation-building has occurred at least four times since the 1860s (1871, 1918, 1933 and 1990) and arguably once in two different German states (1949). The liberal democratic and nationalist revolution of 1848 fell apart in 1849. Bismarck's authoritarian empire collapsed in 1918 (and began to falter in 1890). Democratic Weimar almost disappeared on several occasions before Brüning took power in 1930. He was replaced by Adolf Hitler whose thousand-year Reich disappeared in the devastation of Germany barely thirteen years after its inception.

To write about German politics after 1945 is therefore to aim at a moving target (Germany today and tomorrow), as well as a more stationary one (West Germany yesterday) because the Berlin Republic (as we must now learn to call Germany after unity), precisely because of unity, cannot be the same sort of state as West Germany was before it. 'Bonn is not Weimar' was the title of a celebrated and entirely convincing book on the Federal Republic, written in the 1950s. But if the Bonn Republic was *not* 'Weimar', can the Berlin Republic be 'Bonn'? The last chapter in this book seeks to answer this.

But before setting the present and future alongside the past, we should say what we mean by the term German 'political development'. This is not a book about Germany as an object in international relations, nor about the nature of German post-war economic strength even though both these topics are touched on, and both are valid ways of defining Germany's place in Europe and the world. Here, political development means just that; that the prime concern of this book is the politics of Germany. What, then, are the criteria used here for evaluating this development? How well has Germany done, in a political (rather than a diplomatic or economic) sense, since 1945? What 'performance indicators' should be used to provide a measured answer to this question?

Driving the process of contemporary German political change – which culminated in the founding of the new German nation – is the story of how West Germany made a remarkable, if painful, transition from Nazi dictatorship to republican democracy. East Germany's transition from the Third Reich to Communism and from there to democracy in 1989 and 1990 is, in several respects, an analogous event. It demonstrates, in its own way, the extraordinary capacity of German political life to copy its own patterns and to repeat its own processes.

Introduction

As we shall see, the history of the Federal Republic shows us that what was constructed after 1945 was *not* the product of chance but of a conscious set of policies, deliberately pursued, and with a particular purpose in mind.

This book provides a set of criteria by which to test the democratic reliability of the Bonn Republic and its success in maintaining democratic values over a forty-year period. They are intended to illuminate the deeper framework within which the day-to-day issues of German politics occur, and to provide a perspective which permits a balanced view of the issues, untainted by the not infrequent German political blunder or exaggerated viewpoint. It uses evidence that has been derived from the key episodes which imparted to German politics, in the west, their particular shape at any given time.

I begin with mapping out the legacy of the Third Reich for post-Nazi German politics and end with German unity. The first criterion, then, is concerned with the *political impact* of the Third Reich and the extent to which Nazi values were successfully removed from German life and replaced by decent and democratic ones. The second has to do with the *durability* of these changed values, in the period marked by the end of West Germany's occupation and the growth of a specific West German political identity.

The third criterion has to do with the use German political leaders made of their power to *reintroduce West Germany into the community of democratic and liberal Western states* and their efforts to entrench liberal constitutionalism in the Federal Republic. I stress, in particular, the West German propensity for the *management of political issues*, to produce consensus within Germany, to avoid the exploitation of conflict for political gain, and to ensure that in its foreign policy *in Europe and the world* the Federal Republic would always appear benign and compliant. This account argues that, set against these benchmarks, the Federal Republic has, on the whole, done reasonably well. It has proved to be a good sort of German state.

What is offered, then, is an account of the creation of a particular sort of German state in the west of Germany led by Adenauer (and a particular sort of German state in the east). After this, we look at how West Germany's political leaders made what proved, to all intents and purposes, to be a West German nation (even if this may now be denied). Due attention is paid to Adenauer's policy of total Western integration and Brandt's *Ostpolitik*. There is a discussion of Brandt's successor, Schmidt, and an account of the Kohl chancellorship. This book is mainly concerned with those political leaders who made the West German state what it was, and thus focuses chiefly on Adenauer, Brandt and Kohl. These were the 'Big Three' German chancellors, not so much because of any equal length of tenure of the post (Brandt's five years were considerably less than Adenauer's fourteen and Kohl's thirteen to date) but because of what they were able to do to (and with) the Federal Republic.

Although German politics underwent only a few major internal and external changes during the period from 1945 to the present, those that were made were major and radical departures from German politics in earlier years. The biggest changes – with two exceptions, the process of *Ostpolitik* and unity – were produced in the period from April 1945 until 1949, for they fundamentally affected West German institutions, society and the economy, as well as West Germany's place in Europe and the world. They were effected right at the beginning of the Bonn Republic. The new policy towards Eastern Europe, mainly an external matter when it was conceived, but destined to alter the domestic shape of the Federal Republic as its *unintended* consequence, began to take shape in the aftermath of Adenauer's fall. If this was a further, conscious re-invention of West Germany, the intention was only to consolidate its Western-ness by stabilizing the Federal Republic in the East. The final, most intriguing, change was unification in 1990.

West Germany before 1989/90 was not in fact a 'restless Reich' (as Michael Stürmer mistakenly argued), either internally or in its foreign policy, despite the fact that, in a formal and geographical sense, its frontiers lacked legal demarcation and were uncertain. Whilst thinking members of West Germany's political class liked to make themselves anxious by questioning the health of their democracy, or the nature of their institutions and the activities of their major parties, for most of the past forty-odd years, questioning was all that went on. Most West Germans were, on the whole, passive, even if the generation who became adult in the 1960s and, more recently the Greens, were doughty protestors. Mostly they accepted the changes their leaders thought good for them, even if thinkers and journalists often engaged in vitriolic debate about the meaning of them.

David Conradt wrote that Adenauer wanted the support of the West Germans, but not their involvement. With a very few, if notable exceptions, this became a tradition in West Germany. In any case, 'liberty' and 'freedom' came to mean something different – and non-political – for citizens who soon learned to enjoy the new things that the 1950s and 1960s could offer consumers in the West. Foremost amongst these were an improving standard of living, television, and mass mobility thanks to cheap and reliable motoring, but also antibiotics and the contraceptive pill. For most West Germans it was obvious that the political system appeared to function well and should not be tampered with. Poll after poll showed that most West Germans wanted their country to be like Switzerland or Sweden, and not like the superpower America. This lack of German feistiness or 'attitude' (something the rest of Europe came to value) was taken as a sign of 'normality'. Yet the truth was that West Germany was not a normal nation, even if the ordinary German came to find this abnormality perfectly normal.

Events which disturbed the order in West German political life were dismissed, by most Germans and non-Germans, as insignificant. The terrorism of the Baader-Meinhof Gang and the Red Army Faction or other instances of unacceptable political behaviour – corruption scandals, say – were, it was insisted, atypical. No one believed Nazism could ever regain power. The constant evocation of Germany's Nazi past, particularly by the British media (who could only very rarely make an interesting story out of the apparent core beliefs of the Bonn Republic) meant only that the real achievements of post-1945 West Germany were ignored (often to the disadvantage of West Germany's neighbours). German politics after 1945 and until 1989 were portrayed either (truthfully) as (usually) a trifle dry and ponderous, or, in a biased and inaccurate way, as Nazi-like and sensational.

Almost all serious observers of German affairs regarded West Germany with favour. They saw its government as well-ordered. It was prosperous and well in tune with Western ideals. Almost every study praised its reliability, its constitutionalism and its liberalism. The keynote of its political culture – consensus – was seen as the magic cure to political discord, discord which had haunted Germany in the past (and continued to haunt some of its neighbours). If West German politics had a flaw, it was precisely that, on the whole, they were boring. But, given the circumstances, even this was hardly a flaw. Such positive views were, in fact, justified, because, before unity, it seemed plain that the Bonn Republic was not merely a new departure for German politics, but had very little in common with previous German states.

Most argued that the major theme of this period (1945–89) appeared to be the 'normalization' of (West) German political life. By this they meant that West Germany had not only lost the aggressiveness and urge to dominate which history had associated with earlier, undemocratic, German states, but had managed to become dull, placid and predictable. Furthermore, some commentators suggested that the Bonn Republic had not merely cast off nationalist sentiment (by accepting Germany's division and apparently sublimating its national feeling into the European Community) but also, as a result of having done so for forty years, it had actually become a 'post-national' state, for which nationalism had become an irrelevance. It had been true that the West German Government remained publicly committed to the achievement of some sort of national unity; but, as we see below, this commitment tended to be regarded, by 1989, as little more than lip service to an idea that had passed its sell-by date thirty years before.

Pre-1989 commentators repeatedly stressed that this 'normalization' (in fact they meant 'Westernization', again hardly normal in the German context) proved that the Bonn Republic had successfully overcome the disruptions of the nineteenth and the first half of the twentieth centuries. In this way, a new non-dominant German part-nation was able to develop and to learn to live in a tense international environment and in an increasingly interdependent Western community of states. The post-Second World War settlement had lasted forty years. All believed the issue of German dominance had finally been solved. This was why the West German state, which existed from 1949 to 1989, *was* essentially different from previous German states. In both domestic and foreign terms, the Bonn Republic was another sort of Germany.

As far as the domestic development of Germany before 1990 is concerned, the institutions and political rules established in 1949 were subjected to intensive refinement; but their basic form remained unaltered. The political authority vested in them and their political value within the system as a whole, already enormous, was upheld and strengthened. Consensus ruled – and the rules produced consensus. There was a real and easily verifiable burgeoning of liberal constitutionalism. At the same time, successful management of politics led to a decline in what might be termed true, if old-fashioned, democracy. A huge increase took place in the power of the German state, which means both the power of the unitary element (the *Bund*) and its constituent parts (the *Länder*). The power of the two big parties and of their political managers also underwent a vast increase. Parties, for the first time, were given a place in the Constitution. Party membership became a key factor in advancing the ambitions of the political class and choosing members of public bodies on the basis of their party affiliation became almost synonymous with democratic behaviour. All of the parties established political foundations: the CDU's Konrad Adenauer *Stiftung* and the SPD's Friedrich Ebert *Stiftung* played an ever more important role in managing politics. They identified members, supporters and new policies, and even set up offices and links abroad with like-minded parties, rivalling those of the Republic's foreign ministry.

Curiously, however, and despite the work of the foundations, the ability of the parties to define and articulate day-to-day political concerns began to decline after about 1960. What might be called West German democratic corporatism blunted policy edges. The pre-1933 tendency to develop interest-led policy change through the formation of associations (*Vereinsmeierei*) reappeared. Indeed, 'citizens' initiatives' (these days often funded by local government) began to execute a number of functions previously carried out by the parties. The paradoxes here can be seen most clearly in the fate of the Green Party, which is increasingly called upon to shed its function as a specific interest group and take on the more comprehensive tasks of local and even national political management.

Before unification in 1990, the political institutions of the Federal Republic underwent a number of changes in emphasis. By far the most important of these was in regard to its federal structure. In Britain, it is fashionable at present to regard federalism as being concerned with the amassing of power in the centre to the detriment of the constituent parts. (Previously, the opposition was always between a 'loose confederation' and a 'unitary centralized state'.) For Germans, federalism means something quite different, and at times the precise opposite. The concept of federalism describes a relationship between two centres of power. The one is generated by the German 'nation' (in inverted commas because the Bonn Republic was not a nation); the other by the constituent states or *Länder*, operating as individual states but also conjointly, thanks to the device of their own 'national' body, the *Bundesrat*, or federal council (even though formally this latter institution is a *federal* organ, and must bow to the precedence of the Federal Parliament or *Bundestag*).

The Federal Chancellor, the political leader of the Federal Republic, is conceived, as it were, through the agency of the Federal Parliament and the political parties. Yet his power (it has always been a 'he') is firmly constrained by the power of the *Bundesrat* and the *Land* parliaments. Furthermore, all West German Chancellors have entered 'national' politics via a strong record of achievement in *Land* politics (even Ludwig Erhard had served, for a time, in the Bavarian government before assuming a zonal post). In addition, since 1949 there has been a marked shift of political power from the Federal Chancellor and his government to the minister presidents of the *Länder* and their governments. The net result of all this managing of politics, however, has been that the power of the ordinary citizen, as a political actor, has declined to what is often effective impotence. By 1990, the democratic political parties (with the exception of the Greens), though important, hardly differed from one another any longer, even if there was disagreement about the odd policy. Those with governmental ambitions (the CDU/CSU, the SPD and the FDP) sought to homogenize their defining policies with each other. Even the Greens now find their concern with ecological affairs has become mainstream and they, too, seem to be ready to form a consensus in areas where previously they only wanted to oppose government and be 'alternative'.

Before 1990, in foreign policy terms, the West Germans were adventurous only in seeking European integration because it offered the chance of perpetuating West Germany's westernization. Even the most potentially dangerous problem, the division of Germany, was so carefully managed by the politicians that far from firing heady nationalist sentiment, it served as a warning against it. By 1989 very few West Germans shared their Chancellor's stated desire for national unity. That noted interpreter of German politics, the celebrated French political scientist Alfred Grosser, once distinguished between the French attitude to the loss of Alsace-Lorraine in 1871 (about which the French always thought but never talked) and the West German attitude towards the Communist East German state (about which the Germans always talked but never really thought). Certainly, the view that the division of Germany was probably permanent and that most West Germans were scarcely troubled by this formed the basis for the way in which German affairs were perceived by Germany's neighbours. Both internally and externally, and not just in terms of the treatment of the German question, the political life of the Federal Republic was, on the whole, remarkably calm. Virtually no one, German or non-German, considered unification to be a realistic project, even in the medium term. When unity required the alteration of East German car number plates to the West German model, it transpired that one civil servant, as a hobby, had already worked out what abbreviations to use for place names. Kohl liked to claim that this anonymous civil servant was *the* real champion of unity.

West Germany's first Chancellor, Konrad Adenauer, himself firmly believed that the German unification was desirable only in conjunction with its Western integration, and should on no account be the alternative to it. Integration meant something quite concrete to Adenauer. His aim was to bind West Germany militarily and economically to the West so that its western-ness could not be undermined. This is why Stalin's offer of unity in 1952–3 was, for Adenauer, never a 'missed opportunity' because it was not one he had ever wanted to accept. It has to be said that, as far as Adenauer's stated policy is concerned, German unity in 1990 has met the conditions he always laid down. Unity has indeed occurred with the German nation remaining an integral part of NATO and the European Community. Kohl's office chief, Horst Teltschik, said in 1990 'Adenauer's concept of unity has now borne fruit', and this was a perfectly fair comment. Most West and East Germans seemed, before 1989, to have taken on a bizarre non-national national identity. They came to regard the Bonn Republic and the German Democratic Republic, the GDR, as their respective national homes, the countries with which they identified, along with their regional homes, or *Heimat*.

Even after unification, the mark of these differing identities can be clearly discerned in many areas such as voting behaviour.

It is perfectly true that the Communist states of Eastern Europe took two decades to admit publicly to what they knew privately, that West Germany was not expansionist (only to discover that, with the collapse of Communism, it had in a sense decided to become so). But the allegation of German revanchism made Soviet occupation credible and associated Communism with national defence. Two generations of Western observers, however, agreed that West German leaders of all major parties wanted first and foremost to offer this reliability to their Western allies and to eschew any hint of domestic or foreign domination. A narrative was constructed by them which stated that although there were at times fierce political differences between the two major parties in the first decade of the Bonn Republic (caused chiefly by the Social Democrats' particular concept of opposition), these were subsequently seen to have been damaging and inappropriate. From the early 1960s until Helmut Schmidt's fall in 1982, the leaders of the Centre Right and of Social Democracy sought consensus and, usually, found it. The ultra-fair West German electoral system made it hard for parties to gain overall majorities. This led to the formation of coalitions, which further reinforced consensuality. Politics was mostly conducted in a deliberately low-key way; most Bundestag debates were lack-lustre and unemotional set pieces.

At the same time, the nagging fact remained (even if often ignored) that West Germany was only *part* of Germany, the product of very special circumstances. If West Germany was a model of liberalism, this might have as much to do with the peculiar position in which it found itself after the defeat of the Third Reich as with its constitutionalism. For the Federal Republic had been *constructed* in a certain way. It was but a part-nation.

There is, therefore, a sub-text to this book, a fourth criterion which runs implicitly through German political development before 1990 and becomes explicit after it, when Germany became a unified nation once more. It is the most perplexing one of all, for it is fraught with controversy and concerns Germans and non-Germans alike. It has rather less to do with the early fears of the post-1945 world, that Nazism could somehow re-emerge, and more to do with a different and older concern. It is the fear of German dominance over Europe and political upheaval within Germany. Even the havoc that Nazism was able to inflict on the rest of Europe can be seen as a particularly appalling expression of something that predated Hitler, namely, Germany's potential to dominate Europe. It led twice, in 1914 and then after 1938, to actual German domination over Europe. Since its unification in 1871,

Germany has repeatedly been in a position to exercise economic and political dominance over other European states, whether its political leaders wished this or not.

Before 1933, the nature of German dominance was held to lie in the fact that the driving force behind German power and strength was the inevitable consequence of Germany's economic and political interests. The party of the swastika may have given its own expression to these interests. But it had not invented them. History shows us that, for nineteenth-century Europe, the German 'question' (should Germany become a single nation?) became the German problem (could Germany be contained?) almost as soon as Germany achieved nationhood in 1871. By the turn of the century, the power and influence exerted by Germany had become the major foreign problem for its European neighbours, and particularly, perhaps, for Britain and France.

These interests, it was thought, had been dictated by its great size, its geopolitical location in the European continent and the difficulty in constructing a single German nation, with clear borders, given the vast number of Germans in Europe and the even larger numbers of non-Germans seeking their share of Germany's economic might.

After Hitler, however, what was seen to be wrong with Germany was differently, and more carefully, defined and addressed. In the eyes of Roosevelt, Stalin and Churchill, their successors and their advisers, Germany's bid to dominate Europe and the world was seen as the outcome of a mixture of clearly discernible problems, presenting themselves as both external *and internal* dangers (and not simply German foreign policy needs). Externally, they thought that Germany had a built-in capacity to out-compete most other European nations in economic affairs and in its capacity to wage war. They knew that Germany's political borders had always been ill-defined and that the Germans were uncertain as to who belonged within the nation and who needed to be kept outside it. When the victors of 1945 looked at Germany's domestic political development, they saw a string of wholly unsatisfactory political systems, too frequently given *carte blanche* to articulate an over-assertive and aggressive set of policies. They listed the authoritarianism of Wilhelmine aristocratic and militaristic government, the Prussian reinvention of Germany. They noted Weimar's allegedly excessively democratic democracy and Nazi ethnocentric tyranny. All this seemed to signify the inadequate political competence of the German political class and people and the lack of a real liberal tradition.

The solution to the German problem proposed by the political leaders of 1945 – Roosevelt, Truman, Churchill, Attlee and Stalin – was complex if logically straightforward. It consisted, as we have said, of yet another reinvention. This one was chiefly, perhaps, to be manufactured by Germans, but it was one to which all Germany's victors made a strong contribution and thinkable only because Germany had been defeated. It was predicated on military and political occupation. Federalism (in the German sense) was to be emphasized in order to weaken any central government. In Germany's western part (at any rate) a liberal and democratic form of government was to be installed in which strong liberal institutions were made to possess a decisive role. This produced the unintended, if blunt and effective, consequence that Germany became divided into two political states. The nation of Germany thus ceased to exist.

Two unique German states took its place. They were unique because they both had to satisfy, if they were to survive, domestic German aspirations, at least to a level where the regimes would be tolerated. At the same time all real conflict with their respective occupiers, who actively interfered with German affairs, had to be eschewed. The means employed by the leaders of the two states were, of course, quite different. West Germany's first Chancellor, Konrad Adenauer, in accord with Germany's victors (particularly the Americans), took every opportunity to show that he had established a political system that was well able to promote the fortunes of liberal democracy and cooperate with the West. Communist policies were, on the other hand, almost wholly repressive and propagandistic. Yet both German states were ultimately subject to the real constraints imposed by non-Germans. Brezhnev is reported to have said to Honecker in 1971: 'Remember, dear Erich, our troops are always there, always at your side...Without us, there would be no GDR.' The West had, in effect, delivered the same sort of message to the West Germans.

What had been the German nation became two extraordinary constructs. Indeed, it is the argument of this book that all this meant that, from 1945 to 1989, the German problem had, in truth, been solved. Today, however, Germany is once again in the process of being reinvented. Germany is being changed by unification, even if it is merely a question of extending the West eastwards, and this means reinvention is now underway.

So what will the new Germany be like? How can we arrive at an answer secure enough to be a basis for the policy of all concerned, as well as for proper understanding? One method might be to write a 'national' history of West Germany and test the extent to which the qualities that made the old Federal Republic so reliable can continue to flourish in the future. It is the method employed here. Yet it must be conceded that there are objections to such a history.

There are those who argue that to write a 'national' history of the

Federal Republic is, in itself, fallacious. For some, a national history can only be written about a nation. From 1945 until 1990 no German nation existed. For others, to write about today's Germany *as a nation*, is automatically to perpetuate the alleged myth of the German problem. This, it is sometimes suggested, is merely a convenient fiction used by Germany's neighbours to do Germany down (in the same way that the Russians, before 1914, coined the phrase 'Drang nach Osten' as if it had been German in origin). Why should German affairs be any more problematic than anyone else's? Their solution is to seek to produce a comparative analysis of German politics, within the framework of European political development.

A comparative history or political study might indeed place flaws in German political development into a more rounded perspective. Aggression, Fascism, and even genocide, can be shown to have taken place in other states as well. But the hard truth, epitomized by the words 'Auschwitz', 'Occupation', 'Division' and 'Unity', makes it clear that Germany's political development in the twentieth century has not been the same as that of its Western neighbours.

As we shall see in the final chapter, the critical issue here is undoubtedly how the new Germany's national interest is constructed and how its foreign and European policies affect others. Even if Germany's political landscape is now changing – and for the forseeable future, two political cultures must exist side by side – there is no reason to believe it will become politically unstable. The Berlin Republic has been derived from West Germany. Much of its domestic political life will be taken over into the new state.

Indeed, every German state since 1866 has consisted both of new elements and of old ones. Bismarck's Prussian Germany allowed a liberal constitution and a popularly elected parliament (in many ways was the most modern then in existence) to co-exist with feudal powers and Prussian behaviour. Weimar was haunted (and destroyed) by those who preferred Germanic nationalism and authoritarianism to the liberal and democratic republic then on offer. The GDR could never deny its German-ness nor did it risk abolishing the pre-Communist German past or some of its manifestations. Just as West Germany, as a reinvention, had elements of continuity with previous German states, so, too, are the Bonn and Berlin Republics connected.

Unity in 1990 was not accompanied by a change in the form of regime as was the case with some previous reinventions. As Lewis Edinger has stressed, former reinventions had often proved to be changes of regime and thus profound and radical. 1990 confirmed the strength of liberal democracy and, indeed, of Chancellor Kohl, a committed Westerner and European. Similarly, as we shall see, those who constructed the Federal Republic made systemic change very difficult to achieve. It is important to realize that the Berlin Republic takes its authority, and its legitimacy, from the Constitution of Bonn. Unity produced, on the whole, only cosmetic alterations to it (with the exception of the use of German troops 'out of area'). In practice, therefore, it is hard to see how the Federal Republic could be deconstructed and turned into something else. Thus, one might conclude, West German history *can* be a good guide to the future. Precisely because of the continuities in German political development, many observers now suggest the Berlin Republic will merely be the old Federal Republic writ large. That, demonstrably, is what its current leadership hopes will happen. But continuities are a two-edged sword.

Two caveats must be entered. If there are positive continuities in German political development, there may also be negative ones, connecting this nation to the past. The political culture of East Germany has not disappeared; German Communism is not dead. The biggest difference between the old Federal Republic and the new one is that it is a real nation again. German nationhood exists once more and with it a German national interest, even if still hazy. The very idea of a German nation and the concept of nationhood are deliberate expressions of historical and political continuity reaching back before 1945, symbolized by the choice of Berlin as the new capital.

Whilst it is right, and important, to stress the central continuity of the Bonn constitution, for example, as a link between the Bonn and Berlin republics and a cardinal difference between those republics and what preceded them, it is equally necessary to see that the need for a new national identity for Germany could resurrect different and older continuities. The real question has to do with how permanently liberalism is entrenched at home, and whether German political leaders can continue to frame German national interests in ways which can coincide with the wishes of its neighbours.

In Europe, there are today well over one hundred million people who speak German. Many non-Germans look to Germany for economic prosperity and political support. This was true even before 1990, but it had no real political meaning. Today, however, an increasing number of Germans are thinking about the implications of their nation's power. Some, admittedly a national conservative minority, can even be heard re-asking the old question: how can there be a real German nation if so many Germans continue to live outside its national borders. Once again, the question of German national identity (which so perplexed its nineteenth-century thinkers) is beginning to be debated in contemporary Germany. The apparent simplicity of the concept of the German nation conceals a challenging reality.

Because of this, the Federal Republic has to reflect seriously on two possible changes which could expel it from its secure place in the West. The first is the possibility of a resurgent domination over Europe, which is, at present, unlikely but not impossible. The second, of which there is already hard evidence, is that the national interest of the new Germany may generate conflict with that of its neighbours. The Bonn Republic was a success because it was different both from other Germanies and from other European nations. It had no alternative but to be a submissive state. The new German nation, however, is not obliged to be special, to be different from other nations. The founding generation of the Federal Republic who felt it their historical duty to make another sort of German state have died out, or are dying out. Their places have been taken by others who have been conditioned by different experiences. If the Berlin Republic becomes either more like other German nations, or more similar to its European neighbours, things may become very much more difficult. Even if the story of German political development since 1945 is bright, the future of the united German nation seems darker and more problematic. This book also seeks to illuminate this apparent paradox.

It will be very hard indeed for the leaders of the new Germany to resist the pressures to exercise great national power. These pressures, it should be added, do not, at the moment, come from Germans but from Americans and some others in Europe. Yet if the new Germany does become the European superpower (which seems inevitable), will it always be able to repress its own dominance? Does a unified Germany have any choice other than to turn its potential for dominance into actual domination of the continent? Even if its leaders and its citizens want to continue to be 'Bonn' republicans, to be 'predictable' and Western, they may find that the changes produced by unity have forced them into being 'Berlin' republicans, with new, unclear wants and needs.

Some will doubt that Germany's neighbours will want to fall out with her whatever she does. France and the Benelux states to the west, as well as the new democracies to the east, are so deeply interlocked with the new Germany that they cannot afford conflict. But the pursuit of good relations with Germany is not, in itself, a sustainable policy for any state, if it becomes just another term for German interference in the domestic affairs of its neighbours. This would be an effective occupation. Relations between states are governed by deeper traditions and not merely by perceived economic self-interest. For this reason, this book looks at both domestic developments *and* foreign policy. The critical interrelationship between domestic and foreign policy was a key feature of the Bonn Republic. Even in 1990, as we shall see, the key decision to create a single German nation was a foreign one, taken by the then Soviet leader, Gorbachev (admittedly seeking to fall in with West German wishes). In the end, it is the future of this interrelationship which will define the new Germany's place in Europe and the world and provide the answer to the question of German dominance. Germany as the object of the diplomacy of other major states is thus presented here as a vital topic. Yet it is one that is so vast (precisely because Germany is so important for other nations) that this topic cannot be treated in detail.

There have been at least six attempts at making German nations in recent times. We cannot therefore be optimistic about German political development. If it was not accurate to interpret German politics from 1945 to 1990 through a historical lens fashioned by the fall of Weimar and the horrors of the Third Reich, an analogous warning should be given today. To use the historical lens of the Bonn Republic to examine post-unification Germany must distort the reality of the new and resurgent German nation. Since the German problem, which is the problem of Germany's dominance, was solved for forty years by the expedients of dividing the nation (even if unintentionally) and imposing liberalism upon its people, we may reasonably ask whether the solution of 1945 will continue to stick, given the momentous changes that have taken place in Germany since national unification.

Figure 1. Franco-German Friendship as the cornerstone of the new Europe. President Mitterrand and Chancellor Kohl join hands at Verdun 22 September 1984. © Presse- und Informationsamt der Bundesregierung

Figure 2. Berlin the once and future capital of a new Germany in a new Europe. © Bundesbildstelle

The Nazi Legacy: Hitler and Post-1945 German Political Culture

Post-1945 Germany and its Nazi Past

What, precisely, was the *political* legacy bequeathed by the Third Reich to post-Hitler Germany? We know that post-1945 German politics had a Nazi past; but the actual ways in which it was expressed (and repressed) within the context of German politics is hard to evaluate. The Nazi concept of a 'people's community', or *Volksgemeinschaft*, which was depicted as transcending both social class and the political borders of the Reich in 1937, was, of course, one reinvention of Germany. The institutional arrangements that produced the disordered order which was Nazi governance, relying always on Hitler's personal orders (and thus on proximity to him, whether in Berlin or elsewhere) did not survive their architect. But it is plain that although the institutions may have disappeared, a key dimension of German political life continues to be Germany's Nazi legacy, though there is no common agreement about its true nature or weight in terms of what actually happened to German politics after Germany's defeat. Indeed, there is still no agreement about the place the Nazi reinvention has within the course of German politics and whether Nazism was its inevitable product, or merely a nasty accident that could have happened to any nation.

Today, most observers accept that Nazism was not accidental, in the sense that it came out of the blue, because it was the product of clearly definable failures within the German political system before 1933. As to the effect of Nazi policies on German life after 1933, it is generally agreed that this has been so great that its full impact has only recently come to be understood. What is, perhaps, less fully comprehended is the essential racism of the Third Reich. Whilst it is generally understood that the Nazis hated the Jews, and that this hatred was irrational in the view of any liberal-minded person, the extent to which this hatred was formalized and institutionalized to create a racist German state was often glossed over, precisely because Nazi racism was so murderously irrational. Yet the racist core of Nazi Germany was not merely upheld by many Germans, it was consciously accepted as a central pillar of the Germanic reinvention of Germany after 1933.

Some post-1945 German leaders, like Adenauer and Brandt, believed that West Germany, on account of Nazism, would, for the foreseeable future, never be able to be like other states. Others, like Kohl, desired Germans to move beyond the past (whilst paying due attention to contemporary German history). For the Germans themselves the Nazi legacy has proved a generational problem. For the first twenty-five years of the Bonn Republic, most ordinary Germans found comfort in the idea that 1945 had been a 'Year Zero', a completely new beginning which broke the continuity with the past, and allowed them to start new lives. Those born into the Federal Republic, however, who bear no responsibility for Nazi crimes, have tended to believe that the reinvention of Germany after 1945, whilst politically complete, could not prevent the Nazi experience from influencing German political culture. They are committed to remembering. It is safer for them to do so. Indeed, few people have scrutinized their own recent history with as much effort, and anguish, as the West Germans (and perhaps the East Germans) have now done. Even though this past is often called the 'unbewältigte Vergangenheit' – the unconquered past – today's Germans, by confronting their past, have dared do what many others have not. Even if it was simply something to explore, and react against, the past has continued to exist in the present. Indeed, if anything, the past exists more strongly today than in earlier phases of the Bonn Republic. Yet the ever-present past itself becomes thereby a problem in politics as well as in history.

The concept of a 'Year Zero' was, then, in some ways merely a fiction. Yet it allowed the German people to get on with inventing a new future for themselves. For these reasons the most enduring aspect of the Nazi legacy is that the Federal Republic was never considered a 'normal' state. It follows, dauntingly, that although the Berlin Republic may now seek to lay the ghost of its Nazi past and thus 'normalize' itself, to do so would be dangerous. It has been a paradox that it was only by accepting its essential abnormality that West Germany became a valued member of the West. Its Nazi past demonstrates that German political development could create quite different ways of running German affairs from those adopted after 1945. The Western-ness of the Federal Republic, a unique marriage between Western values and German politico-legal thinking, could only have been fashioned out of the political ruins of the Third Reich. The necessity of understanding this had now been made redundant by unification.

The East Germans were also acutely conscious of the Nazi past but liked to make something different, and far more simplistic of it. Nazism, they claimed, was not something for which Communist Germans bore any responsibility (the GDR Government refused until the 1980s even to consider any financial reparations to the Jews). It was, they said, a general phenomenon of capitalist society, a political doctrine based on a desire by the capitalist classes to destroy the power of the working class. This allowed them to insist that West Germany was and could continue to be essentially fascist.

It is therefore hardly surprising that the trauma caused by Nazism had most impact early on, even if many Germans themselves were coy about accepting the extent of the political and non-material damage done both to Germany and to themselves. At first, then, the legacy found expression in repression and amnesia. The trauma was too distressing to face up to it. The elements in the political life of Nazi Germany which generated most problems after 1945 were those stemming from Hitler's relationship to the German people and the racist nature of the Nazi Germany. The implications of Hitler's establishment of an ethnocentric Germanic state have not always been addressed.

Nazism and Post-War Political Culture

The Nazi past influenced German political culture in two principal ways. The first was by promoting the realization that an aggressive and assertive foreign and domestic policy for Germany had been (and would be) lethal to post-1945 Germans and their neighbours. The second stemmed from the need to understand how Nazism had altered what the people thought about politics and how they should behave politically. This centred on the fact that most Germans had not opposed Hitler but had, one way or another, supported him. This failure was compounded by the obvious weakness of German democracy before 1933. Whether one believed that Weimar had simply collapsed, or had been overthrown, the practical conclusion was the same: any post-Nazi German democracy would have to be reinvented using new methods. It came to be seen that Nazism had permeated every aspect of German public life.

Post-Nazi German political life began to stir remarkably soon after Germany's defeat. Its base was a political culture (and political structures) that had been controlled by Hitler and the Nazis for a little over thirteen years. This was not a long time in chronological terms (and certainly not the thousand years that had been promised). But it was a long time in political terms precisely because Nazism had been so radical.

For Germany's victors, and for the German political leaders of post-Nazi Germany, an awareness of the vast implications of the Nazi legacy, and the damage that it caused, was to prove a key political need. Even if in 1945 they subscribed to the view that the Germans, to put it bluntly, were more guilty than the German people themselves liked to pretend, politically it could prove disastrous to make the point too strongly. All Germany's victors understandably attempted to begin their occupation by getting the Germans to alter their political behaviour by acknowledging their guilt and responsibility. But it quickly became clear that, tactically, it would be much more effective to concentrate instead on shoring up post-war political institutions to make them capable of resisting anti-democratic onslaughts. Responsible German politicians took the same view. From this emerged the emphasis placed on constitutionalism and on a constitution that was both workable and defensible.

Table 1.1. German Elections 1928–33

	20 May 1928	14 Sept 1930	31 July 1932	6 Nov 1932	5 Mar 1933
Electors in millions					
	41.22	42.96	44.23	44.37	44.69
	74.60	81.41	83.39	79.93	84.04
Turnout %					
Nazis	2.6%	18.3%	37.2%	33.0%	43.9%
DNVP	14.2%	7.0%	5.9%	7.2%	8.0%
DVP	8.7%	4.5%	1.1%	1.7%	1.1%
ZENTRUM	11.9%	11.7%	12.4%	11.9%	11.2%
BVP	3.9%	3.0%	3.2%	2.9%	2.7%
DDP	4.9%	3.7%	1.0%	0.9%	0.8%
SPD	28.7%	24.5%	21.5%	20.4%	18.3%
KPD	10.6%	13.1%	14.2%	16.8%	12.3%
Others	14.5%	14.2%	3.5%	5.2%	1.8%

(adapted from A. Grosser, *Germany in Our Time*, London, 1974, p. 24.)

Key:

Nazis	National Socialist German Worker's Party (die NSDAP: die Nationalsozialistische Deutsche Arbeiter Partei)
DNVP	German nationalist People's Party (die Deutschnationale Volkspartei)
DVP	German People's Party (die Deutsche Volkspartei)
Zentrum	the Centre (das Zentrum)
BVP	Bavarian People's Party (die Bayerische Volkspartei)
DDP	German Democratic Party (die Deutsche Demokratische Partei)
SPD	German Social Democratic Party (die Sozialdemokratische Partei Deutschlands)
KPD	German Communist Party (die Kommunistische Partei Deutschlands)

Hitler and the Germans

How popular were Hitler and the Nazis? The votes that the Nazis won after 1928 show that the Nazi Party made spectacular gains but never scored an absolute majority in any free election. The figures in Table 1.1 also show the collapse of the non-Roman Catholic bourgeois centre (DVP and DDP), the erosion of support for the SPD and the increase in support for the Communists. Indeed, if we add the votes cast for the Communists to those cast for the Social Democrats we can readily see that there was a firm and extensive base for the Marxist left. The Nazis did particularly well in rural areas and amongst younger voters. The extent to which working class and women voters were won over continues to be debated. The Nazis gained, however, virtually no votes from the Roman Catholic Centre Party (which had, admittedly, moved to the right after 1930 and did not vote against the Enabling Law) and did better in northern than in southern Germany. All these matters were to prove critical for post-1945 German politics.

Although a majority of Germans did not vote for the Nazis in 1933, most historians now believe that by about 1938 a majority had come to support them. When Winston Churchill insisted that the war was being fought against Germany rather than against Fascism as his predecessor had liked to claim, he had a point. It is clear that National Socialism gave the Germans a sense of national purpose, a feeling that Germany counted again in world politics and pride in their own achievements. When it was attacked to the west and east, and from the air, they willingly defended it, even with their own lives. Many of them genuinely subscribed to racist ideas. Others were motivated by a deep fear of the West, and the modernism it implied. Ralf Dahrendorf and others have often stressed this latter point, implying a Romantic longing for a simpler, pre-industrial age. At the same time, we should not ignore the support that may have come to the Nazis because people feared them; nor should we ignore the significant numbers of Germans who opposed Hitler. Yet even these groups suffered from trauma. Fear, after all, is evidence of weakness. Those who opposed were risking their own lives and those of their loved ones as well as their reputations amongst their peers. It was all too easy to portray anti-Nazis as traitors. Yet all these problems stemmed from the fact that Hitler became hugely popular.

Albert Speer, whilst hardly objective, has provided a telling account of the enthusiasm which met Hitler on his many travels through Germany:

Hitler always sat next to his driver in his 7 litre Mercedes compressor. Behind him on one side sat I; on the other his valet who took maps, sunglasses, pills and sandwiches out of a large leather bag. Slowly in a hail of flowers we drove through the villages of Germany; youths shut the town gates, children climbed all over the car; Hitler had to sign autographs and then only then did they let him pass. They cheered and laughed and Hitler laughed with them. Once he turned to me whilst we were driving and said 'You know, in the whole of German history, only one other German was ever celebrated in this way. That was Martin Luther. Whenever he went on his travels, people flocked from all over everywhere to greet him. Today they come to me.'

What generated this adulation is hard to say. In his circle of intimates Adolf Hitler was considered inspiring, charming, interesting, always well-informed and anxious to do his best for the German public, who idolized him. After 1941 his friends claimed that the worries of war and the machinations of men like Martin Bormann, his secretary, made him become remote and increasingly harsh and bitter. Yet even then, so they stated, he was not a demon, ranting and raving incoherently, as was sometimes alleged (although he would never tolerate the least criticism of anti-Jewish measures).

For these intimates, Hitler was an imaginative and creative man, a man of culture, the author of a remarkable political autobiography, an good artist and architect. He plainly enjoyed the trappings of power; in every way he was a modern head of government, relying on a good communications system and numerous specialist advisers.

Was Hitler a German Nationalist?

In 1933 the German people were presented for the first time since 1918 with a national political leader who was genuinely national and neither a monarch, an aristocrat, a leading soldier or the representative of an executive committee. Hitler claimed to represent every German, of every class (provided, of course, they were not Jewish). Before 30 January 1933, few national leaders, if any, had made a real attempt to forge a direct link between leader and people. At least part of Hitler's appeal stemmed from his ability to project 'German-ness' and offer an enticingly ruthless definition of Germany's national interest. This was sometimes dismissed by his opponents with the claim that he was not a German but an Austrian, or a Bohemian. But to do so was to miss the very point that Hitler could exploit so tellingly. To him Austrians *were* Germans; denying this, proved how right he was to insist upon it. To re-invent Germany along ethnic lines was a manifesto in itself. Indeed, by 1945 the *racist* aspect of Nazi policies came to subvert the *nationalist* aspect almost completely. If before the outbreak of war, the ordinary German regarded Hitler as a German nationalist, by the end of the war it was plain that, to those who wished to see, that the idea of the German nation, or people, meant virtually nothing to him.

There is no record of Hitler's ever having privately expressed genuine affection for the German people. He liked dogs, his old party comrades, certain artists, musicians and ancient cities. He seems to have respected those fighting for him, as long as they were winning, but was always reckless with their lives. He did, it is true, take an interest in local German habits and customs. When told that a quarter of eastern European girls doing labour service in the Reich were found to be virgins, he remarked that this was a far higher proportion than would be found amongst Upper Bavarians. Yet he was always quick to come up with ways his German subjects could be regimented and even intimidated more successfully. In his *Table Talk* he can be seen to be quite impervious to suffering; he jokes about the Gestapo's torture of a murderer; he glibly discusses the execution of a hundred and fifty Jehovah's Witnesses that he once ordered, and delights in an order given to Himmler that all political detainees in the concentration camps should be killed in the event of unrest at home. In addition, of course, the manufacture of Aryan babies in baby farms implied that the Nazis were not fully satisfied with the German people such as there were.

What was certainly Hitler's real attitude towards the German people became apparent only after 1944, through his scorched earth policy. In order to resist the advance of the Allies for as long as possible, and deny them any material fruits of victory, he demanded that Germany be converted back into a pre-industrial state. On 19 March 1945 he decreed that those areas of German territory that would have to be given up to Germany's enemies should be robbed of the infrastructure that was needed to support modern life (analogous orders had already been given piecemeal since the summer of 1944).

Hitler's explanation of this order made his intentions plain:

> If this war is lost, then the German people are also lost. They cannot escape their fate. It is no longer necessary to consider what the German people need in order to survive on even the most primitive basis. On the contrary, it is better that these things be destroyed. The German people have proved themselves to be the weaker ones and the future belongs exclusively to the stronger masses of the East. Those who will remain after the fighting is over are, in any case, those worth less since the valuable ones have all fallen.

In short, whether one looks at the death and destruction that Hitler wreaked upon Germany or his concern with the Aryan race in Europe, rather than the nation states of Europe, Hitler was no nationalist in any conventional sense. Even if we argue that Hitler was mad (which seems reasonable), this scarcely lessens the traumatic impact on the Germans of having a leader, who purported to be a nationalist, destroyed the nation and came to scorn its inhabitants.

A Racist Germany

It is sometimes asserted that anti-Marxism was a far more powerful binding force in Nazi Germany than racism, or anti-Semitism. This is partly, perhaps, because in Cold War Europe anti-Marxism was less unacceptable, partly because it was in human nature to repress the horrors that anti-Semitism had precipitated. Today, however, it seems more clear than ever that race lay at the centre of the political culture of the Third Reich.

Although historians of the Third Reich, German and non-German, have always accepted that for the Nazis themselves the concept of race was central, it was almost always qualified by the claim that the concept itself was meaningless – as meaningless as the Nazi notion of the 'Aryan'. This lack of meaning was then transposed back into the study of Hitler's Germany with the obvious result. If we substitute for the opposition 'Jew and Aryan', the opposition 'German and ethnically other', it becomes plain why Hitler's ideas had far greater purchase on German political culture than Germans and others liked to suggest after 1945. Racism became not the personal madness of Hitler and his henchmen, but a widely accepted statement of German-ness and the German place in a ethnically diverse Europe.

Recent evidence has proved that the war against the Jews was waged not just by fanatical Nazis and Nazi organizations but by all the institutions of the German state, including the armed forces. It implies that 'Aryan' Germans (but also other Europeans) were convinced that Jews were ethnically 'other' and therefore to be denied humane treatment. The *Wehrmacht*, the only body capable of preventing genocide, in fact participated willingly in it. One of many notorious massacres, the murder of almost 35,000 Kiev Jews at Babi Yar was organized together with the military commander of Kiev and the 29th army corps of the Sixth Army. Field Marshal von Reichenau and Generals von Manstein and Hoth were also implicated.

In the Balkans, German army units were ordered to 'take the most brutal actions against troublemakers and hang and not shoot' partisans; during July and August 1941 1,000 Communists and Jews held as host-ages were duly slaughtered. They were to be hanged, one presumes, because it was more painful and more horrible than shooting. By

September 1941 Keitel himself decreed that for every German soldier killed by partisans, a hundred Communists and Jews were to be 'executed'. This time 21,000 were murdered. Keitel specifically stated that the executions were to be carried out by the units which had suffered losses against those who, by definition, had no part in the fighting (because they were hostages).

In addition, many of the peoples controlled by the Germans after 1939 – Poles, French, Dutch, Balts, 'white' Russians and so on – enthusiastically took part in the Nazi crusade against the Jews. No one was punished for refusing to kill Jews. Yet murders and 'executions' became common events in Hitler's new Europe. What was special about Nazi genocide was not simply the numbers involved (plans had been made at the 1942 Wannsee conference to exterminate all the eleven million Jews of Europe at a rate of 8,700 per day) but the fact that Germany was seen, and saw itself, as a cultured and scientifically modern society. The message that the Germans were ethnically superior, the Jews inferior and other, seems to have been widely accepted amongst the highest but also the lowest in the land. One of Hans Frank's sons, for example, has related how his mother took him to visit the Warsaw Ghetto. His testimony is a stark description of ethnic otherness. The boy asked his mother 'why the people had stars and who were the men with whips. When our [official] car stopped, I looked out of the window, and an older boy standing outside, staring at me . . . I made faces at him, he looked very sad and then ran away . . .'

The imposed and invented ethnic otherness of Jews was internalized by quite ordinary Germans. A war diary, kept by a simple Luftwaffe officer, Jürgen Flick, made the following entry for 22 March 1941:

Visit to Warsaw . . . I repeatedly found myself coming up against the walls of the Ghetto and decide to see it. The tram is the only way; it travels through the Ghetto without stopping. The impression I retain is very strong. I've never seen anything like it – people sealed off from other people by walls and gates. How justified it is that they be separated like this is clear to anyone who has seen the Ghetto. Jews, just Jews, forced now to rely only on themselves. From outside you can hear the chanting of Jewish pedlars, praising their wares . . . everywhere people are haggling. Many are selling arm bands with the Jewish star and little bits of cake. The streets were full of Jews. And of the stench that goes with Jews. Jews like a normal European has never seen them. Old ones with beards and fatty, lumpy eyes, eyes dark with evil. Young men, without moral consciences, with hatred and wickedness etched on their foreheads . . . Corpses lie on the pavements. We went to supper to the 'Black Forest' Restaurant. Otherwise nothing special happened today.

Whilst we will never know how much of Hitler's secret war against the Jews was known about, the evidence indicates that many more Germans knew of the killing of Jews than subsequently admitted to this, particularly in the larger conurbations where information was widely exchanged. Even if the precise details of genocide were kept secret as the Nazi leaders intended, the numbers involved in the killing and in the preliminaries to it, were so vast that it must have been public knowledge that organized killings were under way.

The commitment to a racist recasting of the German state was part and parcel of the commitment of very many Germans to the man who articulated it – Hitler. There can be no serious doubt that he personally ordered and watched over the process of extermination and that he provided the energy needed to unleash it. Theories distancing Hitler from this process, popular amongst some West German historians, are inherently implausible and may be politically dangerous, since they could allow posterity's view of Hitler to be revised.

Hitler never made a secret of his wish to subject Jews to 'racial cleansing', and most Germans (and other Europeans) knew something appalling was happening to the Jews, even if their physical murder took place in conditions of semi-secrecy. Indeed, the words 'cleansing' and 'cleanliness' are, eerily, ones that he used himself. He told a Munich journalist in 1922

> when I really am in power, then the annihilation of the Jews will be my first and most important task. As soon as I have the power to do it, I shall, for example, have erected in the Marienplatz in Munich gallows and more gallows . . . The Jews will be hanged, one after the other, and they will stay hanging until they stink. They will hang as long as the principles of hygiene permit. As soon as they have been taken down, the next ones will be strung up and this will continue until the last Jew in Munich is destroyed. The same will happen in other German cities until Germany is cleansed of the last Jews.

Not only does Hitler begin the very first page of *Mein Kampf* with a statement of the significance of ethnic solidarity amongst Germans, but he also gives it a foreign policy value: 'German-Austria must be re-turned to its great German motherland and not for economic reasons. No, no. Even if this union – in economic terms – had not impact, yes even if it was economically harmful, it would still have to take place. The same blood [written in emphasis] belongs in the same Reich . . .' Hitler goes on to relate how, out for a walk in the centre of Vienna, he saw a figure in a long caftan with black curls: "Is this also a Jew?" I asked myself . . . I observed the man secretly and carefully and the more I looked, the more a different question came into my mind: is this a

German?' He goes on: 'The cleanliness of the habits of these people is in itself an issue. That these were people who did not like water could be seen at once, sadly even with closed eyes. Later I often felt sick at the smell of the caftan wearers.'

Hitler's anti-Semitism was not marginal to his public and private acts as Germany's political leader, but almost always central to them. He never changed his views on Jews. Indeed, there is a remarkable consistency about what he said and wrote about Jews for the whole of his political career. Almost twenty years after his *Mein Kampf* outpourings, he could still tell his dinner-table circle that Jews were a virus and that the work the Nazis were doing in exterminating them was on a par with the achievement of Louis Pasteur: 'The discovery of the Jewish virus is one of the greatest revolutions that has taken place in the world. The battle in which we are engaged today is of the same sort as the battle waged during the last century by Pasteur . . .' (22 February 1942). In his final will and testament of 30 April 1945, Hitler repeated his belief that the war had been caused by the Jews and not by him.

His views were shared fully by his close associates and not simply by lunatics such as Julius Streicher. Hans Frank, Hitler's lawyer and later in charge of German-occupied Poland, was seen by early contemporaries as a 'well-educated attorney, highly cultured and cultivated'. He, too, took a clear ethnic line. He told a visiting Berlin journalist 'If I were to have one poster printed for every seven Poles I'm going to have shot, all the trees in Poland couldn't provide the paper . . . After the war, you can make mincemeat out of the Poles and Ukrainians and anybody else hanging around here as far as I am concerned.' On 1 August 1942 he spoke to German troops, and a delegation of Polish and Ukrainian Nazi sympathizers. He thanked Hitler for having given him control of 'this ancient nest of Jews . . . Once, there were thousands of Jews, hideously repulsive Jews, but now I can't seem to find any. Don't tell me you've been treating them badly . . .' The stenographer noted that this audience reacted to these remarks with 'great hilarity'.

Heinrich Himmler explicitly recognized that support for genocide could follow if it was presented as an act of 'ethnic cleansing' rather than straightforward slaughter. Even so, he feared (wrongly) that many Nazis would prove unwilling to see policy converted into practice, enforcing secrecy on this process and acknowledging that this would for all time deny the SS its 'rightful' place in German history.

As he put it to his SS leadership in his infamous speech in Posen on 4 October 1943:

> One principle applies absolutely to every SS man: he must be honest, decent, loyal and comradely to members of his blood but to no one else . . .

As far as the evacuation of Jews is concerned, the extermination of Jews, it belongs to the things that are easy to say. 'The Jewish race will be exterminated' says every Party member 'No question, it's in our programme, removal of Jews, extermination, we'll do it'. And then along come 80 million Germans and each one has their decent Jew. It's clear – the other Jews are swine but this one is a tip-top Jew. But none of those who speak in this way has watched, has had to stand through what you have stood through. Most of you know what it means if 100 bodies lie there, if 500 or 1,000 are there and you, apart from acts of human weakness, have remained decent. That has made us hard. That is a glorious chapter of our history that has never been written and never will be.

Opposition to the Nazis

The part played by terror in keeping the Germans compliant should not be minimized. Active opponents of the regime (as well as Jews) knew that they were certain to be identified and, at best, to suffer beating and imprisonment as a result and, at worst, to be killed for their opposition. In 1942 six Jews blew up an anti-Soviet exhibition in the centre of Berlin. Five hundred Jews were arrested at once; half were shot, the others deported to the East. The warning was intended to be as clear as it was brutal. Many historians have rightly drawn our attention to the horrors of the SS state not just in fighting the war of genocide against the Jews and others but also in using this fight to terrorize perfectly ordinary Germans.

The very large numbers of non-Jewish Germans arrested and executed for political crimes bear chilling witness to the extent of opposition to the regime. By the end of the summer of 1933 about 100,000 people had been arrested, and nearly 600 killed. From 1933 to 1939 some 225,000 people were sentenced to more than 600,000 years in gaol. In 1939 there were 300,000 Germans in custody. By 1945, a million had spent varying periods in concentration camps. In the period from 1907 to 1932, 1,400 individuals had been sentenced to death and 345 executed. But from 1933 to 1945 13,405 death sentences were passed and 11,881 were executed. Some 40,000 people were executed by the peripatetic peoples' courts after 1944. A further 800 were executed in the final weeks of the Third Reich. About 50 per cent of the Nazi death sentences were passed for political crimes. In the military sphere, courts martial passed 9,413 death sentences on members of the armed forces.

All the high institutions of the German state, but most fatefully the lawyers (who were subsequently themselves never indicted for this) caved in to Nazism and themselves used the law to help Nazify Germany. Hitler appointed Roland Freisler to head the *Volksgerichtshof,* which the latter described as 'a revolutionary tribunal to purify the nation' which in fact upheld National Socialism through terror. It handed out death sentences with no qualms – for criticizing the regime, even for telling jokes about it, as well as seeking to overthrow it. Hitler himself directly interfered in judicial decisions on many occasions, happily meting out death sentences or transfers to concentration camps. The law of High Treason was used as one might expect: it was a crime even merely to intend to set up a political organization outside the Nazi Party, to attempt to influence politically the army or the police, to produce anti-Nazi literature or to tune in to illegal broadcasts (particularly those on the German Service of the BBC). The outbreak of war in 1939 brought with it the chance for an even greater radicalization of the law. A criminal code for Poles was produced to punish them 'in the interests of the German people'. The SS and the SD, the security police, were in law now allowed to execute Poles or 'use' them as hostages. After July 1942 membership of the Communist Party triggered off an automatic death sentence. Ordinary people were punished with the greatest severity (often for saying what was obviously true). A Berlin worker was executed for having said Hitler was the greatest butcher of all time – the court's verdict said that 'Everyone knows the Führer did everything possible to avoid this war.'

If the trauma of subservience, and the trauma of recognition were bad enough, they were compounded by the trauma that resistance caused. It required Germans to attack their own government (courageous in a culture where discovery meant certain torture and almost always execution). The bravery of a few made the apparent cowardice of the many even more bitter. The resisters, however, also offered a legacy to post-Nazi Germans. It took a long time to assimilate the existence of resistance into Germany's national consciousness. Resisters acted either individually or as members of virtually every German social and political grouping. They were few in number. But they were nevertheless a light in a time of great darkness. Indeed, recent research shows that the longer the Nazis were in power, the more evil their regime became and the greater the number of people that were barbarized by it. In this sense, those who resisted, whether individually, or as part of a group, deserve greater credit than they have often been awarded because the possibilities for resistance today seem even scarcer than has often been assumed.

The Resistance

Most attention has been paid to the military resistance. They were the most important anti-Hitler conspiracy inside the Reich and they very nearly succeeded in assassinating Hitler on 20 July 1944. Indeed, the armed forces (or some of them) were the only grouping in reality strong enough to take on the Nazis and defeat them. It was not without irony that a group of people who were largely Prussian and of aristocratic origins provided the strongest challenge to the Nazis. These individuals were for the most part not liberal democrats. Some of them held straightforward racist beliefs, even if they utterly rejected the murder of the Jews. They insisted that in post-Nazi Germany Jews should continue to be classified as second-class citizens (even to the extent of being required to live in ghettos and losing their German nationality). They hoped that the overthrow of Hitler would avoid a defeat for Germany and its occupation by the Soviets (which by 1944 was a certainty). Nor did they represent the armed forces as whole. We now know that the war in the east had successfully brutalized most of those Germans involved in it. But the resisters themselves did detest the savagery of the Nazis and believed firmly that Hitler was evil.

This was made entirely plain – much the discomfort of the regime – at the trial of the plotters by the *Volksgerichtshof.* Yorck von Wartenburg managed to blurt out that he was opposed to the murder of the Jews; Ulrich Schwerin talked about 'murders at home and abroad'; von Moltke stated that Hitler was wicked and von Haeften that in 1923 Hitler had tried to do precisely what they had attempted in 1944. Roland Freisler, the prosecutor and judge in the trial, significantly referred to the defendants as 'reactionary slime'. 'Compared to you' he shouted at one stage 'Metternich was a progressive.' About five thousand people were executed in the purge that followed the bomb plot.

It would be wrong, however, to dismiss the words of these courageous Germans as the last gasp of an antiquated class, a view that Hannah Arendt and some German historians surprisingly shared with Freisler. Nor should we regard the plot merely as an attempt to safeguard their own position in German society, which they believed Germany's inevitable defeat would bring about. There was much more to it than this. The important fact is that there *was* a bomb which almost killed Hitler; that had Hitler been killed, the extermination of the Jews and the war in the west could have been stopped considerably sooner; and that it could do post-1945 German politics no harm whatsoever to stress the positive value that could be accorded to dissent and revolt even if it was fortunate for the development of liberal democracy in Germany in 1945 that Adenauer's concept of Western liberalism owed nothing to the resisters' plans for a post-Nazi Reich.

As far as political resisters were concerned, the most significant were the exiled German Social Democrats and the Communists. The rump of the SPD went first to Prague and then in 1938 to Paris. From 1941 to

1946, London was the official seat of the party. They played a very limited part in the war against Hitler thanks mainly to British anxieties about cooperating with anti-Nazis who were also anti-Communist. Whilst it was true that Social Democrats inside Germany refused to riot or resist actively in any significant numbers, there were many reasons for this other than lack of courage.

The exiles in London were led by Hans Vogel (who died in 1945 on the very day that Kurt Schumacher was re-forming the SPD in Hanover) and Erich Ollenhauer (who succeeded Schumacher as SPD leader from 1952 until 1963). Their blueprint, conceived in exile, for a post-Nazi Germany has been termed a plan to 'export British democracy', but to do so is not wholly illuminating. Whilst the exiles valued what they regarded as British 'tolerance', they did not, for example, propose to tolerate the Communists (a pre-1945 concept). They sought a Germany in an international system, willing to make reparation for Nazi crimes and a 'Socialist democracy born out of co-determination' with organized groups in society, particularly the trade unions.

The German Communists set up their major base in Moscow where they developed plans for Germany's future drawn up by Stalin and his colleagues. At times, they provided well-organized and courageous opposition to Nazism, although the Hitler-Stalin pact, which lasted from 1939 until 1941, meant their work was cynically halted (some of them, particularly in the Soviet part of Poland, were actually handed over to the Gestapo). After *Barbarossa*, German Communists quickly saw the logic in Stalin's wish to build a bridge between nationalism and Communism in the post-war world, and they followed his idea to establish a Free German committee in 1943, composed of representatives of all the resisters, in order to set up a broad coalition after Hitler had been defeated. A number of these anti-Nazi German Communists returned to lead the East German state.

Individual resisters or small resistance groups should also not be ignored. Amongst the most important of these were, first of all, the White Rose Group in Munich, who came from a Roman Catholic milieu and distributed anti-Nazi pamphlets amongst their fellow students at Munich University. They were staunch anti-racists and wrote simply about German policy: 'Since the conquest of Poland, 300,000 Jews have been murdered in the most bestial manner. In this we see the most terrible crime against human dignity, a crime not to be compared to any similar one in the history of mankind.' They were wrong, however, to believe their courageous resistance would spark off wider action ('What does death matter' asked Sophie Scholl on the morning she was beheaded in February 1943 'if thousands will be stirred and awakened by what we have done?'). Thousands were stirred and awakened – but alas not in the Germany of 1943. Detlev Peukert has shown that anti-Nazi youth groups (often looking to the United States for inspiration) flourished in several major German cities. Some of them went by the name of Edelweiss Pirates. One of the Cologne group, a 16-year-old named Barthel Schink, was publicly hanged there in November 1944.

The role and history of the resisters was treated curiously in post-Nazi Germany, further contorting the Nazi legacy to German political culture. Many Germans were embarrassed by the existence of resisters; some regarded them as traitors and a few as heroes. Whilst German democrats from all parties generally gave resisters their due, some groups were singled out for special praise (such as the military resisters) whilst others (Communists, for example) were denigrated. It has never ceased to be a fraught issue, often misused for political purposes. Ulrike Meinhof, for example, a leader of the Baader-Meinhof Gang in the 1970s, notoriously compared herself to the anti-Nazi resistance. The acts of violence she and her comrades committed in the Bonn Republic were justified, she claimed, because the opposition to Hitler had proved how necessary resistance was.

Life Inside the Reich

As for all the other peoples involved in the fighting, the war was itself a traumatic experience for the Germans. For one thing, they had to live with the continuous presence of death. This obviously affected different personalities in different ways, but there seems no doubt that its overall effect was to brutalize some and benumb the rest. For the Germans at home, the fact that Germany was at war was brought home to them first by the bombing campaign waged by the British and American air forces, and then by the advancing Allied armies.

In October 1944 one of them, Frau Wolff-Mönckeberg, wrote 'Around Antwerp and Aachen furious battles have raged for days with enormous losses on both sides. Success and defeat alternate. It seems now that the Americans have taken Aachen and Metz. They are fighting for every house, every cellar, every inch of ground . . . in the East battles are raging across the whole front; in the northern part the Russians are at the frontier of East Prussia!' She added: 'The background music to all this is the never-ending noise of droning aircraft passing across poor Germany, leaving havoc in their wake . . . the army bulletin gave out today that Kassel, Cologne and Bonn were subjected to very heavy bombing yesterday. In some of our towns, only a few houses are left; Münster, Darmstadt, Cologne and Frankfurt are almost totally destroyed . . . We, too, have renewed terror raids.' The person who wrote this was a firm anti-Nazi. Yet we note her use of the phrase 'terror raids'.

Bombing was intended to have an immediate impact both on the morale of the German people and on Germany's economic capacity to wage war. There was a widespread belief in the RAF that the destruction of essential industries and German centres of population would together achieve both the collapse of the German economy and of German civilian morale. This would, it was argued, cause the Third Reich to lose the war, and might even lead to the overthrow of the Nazi regime. They ignored the point that Germany was not a democracy and that its leaders were quite prepared to sacrifice German civilians if necessary. For many years after the war had ended, special attention was paid to Sir Arthur Harris, whose name became synonymous with blanket bombing of civilian targets. Harris was certainly one of the most emphatic supporters of mass bombing but his thinking was broadly in line with that of most of his colleagues. In 1928 Lord Trenchard, then RAF chief of air staff, had argued that although indiscriminate bombing of civilians was unacceptable, bombing to 'terrorize' individual groups of workers to absent themselves from their work was not wrong. Having established that enemy morale was a legitimate target, Harris's development of the tactic seemed acceptable.

In the event, bombing did not break the morale of the German people, or cause them to rise up against their Nazi leaders. It certainly generated hatred against the British and the Americans prior to capitulation. There were numerous cases where Allied airmen (quaintly called 'air Huns, in the pay of world Jewry') who had parachuted out of their stricken planes were lynched by ordinary citizens. In July 1944, for example, following a raid on Rüsselsheim, an American airman was beaten to death in the market place by a crowd. The next month a further six were killed as they were paraded through the city. At least one similar attack on *Luftwaffe* personnel is believed to have taken place in Britain. Almost every major town or city was hit. Some – Hamburg, Cologne, Kassel, the two Frankfurts and Würzburg to name but six – were almost totally reduced to rubble. Others, like Berlin, Hanover, Stuttgart, Kiel and Dresden lost over half their buildings. As a consequence, by 1945 there was widespread chaos in Germany. Bridges, railway lines, roads and telephone wires had been blown up. Hundreds of thousands of Germans were killed. Millions were now homeless. Their places of work were destroyed, their water supplies and sewerage ruined.

It was true that the destruction of so many German towns and cities was an unmistakable symbol of what Nazism had come to mean for Germany. It demonstrated the extent to which Germany's victors had been obliged to destroy Nazism physically themselves. What this signified, over and above the deaths and the rubble, was more complex. For the next fifty years, a number of Germans sought to deny the viciousness of their own bombing campaigns in order to regard Germany as a victim. Such denial in fact increased the trauma and caused it to be relived every time Harris's policies were discussed, or the Allied bombing of Dresden was scrutinized. Harris may have overstepped the limit of what was humanely acceptable (and the political reasoning which underpinned his policy was naïve). But it had been the *Luftwaffe* who had provided Harris with the opportunities in the first place.

The Nazi War Economy

Hitler bequeathed yet more psychological damage to the German people. He had undoubtedly got them back to work and rebuilt the German economy (whether on strong or weak foundations did not seem to matter). War and the bombing campaign now appeared to take this gain away. The Germans had, in economic terms, lost in Weimar, done better in the Third Reich and now, by 1945, were losing once more. The reason why the German economy had been transformed during the Third Reich was chiefly, of course, to wage war. The means used to promote the Nazis' goals were massive government spending combined with tight currency controls and the use of barter agreements wherever possible (these were used with great effect in gaining food supplies from Balkan states). Public spending in 1932 was roughly ten billion (thousand million) Reichsmarks. By 1939 it was fifty billions; by 1941 one hundred billions, by 1943 two hundred billions; by 1945 it had reached four hundred billions. Not only was this sort of spending unsustainable over any period of time, but it would also inevitably lead to a high degree of inflation. In 1928 arms spending represented about 1.1 per cent of German gross domestic product; by 1934 it was 6.3 per cent and by 1938 18.9 per cent. Alongside this damage we must set the 2.2 million tons of bombs which were released, of which over 906,000 tons of bombs were dropped on German (and French) targets; 224,000 on oil targets, 319,000 on transportation and 57,000 on the aircraft industry. Six hundred and fifty thousand civilians died in the campaign.

In actual fact, the German economy was undermined far less than appeared to be the case. For one thing, the Nazi leadership were loath to sacrifice Germans' standard of living to war aims for as long as they could avoid it. They understood only too well the part that deprivation and lack of food had played in the events of 1918–19, and were determined that they should not be repeated. They were not. The production of consumer goods in 1942 was only 3 per cent less than in 1939, although this figure was increased to 5 per cent after Speer took over. As late as 29 December 1944 a citizen of Hamburg could still go out for a meal of 'soup first, followed by a large trout fried in real butter. Then we had venison with red cabbage and potatoes and finally ice-cream . . .'

For another, German economic strength combined with this massive expansion of output meant that there was, in addition, a labour shortage, despite the existence of voluntary and involuntary labour recruitment schemes. German factories were not only able to rearm Germany and put the Germans back to work, but also to provide well-paid work for non-Germans. Hitler told Speer that since Germany controlled a population in Europe of 250 millions, labour would never again be a problem for the German economy. Yet amazingly, by 1942 it was estimated that German industry lacked one million workers. Attempts to remedy the situation by the recruitment of female labour, fell foul of Nazi ideology which held that a woman's place was in the home. Hitler was, however, prepared to allow the recruitment of half a million girls from eastern Europe to assist German housewives at home. Jews and other concentration camp inmates were ruthlessly exploited, and in July 1943 Hitler and Keitel gave their agreement to the use of forced prisoner-of-war labour.

Although the air attacks had a cumulative effect on the war economy, the effect was less severe than it might have been until the beginning of 1944. Speer's own ministry in Berlin was totally destroyed in November 1943, but this did not appreciably affect its work. The Germans continued to pay their taxes, even if the tax offices had been destroyed, so that tax revenue was maintained. Bombing factories, the Nazis claimed (apparently with justification) increased the resolve of the German worker to produce even more. Socialist and Communist calls to work more slowly (transmitted by the BBC and Radio Moscow) fell on deaf ears. The US Air Force estimated that bombing before 1944 had caused an overall loss in plant which ought to have generated a loss in production of 9 per cent. Speer claimed that this never occurred because the German workers' readiness to put in an extra effort made up for the missing 9 per cent. Under him the production of arms had, by August 1942, increased by 27 per cent over the February 1942 figure. Tank production was up by 25 per cent and munitions by 97 per cent, an overall increase of almost 60 per cent.

By May 1944, however, German industry was no longer able to replace the arms losses of the *Wehrmacht*. In addition, possession of bases in northern Italy allowed the Americans to bomb southern German industry more successfully, as well as to target fuel production. Bombing at the end of May of refineries and the all-important Romanian oilfields led to a loss of 2,000 tons of fuel per day. By 22 June 1944, 90 per cent of fuel production had been brought to a halt (although within a few weeks it was back to 40 per cent).

In addition, as 1944 progressed, the German economy was increasingly ensnared by Hitler's scorched earth policy. Hitler had insisted – originally for execution on the eastern front – that any withdrawal by German forces should proceed only when the economic infrastructure had been completely destroyed. As the Western Allies approached Germany's western border, he inflicted the same measures there. As a first step, much of French industry was to be blown up (in the event it was for the most part merely made lame rather than destroyed). Then it was the turn of German industry in the west (and the transport system). The beginning of the final Soviet offensive on 12 January 1945 robbed Germany of its last supplies of coal in Upper Silesia, Czechoslovakia and Danzig. The Ruhr had ceased to function by this time. It is usually estimated that bombing destroyed some 10 per cent of Germany's metal-working industry, 10–15 per cent of its chemical industry, 15–20 per cent of its engineering and 20 per cent of its textile plants. This was an important loss, but on the whole not a catastrophic one. Above all, it was a loss of an order of magnitude which made replacement and renewal within five to ten years a difficult task but not a hopeless one.

Defeat – or Liberation?

On 18 September 1944 the order had gone out that every village, town and city on the home front had to be defended with the utmost fanaticism to the last drop of blood, and the Nazi Party organized the *Volkssturm* – or 'people's shock troops', established in October for all males of between sixteen and sixty in every area of the Reich now under threat, both in the Rhineland and in eastern Germany. Soon every city would have a *Volkssturm*. On 12 February 1945 women were called to assist the *Volkssturm* (and on 2 April 1945 the *Werwolf* units were created as an underground army of resistance).

Briefly, during the winter of 1944/45, the Germans suspected they might have succeeded in stemming the advance of the Western Allies. On 16 December 1944 the Ardennes offensive began, taking the Anglo-American forces by surprise. In anticipation of success Hitler even moved to Bad Nauheim to be near the action. But when the offensive collapsed on 15 January, he returned to his bunker in Berlin, never to leave it again alive.

Americans Cross the Rhine

Even though the US armoured tank division commanded by General Courtney Hodges managed to take the bridge across the Rhine at Remagen on 7 March 1945, the German forces did not give up. Troops joined by schoolboy Flak gun operators fought on to try to stem the tide – V2 rockets were even fired from Hellendoorn in Holland in an attempt to destroy the bridge but they missed their target. The new jet fighters, the Messerschmidt 262s which had just been commissioned, were also ordered into action, but to no avail. Within a few days, the Americans had created a bridgehead twenty miles wide and five miles deep on the eastern bank. Their front stretched for more than five hundred miles - from the Swiss border to the south and to the North Sea to the north. On 27 March Eisenhower told Stalin that his aim was to reach Leipzig rather than seek to meet the Russians in Berlin. The Red Army and the US troops in fact met at Torgau (oddly enough, the 'Torgau March' had been one of Hitler's favourite tunes).

The Red Army

At the beginning of March the Soviet front extended from the Baltic to the Adriatic, almost one thousand miles long. In Germany, the Red Army had reached the Oder-Neisse line as far as the border with Czechoslovakia. The Germans had identified three main groups opposing their own Army Group Vistula, with bridgeheads at Stettin in the north, Küstrin (Kostrzyn) and Frankfurt on the Oder to the south.

It had been finally agreed at Yalta in February that the Russians would push to Berlin. The task was given to Marshal George Zhukov; Generals Konstantin Rokossovskii and Ivan Koniev commanded the huge army groups to the north and south. Zhukov believed that Berlin could be taken by the end of April. His opponents were Generals Heinz Guderian and Gotthard Heinrici, who now commanded the Army Group Vistula. General Alfred Jodl masterminded the overall defence strategy for the OKW or *Wehrmacht* high command. In the event, however, Stalin ordered Koniev to take the capital of the Reich. The *Wehrmacht* that opposed him consisted not only of hard-fighting professional units, tough young boys and old men in the *Volkssturm*, but also of phantom forces, such as General Wenck's 12th Army, which did not exist but had been invented to please the Führer. Hitler still held out in Berlin, but without point. In March 1945 the Siegfried Line was breached and US troops moved into central and southern Germany as far as the Alps and the river Elbe. By the end of June US military government was established in Hesse, North Württemberg-Baden and Bavaria. Frankfurt became the headquarters of what was now US Forces, European Theater. It is often claimed the Germans fought harder against the Russians than against the Anglo-Americans, but there is no conclusive evidence to this effect: most Germans believed they were fighting for Germany and fought hard on every front.

The Dönitz Government – First Post-War German Government or Last Nazi One?

On 30 April 1945 Grand Admiral Dönitz, the head of the U-boat force and commander in chief of the *Kriegsmarine* based at Ploen near Kiel, received a radio message from Hitler's bunker informing him that he had been appointed Hitler's successor and that the previous nominee, Goering, had been sacked. Hitler also named several of his ministers. A message was sent the next day that Hitler was indeed now dead, and Dönitz duly became the second Führer of the Third Reich (and not the first leader of post-Nazi Germany, as has occasionally been claimed). He did, however, dismiss three of Hitler's nominees – Himmler, Rosenberg and Ribbentrop – though he kept on Speer, Schwerin-Krosigk who took over foreign affairs, and Franz Seldte, the labour minister and Weimar *Stahlhelm* leader, who achieved the notorious distinction of being the sole survivor of Hitler's first 1933 government.

Hitler had in fact committed suicide in his bunker in Berlin shortly after three o'clock in the afternoon on 30 April. Dönitz, however, told the German people that Hitler had died fighting the Russians. Viewed from the perspective of the Nazis, there was a propaganda value in claiming that Hitler had indeed died as the national leader, defending German sovereignty to the last against the Bolsheviks. In reality, however, Hitler had killed himself (and his wife and dog) to escape being hanged for the murder of millions and the destruction of Germany and other European nations. Dönitz, a Nazi, was clear that the war was over. He did not, however, want to end it straight away, but hoped to make a bargain with Britain and America by offering a peace in the west in return for permission to carry on fighting on the eastern front.

Complete Collapse

But by 1 May 1945 the final collapse of Dönitz's residual authority was simply a question of time, even though he continued to try to delay surrendering until he had evacuated at least some of the 500,000 Germans fleeing from the Russians in the east and the armies cut off in Kurland and West Prussia. He continued to praise Hitler: in a speech delivered on 1 May, he claimed that Hitler, 'working for Germans and for Europe', had been right to fight Bolshevism. He and his cabinet were arrested on 23 May.

On 2 May 1945 Koniev finally took Berlin. On the same day, the German forces in Italy capitulated. On 5 May Field Marshal Montgomery accepted the partial capitulation of all troops in north-western Germany. In fact, he ought to have done no such thing, because there was a firm agreement that the demand for unconditional surrender meant that all Germans everywhere, including those on the eastern front, were obliged to surrender at the same time. This principle was upheld by General Eisenhower. When other German forces in the western theatre offered to surrender, Eisenhower said that either all German forces surrendered or else he would order further bombing. Thus on 8 May 1945, the German forces capitulated unconditionally to the British and Americans at Rheims and at Karlshorst, outside Berlin, to the Soviet Union.

The Dead

Hitler's war had caused the deaths of:

	Soldiers	Civilians
Germany	3,250,000	3,250,000
The USSR	13,600,000	7,000,000
The USA	225,000	
Belgium	12,000	76,000
Bulgaria	10,000	10,000
Denmark	400	1,000
France	250,000	350,000
Greece	20,000	140,000
Great Britain	326,000	62,000
Italy	330,000	80,000
Ex-Yugoslavia	300,000	1,400,000
Holland	12,000	198,000
Norway	6,000	4,000
Austria	230,000	104,000
Poland	100,000	5,700,000
Romania	200,000	260,000
Czechoslovakia	150,000	215,000
Hungary	140,000	280,000

These figures include the six to eight million Jews and Gypsies killed in the war of genocide.

The Survivors

Since Hitler had refused to countenance the possibility of a German surrender, German troops were not given any rules on how to hand themselves over. When they did, their victors found themselves swamped. From 15–20 April 325,000 German troops surrendered to US forces: this was more than the total of those who gave themselves up at Stalingrad. By 22 June 1945 the Americans alone had taken 3.4 million German prisoners-of-war (there were 7.6 million in the west as a whole). At first, many of those captured were subjected to physical abuse. The Western Allies were not only not prepared in a logistical sense for what they had to deal with; they were also not prepared for the evidence of massacres that they uncovered.

Many mass graves of foreign workers and other resisters were opened, and German POWs were forced to rebury the dead. None of Germany's victors found it easy to deal with such numbers of ex-enemy personnel in a humane manner, not least because of what they found. Alfred Hitchcock, the British-born Hollywood director, was asked to film the liberation of several concentration camps. His film was so horrific that it was not screened publicly for forty years.

There was undoubtedly abuse of German POWs. Some of the complaints that the prisoners made, particularly against the American troops, were frivolous (that they offered only white bread). At first, anyone found trying to escape was shot at once. Yet POWs were also given their first taste of the West. Education, particularly about the horrors of the Third Reich, played a part: many POWs claimed that it was only in captivity that they discovered the facts about the war of genocide. The claim that has been advanced recently, that up to one million German soldiers were killed by wilful neglect, has been treated with much scepticism. Yet it is clear that thousands died at this time, and some as a result of inhumane treatment. Those Germans not in uniform also suffered, particulary the young, the sick and the women. Tens of thousands of German women were raped without mercy by Red Army soldiers. The first wave of troops, often the élite, were usually well behaved; the second wave, however, were younger and poorly disciplined. Stalin himself told Djilas that soldiers who had risked their lives 'deserved fun with a woman' (Hitler took a similar view).

Just Another Beginning or the Year Zero?

The 'Year Zero' signified the time when Nazism finished and a fresh start could be made. For the practising politician and for the morally troubled citizen as well as for the ordinary person who just wanted to get on with living, the idea of a new beginning contained many attractions. In order to re-build Germany, its occupiers had to understand what now needed to be altered and what could be retained. The Germans who survived, however, were 'the Germans' both before 8 May 1945, and after it. They were the building blocks, however damaged, from which the new nation had to be built. Political leaders and political parties knew this only too well. The people had been changed and conditioned by Nazism, and anyone seeking to make a new, and above all democratic, Germany was obliged to accept this. The end of the war meant that there was now a realistic chance for those who lived that they might continue to live, providing, of course, that they could find food and shelter and stave off disease. The German nation had gone into abeyance. In its existing political form, it had been totally deconstructed into *Länder* and zones of occupation. There was, of course, still a geographical entity called Germany but its precise outline was now hazy. It was clear to the German political class and to Germany's victors, that capitulation had not only ended a regime but had thrown open the very future of the German nation. If German nationalism had generated Nazism, then Germany's future as a nation would have to be carefully scrutinized. The German economy had been very badly hit but, as we have seen, not devastated, even if it would require vast resources of cash and manpower to begin to rebuild it. German society, however, continued after May 1945 to be composed of the same groups as before although death and devastation had taken their toll and the Nazis had done much to weaken the standing of every class and every single social institution.

If 'Year Zero' is taken to mean *tabula rasa*, Germany in 1945 did not experience one. It could not have done so. But if 'Year Zero' simply means a condition in which people *imagine* a new beginning for themselves, and a new German state or states became thinkable, then indeed, this happened to the Germans now. In many ways, creating the 'Year Zero' helped conceal the Nazi legacy. Despite this, the next fifty years showed how important it was in reinventing a West German state.

The Occupation of Germany

Germany After Defeat

The policies pursued by Germany's victors from 1945 to 1949 constitute the second – and perhaps the most important – of the five processes which formed the Bonn Republic. Occupation in fact continued in one form or another until unity in 1990. The Western Allies retained important rights over West German security and, of course, in West Berlin. Even if there was a move away from occupation to cooperation, even if American, British and French forces became allied forces, it was occupation that gave the Bonn Republic its truly distinctive cast. The most significant changes in German political development, both in the west, and in the east, were thus the changes made during the years of occupation, by those who had fought against Hitler's Germany, rather than by the Germans themselves. In the west, it was the Americans who ultimately did most to shape the Federal Republic; in the east, the Soviets constructed their model German state.

It was the occupiers who now defined German interests and framed German affairs, both domestically and externally. On paper, with certain exceptions, this came to an end after a decade. In reality, what was created lasted for two generations at the very least. The first phase of occupation was hallmarked by a punishment paradigm. A punitive and colonial system was imposed on Germany, which employed new legal means to criminalize Hitler's most wicked racist supporters, along with the state they had created.

Once this was done as well as it could be (even if not well enough), a second phase began. As far as the west of Germany was concerned, this was characterized by constructive occupation, leading to real cooperation and then partnership. The Western Allies now began to impose democratic political structures – parties and political institutions – on the Germans. As we shall see, the full force of these actions is hard to estimate; what was done was, generally speaking, not the result of any stark, *new* invention. West Germany was different from other German states, but it was German and not American, British or French.

On the whole, German political and institutional forms were adapted, and filled with Western liberal contents. In the west, at any rate, it was, therefore, a veritable *reinvention* of Germany. It secured German democracy and ensured the new Federal Republic would be the ally of the United States, France and Britain and that is political life would be Westernized and Americanized. It is possible that the Germans would, after 1945, have done all of this had they not been occupied but it is not probable. But in any case, Germany's victors were determined to totally occupy Germany so that this matter would never be put to the test.

As one might expect, once Germany's victors found that they were able and obliged actually to make and execute policies for Germans, matters became very complex. The wartime Allies had different political ideas and competing security interests. What had been Germany was now affected by at least five different external entities. These were the occupation policies of the individual victors in their own zones, and the jointly agreed policy on Germany, as a whole, to which must also be added a domestic German input (an input which could only lead a political decision if it enjoyed the support and gained the final approval of the occupying power for each victor retained ultimate authority over legislation). Each of these inputs had its own special aspect. Out of them, two new German states were fashioned and German political life thereby assumed a new and very difficult shape.

We thus need to pay regard both to policy agreed between the Allies, as formulated at Potsdam (to which the French were not invited) and at the Council (or other formal meetings) of Foreign Ministers (in which France did participate) and to the individual agendas of the Allied Powers. Over and above all of this, we must bear in mind that the two German states were forged out of superpower conflict, against a backdrop fashioned by the fear of nuclear, and after 1953, thermonuclear war. Atom bombs and then hydrogen bombs, added huge danger to all differences in policy. These bombs, which were able to crack open the earth's outer mantle, ended up solidifying the political geography of the two parts of Germany. Neither superpower dared interfere with the other. In this way, after Germany's defeat, the differences in intention between the superpowers and the ensuing Cold War meant that by 1947 it became the determining factor in their respective foreign policies and their policy on Germany.

Some younger West German historians have questioned the implications of this upon the course of West German politics. In particular, just as some of them regarded the failure of the 1918–19 revolution as a missed opportunity for German democracy, so they suggest that the Federal Republic might have been a more satisfactory state if socialism, rather than occupation, had been its guiding principle. It could be claimed a socialist revolution would have re-created a united Germany along lines more acceptable to the Left, looking, perhaps, not to America but to the Scandinavian tradition of social democracy. It is true that the Western Allies did not promote a socialist revolution and showed no favour to social democracy. But by refusing to give it any special status of any kind, they both facilitated the development of democracy and avoided lumbering any one party with the responsibility for Nazi crimes, or making peace.

It was occupation that made democracy viable. A Germanic form of democracy whether of the Left, or the Right, was simply not permitted to take root. All the occupiers shared the basic wish to ensure the survival of the German people but soon went their own ways. It is obviously important to examine all these inputs in turn.

The Potsdam Conference

The Potsdam Conference – appropriately code-named 'Terminal' – was held in what was considered the home town of Prussian militarism (in a mock Tudor palace). It did not lead to a treaty, but to a protocol, a report upon which there was Allied agreement. It ended one sort of German nation and planned for another.

The rump government of Grand Admiral Dönitz had been formally dissolved on 5 June. There was confusion as to whether this meant that Germany itself had ceased to exist: the political reality (which was that the German nation state had effectively been destroyed) conflicted with the legal and historical need to confirm the continued existence of a German Reich, albeit one which no longer had any ability to exercise control of any kind, since without one, no peace treaty could be signed. Whether the German state as such continued to exist is a matter of academic debate. Historically, the Third Reich had ended as of 9 May 1945. Yet legally it could be argued that a German state, admittedly one under foreign occupation, remained intact, even if occupation prevented it from exercising its functions. There was confusion, too, as to whether the capitulation had been a military act, affecting the armed forces, or whether the armed forces had, on 8 May, represented the legal and polit-ical state. Carlo Schmid, himself a lawyer, soon to become a leading figure in the SPD argued that the German state had not ceased to exist in 1945 but had merely temporarily lost its ability to act as a state.

The Allied view seems to have been that one German state had ceased to exist and that in due course another German state would be established, and that the form this process would take would ultimately be the subject of inter-Allied and not German decisions. The Potsdam Conference was designed to initiate the process.

The Victors

The new American President, Harry Truman travelled to Germany by boat (a week's journey) arriving in Berlin on 15 July, on the same day as Winston Churchill and his Deputy Prime Minister, the Labour leader, Clement Attlee. The British leaders had, in fact, just fought a General Election against each other, the result of which was still unknown. To the surprise of many, Labour went on to win. In terms of foreign policy, however, there was not much to choose between the line taken by Churchill's coalition and Attlee's Labour administration. Stalin arrived in Berlin in a special train on 17 July.

The Conference

The Potsdam Conference produced quick agreement on the 'five Ds' (the Soviets, amusingly, merely talked about the 'three Ds', forgetting the final two): demilitarization, de-Nazification, disarmament, democratization and decentralization. Stalin had three main aims; to take receipt of the $10 billion in reparations he had been secretly promised at Yalta, to gain four-power control over the Ruhr, and to gain recognition of the Oder- (western) Neisse line as the new Polish-German border. Local self- government on democratic lines was to be introduced speedily. Indeed, the Commander of the Soviet Zone in his 'Order no. 2' of 10 June 1945 had already permitted the formation of four political parties. But the Americans and the British could not agree to the Soviet demand for reparations as it stood. Payment was to be made in German industrial machinery (taken from the whole of Germany) rather than actual cash. The term *démontage*, that is the dismantling of factories, was to become virtually synonymous with reparations. Stalin also insisted that Russia needed the enforced services of 2–3 million German workers, to be recruited from former war criminals, Nazi party members and the unemployed.

The USA (and Britain) feared that to comply in full with the Soviet wish for reparations would disrupt economic and political life in their own zones so radically that political chaos would ensue. The US Secretary of State James Byrnes suggested a compromise in which each occupying power could take reparation payments from their particular zone, with the Soviets getting an additional 10 per cent from the Western zones and a further 15 per cent in return for delivering supplies, especially food to the western part of Germany.

It was decided that economically Germany was to be treated as a single unit. It was also agreed that the Allied Control Council meeting in Berlin would take unanimous decisions on all matters affecting

Germany as a whole (although within their own zones, the military Commanders-in-Chief had full authority). Finally, the Potsdam agreement established a council of foreign ministers (which was to be joined by the French foreign minister) to meet at regular intervals. It was charged with special duties for the process of making peace in the future, especially with the future German state.

Despite their apparent personal wish to see the deconstruction of German national unity, neither Roosevelt nor Churchill were willing to build this into their respective national policies on Germany. There was agreement that the power of a central German government needed to be curtailed, given Germany's inherent strengths which would, one day, reappear. But this was not the same as suggesting that Germany be split up into separate states. As late as July 1944 Frank Roberts (later to become a leading British expert on Germany) complained in writing that 'planning on Germany has had to go ahead without any Cabinet policy directives. For example, the fundamental question of dismemberment has never been tackled.' Indeed, the extent to which Germany's dismemberment was not high policy is surely demonstrated by an examination of all the agreements reached at Potsdam. The dismemberment of the nation itself was never a sixth 'D'.

The Potsdam protocol, finally signed on 2 August 1945, laid down the basis for the political and economic control of Germany under occupation. In the event, its writ disintegrated within two years. Some German historians have argued that as a consequence of that the agreement was a work of fiction and that the decision to treat Germany as separate units for the purpose of reparations in effect created two German states. This is not plausible. The underwriting of the existence of a four-power Allied High Command in Berlin to coordinate policy in all the zones of Germany, as well as the decision that economically Germany was seen a single unit, can be seen as the outcome of a clear intention to retain an element of all-German government.

It would be quite wrong, therefore, to regard Germany's division as decided upon at this juncture, let alone before 2 August 1945. Yet allowing the Soviets to take what they wanted from their zone without regard to the economic consequences of this to the whole of Germany was bound to make the creation of a new German state harder to achieve, doubly so, given the Western toleration of the establishment of a Communist system there.

Even after the Cold War had properly broken out in 1947, both the West and the Soviets continued to hope for a single German nation. Both blocs had the same interest, namely the building of the German nation into their own social, political and economic system. Both the West and the Soviets believed a future Germany ought to mirror their respective systems. Yet even after the end of formal occupation, as, for example, in 1953, when with Stalin's death a real chance for reunification of sorts presented itself, the West (aided by Adenauer) always preferred a divided Germany, with a strong Federal Republic as a part-nation, to a united but neutral Germany, which might come under the sway of the Soviet Union.

Common Allied Policies

The Punishment of Nazi War Criminals: The Nuremberg Trials

The first step in the abolition of Hitler's ethnic order was to criminalize those who had directly executed it and tear up the laws that had upheld it. There had been eight-and-a-half million NSDAP members and four million members of associated organizations. The Allies had to set up 545 courts (staffed by 22,000 officials) to process the three and a half million questionnaires completed by former Nazis.

The evolution of a common Allied war crimes policy contained many twists yet its effects on politics in western Germany (as well as its effect on the rest of the world) should not be underestimated. The effective criminalization of Nazi party members and sympathizers (even if only on paper) permitted a distinction to be drawn between Nazis and Germans – to the huge advantage of the latter. Not every Nazi had been a war criminal but Nazism itself became illegal. It enabled western Germany to be purged to a relatively satisfactory degree (it is doubtful whether the Germans themselves would have conducted a satisfactory de-Nazification process). From 1945–92, 103,823 people were investigated for Nazi crimes, the vast majority by the West Germans. But only 6 per cent were ever convicted. Of these, 85 per cent were found guilty of minor crimes only. It has been estimated that only seven out of every thousand were brought to justice, and only five out of every thousand punished in any way at all. Allied actions, however, allowed West Germany to enter the community of Western liberal states far quicker than would otherwise have been possible. And, with one or two relatively minor exceptions, 1930s Nazism was successfully excluded from German public affairs. This was a tremendous achievement.

Initially, Churchill (and not Stalin, as is often supposed) believed that these major war criminals – he thought there were from fifty to a thousand of them – should be shot at once; Stalin, however, much to the West's surprise, insisted on trials. In 1945 an international conference was called in London to discuss these trials, and it was agreed to set up an international tribunal, operating with its own laws, at Nuremberg (seen as the chief spiritual home of Nazism). Both the United Nations

War Crimes Commission and another body known as CROWCASS (the Central Registry of War Crimes) produced extensive lists of suspected war criminals. All Allied forces were ordered to seize any war criminal they uncovered. Captured German personnel were supposed to be checked off against these lists, though under the circumstances it is clear that the process could at best be only partially successful. Figures supplied by a Canadian government report stated that in 1946 Britain had 5,900 active war crimes files and a list of 1,085 suspects; it had passed 240 death sentences. The French, by 1950, had produced 5,000 convictions and 104 death sentences; the United States (to 1949) had tried 2,125 suspects, passed 267 life sentences and 348 death sentences.

The Nuremberg Tribunal generated 13 separate trials involving 177 people and passed 20 life sentences, 25 death sentences and 35 acquittals. They were charged on one or more of four counts: the common plan or conspiracy, crimes against peace (the planning and waging of aggressive war), war crimes (here defined as shooting prisoners of war), and crimes against humanity (here defined as the persecution of Jews and the destruction and exploitation of occupied territories). The Americans handled the count of conspiracy, and the prosecution of organizations like the SS; the British dealt with the second count; the Russians and the French with the third and fourth (the former dealing with eastern, the latter with western Europe). The defendants were prosecuted by lawyers from the four allied nations; the chief prosecutors were Robert Jackson (USA), Sir Hartley Shawcross (the attorney general) and Sir David Maxwell-Fyfe (who did much of the former's work) and General Roman Rudenko (USSR).

Goering was convicted on all four counts, as were von Ribbentrop, Keitel, Rosenberg and Jodl. They were hanged with the exception of Goering, who was able to commit suicide. Von Neurath was found guilty on all four counts but received fifteen years in gaol. Kaltenbrunner, Frank, Frick, Streicher, Sauckel and Seyss-Inquart (and Bormann in his absence) were also sentenced to hang. Raeder received a life sentence; Hess (guilty on counts one and two but innocent of three and four) got life; Speer, guilty on three and four but innocent of one and two got twenty years. Funk, Dönitz and von Schirach got between ten years and life; Fritzsche, Schacht and von Papen were acquitted. The leaders of the Nazi political élite were thus dealt with unequivocally. The ashes of those who had been hanged and cremated were cast into the river Iser.

In addition, the tribunal declared the political leadership corps of the Nazi Party (*Gauleiters* and the like), the Gestapo, the Security Service (SD) and the SS to have been criminal organizations. Further trials dealt with leading officials of the foreign office (including von Weizsäcker, head of the Nazi Foreign Ministry, found guilty of assisting in the extermination of Jews), directors of I.G. Farben the chemical concern, SS doctors and concentration camp guards.

At Potsdam it had been agreed that all members of the Nazi Party who were more than nominal members were to be dismissed, and for the next one-and-a-half years almost one million Nazi Party members had to resign from the bureaucracy. By the end of 1946 the British had interned 64,000 'dangerous Nazis', the Soviets 67,000, the French 19,000 and the Americans 100,000. Almost half a century later, however, it became clear that many of those responsible for appalling acts of cruelty, both German and non-German, remained unpunished. All Western powers in due course passed de-Nazification procedures to German officials and courts. Every German over the age of eighteen had to complete a questionnaire and wrong-doing was punished in a variety of ways, including detention in labour camps (for a maximum of ten years), fines, loss of pension rights and exclusion from certain professions. The law differentiated uniformly between five categories: major perpetrators, perpetrators (defined as activists), minor per- petrators (whose sentence could involve two to three years' probation), fellow-travellers and those who were blameless. Those under investigation sought to obtain statements of support from recognized anti-Nazis and others which assisted them in establishing innocence. Up to 1950, more than six million cases were investigated in the three Western zones. 1,667 people were classified as major, 23,060 as minor and 150,425 as perpetrators; 1,005,854 as fellow travellers (of whom two-thirds were punished in some way) and 1,213,873 as innocent. In another four million cases, amnesties were given for various reasons (including youthfulness).

Common Economic Policy

As we have seen, whilst severely damaged, the German economy was not devastated. Recovery was feasible. Indeed, in a bizarre way, it was possible to argue that Germany came out of the war in a better position than Britain with its $20 million war debt. German industry, where it had not been destroyed, was better equipped in 1945 than in 1939. It was true that in 1945 coal production was but one-tenth of its 1939 level. But the coal was in the ground and all Germany's victors saw it – quite rightly in a pre-oil era – as the cornerstone of the German economy. By January 1946 coal production had been increased fivefold. Yet this coal was for the present to be used for the benefit of the victors rather than the Germans themselves.

On 26 March 1946 the Control Council published its plan on

reparations and the post-war level that the German economy was to be allowed to attain. Its basic principles were that the population of Germany was to be reckoned at 66.5 millions (the implication being that Germany was one nation); that, as Potsdam had declared, Germany was to be treated as a single economic unit; and, finally, that German exports should have access to the international market. On 1 April 1946 the economics directorate of the Allied Control Council duly published a list of factories to be dismantled. There were over 400 of them, ranging from iron and steel mills, aircraft and munitions factories and shipyards to optical and chemical concerns (262 in the UK zone, 130 in the US zone and 23 in the French zone). This was tantamount to a massive impoverishment of the German economy.

The Russians consistently refused to account for the reparations in their zone, partly because they did not need to, and partly because they were vexed they had still not been given the original $10 billion they had requested at Potsdam. They had been given 10 per cent of the value of reparations, as well as a further 15 per cent in value as a trade-off against delivering supplies to the western zones (which were in fact never delivered). The deliveries to them from the US zone began in September 1945, but were stopped in May 1946 because the Americans did not believe the Russians were fulfilling their part of the deal. Yet *démontage* itself still continued, and became, not surprisingly, a central issue in the emerging agenda of West German political life.

The socialization or state ownership of industry that each victor was free to embark upon (and which the Soviets and the British proceeded with) nevertheless had implications for every occupying power.

The Ongoing 'Potsdam Process', 1946–8

As we have seen, the Potsdam agreement provided that there should be regular formal meetings of the foreign ministers of the four victorious powers in order to work out how Germany was to be restored to nationhood and how the new German nation was to fit into the political and economic structure of Europe. Since this process ended in failure – in the sense that Germany could not be restored as a nation – more attention tended to be concentrated on the disagreements between the powers than on their ultimate goal, which was that once Potsdam had been enacted, and Germany reinvented as a nation, they could go home.

German national unity was discussed in April, May and June of 1946 by the foreign ministers. There were agreements and also disagreements between the Western Allies as well as between them and the Soviets. Britain, for example, made it plain that it opposed the French policy of seeking to separate the Rhineland and the Ruhr from the rest of

Germany. Similarly, the British had problems with American policy. Whilst conflicts between the West and Russia emerged, causing the Americans to believe the occupation of Germany would have to continue for an undefined period, this – significantly – was seen as a way of keeping German intact rather than breaking it up.

The Creation of the Bizone

Against this background, the Americans, followed by the British, decided to address the growing economic problems of western Germany by setting up the Bizone on 29 May 1947 (the final agreement on the measure came on 17 June 1947, the treaty being signed on 17 December). The aim was to create vitally important economic unity between the US and UK zones, in order to restore the German economy in the west. They wished to reduce the expense of occupation and transfer virtually all the occupation costs from Britain on to the US until the western German economy had recovered. To expedite this, an Economic Council was to be set up, with representatives to be chosen by the *Land* parliaments. It met on 25 June 1947 in the Frankfurt stock exchange (with 21 CDU members, 20 SPD, 3 KPD, and 3 FDP, and other assorted splinter groups). From the domestic western German standpoint, the Economic Council was a body of great importance – virtually a shadow federal government. In 1948 Ludwig Erhard (1897–1977), western Germany's most influential economic thinker and policy maker (who had been supported by the Americans ever since 1945) became Economic Director of this council. From 1929 until 1942 he had worked at the Institute of Economic Research of the Nuremberg Technical College; his work inherently contradicted Nazi policies of state interference in industry.

This Anglo-American move has, in retrospect, sometimes been seen as the decisive stage in the formation of a western state in Germany; but by sovietizing their zone, it was initially the Russians who had created the preconditions for the evolution of two German states, and the Americans and the British merely set the seal on this process. In Moscow, meanwhile, the foreign ministers debated the future form of the German government, the kind of economic system it should have, the borders of the new German nation and their own future role. During the July–September 1946 Paris council, various German issues had been raised but it was already accepted that the German problem was in a class by itself, and that unless the West could be satisfied that the Soviets would cease sovietizing eastern Germany, German unity would in the foreseeable future be impossible to achieve. To underscore this, the British Foreign Secretary Ernest Bevin produced a plan of his own on 27 February 1947 that appeared to support continued four-power control of Germany but severely limited the already minimal effect the Soviets could have on its western part. As Bevin told his Cabinet colleagues, his aim now was 'to keep the iron curtain down (unless we get satisfaction [from the Russians] on all our conditions) and build up western Germany behind it'.

Germany's future division became inevitable after the failure of the Moscow council of foreign ministers from 10 March to 24 April 1947. Yet it is important to realize that this was still more of a slide into keeping Germany divided than a positive wish to have two German states. Many areas of agreement emerged, particuarly between the Soviets and the Americans. The Moscow meeting was, however, already overshadowed by the enunciation, on 12 March, of his celebrated Doctrine by President Truman, one of the most significant policies of the twentieth century because it actively promoted the westernization of West Germany and other European states.

The Truman Doctrine and Marshall Aid

It was America's belief that a new economic order was necessary, not only to lay the foundations for future prosperity, but also to permit western-style democracy to flourish. On 12 March 1947, in an address to Congress, President Truman called for a $400 million economic and military aid package to Greece and Turkey, adding the keynote phrase that 'It must be the policy of the United States to support free peoples who are resisting attempted subjugation by armed minorities or by outside pressures, primarily through economic and financial aid, which is essential to economic stability and orderly political progress.' This was followed on 5 June 1947 by a speech made by Secretary of State George Marshall at Harvard University, initiating what became known as Marshall Aid. Its political and economic effects were enormous. They not merely led to the economic regeneration of western Europe, and the creation of a European Economic Community, but also confirmed the political division of the continent.

Marshall pledged the USA to fight 'hunger, poverty, desperation and chaos'. His deputy, Dean Acheson, had already provided a highly significant pointer as to the direction the Americans wished their policy to take when he stated that 'the achievement of a co-ordinated European economy' was a fundamental objective. In due course an Organisation for European Economic Cooperation was set up to administer the scheme which distributed $6 billion over its first fifteen months. It also regulated the various devices which prevented the American dollars from causing financial problems for the various economies, thus promoting European integration and industrial renewal at the same time.

It is hard to exaggerate the importance of this American policy which had such a profound impact on the shaping of Germany's future. Marshall Aid was used not just by West Germany but by the sixteen western European states who received it in a variety of ways; western Germans used it first for food and then for modernizing their industrial base and building homes. The impact this act of American generosity (the aid was a gift, not a loan) had on western Germans was enormous; it played a key part in locking West German democracy into the Atlantic relationship – and, by producing such prosperity, ultimately proved to the people of Eastern Europe and the Soviet Union that Communism could not compete with Western economic ideas.

The Plan to Found a West German State

By 1948, the Americans (and the British) felt they could openly develop western Germany into a state which could be part of the Western community. This policy was predicated on the growing conviction that Stalin's chief aims included the wish to extend Soviet power and influence as far west as possible. It is true that some individuals (most notably Winston Churchill) argued the Soviet Union was chiefly concerned with security rather than expansion or domination. Given the danger of nuclear war, however, the wisest policy seemed to be to err on the side of caution. The issue of German unity was, of course, subsumed in this wider struggle. 1948 was a turning-point in other ways as well: the first stirrings of Communist aggression in Korea and the Communist-led *coup d'état* in Prague in the second half of February indicated that Stalin had decided to drop the last pretences of democratic behaviour. On 22 January 1948 Bevin urged the Benelux states to form a defence union against Communism (Britain was still the leading West European power).

From 23 February to 6 March 1948 the three Western Powers and the Benelux states deliberated in London upon the German issue independently of the Soviets. They agreed that their three zones should participate fully in the American recovery plan, and in effect the Bizone became a Trizone. Virtually contemporaneously on 17 March the same countries signed the Brussels Pact, which on paper said that they would join to defend themselves against a renewal of *German* aggression, but they meant Soviet aggression.

At a further London conference of the same group of states on 1 June 1948 it was announced that it was now 'necessary to give the German people the opportunity to achieve on the basis of a free and democratic form of government, the eventual re-establishment of German unity at present disrupted'. To achieve this end, the military governors were ordered to hold meetings with the minister presidents of the western zone to convene a constituent assembly with the task of preparing a West German constitution.

Within their zone, the Western Allies were urgently seeking to reorganize the governance of the Economic Council following an agreement on 17 December between Bevin and Marshall, formally giving the USA the greatest say in the development of the German economy. A *Länder* council was established on 9 February alongside the Economic Council which was itself doubled in size (to include 104 members). Shortly after this, the Allies established a German bank (*Bank deutscher Länder*) and a German supreme court (*Obergericht*) in Cologne.

Meanwhile, in their zone, the Soviets formed a German economic commission, led by Heinrich Rau. They had already established political parties and begun to exhort and coerce Social Democrats in their zone to merge with the KPD and form the Socialist Unity Party, or SED. Rau was an SED member. On 20 December the Soviets dismissed Jakob Kaiser and Ernst Lemmer as leaders of the (eastern) CDU on account of their opposition to the form of parliament – a people's congress – which the Soviets had put forward. In April the Soviets formed two new parties, the National Democratic Party, based on the National Committee for Free Germany and supported by officers and soldiers who had been part of it, and the Democratic Farmers' party. Both were simply front organizations for Communist dominance; yet deemed necessary in the German context.

On 17 and 18 March a people's congress was convoked in East Berlin with 2,000 delegates, claiming for itself the sole right to represent Germany (indicating, yet again, the Soviet interest in German unity), announcing a plebiscite on unity and recognizing the Oder-Neisse line. It established a people's council (*Volksrat*) led by Wilhelm Pieck of the SED. Accordingly, on 20 March 1948, General Sokolovsky, the Soviet military commander of Germany, walked out of a meeting of the Control Commission in Berlin in protest at Western policies. The four victorious Allies were not to meet again in the Commission for another forty-two years; but meet again they did, and this time it was to reunite Germany rather than divide it.

Currency Reform

In order that the three western zones of Germany should be able to participate fully in the Americans' European recovery plan, it was necessary to deal with German inflation. In 1938 there were about RM 60 billion in circulation; by 1945 RM 300 billion. In addition, Germany's war debt amounted to some RM 400 billion. The occupiers had of course also printed money (the Soviets were particularly profligate). Increasingly, the cigarette had become a unit of currency (1 cigarette being worth 7 Reichsmarks and, when in packs of ten, having a decimal value as well). It was thus vital to restore real money to western Germany. This was done in a series of four laws, of which the most obvious was the German currency law of 18 June 1948 (to take effect on 21 June 1948), which gave every individual 40 units of the new money, the Deutsche Mark, or DM; later they were to get another 20. Within ten days all old Reichsmarks had to be handed in and changed at a value of 10:1, although half of this had to be kept in a closed bank account. This huge (and inevitably secret) operation was masterminded by Ludwig Erhard, in charge of the West German end, and the Americans.

On 23 June 1948 (the day after the western currency reform) the Soviets instituted their own reform. The old RM was exchanged at a 10:1 ratio; each eastern German received DM 70. But in reality the eastern German currency was worth far less far sooner than the western currency, not least because of the inflationary policies of the Soviets and its lack of value in Western hard cash. On 24 June 1948, meeting in Warsaw, the Soviet Union, Albania, Bulgaria, Czechoslovakia, Yugoslavia, Poland, Romania and Hungary joined a mutual defence pact, known as the Warsaw Pact.

The Berlin Airlift

The Soviet response to western currency reform was crude; it now sought to detach West Berlin from the West. At the beginning of 1948, the Soviets had begun to interfere with transports to West Berlin. Since all land access and all three air corridors went through Soviet controlled territory, it was clear that their power to blockade Berlin was enormous. On 24 June, in an attempt to prevent the transfer of the western Deutsche Mark into West Berlin, Soviet forces imposed a complete halt on western land traffic to Berlin.

Stalin's aim was plainly to starve the two million inhabitants of West Berlin into surrendering to Communism by accepting the eastern DM. Whilst the Americans had atom bombs as a deterrent, they were, for obvious reasons, of little use in this case; and the advice that General Clay, the US commander in Germany, was giving to the American President was that Stalin, too, did not wish to have a nuclear war over West Berlin. The Western Allies decided to defeat the Russians not through military force but by a demonstration of their technical superiority.

As a result, Operation Vittles – the airlift of food and fuel – was initiated on 7 July and, within a few days, 3,000 tons were flown in; on one day, 13,000 tons of food were transported in 1,400 flights to Tempelhof, Gatow and Tegel (British seaplanes even landed on the Havel). There could be no more basic or emotive illustration of the Western commitment to the German people than an airlift whose purpose was not military but to keep people alive and to prevent them from being blackmailed. General Montgomery had been right when he had said that the strategic significance of Berlin was minimal; but entirely wrong to deduce that it was therefore not worth fighting for. The point that those who had three years previously been the mortal enemies of the West were now treated as its allies, escaped no one in the West or the East. The Berliners themselves came out of it with much praise, not least because of their humour ('good that the Russians are providing the blockade and the Americans the airlift, rather than the other way round'); but it should not be forgotten that in the process of making 300,000 flights (and delivering 2 million tons of goods), 39 British and 31 American servicemen gave their lives.

The Soviet authorities also attempted to interfere with the democratic life of the western part of the city when elections in Berlin began to demonstrate the unpopularity of Communism. Berlin's City Hall (situated in the eastern sector) was the scene of violent demonstrations organized by the Communists and a Communist government for all of Berlin was imposed towards the end of November 1948. The Western response was to give West Berlin its own administration with an elected mayor (under their authority). Ernst Reuter, a Social Democrat, became the first governing mayor. The blockade did not come to an end until an agreement with the Soviets was reached on 12 May 1949.

Occupation Policy in Germany: The USA

US policy on Germany and its zone (the dominant policy, thanks to American power), was constructed around the Joint Chiefs of Staff Document 1067, usually referred to simply as JCS 1067. This policy statement was first drawn up on 22 September 1944 at the time of the Quebec conference.

Roosevelt's harsh line on Germany, particularly his support of the Morgenthau Plan, had come under fire. Henry Morgenthau, Roosevelt's Treasury Secretary, took the line that in order to punish the Germans, and prevent them from ever again being strong enough to wage aggressive war, it was necessary to de-industrialize, to pastoralize Germany and to dismember its national unity.

Although Roosevelt sought to distance himself from this plan, he did derive a number of ideas from it. The American President was entirely serious about not simply eradicating Hitler's ethnic order but attempting to alter the basic social, economic and political structures which it was believed had given birth to Nazism. Thus JCS 1067 came to possess the clear mark of Morgenthau. Roosevelt's successor Truman signed JCS 1067 (in its eighth version) on 14 May 1945. He also continued his predecessor's policy of seeking to cooperate fully with the Russians. General Eisenhower was US Military Governor in Germany until November 1945 (when General McNarney replaced him). Eisenhower, too, firmly believed in the value of cooperation with the Soviets and felt considerable bitterness towards the Germans ('I won't shake hands with a Nazi', he once declared). After his departure, real power was exercised by General Clay, first as Deputy Governor and then, in March 1947, as McNarney's successor.

Clay's initial attitude was clear. He told his staff they were in Germany to punish it and 'hold it down the way it should be'. But he soon softened his approach, impressed by the way in which the ordinary German people were seeking to tackle the devastation the war had left behind. Clay (sometimes called 'proconsul of western Germany') had a clear sense of America's mission there. He actively intervened in all the important political matters. It was he, for example, who obliged Erhard to adopt a harsh rate of exchange for the DM, understanding that he, Clay, could dare to do what a German politician could not. It was Clay, too, who insisted the constitution makers accepted American ideas. He once told his interpreter that he was proud of the beneficial impact he believed he had had; he regretted only his failure to totally abolish class, the power of banks and of bureaucrats.

JCS 1067 was a compromise policy, and successive governors were given considerable latitude in interpreting aspects of it. Its most consistent theme was punishment. It declared that it should be brought home to all Germans that it was Nazism that had destroyed their country and their economy and brought inevitable suffering as a result. 'Germany' it added 'will not be occupied for the purpose of liberation but as a defeated enemy nation.' The aim of Allied policy was to 'prevent Germany from ever again becoming a threat to the peace of the world'. The Germans were to be punished by reducing drastically their standard of living and by capping their economic strength. This policy remained in force until July 1947. As one of its many critics (an adviser to Clay) said, JCS 1067 had been 'assembled by economic idiots. It makes no sense to forbid the most skilled workers in Europe from producing as much as they can for a continent which is desperately short of everything.'

US Policy on Political Parties

It is interesting that pressure to form political parties began to build up in all the zones so soon after Germany's capitulation. There were several reasons for this. First, German democrats chose to perceive the Third Reich as a hiatus in German political life. They were keen to prove this by becoming active at once. Secondly, parties represented organized opinions and interests. However downtrodden and submissive the German people had become, there were some Germans with opinions. All of them had interests. Even where there was so very little to be consumed (perhaps precisely because there was very little), competition, for what there was, could be best articulated through parties. Above all, the Americans believed in democratic politics. They permitted licensed parties to start operating on 13 August 1945 (this was, as we shall see, more than two months after the Soviets granted licences in their zone). On 27 August, however, this permission was restricted to activities at *Kreis* level only, zonal activity being allowed again in November.

At local level (as shown, for example, in Bavaria) the US intervened with a firm hand, first to punish and then create democratic conditions. US polls of POWs in Bavaria had shown that about 35 per cent of them were still active Nazis, 40 per cent passive ones, 15 per cent passive resisters and 10 per cent active resisters. The high figure of active and passive Nazis caused understandable alarm. Security demanded that Nazism be extirpated from German political life. JCS 1067 laid down that anyone who was more than a nominal Nazi would have to be dismissed.

In practice, it proved very difficult to de-Nazify the US zone and govern it at the same time. The waters were muddied somewhat by General Patton's famous observation (that 'the Nazi thing was just like a Democratic and Republican election fight'); against this background the man appointed minister president, Fritz Schäffer (a former Dachau inmate) had proposed that ex-Nazis should be allowed to serve in the bureaucracy for a three-year probationary period. However undesirable, there was little alternative to this policy if the administration was to be started up again.

The Americans were strongly opposed to the policy of state owner-ship of key industries. They believed that far from endangering democracy, capitalism nurtured it and that governments should stay out of it. In 1945, learning about Erhard's views on the free market, they appointed him to the Bavarian government. His concept of free-market activity combined with social responsibility contained, in their view, the only sensible basis for the economic future. When the people of Hesse, in the US zone, voted in June 1946 for a constituent assembly that decided to nationalize 169 coal and iron companies as well as the transport system, General Clay refused to accept the decision, and ordered what in effect was a plebiscite on 1 December on this issue. When this vote showed a 70 per cent majority for nationalization (most of the Hesse CDU were in favour of the policy) Clay agreed to keep the clause in the constitution, but denied permission for it to be carried out.

British Occupation Policy

The British, as was perhaps to be expected from an imperial and colonial power, were determined to take occupation very seriously. The British zone was to be run as if it were a colony. Yet this does not mean quite what it seems. The colonial principle was to maintain overall control but devolve actual decision making, and to encourage the emergence of domestic leaders whose aims ran parallel to those of Britain. Apart from the central themes of occupation laid down at Potsdam, the British, more than any other power in Germany, were content to let Germans shape their own destinies.

The British element of the Control Commission for Germany was headed by Field Marshal Montgomery. His deputy, General Sir Brian Robertson, succeeded him in 1947. In October 1945 a Minister for Germany, John Hynd, was appointed (his real title, which must have amused the Germans, was Chancellor of the Duchy of Lancaster) and almost 55,000 people were employed by the Control Commission for Germany (29,000 of them in the UK Zone). By early 1946 this was costing £80 million per year.

Cost was a major British concern not least because the Labour Government of 1945 had embarked upon an over-ambitious programme of nationalization. Another worry was the growing perception that the Soviets did not want to cooperate with the West, but were intent on extending the power of Communism. Sir William Strang, political adviser to Montgomery, defined British tasks in what became the four British *Länder* as being first and foremost concerned with food, coal, displaced persons and public safety. The politics, he believed, could wait. He was agreed with the plan to 'rebuild the life of the people on humane and decent lines'.

The situation facing the British in Germany was, of course, the same as that which faced its allies, one of complete and utter chaos. Millions were on the move as refugees, displaced persons uprooted by the Germans and used as slave labour, Germans seeking to escape the control of the Red Army, and Nazis trying to escape capture. People were starving. Just as in 1918/19, horses killed during the fighting were quickly reduced to hooves, skin and hair by men and women wielding knives, taking as much as they could carry. It took a generation for the Germans to forget how hungry they had been during these years. Millions were without a roof over their heads.

The supply of food was indeed a horrendous problem. One-quarter of all food production had been lost with the lands east of the Oder and Neisse. The British laid down a food norm for Germans of 1,550 cals per day although the League of Nations limit was 2,400; JCS 1067 envisaged the use of the Allies' food only to prevent starvation, plague and civil unrest. An early task in the summer of 1945 was to bring in the harvest. In the British zone of occupation, General Montgomery himself had noticed that no one was working in the fields, work previously done by slave labourers or Allied POWs. It was decided now to use German POWs in British hands. The first harvest of peace was duly brought in.

By March 1946, however, it had become clear that there was not enough food to last until the next harvest so a cut in rations was ordered. A hard winter in 1947 was followed by a dry summer leading to a further decline in food production. The calorie allowance went down to 1,103 and in some places like Essen only 1,056. This meant – per day – a ration of four slices of bread, 14 gm of meat, a small cup of skimmed milk and tablespoons of cheese, fat and cereals. In order to stay healthy, it was considered necessary to have at least 50 gm of fat a day, not to mention vitamins and mineral supplements.

The British believed that a centralized system of food control would offer the best chance of averting a major famine and bizarrely used a Nazi institution to organize supply (the *Reichnährstand*, the Reich food authority, was dissolved only on 21 January 1948). Their Western associates disagreed: both the Americans and the French wanted a decentralized system. As late as December 1948 the British food supremo, Hans von Schlange-Schöningen attacked Ludwig Erhard for suggesting that West Germany under a market economy would be able to feed itself. In fact, the Hamburg food office depended on massive food imports – 'out of the ship and into the mouth' as Schlange-Schöningen put it. Even so, there was not enough to eat. By 1946 the incidence of tuberculosis was four times the 1938 figure and all the Allies realised they would have to modify their stance on the importing of their own food, the Americans taking the lead. From October 1946 for the next ten years, 8 million care packages were sent from the USA to Germany; by May 1949 5 million German school children were getting meals from America.

In due course, the British began to fear that starvation and disease might promote political unrest or further the aims of Communism. In addition, many in Britain found it hard to understand why they should have to put up with food shortages at home in order to feed the Germans. There was another aspect to this matter: coal. There was plenty of coal in the British zone; but the German miners needed food in order to be able to extract it, and, in order to export it, an adequate transport and communications system was needed. An additional difficulty was caused by the order to remove Nazis from management positions in the coal industry. On 5 September 1945 a decision was taken to arrest several coal barons; Strang, who favoured this decision, suggested that the failure to act against Nazis in the coal industry was lowering the morale of the miners. The British then went even further: on Bevin's suggestion, the Control Commission assumed ownership of the Ruhr mines in December. His aim, consistent with his Socialist beliefs, was to 'eliminate the present excessive concentration of economic power' in the hand of the Ruhr magnates, as well as to show the Ruhr miners that they were committed to bringing about socialism in the zone.

The fact that the British government of the day was a Socialist government contributed in large part to the decision to transfer parts of industry in their zone to so-called public ownership. The British cabinet decided on 19 November 1946 to nationalize the Ruhr industries. The British adopted a complex and costly three-stage policy: the first stage involved the establishment of boards of trustees to manage the earmarked companies; next, they were to be transferred into public ownership by means of committees set up after elections to the *Land* parliament; and, finally, once a German nation had been created, the companies were to be placed under its authority.

The Americans and French disliked this policy because they believed the British were taking decisions on a *Land* level which they did not like, but would nevertheless influence Germany as a whole. Yet William Asbury, the British regional commissioner for North Rhine-Westphalia, pushed ahead regardless, and together with Erik Noelting, the SPD finance minister, produced a list of trustees, headed by Viktor Agartz, the SPD's chief economic specialist and head of the central office for the economy in the British zone in Minden, but also including some CDU figures. Increasingly, however, the Americans were prepared to insist the British heed their views. The net effect of this was a go-slow on nationalization. Thus despite the fact that the North Rhine-Westphalian *Land* parliament voted in favour of the state ownership of the coal industry on 23 August 1948, the British now refused to accept the bill.

British Policy on Political Parties

Political parties had been permitted to establish themselves under licence since 6 August in the UK zone. On the whole, of all the occupying powers, the British seem to have given least thought to this particular matter. They considered Berlin to be the real centre of German political life and initially had relatively little understanding of or sympathy for those political groups whose roots lay not in national but in provincial political life. The British were also determined at an early stage to break up the unlicensed *Antifa* groups, the anti-fascist associations that had sprung up in the wake of Germany's invasion, often composed of Communists and Social Democrats for the simple reason that they were a challenge to military authority.

Britain took a special interest in trade union affairs. They saw that General Zhukov in his Order No. 2 had established a 'Free German Trade Union' but noted quickly that this was to be Communist. Even before 1945, British ministers, in particular Ernest Bevin (then Minister of Labour), had given thought to how to manage German trade union affairs. In Bevin's eyes, the strong support (as he saw it) that the British trade union movement was able to give the Labour Party was an important reason why the Labour party was not the SPD.

Together with Sir Frederick Leggett (an industrial conciliator) and Sir Walter Citrine (TUC General Secretary), Bevin planned for a genuinely free German trade union system which would teach (as he saw it) the Germans how to be democrats. Many pre-Hitler trade unionists had survived. Between 1945 and November 1946 the number of trade unions in the British zone increased from 17, with a membership of 145,000 to 192, with a membership of 1.7 million. In Hamburg alone there were 13 organized groups, and in Lower Saxony about 80 general unions.

The British aim was not, as has sometimes been supposed, to form a single trade union for all workers which they (rightly) regarded as a Communist concept. In November 1945 a Trades Union Congress delegation led by Will Lawther and Jack Tanner visited German trade unionists and despite much acrimony (the Germans were accused of having caved in to Nazism), Tanner told the Germans to come to their own conclusion about the best structure to adopt. The British were, however, adamant that there should be only one high trade union authority, and supported strongly the ideas of Hans Böckler that there should be one German trade union federation (DGB) and that it should consist of 13 autonomous industrial unions.

The most complete demonstration of Britain's colonial attitude was the decision to form a new German political entity by the creating a

Rhine-Ruhr 'super' state, the *Land* of North Rhine-Westphalia. They believed that this conglomerate, with its proposed state-run industries, would be adopted as a model by other *Länder*. By July 1946 the British were ready to discuss the proposal with influential Germans. The CDU were not against it, since they saw in it a source of future federal political strength. The SPD, on the other hand, disliked the idea for the same reason. On 17 July 1946 the plan was made public, and a week later Rudolf Amelunxen, the *Oberpräsident* or chief executive of Westphalia, was appointed minister president of the new *Land*. On 23 August the British formally dissolved the Prussian western provinces and instituted the new *Länder* of Schleswig-Holstein, Lower Saxony and North Rhine-Westphalia. North Rhine-Westphalia proved (without state ownership of its industries) to be a highly prosperous unit which went on to provide much of the Federal Republic's economic prowess. The first *Land* elections in the British zone were held on 20 April 1947.

Trade unions seemed easier to develop than the appropriate political parties. What the British ultimately decided to do about the rebirth of democratic politics was to speed up the process of political development within the British zone. The first clear statement of policy on this was made at the Control Commission conference in October 1945 – five months after the Russians had started to do this – and to re-examine their commitment to a central administration for all of Germany. The British now argued that the line taken at Potsdam – that Germany should be treated as a single economic unit – put power at the centre, in Berlin. Yet if the same principle were to be applied to political power, the Soviets would be given the chance of influencing political life over all of Germany. The antidote was obvious.

On 3 May 1946 the British Cabinet were given a paper produced by Bevin discussing the merits of a unified if federal Germany versus a western German state 'more amenable to our influence' to be set up in view of the 'Russian attitude and the danger of Communist domination of western Germany'. The reactive nature of this policy is worth stressing, as is the fact that the British were following the Russian lead rather than pre-empting it. At the same time, in order to sweeten the Germans in their zone, the Foreign Office proposed an increase in food rations and assurances of continued US support for western Germany.

De-Nazification

The British believed that by weeding out all former Nazis and then immediately putting most of them back into office, the Americans were swinging from one extreme to the other. They wished to be more consistent and thorough. Both British and Americans were helped by the fact that the records of the Nazi Party were discovered at a paper-pulping factory still intact. They were taken to Frankfurt (in the US zone), where a card index was drawn up and thence to Berlin where the Berlin Document Center was established under American leadership (it was handed over to the Germans in 1994). By 1950, it held about 20 million files, relating to about 13 million people; 85 per cent of Nazi Party members' records, as well as SS personnel office files had all been preserved.

But many British officers disliked the de-Nazification process for bureaucratic reasons and found relatively simple issues hard to resolve; whether, for example, someone who had joined the Nazi Party after 1933 was more or less guilty than someone who had joined before Hitler took power (the conflict arising from the fact that although certain categories of people had been obliged to join after 1933, the Nazi Party in power had of course been more wicked then).

General Robertson argued that if all Party members were to be removed from their posts, not only would there be no German civil servants for the British to use, but the vast numbers of people put out of work (some 1.5 million Germans in all zones) would create appalling security problems. The assumption was that an unemployed ex-Nazi might well conspire against the military occupation but an employed one would be prepared to toe the line. Strang, however, refused to accept this reasoning, reminding the military chiefs that 'The primary purpose of the occupation is destructive and preventive.'

In June 1947 the British Prime Minister decided that the time had come to stop further war crimes investigations in the British zone, and that after 1 September 1948 no further registration of alleged war crimes would be accepted.

The Bureaucratic Machine

British attempts to reform the civil service in their zone were subject to exactly the same constraints experienced by the Americans and French. The fact is that the professional German civil service managed, in the western part of Germany, to emerge from the Third Reich unscathed despite the many calls made for its complete reform. The German civil service regarded itself as an organization designed simply to execute political decisions without regard to their party-political aspects, implying it would faithfully execute British policies. Whilst this was not unconvincing, it allowed the civil service to escape a root-and-branch reform, desirable since the same logic had allowed Nazi laws to be executed. Some Germans wanted greater party political control over the bureaucracy as an antidote. Subsequent experience showed that the post-1945 civil service behaved quite properly and did not need greater politicization to achieve what its political masters required it to do.

New Thinking on the Economy

Finally, due not least to anxiety about the Russians, there soon emerged a widespread belief that to continue to do punitive damage to the German economy would harm the other European economies and promote the fortunes of Communism in the western zones of Germany. An economic adviser to the Control Commission wrote at this time that Germany was the 'hub of the entire European economy and that upon her prosperity the prosperity of Europe in large measure depends'. To 'beggar' Germany would be to move it inexorably into the Russian orbit. The Soviets, the British believed, sought to prevent the creation of a unified and stable Communist Germany; to keep the Ruhr's riches out of the hands of the western democracies and bind Germany to themselves. By May 1946 Ernest Bevin could speak of 'the danger of Russia' being 'as great as, possibly even greater than that of Germany', and officials began to draw the obvious conclusions from this view, namely that a western German state should be constructed upon the Western zones of occupation. Yet just one month earlier, on 26 March 1946, economic production had been fixed at just 50 per cent of its 1938 figure and 1,800 factories were being dismantled.

French Occupation Policy

The French zone was the smallest. About six million Germans lived in it, but it had, as Alfred Grosser points out, the largest number of occupation personnel, because the zone was so close to France. According to his critics, the French commander at Baden-Baden ran the zone as if it were a personal fiefdom, and there was much German resentment at this as well as the many instances of rape by some of the North African troops.

Of all Germany's Western occupiers, France pursued the most consistent line towards Germany. France had not been at Potsdam but it was part of the Control Commission. Its aims were straightforward: it wished to gain security for itself by blocking the creation of a German national government, getting access to Germany's economic riches and at the same time separating both economic and political control of those riches from Germans in so far as that was possible. To this end, the French attempted to separate their zone from the other two western zones (setting up a 'silk curtain' between them). Most notoriously, perhaps, the French attempted to detach the Saar-Rhine-Ruhr area from

Germany. Indeed, it was the French who vetoed the proposal for German regulators of transport and finance, as stipulated by Potsdam, because they did not want German unity.

Démontage affected Württemberg badly. There was watch-making in Tuttlingen, and technologically advanced companies were found in the Swabian Alps and Black Forest. The Dornier and Zeppelin aircraft works were located on Lake Constance. All of these factories were requisitioned for removal to France; but Carlo Schmid, himself half-French, and the leading SPD figure in the zone, was able to hinder this in part. The French continued to regard the Germans in their zone as enemies until the end of 1947. Schmid himself was told by General Koenig that no Frenchman would ever trust the Germans again (Schmid replied that trust was the only way to make a future that was better than the past). This was a point he made both to Pierre Schreiter, the French minister for Germany, and Alain Poher. Three of Schmid's aides rose to prominence later on: Karl Carstens, Walter Seuffert and Hans Jochen Vogel.

The Saar, treated as a distinct area under its own military governor, had long been a bone of contention between France and Germany, and the French were determined now to settle old scores. It had been separated from Germany by the Treaty of Versailles, but voted for reunion in 1935. In December 1946 a customs barrier was established between it and the rest of the French zone. In the elections of October 1947, 97 per cent of the voters supported parties which had endorsed a constitution whose preamble had insisted the Saar be made an autonomous territory linked to France by economic union. On 14 November 1947 the Franc was introduced as the only legal currency.

Under these circumstances it may be considered surprising that the Germans came to cooperate with the French more closely and more creatively than with any other European nation. This was partly because the French insistence on access to Germany's natural resources allowed Adenauer to make a virtue out of this necessity (which he himself accepted as desirable), and partly because this led to the creation of common, supranational economic and, later, political structures. One could be forgiven for having assumed that the legacy of France's occupation would have been the most bitter; in fact, thanks chiefly to Adenauer and Schmid, it proved as sweet as America's.

The Policy of the Soviet Union: Propaganda and Reality

In their own way, the Soviets also embarked upon a reinvention of Germany. They, too, had to operate within a German political culture which had been deeply traumatized by the Nazi legacy. They, too, were able to exploit the submissiveness of the Germans to their own advantage. Yet Soviet policy towards its own zone of Germany was not always easy for others to interpret. This was partly because before 1990 there was an absence of archival evidence (either from East Germany or the Soviet Union) and partly because the study of the Soviet Zone in both east and west was sometimes contaminated for political reasons.

Most of all, however, the German Communists and their Russian masters quickly produced a befuddling, but internally consistent, explanation for political, social and economic events in their part of Germany to camouflage the establishment of Soviet-style totalitarianism. A rich lexicon of empty phrases was invented in order to present a picture of East German affairs that bore little, if any, relation to reality. Up to 1989, analysts could be found who asserted that the Soviets, because they could rely on German Communists, did not *impose* a Soviet-style state on East Germany. They alleged that there were important differences between the composition of the Soviet state and the Communist German state. Yet when the various frills were removed, the only differences stemmed from the reality that, generally speaking, the Russians gave the orders and the East Germans took them. It was true that a pretence of multi-partyism was maintained for the whole of the GDR's life, but it was a pretence. Power was wielded by Communists, using all the apparatus at their command ruthlessly in order to extend their control.

East German Communists maintained ten former Nazi concentration camps for use as internment camps, for ex-Nazis, war criminals and political opponents. The most obscene cases were those of Buchenwald and Sachsenhausen where from 1945 to 1950, 122,671 people were so interned. Almost 43,000 people died in them. The Soviet NKVD (later KGB) had its own camps until 1950. It has been estimated that some 130,000 people were interned in them (of whom about 50,000 died and 20,000 to 30,000 were deported to the USSR). Until the State Security Ministry (the Stasi) was founded in February 1950, the NKVD did much of the secret police work in the GDR. Even if some of those who were involved in this process did so from a conviction that Communism was morally better than capitalism or that Communism alone could destroy Nazism, it should not be forgotten that many of them were criminals of Nazi ilk. The torture chambers of the Communists, for example at Hohenschönhausen in Berlin, were no less repellent than those of the Nazis.

The Communists were successful in holding on to their part of Germany for forty years because, first of all, they had the use of Soviet power, the Red Army and the KGB. They also controlled the press; there was no outlet for public opinion. Finally, the Communists could rely on the support of many intellectuals, academics, those with ambition and even the clergy of the Protestant Church. Their early insistence on the coalition of all democratic forces opposing Nazism, and the structure of Socialist ideas to which they could lay claim, undoubtedly helped them to win over the hearts and minds of many Germans who sincerely wished to avoid a repeat of Weimar and the Third Reich.

The Aims of Soviet Policy

There is significant circumstantial and empirical evidence to suggest that of all Germany's conquerors, the Soviets had the clearest idea of what they wished to achieve in Germany and the most carefully developed plans. Stalin told the Yugoslav Communist leader Milovan Djilas in 1945 that 'this war is not as in the past: whoever occupies a territory, imposes his own system as far as his army has power to do so. It cannot be otherwise.' At a further meeting, Stalin both expressed his admiration for the atom bomb but insisted that because the West had the bomb, Germany would now remain divided ('We shall turn Eastern Germany into our state').

Stalin's ideas on how to ensure that the Soviet system was extended into central, eastern and south-eastern Europe were, it seems, developed well before the Soviet Union began to be seen to be winning the war. Despite those who have argued that Stalin was a pragmatist, out only for what he could get, the record indicates otherwise. His treatment of the Baltic states and that part of Poland that fell to him as the fruits of the 1939 Nazi-Soviet pact, shows clearly that he was very happy to use the most brutal methods to impose Communist rule on subject peoples. He also understood better than many others that Communism and nationalism were not necessarily the antithesis of each other, but could be brought into productive conjunction and would inspire helpful propaganda, unchallengeable in public. It was not merely Germany that was the object of his interest but also China, Indo-China and elsewhere.

Moscow's Exiles

The establishment of a National Committee for a Free Germany has already been described. We also know that the Soviets taught statecraft to a number of leading exiled German Communists and fellow-travellers in the so-called Agricultural College in Moscow. Many German Communists, it must be stressed, had played a courageous part in anti-Nazi resistance. A large number of the East German élite had seen active service in the Spanish Civil War; very many of them had been incarcerated in concentration camps (prominent examples were Hermann Axen, Hilde Benjamin, Franz Dahlem, Robert Havemann, Bruno Leuschner, Alfred Neumann, Karl Schirdewan and Horst Sindermann).

It had been decided that the Communists would not make an open bid for power immediately, but would work together with others, under the aegis of the Red Army and Soviet security apparatus. In public affairs, they would not seek what were usually regarded as the leading positions in local government, but concentrate instead on the apparently less significant posts of personnel, welfare, education and the police.

There were three main exile groups. One – the Sobottka group – arrived in Stettin on 6 May and followed the northern Red Army thrust into Germany, ending up in Schwerin in July. The second – the Ackermann-Matern group – arrived in Dresden on 1 May and the third – the Ulbricht group – arrived in Kalau on 30 April 1945 from Moscow. They began work in central Berlin on 2 May.

Soviet Policy on German Nationhood

One of those involved in this process, Wolfgang Leonhard, estimated that it took but fourteen days from the arrival in eastern Germany of the first planeload of Communists from Moscow to complete effective Communist control of the Soviet zone. This gives some idea of the extent to which Communization, at the very least of the Soviet zone, had been decided on long before Potsdam. From this evidence, it follows that Stalin's expressed wish not to dismember Germany (if that wish were, as it would seem, quite genuine) was motivated by his belief that a united Germany – run from Berlin – might one day become a Communist Germany. In the meantime, a Communist Eastern zone, built around Berlin, might one day become a springboard into all of Germany.

One of the most important Soviet statements on Germany was made on 10 July 1946 in Paris by the Soviet foreign minister Molotov. He argued that although the Russians were not motivated by revenge, their huge losses required them to take an active role in defining Germany's political and economic future. There could, he said, be no sense in turning Germany into a rural society, because that would lead to wider economic disruption in Europe. Thus a political solution was needed to ensure that a unified Germany kept the peace. The Soviets, he declared, had no interest whatsoever in dividing Germany; and, once nationhood had been achieved, they would press for a peace treaty with the new state.

Soviet Policy on Political Parties

On 10 June 1945 the Soviet Military Administration for Germany (SMAD) under Marshal Zhukov (replaced by Marshal Sokolovsky in April 1946), at Karlshorst in Berlin, issued its Order No. 2. This permitted the formation of anti-Fascist committees, non-Fascist and non-right-wing political parties and free trade unions. On 11 June the KPD and its two chief Moscow exiles, Wilhelm Pieck and Walter Ulbricht, made its first declaration (it had been composed by Ackermann in Moscow). It stressed that, despite Communist warnings, 10 million Germans had voted for the Nazis in 1933, and would have to be punished for this. The Communist leaders sought what they called the democratization of Germany and (to show awareness of the continuities in German history), the completion of the bourgeois democratic revolution that had begun in 1848. They wanted land reform, a democratic civil service, the establishment of a new education system, but not, they insisted, the sovietization of Germany. The 'present conditions of development in Germany' did not support such a move, they said; instead they wished to go down a 'different path' by constructing a broadly based anti-Fascist regime in a parliamentary democratic republic with a guarantee to all citizens of full democratic rights and liberties, including free trade, private enterprise and a respect for property. On paper, the first GDR constitution looked very much like the West German one. It bore a close resemblance to the Weimar constitution. A number of rights and liberties were guaranteed: in particular, the rights of free assembly, to strike and to hold property. But article six permitted the prosecution of political crimes, and the death penalty was retained.

The paper similarity to the Basic Law produced an unforeseen consequence. The German Unity Treaty of 1990 allowed the courts of the Federal Republic to try only those human rights violations that were illegal under East German law. Since the latter was liberal, even if only on paper, the scope for redress has proved greater than many believed was possible.

On 15 June 1945 the SPD re-emerged under Otto Grotewohl and Gustav Dahrendorf; on 26 June an eastern CDU was formed by Jakob Kaiser, Ernst Lemmer, Andreas Hermes, Heinrich Krone, Ferdinand Friedensburg and Otto Nuschke. On 5 July the eastern Liberal party was founded. All four parties formed an 'anti-Fascist block' on 14 July 1945 whose aim was to 'save the German nation' by a fundamental change in German political life.

This corresponded not merely to the ideas which had underpinned the formation of the 1943 National Committee for a Free Germany in the Soviet Union, but also to what the KPD had been openly urging since the beginning of 1945, when it called for the creation of a 'block of democratic parties' and a 'people's democracy'. What this meant, in effect, was, first, that the KPD knew it could not gain majority support by itself and, second, that the Communists could 'block' any decisions they did not like so that their own proposals, supported as they were by the Soviets – who legally had the ultimate say – were all-powerful. It is an indication of the confidence of the KPD that they were prepared to go as far as they were in cooperating with other parties who were still non-Communist. Although they had little choice since they wished to maintain the fiction of democratic legitimacy but had failed to win majority support, some KPD stalwarts are reported to have challenged Ulbricht on aspects of this programme, arguing that the KPD was losing its chance of influencing events. Ulbricht's response was that they should wait and see.

Reforms and changes were needed as much as they were in the western part of what had been the Reich: three-quarters of all German schoolteachers had been Nazi party members and the universities, too, had first been purged of the Nazis' enemies and then stocked with Nazi supporters. Over 400,000 people were dismissed from administrative or economically significant posts although run-of-the-mill Nazis were not punished, and on 16 August 1947 Sokolovsky halted all proceedings against those not accused of specific crimes.

On 15 June 1945 a meeting took place in Berlin to set up the 'free' trade union movement, the FDGB. By the time of its first congress in February 1946 it already possessed 2 million members. The Free German Youth organization (FDJ) was of equal systemic importance. At first it claimed dishonestly to be without party affiliation; but at the second FDJ 'parliament' in 1947 it was decided that all members should be uniformed, and by 1949 the FDJ was ready to openly espouse the aims of the Socialist Unity Party. From 1946 until 1955 Erich Honecker was the FDJ leader. Many young East Germans found pleasure and fulfilment in the organization.

Order No. 17 of the Soviet Military Adminstration (27 July 1945) established 'central administrative units' to restructure the eastern German economy. In September a wide-ranging land reform package was announced: all those who possessed more than 100 hectares of land were required to give it up without compensation. Roughly two-thirds of the land was then redistributed amongst about 500,000 peasants and small farmers; one-third was taken into public ownership and given to local authorities. All banks had been nationalized without compensation in July. Local governments were set up in Saxony, Saxony-Anhalt, Mecklenburg, Thuringia and Brandenburg, with Communists in all key posts (usually dealing with police and justice, education and welfare).

In June 1946 the Soviets seized 213 of the most important industrial units which produced about a quarter of all goods in their zone, and, designating them as reparations, transferred them to Soviet ownership. In the same month, perhaps to forestall any criticism of this move, they organized a plebiscite on the proposed public ownership of factories in Saxony alleged to have belonged to active Nazis or war profiteers: 77.6 per cent apparently supported the measure. Even so, a comparison between the autumn 1946 elections in the Soviet zone (which produced a vote of 57.1 per cent for the SED) and the free Berlin elections at the same time (where SED gained only 19.8 per cent but the independent western SPD received 48.7 per cent) showed that support for the Communists was not what it seemed. The following year, the German Economic Commission was established as an Economic Council analogue: it became the core of the new East German government set up in October 1949. Otto Grotewohl was its head. In July Walter Ulbricht was elected general secretary of the SED, in September the GDR joined Comecon and in October 99.7 per cent of the electors appeared to vote for candidates on the unity list. In January 1951 the first five-year plan was announced and the Stalinization of eastern Germany was completed.

The SPD and the KPD

The Social Democrats in Berlin (whose leader was Grotewohl) responded to the KPD's declaration in favour of union on 15 June 1945, expressing pleasure with it. By July, the KPD, the SPD, the (eastern) Christian Democrats and the (eastern) Liberals formed a united or national front. At the same time, the KPD urged the SPD to merge into a new party of the Left. Although a majority of SPD members in Berlin (two-thirds of which, of course, was under Western SPD control) voted against this proposal, negotiations continued and a special conference was called for 21 and 22 April 1946. At the conference, the Socialist Unity Party, the SED, was established with the apparent support of most Social Democrats in the Soviet zone.

That they should have agreed to this was partly the result of Soviet strong-arm tactics and intimidation. But it would be wrong to deny that significant numbers of Social Democrats believed that a divided working-class party had 'let Hitler in', and they were ready to try a new way of realizing their socialist ideals. The Communists refused to have a free vote on union. A referendum held in West Berlin, however, showed that although 82 per cent opposed an immediate union, 62 per cent favoured close collaboration.

Within the new party, there was to be complete parity – on paper – between Communists and Social Democrats. Yet it was, of course, the Communists who were in direct contact with the Russians, the source of real power. Pieck, a veteran Communist, and Grotewohl were elected joint chairmen, Walter Ulbricht and Max Fechner vice-chairmen and the eighty-member executive, elected by party congress, was similarly divided. A central committee was then formed out of the executive. The SED at first insisted that it was not a Leninist party, perhaps because 53 per cent of its new members had been Social Democrats (although it cheerfully stated that it was a Marxist one). It has been estimated that the party membership consisted of 680,000 Social Democrats and 620,000 Communists. By the time of the second party congress in 1947, it was claimed that the SED had become a 'party of the new type', that is to say a Leninist elitist party. This Soviet reinvention of Germany was later underpinned in June 1952 by the abolition of the East German *Länder* and their replacement by fifteen provinces.

What Did Occupation Achieve?

The case has sometimes been made against the Western occupying powers that they apparently failed to change the fundamental nature of German political life. If this means that there was no support for radical socialist measures, then, on the whole this is true. But it is not the case that West German politics was not given a wholly new form. It is clear that there were many elements of political continuity, connecting the Weimar and Bonn Republics. These were exemplified by the personal careers of men like Adenauer and Schumacher, politicians in both systems or the institutional analogies. Yet the fact is that Western occupation policy wrought the most tremendous and positive changes on German politics. It secured the fortunes of a genuine liberal democracy in Germany. It purged and criminalized Nazism. It supported, in the end (chiefly thanks to the Americans) an economy that was liberal, market-oriented and basically open. West Germany and its values were products forged by the Western Allies (in particular the United States) to a far greater extent than either they or the West Germans would subsequently accept. The political origins of what would become a West German nation, in all but name, lay more in Washington, London and Paris than in Bonn (or Berlin). To those who argue that what the West did was therefore no different from what the Soviets did in their zone of Germany, it must be pointed out that Soviet policies were predicated on coercion. What the West offered was a reinvention through consent.

The Establishment of a Separate West German State

When it became clear that a reunified Germany could not be formed, the United States, as we have seen, insisted that a separate treaty should be negotiated with the western German *Länder* with the aim of setting up a West German state. On 1 July 1948 the so-called Frankfurt documents were delivered; these consisted of three notes handed over by the governors to the minister presidents. One dealt with plans for a constitution which should be democratic and federal, one with new territorial arrangements and the third with an occupation statute.

The Parliamentary Council

Thus the Western Allies gave the minister presidents rather than the party leaders the task of convening a constituent assembly of representatives from the *Länder* to stress the federal setting of the new state. The occupation statute stipulated that German foreign trade was to be controlled by the military governors (to become High Commissioners), as was the administration of the Ruhr, reparations, the level of industrial production, decartelization, disarmament and demilitarization. They were to retain the right to observe the federal government and the *Länder* governments and to give them advice on the pursuit of democracy and social issues.

On 8–10 July 1948 the minister presidents met at the Rittersturz in Coblenz, together with their political advisers and lawyers. They decided to invite the leaders of the major parties to join them. The SPD sent Ollenhauer (Schumacher was ill). Adenauer attended as CDU leader (Josef Müller went for the CSU). A major concern, of course, was German national unity. The minister presidents argued that they could not compose a constitution, only a basic law. Schmid, there as a deputy minister president, said that a West German state could only be created if there were a West German 'state nation'. None of them, he said, believed in such a thing. Nor could they make decisions for those in eastern Germany. Thus whatever they decided to do, it could be only a provisional solution to the issue of German statehood.

The minister presidents met again in Frankfurt on 20 July 1948 with the military governors, who insisted on a constitution rather than a basic law. The minister presidents then went off to Niederwald Castle. There Reuter argued that they should accept the governors' proposals for the sake of Berlin. The people of Berlin and indeed of the Soviet zone saw the consolidation of a West German state as their only salvation. Although Schmid argued against this, the minister presidents were convinced and, at their third meeting with the governors on 26 July

1948, they agreed to produce a constitution and enacted a law to this effect in August.

A parliamentary council was to be established for 1 September 1948, with a preliminary meeting at Herrenchiemsee for 10–23 August. The delegates to the council were to be elected by the *Land* parliaments (emphasizing once again the federated nature of the assembly) on the basis of one delegate for every 750,000 inhabitants. It was therefore a constituent assembly, but one only indirectly elected by the western German people. It had 65 members, including 27 CDU members, 27 SPD, 5 Liberals and 2 Communists, and 5 delegates from Berlin, including Jakob Kaiser and Ernst Reuter. It sat from 1 September 1948 to 8 May 1949 in the Koenig Museum in Bonn.

It was a curious convention for none of its members represented – officially – their parties; indeed, some were civil servants or professors or diplomats. There were outstanding individuals here: Schmid, a humane and enlightened lawyer; Hermann Brill from Hesse; Justus Danckwerts, Theo Kordt, Adolf Süsterhenn, the minister of justice from the Rhineland-Palatinate and Fritz Baade from Kiel. This convention generated a brilliant medley of views. But every constitution-maker was determined that the new state should not suffer from the same fatal flaws as Weimar.

A minority believed that final constitutional power ought not to lie with the federal government but with the *Länder*, who should carry the state until unity came about – a federation of German *Länder* rather than a federal republic of Germany. The eleven *Länder* represented at this conference also wanted their borders to be guaranteed; they did not wish to be mere administrative units but political ones as well. The *Länder* and the federal government, they argued, should have separate finances and laws were to be made by them acting together, except that the federal government was to have priority in about 38 instances. Some, like Schmid and the SPD, wanted a senate as upper house to strengthen central government; others, like Adenauer, preferred a Federal Council or *Bundesrat*.

The importance of the constitution can hardly be overemphasized. It quickly became the very rule book of German politics which defined the entire basis of public activity in the new state. The federal government was to make each individual minister responsible for his or her own duties but the Federal Chancellor was to be empowered to provide policy directives, to state the goals and specify the methods of realizing them. In this way, the Chancellor was to have a special status, unhindered here by parliament. Indeed, it was extremely difficult to remove him, except by a vote of no confidence where a successor, who possessed a majority, had already been identified (such a vote was called only four times in forty years; in 1966, in 1972, and twice in 1982). The importance of jurisdiction and judicial review was stressed. Justice was to be a *Land* matter, but the federal government was to ensure the uniformity of the law. There was to be a federal constitutional court to oversee these processes. Fundamental rights could not be abolished. Those aspects of the basic law that could be altered required a two-thirds majority to do so.

The SPD decided to vote against the basic law unless the federal government was given greater powers. The governors refused, insisting on all or nothing, and on 10 April handed the occupation statute to them. The statute was to enter into force simultaneously with the Basic Law. It stated (once again) that supreme authority was retained by the governments of the United States, Great Britain and France, but that subject to certain exceptions, the new federal state should have 'full legislative, executive and judicial powers'. The exceptions concerned disarmament and demilitarization (including arms research and production), the Ruhr controls and, by no means least important, foreign affairs and international agreements. Interestingly, the Basic Law itself makes no mention of these restrictions. This may have been because they were seen at the time as restrictions that could be negotiated away in due course. Yet neither the Western Allies nor, indeed, the western Germans could have any interest in over-emphasizing the extent to which the Federal Republic had been established at the behest of the occupiers. There could be no sense in conveying the impression that West Germany was simply a puppet state, of the West, even though – in 1949 – in many ways this was what it was.

As far as the electoral law was concerned, the Allies had at first intended each *Land* to have its own law; all the Basic Law said on the subject was that there should be free and equal adult suffrage; that members of the Bundestag should not be mandated; and that governments should last for four years. The CDU favoured the British electoral system, which they believed would give them an absolute majority; the SPD was divided. A compromise, apparently mixing the two, was finally accepted.

The first section of the Basic Law listed the civil and political rights of citizens. As a normative document, describing what the Germans called the *Rechtsstaat*, a state where law prevailed, the constitution set out what was allowed rather than what was not allowed (with the implication that anything not specifically allowed was not permitted). Some areas of legislative competence were reserved solely for the central government in Bonn; they included foreign and military affairs (when these should prove appropriate), monetary policy, citizenship and immigration, posts, rail and air travel, telegraph and telephone systems.

Other areas of legislation could be assumed by the central government in order to uphold uniformity; but on its failing to so assume them, they then fell to the *Länder*. These areas included civil, criminal and labour law, public health and welfare, prevention of economic domination, and the construction of roads. Taxation was divided between the centre and the *Länder*. All other areas of legislation fell to the *Länder* (except where there might be implications for other states). Thus education is a *Land* affair except where it could affect other *Länder*. This then becomes a federal matter, usually resolved by giving federal interests (that is the interests of all the *Länder*) precedence over the concerns of one of them. Meanwhile, elections were scheduled for 14 August 1949.

Parties were made more than mere electoral associations and almost organs of the state. On 10 May the vote was taken for the future capital, Frankfurt or Bonn (the latter won). The draft Basic Law was finally accepted by the Council on 8 May 1949, five years to the day since Germany capitulated. Other tasks were completed by the end of August and on 31 August the minister presidents accepted the draft. The Western Allies, it should be noted, insisted that unity, when it came, should be established by the eastern states' accepting the Basic Law. To this end, the US, British and French foreign ministers met in Paris and issued a declaration of unity on 28 May 1949 in which they called for unification on the basis of full democratic freedom for all parties, the freedom of the media, and a basic package of human rights (including a ban on arbitrary arrest and political policing).

The new Federal Republic consisted of the *Länder* of the UK, US, and French zones. Of these *Länder*, only a few had a history as political units that stretched back into the nineteenth century (the Hansa cities, Bavaria and Saxony). The Saarland was the outcome of French separatist policies after 1918. Hesse, Schleswig-Holstein, Lower Saxony, North Rhine-Westphalia, Rhineland-Pfalz, Württemberg-Baden and Württemberg-Hohenzollern were all created by the occupying powers. In 1951 Baden-Württemberg was formed out of Baden and the two Württembergs, and in 1957 the Saar joined the Republic as a result of the plebiscite. Berlin was declared to be part of the Federal Republic; but, in view of the rights retained by Germany's victors, the constitution only applied here in part.

The point to be made is both an historical and a political one. Even if only a minority of the *Länder* had been political units long before 1949, that does not of course mean they did not possess a distinctive history, or political culture. Once again, it is right to speak of a re-invention. In 1789 there were over three hundred political units in German lands; by 1817 there were thirty-nine. What is more, their political culture varied hugely, not just between those in the east, the west, the north and the south, but even where they were in close proximity to each other (Baden, Württemberg and Bavaria being just three examples). Governing diversity on this scale was therefore a very complex political problem, as German history before 1933 had demonstrated only too often. Federalism was, therefore, not just a democratically sensible form of governance but a political necessity. The post-1945 construction of *Länder* was motivated, therefore, by a desire to divide power and stabilize democracy more than any wish to preserve historical tradition.

The Basic Law also claimed the right to speak for all Germans until such time as German national unity should be restored. It did not recognize the legitimacy of the East German state, and all East Germans could automatically obtain West German citizenship. It adopted as its national colours the black, red and gold of the revolutionaries of 1848 and the Weimar Republic (the same colours that were used by the German Democratic Republic). The national anthemn was the *Deutschlandlied* by Hoffmann von Fallersleben (although only the third verse – 'unity, the rule of law and liberty. . .' was sung since the first verse 'Germany above all other things' had been misconstrued as meaning that Germany was better than any other country, which technically it did not).

Limited Sovereignty

With the passing of the Basic Law, the military governors (Clay, Robertson and Koenig) moved to Bonn. Robertson continued as British High Commissioner but President Truman gave the American job to John McCloy, and the French replaced Koenig with André François-Poncet who had been the French ambassador to the Third Reich.

On 28 December 1948 the Ruhr statute, establishing an international authority for the Ruhr, was announced. The production there and the supply of raw materials was to be under Allied control. In effect, this statute took away a very large measure of the new German state's economic freedom (the 'Allied hand at the throat of Germany' as Schmid termed it). The new state was also to be completely disarmed, and on 17 January 1949 a military security board was set up in Koblenz to ensure that disarmament and demilitarization continued (the board existed until 1955, even though the decision to remilitarize Germany had been taken in 1950). The three Western Allies also declared that they retained supreme authority over Germany as assumed in Berlin on 5 June 1945.

The First Federal Election

Sixteen parties took part in the first campaign. The economy was one major issue. The CDU's social market policy (enshrined in the Düsseldorf principles of July 1949) was under scrutiny. The currency reform had led to an increase in unemployment (over 10 per cent), although the CDU, through Ludwig Erhard, said that the hardship induced by the market economy would shortly pay dividends. The CDU/CSU obtained 31 per cent, the SPD 29.2 per cent, and the FDP 11.9 per cent. The twelve other parties got almost 30 per cent. This gave rise to the justified fear that the Bonn Republic might try to go the way of Weimar, where the existence of splinter parties made parliamentary democracy very difficult to achieve. In fact, the smaller parties soon lost support, gaining 16.5 per cent in 1953, and 10.3 per cent in 1957, and disappearing altogether from 1961 until 1983, when the Greens entered the Bundestag for the first time. Despite the general anxiety about the Soviet Union the KPD got 15 seats and 1.3 million votes; the right wing, however, managed to gain only five seats.

The West German state had been made.

The Re-emergence of German Political Life in the West, 1945–9

Adenauer's Part-Nation

A massive change was now taking place in German political life. It was being promoted by Germany's conquerors, American, Russian, British and French. There was vast and active non-German interference in German domestic affairs, unique for any European state. By 1949, however, in the western part of Germany, this process had undergone a substantial redefinition. What had started off as punitive and vengeful instrumentalism now became something more akin to cooperation between senior and junior partners. The western zones began to be sized up as a potentially vital component of a Western liberal grouping of states. There were both economic and political reasons for this. Above all, the West feared that the Soviet Union might seek to alter the status quo in Europe; and as a hedge against such a catastrophic development, the creation of a West German state seemed to be required.

Even if each of Germany's victors still hoped to establish, if they could, a single German state whose aims ran parallel to their own particular interests, in the West it was decided that this should be achieved with the consent of the Germans rather than by coercing them. Whereas the Western Allies had, after 1945 but before 1947, wished the whole of Germany to be a barrier against the Russians (Churchill's famous Iron Curtain speech in 1946 had located the barrier to the *east* of the Soviet zone: 'from Stettin in the Baltic to Trieste on the Adriatic'), they now accepted they would have to satisfy themselves with a barrier across Germany instead. This meant there could be no question but that the western German state had to be part of the West.

Given the system now being constructed in the western part of Germany, it was necessary for domestic German political leaders to enact the German side of the process. Having completed, more or less, the punitive phase of occupation, the Western Allies were quite genuine in their wish to see the Germans they trusted (the qualification was important) exercise some democratic power.

Figure 3. Konrad Adenauer. ©Presse- und Informationsant de Bundesregierung

Their intelligence officers identified democratic politicians, worthy of patronage (and, of course, Nazis who required exclusion from politics). In Britain's case men like Noel (Lord) Annan, Michael Thomas, and Lance Pope played a major part in the discovery and promotion of individuals. But the Western occupiers also used financial resources and the licensing process to promote the fortunes of people and parties whose aims coincided with their own. Licensing, in particular, was a powerful tool for forming post-war German political culture. What the Western occupiers looked for were men (and, occasionally, women) who had been anti-Nazi or at least non-Nazi. This included figures from the Weimar Republic, but only when they were deemed to have broken with the past (Carl Severing, for example, a very prominent Weimar Social Democrat, was cold-shouldered for this reason). Next, these people were required to have a political line which fitted in, broadly, with what the Western Allies wanted for Germany. Finally, they needed to demonstrate that they were able to speak for the Germans themselves.

The possible contradiction between the second and third aims proved the critical factor. The Western Allies knew that the creation of a real democracy in western Germany implied not merely that conflicts between them and their German counterparts would inevitably occur, but that such conflicts could be exploited for party political gain, especially when the occupiers were perceived as being in the wrong (which might often be the case). This could threaten the position of the occupiers. On the other hand, unless freedom to criticize was granted, occupation might appear to be domination, with dangerous consequences. The trick was to get the mixture right. West German political life became even more complex than it already was, given the need to work through the trauma of Nazism. Every budding political leader was obliged to fit in with the occupiers' plans, to gain and keep the confidence of their German supporters and develop party political life by addressing meetings. The occupying forces, however, always retained the final say. Clashes between them and the German parties on individual policies were almost always resolved on the terms of the occupiers. But by ensuring the political institutions in the nascent democracy were liberal and strong, the Allies could do much to ensure that the Germany they got was the Germany they wanted.

Remarkably, a number of outstanding German political leaders emerged who were able to fit these various requirements. They were very special men and women, sometimes extremely brave, who had been shaped by their experiences of the Third Reich. Both the two major figures of these years, Adenauer and Schumacher, shared a belief in the necessity of constructing a new Germany, even if, ironically, it was the older and more conservative Adenauer who was the more radical and progressive of the two. It was Adenauer who from his earliest political stirrings after defeat proved more flexible and adaptable than the doughty but traditional Social Democrat, Schumacher. Adenauer's ascendancy was not immediate; but it was not fortuitous. As we shall see, his wide political experience and his ability enabled him both to accept occupation and Westernization (particularly from the Americans who – luckily for him – ran another zone) *and* to speak for the German people in the west. Most important of all, he and not Schumacher was most convincing in defining and articulating a new 'unnational' national German interest. It was Christian, democratic, liberal, ultimately capitalist, anti-Communist, but above all Western.

Adenauer's achievement, therefore, was immense. He not only made a decisive contribution to the creation of his political party, the Christian Democratic Union (CDU). By working with the occupiers, he was also able to make his norms (and the norms of the CDU) the values of the new Bonn Republic.

Konrad Adenauer: Grandfathers and Fatherlands

Any modern state is the product of multiple material pressures, conflicts as well as the lust for power of ambitious men and women. Yet it is hard to doubt that, at the high policy level, West Germany came to bear the mark of one man more than of any party, institution, or association. That man was Adenauer, born in 1876 and died in 1967. At a time when some analysts of politics and history like to downplay the significance of individuals and to stress the importance of broader social, economic and political factors, it may seem odd to look to one man as the decisive shaping force behind the new Germany's political culture. Indeed, it may seem even odder to do so when one bears in mind that the man with whom is dealing was a regional, even local, politician by training and experience, and hardly a national figure, and that he was well into retirement in 1945. How could such an unlikely figure indulge in statecraft so radical and so all-embracing? How was Adenauer able to create a new sort of Germany, this German state in the west?

It was bizarre that Adenauer, of all people, should prove so open to new thinking and new influences, since he was such an old man. Yet, as the documentary evidence of his pre-1949 activity demonstrates, Adenauer saw clearly, and very soon, that German domestic political life would both be conditioned by the foreign policy of its victors, as occupiers and as adversaries in the Cold War. He wrote in the summer of 1945 that he was sure the European continent, and with it Germany, would be divided between the West and the Soviet Union. He understood that the US, and not Britain, was now the dominant Western power. The Soviet zone of occupation was – quite rightly – perceived by him as belonging for the foreseeable future to the Soviet world.

That Adenauer became the dominating figure in the new West German state is beyond dispute. How he did so, however, *is* a matter of debate. Ought he to be regarded as a Machiavellian figure, single-mindedly manipulating people and events in order to struggle to the top? Or did he slip into power for apolitical, administrative reasons? Was his age a source of political authority, allowing him to shape events? Or was his age a reason why others who were younger felt able to allow him to take the chair in the belief that he would be a temporary and provisional leader, whilst they had time to develop their own bids for power? The answer almost certainly lies in his ambition and his ruthlessness, often concealed in a cloak of bourgeois respectability. There was old lace, certainly; but much arsenic as well.

Despite his local and provincial background, Adenauer was a highly skilled politician. The extent to which his aims mirrored those of Germany's Western occupiers certainly explains part of his success. Equally, however, he had a personal commitment to the reframing of German political life along Western (and West European) lines. In complete opposition to the SPD, Adenauer and his circle had no detailed holistic blueprint for a democratic post-Weimar Germany, even though the broad logic – liberal and Christian Democratic (whatever this might mean) – was plain. This of course made him inherently acceptable to the West. Secondly, however, Adenauer was driven by a very real hatred of Communism. This made him even more popular, especially with the Americans, and became a vital pathway connecting the Western Allies to the emerging new political class of West Germany. Finally, Adenauer possessed a canny political sense. This told him precisely how far to go, not only in exploiting Germany's pre-1945 political experiences, but also in attacking, for domestic effect, the policies of Germany's occupiers (in particular the British, whom he soon recognized as weak, and under the political control of a Socialist government). Yet he comprehended that his ability to change and reform Germany was directly dependent on the extent to which he was able to follow the Western line. Indeed, Adenauer became so adept at this that by the end of his career, he came to believe that he had a duty to instruct and lead the West, rather than be led by the Americans, still less the British. His distrust of Kennedy (and Macmillan) and his bitter disagreements with them over *détente* examined below, represented the final flourish of this process.

He was also empowered by the reality that Germany's collapse meant that all the old German institutions had, even if only temporarily, lost their civic authority. Each one had been tarred with Nazism, whether they were composed of military men, of academics, or of

GERMANY UNDER ALLIED OCCUPATION

Map 2

bankers and industrialists. There was a real opportunity for reform. Although Adenauer came out of local politics, it would be foolish to dismiss this fact as displaying a lack of aptitude for national politics. There is no reason why a career devoted solely to politics, conducted in a national parliament, should be considered a better qualification for power than actually running a major city as a local party boss. Indeed, in 1921 and 1926, Adenauer had been considered sufficiently weighty to be one of several candidates for the Chancellorship of the Weimar Republic.

He had preferred to stay in Cologne, where he continued to be a prominent member of the sectarian, Roman Catholic Centre party, steeped in the political culture of his Rhenish community. The Adenauer family were loyal Prussians (the Rhineland belonged to Prussia) and the suggestion that Adenauer himself had been a separatist, favouring independence from Prussia after 1918, cannot be substantiated. Indeed, Adenauer himself repeatedly pointed out that it was an allegation that the Nazis investigated thoroughly; and since they had every interest in trying to depict him as 'unnational' they would have left no stone unturned in proving this charge. They never succeeded in doing so, although it seems plain that Adenauer did maintain close political contacts with those who favoured separatism, and that the idea being promoted by the French – that of a western German state, no longer a Prussian province but simply part of a German confederation – was something which Adenauer was prepared to contemplate. He certainly told Noel Annan that the granting of the Rhine province to Prussia after 1815 was the biggest mistake British diplomacy had ever made.

His health was always poor; he was not well enough to do military service (and too old for it by 1914); and when in 1904 Adenauer married for the first time, he failed to get life insurance since he was such a bad risk. He suffered from diabetes. His first and second wives died at a young age; the second, Gussie, in 1948 from what seems to have been leukaemia (an illness which Adenauer believed had been contracted whilst she was being interrogated by the Gestapo in 1944). In March 1917 he was very badly injured in a car crash; fractures to his face gave him his oriental appearance. He loved property and wealth (his pride in his villa overlooking the Rhine at Rhöndorf was but one example of this); yet he was not always wise about his personal finances. In 1928 he met someone at a dinner party who advised him to speculate on the American stock market: Adenauer took further advice, and then borrowed heavily to buy shares. After the Wall Street crash in 1929, a personal fortune of RM 1 million (in addition to the large house he owned in Cologne) turned into debts of RM 1.4 million with the Deutsche Bank alone.

In 1906 Adenauer became one of twelve town clerks in Cologne, in charge of taxation and finance; he prided himself on his good relations with the city's bankers, and shared many of their bourgeois and imperialist values. Wilhelm Sollmann, who later emigrated to the United States, and who was the Rhineland's leading Social Democrat, gained an early respect for Adenauer which he never lost: although Adenauer was a Roman Catholic, he was no bigot, and, despite being utterly bourgeois, he had no contempt for working people.

Bolsheviks in Cologne

Germany's defeat in 1918 brought revolution to Cologne. Although Adenauer welcomed back the servicemen 'unvanquished and undefeated', he realized only too well that a new chapter in German history had begun. He saw it as his task to ensure that whatever political upheavals there might be, the government of the city carried on: together with Sollmann and Louis Hagen, a Liberal, Adenauer sought to keep the fabric of the city more or less intact. Two aspects of this period should be stressed. First, the concept of revolution – and a Bolshevik one at that – was something that Adenauer had himself experienced at first hand. It was a real and concrete phenomenon, not a vague bourgeois fear or some shorthand for other illiberal political beliefs. Secondly, the Rhineland was occupied (by the British as far as Cologne was concerned) from the winter of 1918 until 31 January 1926. In the event, despite the humiliation of occupation, Adenauer understood clearly that he had to coexist with the British.

Nazis in Cologne

Meanwhile, the political situation in Germany was deteriorating to the advantage of the National Socialists and Hitler. Adenauer loathed both; but by 1932 Cologne was virtually bankrupt and 87,000 of its citizens were unemployed. Adenauer had no plausible solution to Germany's problems. When in 1932 Franz von Papen (a colleague of Adenauer's in the Centre Party) began his fateful negotiations with Hitler, Adenauer was not included and went to Switzerland for his annual holiday. When Hitler announced that he would be visiting Cologne in February 1933 and expected an official welcome, Adenauer refused to put up swastika flags and when the Nazis flouted his ruling, he ordered the police to take them down again.

Adenauer – No Resister

Not surprisingly, the year 1933 seemed the end of Adenauer's political life. Sollmann was 'arrested' by the Nazis and badly beaten up; Adenauer himself (legally contracted to be mayor until 1941 and president of the Prussian State Council) had to flee to Berlin, where he correctly assumed no one would know or care who he was. Anxious to secure his pension, he arranged an interview with Goering, now minister president of Prussia. But Goering accused him of embezzling RM 5 million. Meanwhile, Cologne was being Nazified and the Rhineland given a *Gauleiter*, who summarily dismissed Adenauer in a letter which proved to have a fateful echo thirteen years later. Adenauer was accused of crimes against his people (and his religion and his family). He was to be investigated and his pension cut by 50 per cent. Those who had once been pleased to know him, now deserted him. Only Pferdmenges, a Jewish businessman called Dannie Heineman, and a Jewish professor stood by him (and offered him money), something Adenauer never forgot. In 1934, during the Roehm purge, Adenauer was arrested for three days, but released. He decided to retire totally from any political activity. He refused to have anything to do with those who sought to oppose the regime by active or semi-active means. In 1936 Jakob Kaiser came to see Adenauer, wanting him to join a dissident group of generals, but Adenauer did not believe they would act; when in 1943 and 1944 Kaiser asked to see him again, Adenauer refused even to let him enter his house.

Adenauer believed that internal resistance was not merely useless but suicidal. Despite ignoring the anti-Nazi resisters, the Gestapo was not willing to ignore him. He was arrested again on 24 July 1944, on the erroneous and unfounded suspicion of complicity in the plot against Hitler. He managed to slip away to Bonn where he hid. But the Gestapo forced his wife to reveal his whereabouts. He was rearrested and imprisoned in Brauweiler gaol. His cell was situated above a hall where executions were carried out and whilst he was being held, twenty-seven people were hanged, a number of them children. He later wrote 'I could hear everything; before that time I never really believed that the Devil actually exists, that evil truly has power.' Adenauer was released on 26 November and returned to Rhöndorf.

The Americans Find Adenauer

On 7 March 1945 US troops captured the Rhine bridge at Remagen and the next day they were to reach Unkel, near Rhöndorf. A fortnight later, a US intelligence officer came to interview him. Adenauer's name, as

Adenauer liked to relate, was number one on 'the White List for Germany', designating him as someone recommended by anti-Nazis who could assist the Americans. (In fact, Adenauer may have been the first name for alphabetical reasons and the list seems to have been for the Rhine province rather than Germany as a whole.) At any rate, as early as 30 July 1945 Robert Murphy, the political adviser to the US Military Governor, referred to Adenauer as a 'prominent anti-Nazi', adding significantly 'He is a sympathetic exponent of our point of view.'

Adenauer told Erich Brost, a senior figure in the emerging SPD, that he had received another visit from the Americans on 2 August 1945. He had been asked to nominate future national leaders (he had suggested Heinrich Brüning), but that it had been 'made clear to him that if he wished he could play a very influential role in the new government'. Adenauer replied that his aim was to create a large, broadly based, new political party, a *Sammlungspartei*, consisting of people from the conservative right to the right wing of the Social Democrats. He co-operated closely with his American liberators, first as adviser and then, when Hitler was dead, as governing mayor (he feared reprisals against his sons, serving in the *Wehrmacht*, were their father designated a traitor). Cologne had been devastated by the bombing. When the US entered the city, only 40,000 people were still inhabiting the area on the left bank of the Rhine (although by the end of September the figure had grown to about 400,000), and at least one-third of these lived in cellars. The problems arising from this – problems of food, of housing, of communications, and of seeking to get even a primitive economy under way – were overwhelming.

The British and Adenauer

On 21 June the British took over from the US forces. In accord with wartime policy, the Rhine province was removed from Prussia and divided into a northern state, to include Düsseldorf and Cologne and a southern one, to include Koblenz and Trier, which was then ceded to the French as part of their zone of occupation.

Adenauer found it hard to get on with the British, despite his previous experience of them. To the Americans, however, he sent several memoranda on reform in local government, attacking British plans, and on the effects of the 'Iron Curtain' (the phrase had been used by Goebbels). To establish his political credentials and because he disagreed with British policies, Adenauer went public on his differences with them. In September, for example, he attacked coal restrictions imposed by the British; he said people would die, and this might lead to a Nazi revival or a revolt. On 6 October 1945, not surprisingly under the circumstances, Adenauer was sacked by the British military governor, Barraclough, at the insistence of General Templer, for what seems to have been a combination of insubordination and inefficiency. He was ordered to cease all political activity at once. The words used to dismiss him were virtually identical to those used by the Nazis, a point Adenauer was happy to make. Only someone as tenacious and artful as Adenauer could seen this blow as a means of actually adding to his power.

Adenauer and Christian Democracy

Adenauer now used his time to transform his political position. He seems to have believed that his age and experience met the needs of the time: the Germans had lost an evil father – Hitler – and they now needed a good one, almost seventy years old. To this end, he began to work on the organization of the new party he (and others) conceived of, called provisionally the Christian Democratic Party, the CDP. Adenauer's overriding concern was (West) Germany's Westernization. To participate in this process, doubly so if he wished to guide it, it was necessary first to have a democratic political party to take him to power. Westernization, in fact, had both a domestic and a foreign policy perspective. The two were closely intermeshed and driven by each other. We shall examine the foreign dimension later. Here we need to consider the domestic political changes that were beginning to take off.

It is important to understand that the CDP, soon to become the CDU, and its Bavarian associate, the CSU, were not formed in isolation but against the existence of the SPD. Despite possessing a multi-party electoral system (which, contrary to popular belief, helped rather than hindered party formation despite the minimal five per cent barrier), the West Germans were beginning to move towards the creation of two major parties. One reason, of course, was the Nazi legacy which had undermined the relationship between class and party, opening the way for larger and broader parties. Another was Allied pressure. Finally, as the Centre Right began to deliver, electors showed that they wish to reward it. At the time of the first federal election in 1949, the CDU and SPD were running neck and neck, each gaining about a third of the vote. By the second, the position had changed with the begin of a breakthrough for Adenauer. The notion of a party of government, and one of opposition (an Anglo-American concept), was injected into German political development (although today it seems less secure). This, in turn, seemed, at the time, to imply a need for clear alternatives, in the British manner (but as we shall see, this concept was dumped by the major parties after little more than a decade).

What Adenauer gambled on – and won with – was the idea that a majority could be gained for broad, liberal and Western policies, at home and abroad. In addition, he was helped hugely by this complex electoral system which the West Germans designed with Allied help. This allowed a multiplicity of parties to emerge, which effectively produced coalition government. Coalitions, however, implied consensual rather than adversarial politics, and rewarded with power those parties which not only had the broadest appeal but also were most ready to coalesce. Christian Democracy won twice over since, by its nature, it was a consensual and broad doctrine, well-suited for winning new voters but also for coalition-building.

Social Democracy's leaders, however, in their post-1945 policies, made a severe miscalculation by leaving pragmatism to their enemies, the CDU/CSU, and believing that an oppositional stance would bring electoral advantage. Even though West German elections themselves were very bitter (and the SPD repeatedly, and for very many years, was attacked for being, as it was, Marxist), the harsh reality was that once the CDU/CSU (in 1949) had won an initial (if very modest success), it could exploit the desire for consensus by attacking the SPD for being an opposition. In this way, the CDU/CSU won twice over (by attacking Socialism *and* dissension), whilst the SPD lost twice over. Its early total opposition to the CDU/CSU merely compounded its failure to break into the centre, where the votes it needed now lay. The SPD hoped to copy British Labour (who had, after all, just won a massive majority); it failed to see this victory depended not least on both a class and an electoral system that the West Germans did not possess.

Christian Democracy and West Germany

Christian Democracy itself was a remarkable, post-war idea, relying on the fusion of the political centre with the religiously inspired Catholic and Protestant culture and the by now residual conservative forces. It could only have been created out of the very specific historical circumstances of destruction and defeat and the demands of Western-ization. It combined broad principles with a pragmatic approach to specific policies. Its political backbone consisted for the main part of the Rhine-Ruhr business class and the Roman Catholic bourgeois milieu of small-town western Germany.

The parties of what became the Bonn Republic had, of course, to operate on political ground only recently vacated by the Nazis. All of them sought to understand the reasons for the effectiveness of the NSDAP and draw the appropriate conclusions from the Nazi experiment. At first sight, the one party (the CDU) seemed new, the other (the SPD) old. As we have seen, in the Soviet zone, the old KPD re-emerged but even it understood that it could not gain power unless it adapted to the political legacy of Nazism. Its main response was its merger with the eastern SPD.

In the west, amalgamations and take-overs occurred as well – chiefly led by the CDU. As political institutions, all the parties were new, perhaps most importantly in the *way* in which they were led. Yet some parties were, in an overall sense, newer than others, even if all of them had links with parties and political ideas that had existed before 1945. The SPD itself, whose identity, programme, leader and deputy leader were continuities from Weimar days, was, as a party, soon run in a new way. For the first time, it had a real leader. The CDU and the FDP were certainly newer than the SPD. And yet when the personnel of the post-1945 parties is taken into account, it would, perhaps, be more correct to speak of old wine in new bottles, rather than new wine in new bottles. The main leaders of the new West German state were, with only a few important exceptions, members of the reserve team in German politics, the men (and sometimes the women) who from 1933 to 45 had been banned from active life but had not gone under.

As far as their attitude towards their traditional support was concerned, there were obvious differences between the Christian Democrats and the Social Democrats. Most leading figures who saw themselves as belonging to the Christian Centre believed implicitly that there was a need for a new centre-right party that would bring together the groups who had previously supported several distinct parties. 1945 presented them with the opportunity of rectifying many of the shortcomings of the German party system before 1933. The Roman Catholic Centre Party, the *Zentrum*, had been powerful but with self-imposed limits to the support it could canvass. Many former Centre Party leaders wished to make a break with this legacy (although some tried to carry on with the old party). No one saw the need for a decisive break more clearly than Adenauer, although others had come to the same conclusion and had almost certainly acted earlier than Adenauer himself. According to Leo Schwering, he and Cardinal Frings decided to establish a Christian People's Party even before the arrival of the US forces. It seems likely that throughout Germany others did similar things. But Adenauer's actions were different.

In this way, both the two main mass parties, CDU/CSU and SPD, came to bear the heavy imprint of the men who first led them after capitulation, Konrad Adenauer and Kurt Schumacher. Both leaders had suffered badly at the hands of the Nazis (though Schumacher had suffered more); both had plainly been damaged by the experience, and both displayed remarkable qualities of leadership. It was not hard for Adenauer to be pragmatic about policy. He had no great faith in people and did not believe that carefully honed philosophical positions were needed to please them. He once said to Carlo Schmid that what separated them from each other was the fact that Schmid had faith in people. Adenauer declared 'I do not believe in them and have never done so.'

Adenauer knew his first gambit was for leadership of the CDP. It had been founded in several places at local level – on 19 August 1945 in Cologne, on 2 September for Rhineland-Westphalia – and he saw that what was needed was someone or something that could bring the party together to form a single provincial unit. He possessed authority by virtue of his previous position in Weimar. But he was by no means the only individual to do so. There was also Berlin-based Jakob Kaiser, well-liked by the British. Andreas Hermes (also in Berlin), Hans von Schlange-Schöningen, Karl Arnold in Düsseldorf, Robert Lehr, Rudolf Amelunxen were also senior figures making a name for themselves after May 1945, and obvious rivals along with Josef Müller in Munich and even Heinrich Brüning, still in the United States.

Ever since September 1945, Adenauer had openly declared himself opposed to any revival of the Centre Party. In January 1946 he told Hans Schlange-Schöningen (by now the food commissioner in the UK zone) that the Centre had always been 'ultramontan' – that it had, in effect, represented external interests. Instead, he at once spoke up for the creation of a broader political movement, no longer exclusively Roman Catholic, but based firmly on what Adenauer called Christian principles, principles which had evolved over hundreds of years in European affairs and were to bring together Protestants as well as Roman Catholics. It was to be a democratic party with an accentuated emphasis on progressive social reform and on social welfare. It was not, however, to be a socialist party, but to stand in outright opposition to socialism. The fight against the old Centre, which for Adenauer was the pre-requisite for modernizing the centre right, was a hard and potentially hazardous one, which could have produced considerable internecine feuding. But he held firm to his belief.

There must be no return to party splintering, he argued. The German people, Adenauer insisted, could achieve political health only when the Christian principle governed their public affairs; only the Christian principle could oppose the ideas on government and morality now coming from the East, and only the Christian principle could provide the basis for a new cultural and ideological foreign policy in Western Europe. Over and above these broad guidelines, Adenauer eschewed a precise manifesto. The important thing was to concentrate on the fundamental ideas and seek to win over well-known public figures who in turn would attract voters from the right of the SPD, from the Centre Party and beyond. All Christian and democratic forces now needed to be ranged against the threat from the East. Early ideas on the economy supported by Christian Democrats involved the nationalization of some parts of German industry. The all-important notion of a 'social market economy' (which Adenauer, no economist, came to value) was something he specifically wished his party to support at an early stage. Adenauer was very keen to attract Ludwig Erhard into his party's ranks, not least because the Americans had such faith in him.

Adenauer did not attend the Rhineland CDP meeting at the beginning of September; but he had already been elected to the executive committee of the Party on 28 August. By 1 September 1945 Adenauer could write that the *Land* Party was growing fast, not least because of what he called the 'agitation' of the SPD. There was not only a CDP in Cologne for the whole of the Rhine province but one for Westphalia as well. Protestant political groups were working hard in Elberfeld and Essen. Some opposition to this was being expressed by a number of former Centre Party members who wished to revitalize the Weimar party. The Roman Catholic clergy were not committing themselves, although Adenauer was given to understand that they were ready to come out on the side of the CDU. In the event, the battle for the Centre's voters continued into 1948.

The struggle against the old Centre Party was not the only fight he had on his hands. The position in Bavaria (in the US zone) was unfavourable for Adenauer. An attempt had been made by Alois Hundhammer to revive the old Bavarian People's Party; but Josef Müller and his friends were able to build up a Bavarian Christian one, the Christian Social Union. The CSU was, in a number of ways, a potential rival to the CDU, although it could always be explained away as a Bavarian peculiarity. But the most important challenge to Adenauer personally and to his dream of a West German CDU came from Berlin, the once and future capital of Germany. With surprising speed, Adenauer realized that, contrary to expectations, Berlin was not the place to be. The Soviets seemed bound to stay there and interfere in politics. In addition, the new politics of Bonn was certain to be federal, rather than central. The very idea of old-style national politics, brokered in Berlin, had, he reasoned, become redundant. When, on 22 January 1946 at Herford, Adenauer became provisional chairman of the CDU in the British zone (he took the chair as the oldest person present) he began at once to freeze out the Berlin CDU. He told colleagues privately that even if the Soviets moved out of Berlin, it should never again be the centre of German political life. In February 1946 he insisted he wished to uphold

German national unity but Germany would have to be a federal state and, with the presence of the Soviets, its capital could not be Berlin.

At a meeting in Stuttgart on 3 April 1946, the Christian Social Party of Bavaria, the CDUs of Württemberg, of north Baden, and of Greater Hesse and the CDU in the British and American zones all resolved to form a union. It was to prove a defining moment for West Germany. They not only agreed that Berlin could *not* become the official seat of the party but they rejected Kaiser's political line. It directly contradicted Adenauer's own and would, had it been accepted, have moved the CDU (and West Germany) in a non-Western direction. Kaiser had declared that 'east should meet west', that (as frightening to Adenauer) the 'bourgeois era' had now come to an end; and even that the Communist manifesto 'was a major event in history'. The final blow against Kaiser was delivered in February 1947. When Kaiser demanded the chair of the foreign policy committee of the CDU, Adenauer simply walked out of the meeting. Within a few months, Kaiser and Hermes had to flee Berlin. Adenauer's stand seemed more than justified, and the challenge to a Western CDU evaporated.

Adenauer as CDU Chairman

On 5 February 1946 Adenauer was elected chairman of the *Land* executive of the Rhine CDU and on 1 March at the Neheim-Hüsten conference his position in the CDU in the British zone was confirmed. Here Adenauer also managed to get the CDU to move away from its support for the 'principles of Cologne' of June 1945, which rejected the idea of the market in favour of a socialized economy (whilst agreeing to state ownership of mining). This contorted line was designed to retain the support of Ruhr industrialists and Roman Catholic trade union members alike. In the same month he joined the nominated zonal advisory council (*Zonenbeirat*) which met in Hamburg.

Party work now became increasingly complex. It was at this time that Adenauer began to assemble a core group of advisers and aides who were to help him attain the Chancellorship (when it presented itself) and secure it for another fourteen years. Perhaps the most important of these early helpers was Herbert Blankenhorn (1904–91) who had been a career diplomat, joining the German foreign office in the dying days of the Weimar Republic. He at first lost his job, but then, in 1935, became a member of the German Embassy in Washington and of the Nazi Party, although he had reasonable anti-Nazi credentials. Adenauer would have liked him as foreign minister, but his Nazi past ruled this out. In 1946 Adenauer appointed him assistant general secretary of the CDU in the British zone.

In October 1946 the town and district elections in the UK zone took place. The CDU gained 48.5 per cent, a brilliant victory; the SPD 31.3 per cent, the KPD 7.4 per cent, the Centre 5.5 per cent and the FDP 2.7 per cent. Adenauer seemed well on his way.

Adenauer's Bid for Power in West Germany

In December 1946 the CDU held its first party conference in Düsseldorf. Adenauer made a speech criticizing British policy yet again (suggesting now that nationalization of German industries would increase centralization in Germany) and he was duly re-elected chairman. The party programme, however, accepted a mixed economy for the British zone. Adenauer continued to attack British policies. Students at Bonn, for example, were told that although the British controlled zonal affairs, they were incapable of administering them (and thus those Germans who worked for them were not collaborators). A highly developed and heterogeneous people like the Germans could never be governed by another people. England, he said, would never be able to do so. He attacked the British for permitting – he alleged – the North West German Radio to make propaganda for the SPD. He was required to apologize for this (and did so).

In discussing an electoral law for North Rhine-Westphalia, the British seemed to be yielding to SPD demands to include a proportional element (in between 33 and 40 per cent of the seats were to be allocated in this way). The CDU strongly favoured single-member constituencies, to provide working majorities in Parliament. It also spent some time spelling out its economic policy: it wanted to create a 'relationship' between workers and industrialists, but it was not keen to nationalize industry.

The April 1947 elections for the North Rhine-Westphalian *Landtag* did not bring the CDU the result for which it had worked: although it gained the largest number of votes (37.5 per cent), the SPD won 32 per cent; the KPD managed 14 per cent (taken as a warning to get the economy moving again); the Centre achieved 9.8 per cent (equally dangerous to the CDU), and the FDP 5.9 per cent. Adenauer was vexed by the Centre's attacks on the CDU for 'protecting capitalism which had pushed Germany into two wars'. This confirmed Adenauer's view that the CDU needed an economic policy supremo who might gain real support for market capitalism. Indeed, economic issues were now the main item on the agenda (not least because of the importance the Americans attached to liberal market conditions).

Ludwig Erhard

The supremo was Ludwig Erhard. His standing now was that of a gifted and influential academic economist, who enjoyed American support as well as popularity in the FDP (who had helped to get his important post in charge of economic administration in the Bizone in 1948). Adenauer himself had a relatively limited understanding of the technical aspects of economics (although he appreciated only too well what their practical effects might be). Indeed, in October Adenauer complained to Erhard about price increases and insisted he do something to cut them (a wish not entirely consistent with the theory of the market economy). Under Erhard, means were invented of bringing out the inherent strength of the West German economy, chiefly by liberating German industry from controls of any kind. Erhard's economic understanding undoubtedly helped to make West Germany prosperous (and this prosperity hugely assisted both the CDU and the commitment of the West Germans to the West). Economists cannot agree, however, whether Erhard's reforms, and the measures taken by the Allies (in particular the new Deutschmark), were the cause of West German economic strength (which predated 1945), or merely a useful kick-start to it.

Adenauer and Statehood

In April 1948 (shortly after the death of his wife), Adenauer began to develop his international and European reputation with a series of visits. He went to Belgium to discuss the future of Christian Democracy with Belgian counterparts, and in May he attended the founding session of the Council of Europe in the Hague. There he met Alcide de Gasperi, Winston Churchill and Edouard Herriot. In August he was summoned to the second day of the Rittersturz conference of the various minister presidents of the *Länder*.

On 18 November 1948 he was told by Generals Robertson and Steel that in view of the international situation (the Berlin airlift was of course still under way) the three Western military governments were in agreement that it would be highly desirable if the new West German state came into existence as soon as possible. Berlin, he was informed, would not be part of the new state since it had a special status flowing from agreements with the Soviet Union. He was told to prepare for the writing of a constitution and elections which would follow it.

In November, Adenauer made a rare speech in Berlin. He significantly dismissed SED supporters as being no longer Germans. The decisive relationship within Europe, he declared, would be the Franco-German one: no real German would ever want to go along with the

Soviets. At the same time, he concluded, Europe itself could only be saved by the USA. He told Swiss journalists a little later that he was not a nationalist but a patriot. East Germans, however, needed nationalism in order to resist the Communists. These views, were in a nutshell, to be Adenauer's message to the Germans for the next thirteen years.

Adenauer and the Genocide of the Jews

Adenauer wrote in May 1945 that he fully accepted the guilt of the German people for the 'misfortunes' ('Unglück') that had befallen it, but that every sin must be capable of expiation. His general line was the German people had to accept responsibility for what had been done in their name, but that this did not mean they were responsible *for* it. In February 1946 he spelt out – in private – his real views on the behaviour of the Church during the Third Reich. They were sharp:

> In my view, the German bishops and clergy must bear a large burden of guilt for what happened in the concentration camps. It is probably correct to say that, once the camps came into existence there was not much that could have been done about them, but the German people and the clergy allowed themselves to be Nazified without any offering any opposition. It is in this that their guilt lies.

'In general', he continued

> even if people did not know exactly what was happening in the camps, people knew perfectly well that personal liberty and the rule of law was being trampled underfoot, that terrible cruelties were being perpetrated in them; that the Gestapo, our SS and part of our troops in Poland used unparalleled cruelty against the civilian population. The Jewish pogroms of 1933 and 1938 took place in public. We officially announced the murders of hostages in France.

He concluded:

> I believe that if the bishops had all spoken out together on one particular day much could have been prevented. They did not do so, and they have no excuse for not doing so. Indeed, if the bishops had been sent to the camps that would not have been a bad thing: quite the reverse. But since none of this happened, the best thing now is to stay silent.

This conclusion motivated Adenauer's attitude to a number of former Nazis. He was happy to exonerate anyone who was merely a coward (although the testimonials he wrote as an acknowledged anti-Nazi sometimes strained credibility as in the case of a former professor who had joined the SA 'because he was prevented from resisting his entry').

In June 1946 Adenauer wrote that it was wrong to consider officials either Nazi or innocent; there was an in-between stage that a fine could adequately address. In October 1946 he wrote about the Nuremberg trials that too little was being reported to permit a German to form a proper opinion but that although he welcomed the concept of the trials as 'an advance in the struggle for human rights', he wished to see the concept applied to other states and not just to Germany. He was, after all, a German politician.

If this was Adenauer's attitude towards Germans and Nazism, his position towards the Jews, and Israel, was plainer still. He believed that Nazism put those who had survived, and those who sought to represent the interests of the victims, in a very special category and that exemplary retribution should be made. There can be little doubt that his handling of this most sensitive issue in contemporary German history reflects extremely well upon him and, by implication, on the state that he led.

Adenauer had first considered the issue in 1949. In January 1951 the new state of Israel asked the United States, the United Kingdom, France and the Soviet Union to support its claim for compensation against the West German state (East Germany refused to acknowledge any responsibility whatsoever for Nazi war crimes). The West agreed but the Soviets did not respond. On 12 March the Israeli government lodged a request for $15 Billion for the state of Israel for the German Jews who had escaped from Germany before 1950, and a claim for $6 billion for individuals. Herbert Blankenhorn, Adenauer's chief foreign policy adviser, met European representatives of the World Jewish Congress in London in March 1951 and advised his master to enter into direct negotiations with these individuals.

Accordingly, in April 1951, Adenauer had a secret meeting with the director of the Israeli finance ministry and later that year, in September, he declared that although he would not pronounce the entire German nation guilty of the crimes against the Jews, he was ready to accept German responsibility for restitution to the Jews for what had been done to them. Nahum Goldmann, the president of the World Jewish Congress, then met Adenauer at Claridges Hotel (again in secret) on 6 December 1951 and urged him to accept an immediate claim for $1 billion. It was necessary, he said, to offer an enormous sum because of the enormity of crime in question.

Adenauer agreed to negotiate on the basis of the request that Goldmann had made. In so doing, he was forced to accept bitter criticism from many of his colleagues in government, in particular from the finance minister, Fritz Schäffer, who argued that the precariousness of the West German economy could be dealt a mortal blow by reparations of this size. On 21 March 1952, talks started at The Hague in Holland between the two countries. Adenauer insisted that claims made by Jews were to be treated as special and not taken together with other demands for reparations. Furthermore, he said the monies should not be considered indemnities but a token of reconciliation. Abs, the eminent banker and personal friend of the Chancellor, said that DM 10–15 million per year was all the Federal Republic could afford. Erhard disagreed: he reckoned a sum of DM 200 million per year was possible.

In the event, there was considerable discussion about the astronomical sums involved. But in two meetings with Adenauer in Paris, on 28 May and 10 June, the Israelis were able to agree a sum with him. It was accepted by the Federal cabinet on 17 June 1952 and incorporated into the two Hague Agreements with Israel of 1952. West Germany was to pay, for the next fourteen years, DM 3 billion for Israel and provide additional goods valued at DM 450 million. By 1980 the sum of individual restitution payments was DM 80 billion, and will probably become DM 1000 billion by the end of the century.

The Federal Government also signed agreements with sixteen other states attacked by the Nazis (though not with the four victorious powers who had taken reparations for themselves). It has been argued that Adenauer agreed to all of this for two simple reasons. First, he understood that there was a moral dimension to restitution: nothing could ever make good the crimes of the Nazis but that did not mean that Germans should not attempt to make them good. Secondly, he himself had benefited from the generosity of two Jews in 1933. Although the point was never stressed, Adenauer's actions also added considerable weight to West Germany's insistence that it alone represented all Germans; this was one area where the moral issue mattered. He was not found wanting.

For his part, the SPD leader Schumacher stated that the SPD refused to recognize a 'general collective guilt' of the whole people and that if guilt was to be attached to the Germans, then it should also be attached to those countries who had 'permitted Hitler and his generals to think a world war would be acceptable'. Nazis, he held, were class enemies of Socialists and Jews; Socialists therefore had no responsibility for what the Nazis had done. Furthermore, the SPD had fought the Nazis since the early 1920s, rather longer than anyone else. Adenauer was, however, able to count on the full support of the SPD in the Bundestag to pass the necessary legislation. A sizeable number of deputies chose to be absent for the votes: almost 40 CDU members voted against him with 86 abstaining (including Franz Josef Strauss and Schäffer himself). It can be seen, once again, how strong was Adenauer's personal part in the re-invention of Germany.

The Social Democratic Party

If the key to understanding the CDU/CSU was its readiness to reimagine German politics and its part in them, the SPD presents a quite different picture. Both because of its positive self-image, and its clear potential to regain traditional support, it saw far less of a need to adapt to the new world situation or reflect seriously about whether its Marxism suited the sea-change that had come over Germany. Its proposed reforms were, as a consequence, often seen as outdated (quoted examples were its wish to centralize the political system and its desire that the state should take over key industries). Indeed, it took ten years for the SPD to understand fully why the CDU, which was so short on grand designs, apart from Westernization, had been able to take from the SPD what it regarded as its historical and political right to run the future Germany. So much of what Hitler had done, had been done against Social Democracy (even the name National Socialism was an attempt to wrong-foot it). At a *Land* level, many Social Democratic leaders would prosper. Yet their insistence that 'after Hitler, us' proved painfully misplaced.

In one area, however, the SPD did read the writing of the times. This was in its utter opposition to, and contempt for, Communism. No one expressed this more fervently than its leader, Schumacher, who was born in 1896 and died in 1953. Yet this was hardly a new departure for the SPD, since it had been policy ever since 1919. There was, however, a crude political contradiction between the SPD's anti-Communism and its Marxism. Although a theoretical case could be made to defend its position, the truth was that, politically, it was hard for the ordinary German (who liked neither Communism nor Marxism) to understand how the SPD could make a distinction between them. Alongside this failure to understand the real way in which Germany was currently being remade ran a lack of sensitivity towards the new economic realities that would go with Westernization. Rather than look to the US (the real source of this), German Social Democrats liked to look at Britain and its plans for the nationalization of British industry and a welfare system that only the richest of nations (and not Britain) could properly afford.

Kurt Schumacher

Schumacher was born in Kulm (Chelmno) in East Prussia although his parents moved to Hanover when this territory was handed over to Poland in accordance with the Treaty of Versailles. He had been eighteen when the First World War broke out. In December 1914 he lost his entire right arm in fighting on the eastern front, was invalided out and became a student and a committed Socialist. In 1918 he joined the Berlin Workers' and Soldiers' council. He then became editor of a local party newspaper in Stuttgart. He was a fierce left-wing critic of the 1928 SPD-led government. In May 1930 he was elected to the Reichstag and in 1932 to the *Fraktionsvorstand*, or parliamentary party committee.

Both in the Reichstag and outside it, Schumacher increasingly clashed with the Nazis. In February 1932 after Goebbels had said that the SPD was a party of 'deserters and Jews', Schumacher (a volunteer in 1918) not only defended the SPD but added that Germans would require a decade to heal themselves from the Nazis' 'continuous appeal to the inner *Schweinehund* in man'.

Dachau

This and incidents like it ensured that, after 30 January 1933, the Nazis would seek to settle their scores with Schumacher. He refused to flee Germany and was arrested in July, spending the next eight years in Dachau. The Nazis hoped to deal with him through their policy of 'extermination through work'. Schumacher refused to work, however, and went on a month-long hunger strike. He was proud of the fact that no guard ever dared to strike him to his face; he was always ordered to turn his face to the wall before being beaten. Although a non-Jew, he was never given a position of authority in the camp by the Nazis. On 16 March 1943 Schumacher was released from Dachau, and went to his sister in Hanover; it was thought he had been so broken that there was no longer any point in detaining him.

1945

Schumacher had been rearrested in the aftermath of 1944 plot against Hitler, but released in October. As soon as Hanover was occupied (by US troops on 7 April) Schumacher resumed his political career (though his audience had no idea of who he was, or had been). An early line of his was that although the Germans might want to go back to 1933, where they had left off, they could not do so. They had changed, and the world had changed. He also very quickly developed the notion that the new SPD had to be a party open to all Germans, based on a belief in social justice, liberty and tolerance. Whilst saying that the party needed 'all those who have been clean for the past 12 years', he accepted that younger members were equally vital, whether or not they had been Nazis. Yet he rejected capitalism as harshly as he had done before 1933. Even though he claimed (correctly) that the world had moved on, neither he, nor his ideas, had actually moved with it.

Schumacher, now fifty, at once demanded for himself the right to speak for the SPD. On 19 April 1945 General Eisenhower permitted the Germans to establish a reconstruction committee and democratic party politicians were instructed to serve upon it in accordance with their Weimar strength. Schumacher quickly advanced the case for the SPD and against the Roman Catholic Centre Party and the Communists, who claimed the lion's share of seats. His office soon became the *de facto* headquarters of the SPD in western Germany. Berlin and the Soviet zone also had an SPD headquarters from the end of June 1945. Schumacher's main aim now was to make himself the uncontested leader of the SPD.

Schumacher as SPD Chief

Like Adenauer, Schumacher had to rid himself of his rivals to become party leader. Several of these were very senior Social Democrats like Wilhelm Keil, Carl Severing and Paul Löbe. In the event, none of them posed a real threat. Severing was disliked by the British because they thought he had compromised with the Nazis, and Löbe was forced to retire in 1947 when he spoke in support of an SED initiative on dealings with the occupying powers. More serious challenges came from Wilhelm Hoegner (Bavarian minister president for a short time), Wilhelm Kaisen (governing mayor of Bremen) and Ernst Reuter (governing mayor of Berlin). In their own ways, these three men were far keener than their leader both to cooperate with the occupation forces and to coalesce with the so-called bourgeois parties (chiefly the CDU/CSU and the FDP). Kaisen strongly objected to Schumacher's line on the European Coal and Steel Community (ECSC), and accused him of opposition for the sake of opposition (a charge that, on the whole, was well-justified). Both Reuter and Kaisen disagreed with Schumacher's rejection of the draft Basic Law. The most serious challenge, however, came from Berlin, just as it had for Adenauer, where, as we have seen, a number of Berlin Social Democrats led by Otto Grotewohl were keen to move the SPD towards some form of cooperation with the KPD.

Where Adenauer insisted on a broadly based party, grouped around a few ethical propositions, Schumacher regarded a political party as something far more monolithic. According to his close associate, Carlo Schmid, he dismissed the CDU as 'not a party, merely a collection of interests, bound only by hostility towards Socialism and fear of any basic changes in the economy or society'. The SPD, on the other hand, 'Die Partei', as Schumacher usually called it, required loyalty and discipline. The basis of its identity was national rather than regional, and leading it meant dominating it. Schumacher turned down an early invitation to enter the government of Württemberg in 1945, because for him party was more important than government.

The Re-emergence of the SPD

Although many Social Democrats became important leaders of the Bonn Republic at *Land* level, the failure to gain power in Bonn, particularly in 1949 and in 1953, meant that the SPD lost, for all time, the opportunity of giving the West German state, in the widest sense, the imprint of Social Democracy. It did contribute to the making of the system, but only by achieving changes of detail. Since the most important decisions on West Germany's future were taken at the beginning, and since the SPD was excluded from shaping it after 1949, it reaped a meagre harvest. This perpetuated the idea that the SPD was not suited to govern the re-invented German 'nation' in the west. Even where the occupation powers were inclined towards fair treatment towards the SPD, they failed to produce the sorts of policies they – particularly the Americans – believed were right for the new West Germany. On the other hand, it should not be forgotten that the SPD was in achieving government successful at *Land* level, and in West Berlin. Indeed, the idea of an SPD *Land* government coexisting with a CDU/CSU/FDP government in Bonn pleased many Germans in theory as well as practice, since it was proof of political decentralization, whilst allowing the Centre Right to determine overall policy. It was thus not surprising that in the forty-five years of the Federal Republic, the SPD has ruled in Bonn for only sixteen and as senior partner for only thirteen. Furthermore, when the SPD finally had the chance to take power in Bonn, significantly, its policies were shaped to fulfilling foreign policy goals that Adenauer had allegedly failed to realize.

Schumacher's impact on the SPD is open to two quite different interpretations. There are those who argue that his authoritarian style and his unshakeable conviction that the SPD should always, at its centre, remain a working-class party, had the simple – but unwanted – effect of allowing Adenauer's CDU to become Bonn's natural party of government. Others, however, point to the fact that without Schumacher's rigid leadership, the SPD might have done far worse in West German politics than it actually did, not least because most of its repositories of support lay in what became, after 1945, the Soviet zone. It was not his fault, it is claimed, that the success of Rhenish liberalism squeezed Social Democracy.

The SPD certainly gained from Schumacher's organizational talents: his office in Hanover very soon became the centre of an effective party structure, and his establishment of a 'national' network for it in western Germany soon made it a mass party. It also reinforced his own position within. His fierce opposition to German Communism and to the Soviet Union proved beneficial as the Cold War began to break out and his deep commitment to democratic principles gave the Bonn Republic a loyal opposition. He was also a very brave man, a hero for a political culture short on heroes. Adenauer had kept his head down during the Third Reich. Schumacher had held his head high.

A recent book argues that, given the failings of the SPD leadership in exile, it was inevitable that the leading role in the new party should pass to Social Democrats who had spent the Third Reich inside Germany. In fact, the position was by no means as straightforward as this. It actually had far less to do with the exiles' failings, far more to do with the real political problems which flowed having sought exile, in particular, fear of the accusation that the exiles had been fighting on the wrong side.

Erich Ollenhauer, the effective leader of the London exiles, became Schumacher's deputy in 1946 and, after 1952, leader in his place. Many other London exiles played important roles in the party. They included Waldemar von Knoeringen, Fritz Heine, Willi Eichler (chief author of the 1959 Godesberg Programme) and Wenzel Jaksch. Other – non-London – exiles of major importance included Willy Brandt and Ernst Reuter. The Austrian Social Democrat exile Bruno Kreisky (who had sought refuge in Sweden) became Chancellor in post-war Austria.

The Wennigsen Meeting

Schumacher decided to call a national congress (*Reichstreffen*) of the SPD for the autumn and on 5 October 1945 leading Social Democrats assembled at Wennigsen Abbey near Hanover. His aim was to breathe new life into the SPD, to legitimate his own bid for supremacy and to marginalize the Berlin SPD. At first, the British had tried to prevent the meeting and attempted to restrict participation to Social Democrats from the British zone. But they were prevailed upon to change their minds (although no delegates from the French zone were permitted to attend). Indeed, Ollenhauer, Heine and Erwin Schoettle were allowed to fly in from London and Otto Grotewohl, Max Fechner and Gustav Dahrendorf came from Berlin as the representatives of the SPD in the Soviet zone of occupation.

At Wennigsen, it was decided, unwisely and inappropriately, to stick to the 1925 Marxist programme. Mines, heavy industry and energy were to be nationalized. But perhaps the chief aim of the meeting was to allow Schumacher to present himself as SPD leader. His claim was challenged by Grotewohl, the Berlin SPD leader. His candidature was rather stronger than many western SPD members said, not least because the party there could boast 70,000 members.

Half Schumacher's keynote speech was devoted to destroying the credentials of eastern German colleagues. Yet their Berlin central committee was no less legitimate than his Hanover office; like Schumacher, Grotewohl had been a young SPD Reichstag deputy and had even been a minister in Brunswick; he, too, had not gone into exile. Schumacher attacked them for their willingness to work with the KPD, and stalled any attempts to decide the matter there and then.

Towards the end of 1945 Schumacher's office was renamed the office of the 'representative of the SPD for the three western zones of occupation' – still not the headquarters of the SPD, but a step nearer that goal. His office was managed by Anne-Marie Renger, a war widow, who became his companion. He was soon joined by Alfred Nau, Herbert Kriedemann and Egon Franke (all from Hanover). Stefan Thomas, who had also been in London during the war, began to build up an eastern office, or *Ostbüro*, for the SPD whose aim was to establish contact with Party members in the Soviet zone and supply the leadership with first-rate intelligence about the GDR.

On 6 December 1945 the SPD at last gained official permission to undertake party political work in the Hanover area. By February 1946 the party possessed a zonal organization, and permission was given for a full-scale party conference to be held in Hanover on 9 May 1946. Erich Ollenhauer, Fritz Heine and Herta Gotthelf had returned from their London base in February, and they formally gave back to the party in Germany the mandate they had received in 1933.

At the congress, Schumacher was unanimously elected chairman of the party and Ollenhauer, Heine, Nau and Kriedemann elected to paid executive posts. In addition to this executive committee (*Geschäftsführender Vorstand*), there were a further twenty or so members of the executive (*Vorstand*) who played virtually no role in the formulation of policy. Schumacher took specialist advice from individuals he trusted: his economic advisers, Viktor Agartz, Fritz Baade and Eric Noelting were always carefully listened to – too carefully, perhaps, since they failed to appreciate the consequences of the new interest in market capitalism in West Germany.

Schumacher's Marxism

Schumacher always (and tediously) sought to justify his role with Marxist theory. He denied any ambition, claiming to be merely the person who articulated the analysis which would bring power to the

SPD. Schumacher once referred to Marxism as 'an indispensable analytical method in the fight for the liberation of the workers'. In May 1947 he spoke at the re-opening of the Karl Marx house in Trier. 'In other countries', he said 'we have seen the growth of non-Marxist labour movements. But they have all, after a time, proved incapable of surviving.'

Schumacher was convinced that of all the western German political parties, it was only the SPD that possessed the moral right to govern. It had stayed firm against Nazism and Communism. Yet, moral or not, the truth was that the popular appeal of non-Communist Marxism was declining, given the Red Army's defeat of German forces in the east in 1944–5, and the Communists' blatant attempts to take power in their zone of occupation. Schumacher's line obviously precluded any serious thought on coalition-building with the Centre Right, the only means to power in Bonn (as history was later to prove).

Much of Schumacher's analysis of National Socialism was simplistic, over-polemical and unconvincing. Nor were they likely to be satisfied by his analysis of Germany's future part in European affairs. Whilst one could appreciate the logic of Schumacher's strategy (promoting the idea that the working classes had been crushed by big business in Nazi guise was good for the morale of organized labour), this theory of Nazism – which was in essence the old Weimar theory – was neither the full story, nor did it meet the needs of politics after 1945.

It was, however, not only his Marxism that proved outmoded. Schumacher (and most of his colleagues, with the exception of Carlo Schmid) tended to confuse political questions with organizational ones. It was deemed more important to organize existing members, than think about ways of gaining new ones. This obsession with bureaucratic organization at the expense of innovative politics was a time-honoured SPD error. By itself, good organization would not lead to power.

In one specific area, however, the question of organization was genuinely significant in an immediate political sense: this was the relationship between the SPD and the KPD. As we shall see, in order to have a truly democratic Social Democratic party, Schumacher and virtually every single leading Social Democrat in the British and American zones believed the western SPD needed to be organizationally distinct from the SPD office in Berlin, which for geographical and political reasons was already under pressure from the Communists. Here, then, being a separate organization from the eastern German SPD would not only allow the western SPD to stay anti-Communist, but would keep the Party independent.

On 3 January 1946 a meeting of delegates of the SPD in the British zone voted unanimously to oppose the unification of the SPD and the

KPD, and on 6 January SPD delegates from the three *Länder* of the US zone voted 144 to 6 to do the same (the SPD was still forbidden to meet on a supra-zonal level). It should, however, be noted that one out of three western SPD supporters would have supported the SED had it been the only Socialist party, (and it should be recalled that even in the West Berlin vote of 31 March 1946 over 60 per cent said they supported cooperation between the SPD and KPD). The formal refounding of the SPD took place from 9 to 11 May 1946 in Hanover, actively supported by an influential British officer named Lance Pope.

In February 1946 Schumacher and one of his chief aides, Herbert Kriedemann, met Grotewohl and Dahrendorf again at Brunswick, near the zonal border. Schumacher urged the Berliner to dissolve their committee in order to forestall the Communist plan for a unity party. They refused; it was claimed they said this was because SPD members were already been arrested by the NKVD/KGB, and to go against the Soviet Union would precipitate a terrible slaughter of SPD members in the Soviet zone.

Schumacher was flown to Berlin by a British aircraft on 11 February 1946 in a final attempt to persuade organized labour to stand firm against the Communists. He had meetings in the Soviet zone (the first and last time he was there); his theme was that there could be no true socialism without democracy. But too much had already happened for him to be heeded.

In the event, as we have see, Stalin was not to be diverted. It is to state the obvious to say that Schumacher hugely regretted the loss of the eastern Social Democrats (even if there was little that they could do at present to support the party): Thüringia, Saxony, Brandenburg and Mecklenburg had been very strongly Social Democratic; the population of western Germany, however, was on the whole more likely to go for Christian Democracy. Forty-four years later, the first free elections in eastern Germany since 1933 showed that the SPD's traditional strengths here had been destroyed by the 'real, existing Socialism' practised by the SED.

On 20 October 1946 elections took place in Berlin. The SPD's decisive victory was seen as a victory for Schumacher's line. The SPD by 1948 had 800,000 members (200,000 more than in the Weimar era). In the *Landtag* elections in the British zone on 20 April 1947 the SPD gained 36.8 per cent, and the CDU 32.2 per cent, with the SPD doing particularly well in Lower Saxony (43.4 per cent), and Schleswig Holstein (44.4 per cent). Yet the real power to shape the emerging West German state could only be found in the federal government, not at *Land* level.

Schumacher's Nationalism

Schumacher's anti-Communism almost certainly led him to develop his nationalist standpoint. It is fashionable to define patriotism as something positive, implying a beneficial and passive love of one's country. During Weimar, he had certainly expressed patriotic opinions although he was no chauvinist (that is, he did not think Germany was better than any other nation). After 1945, however, he quickly became a nationalist in that he vigorously and actively pressed German national self-interest, paying little heed to difficulties this might cause or the obstacles it might set up in the way of genuine cooperation with West Germany's neighbours.

Tactically, he believed, there was considerable electoral advantage to be won from ardent nationalism. Germans had been schooled in it by the Nazis, and it was not foolish to seek to give them a sense of their own worth again. Yet no party had suffered more from the poisonous political fall-out of nationalism than the SPD and no German party had stronger international credentials, particularly in the West, of course. In addition, by 1950 Adenauer had developed his own supra-nationalist line, and it was not certain that the German voters would follow it.

Schumacher reasoned that nationalism would provide a comprehensive means of establishing the SPD's credentials as an anti-Communist and anti-Soviet party, as a party of all of the German people (and not just those in the western zones) and it would lay the ghost (evoked by the Kaiser and Hitler to name but two) that the SPD was anti-national (that is, international) and anti-German. But his theoretical distinction between genuine nationalism and chauvinism was neither clear nor easily understood: 'To be national is a matter of honour, to be international is a duty, and to be a nationalist is to be the deadly enemy of the German people.'

It was to prove yet another miscalculation. Adenauer was able to offer German electors a far more sophisticated line: that it was in Germany's national interest to be internationalist. Where necessary, Adenauer could always make the required nationalist noises (which he often did) and seem consistent. When Schumacher did the same thing, he seemed either believable and dangerous to the West, or to lack credibility.

Schumacher's line caused trouble with the British. Whilst they expected Adenauer to appear to be a nationalist (and told him off when they thought he went too far) they expected Schumacher to be more pro-Western than he was. An example was a speech delivered to students in Cologne in the autumn of 1945 in which Schumacher said the SPD would never accept the Oder-Neisse line and would fight 'with peaceful means' to liberate it. Furthermore, since the British Labour Party had never actually accepted that the SPD was as internationalist as it and its German opponents insisted, Schumacher's outbursts simply reinforced the line that of all parties, the SPD could be trusted least.

Schumacher's nationalism ensured his fierce opposition to the Allies' policy of *démontage*. But he also spoke out angrily against Western Allied refugee camps ('Bergen Belsen without the SA and SS'). He took on de Gaulle, who had said the Germans would have to get used to the separation of the Rhineland and Ruhr from the rest of Germany (Léon Blum, the SPD's old friend, as well as the French Communists, opposed this plan) and he was also highly critical of the notion that western Germans should contribute to their own defence ('no German should be cannon fodder for the Allies').

Whilst Schumacher objected to the idea that the new Germany should be pushed into the Soviet orbit, he strongly opposed tying it to the West. When he visited London in November 1946 it was his nationalism that generated most of the interest. His demand made at a press conference, that the *Anschluss* of Austria be permitted produced much hostility, and was widely seen as a serious error. Both in 1946 and on a subsequent visit in 1948 the Foreign Secretary refused to receive him (despite the fact that they were both Socialists). When in 1949 Bevin finally agreed to see him, nothing good came out of it (indeed, when Schumacher and his advisers went to see Bevin at the Foreign Office, Bevin neither stood up nor shook their hands as they entered his office).

Bevin's unpleasantness was caused by his more general hatred of Germans ('I tries 'ard, Brian, but I 'ates 'em' was his well-known comment on the Germans to General Robertson). But Schumacher was considered very heavy going even by those with no in-built animosity towards him. US Secretary of State Dean Acheson was taken to meet him in 1949 and found him peculiar. Sir Ivone Kirkpatrick, who became British High Commissioner in 1949, got on famously with Adenauer but found Schumacher so difficult to deal that in due course they were 'barely on speaking terms'.

Running the Party

The party by now consisted of nineteen district organizations. These were headed by officials paid for by the districts (and not, as before 1933, paid for by the national executive). It was they who collected the membership charges. The post-1945 SPD was no longer in receipt of trade union funds, since the unions had been formally separated from the party.

Several regional political leaders played a very significant role in the development of the SPD. They included Franz Neumann in Berlin, Erwin Schoettle in Württemberg and Waldemar von Knoeringen in Bavaria. The Weimar party had possessed the benefit of a large press: in addition to its daily newspaper, *Vorwärts*, it could count on more than 200 newspapers taking the SPD's line. After 1945 the situation was very different. It became increasingly difficult to put the party message over (it was Fritz Heine's job to attend to the party press) although some papers like the *Westdeutsche Allgemeine Zeitung* in the Ruhr were a strong source of support. Yet as Heine himself wrote, newspapers were increasingly read for amusement, not information or to form opinions. Socialist papers were therefore forced to choose between sensational reporting and retaining their readers, or serious political comment and losing them.

As has often been pointed out, the membership of the SPD after 1945 was not merely ageing (in 1946 two-thirds of the members had been members before 1933) but also declining (from 875,000 in 1947 to 627,000 in 1952).

The SPD and Statehood

When it became clear that the Western Allies wished to see a separate West German state, Schumacher and the SPD were concerned that this state should be viewed only as a provisional entity. Schumacher's ardent nationalism prescribed this course of action, and the SPD was determined that its national credentials should not be called into question. In March 1949, Schumacher, seriously ill, opposed the Allies' wishes on decentralization. He believed that without central control, West Germany could not be socialized. He insisted that 'one could not a patriot with eleven fatherlands'. But his view could not be upheld, given the strength of the Allies' feelings and Adenauer's compliance. He nevertheless believed that his stand would find wide support amongst the West Germans. His health improved sufficiently for him to appear at the Hamburg local party congress in 1949, with his arm around Frau Renger, who supported him as he hobbled into the hall. He received a standing ovation, and the membership burst into one of the old party songs.

Yet the first Federal elections on 14 August 1949 were a desperate disappointment. The SPD gained 6.9 million votes, the CDU/CSU 7.3 million. This small margin, however, gave the CDU the right to form the first federal government. Schumacher decided to stand as Federal President in order to gain at least something; but he lost to Theodor Heuss by 312 votes to 416.

The SPD and the Bonn Republic

Schumacher's first speech in the newly elected Bundestag on 21 September 1949 was intended to lay down markers for the next four years. He praised nationalization in Britain, and promised to fight for a socialist economy in the Federal Republic. The SPD, he promised, would be an opposition, but an opposition *loyal* to the democratic Republic (a factor which distinguished the Bonn Republic from the Weimar Republic in an extremely important respect). He continued to accuse Adenauer of selling Germany out to the Western Allies, and singled out the Ruhr statute for special attack. The statute set out the way in which the Ruhr authority was to distribute Ruhr coal to the international community. The parliamentary debate on the issue that took place on 24 and 25 November 1949 proved to be a watershed in post-war German political development. As Adenauer expounded his Western policies, uproar broke out in the Bundestag, and one SPD member called out 'Is the Chancellor a German chancellor?' Schumacher himself then shouted 'He is the Federal Chancellor of the Allies.'

These words (for which Schumacher was suspended) were symptomatic of the extent to which the SPD leader had left political reality behind. In one sense, Adenauer was of course the Allies' Chancellor (though his opposition to many British policies showed this was not so in every case). But in another, more important one, western German politics demanded that this distinction be made meaningless. What was in the Western interest was now also in the German 'national' interest. It was a sign of the abnormality of German political life and the damage done to it, with which all parties had to live.

The SPD's line on European integration and on European defence was part and parcel of the same massive miscalculation. Schumacher rejected the common plan for coal and steel production. On 8 November 1950 in relation to the Pleven plan, a European Defence Community was debated in the Bundestag. Schumacher was no pacifist, as his own war service proved. Yet his argument, that a new German defence force would perpetuate Germany's division, was inappropriate. Not only was there no other road for West Germany to follow but the lack of a real defence force could have opened all of Germany to Communism by means of the power of the Red Army. Schumacher's policy was unsustainable. On 9 October 1951, in a speech in Hamburg, he dismissed Adenauer's plans as an 'illusion'. The real illusion, however, was his own.

On 21 December 1951 Schumacher collapsed in his office, blood flowing from his mouth. He suffered another massive stroke in his sleep on 20 August 1952, and died at once. He was 56 years old. The SPD gave him what amounted to a state funeral. Adenauer did not turn up. Ultimately, however, what made Schumacher the right leader for the SPD in 1945 made him the wrong leader by 1952. His inner certainty, his uncompromising belief in the value of party discipline and his refusal to shed Social Democracy's traditional idea of working-class aspirations all allowed the SPD to re-establish itself quickly. But his hold on the party arrested its development, preventing it from adapting to the fundamental changes that were taking place in West German political life whether the SPD liked them or not.

—4—

Adenauer's High Policy

The Problem of Limited Sovereignty

Adenauer's central achievement was to give a precise meaning to the idea of a reinvented German state in the west, one which was *integrated into* the West. The key components of his reinvention were domestic liberalism (to be based on political and economic liberalism), complemented by a clear policy of economic and military cooperation with the Western Powers.

It is important to understand how very radically this changed the course of German political development. Occupation had established the basis for this. It had, so to speak, staked out the plot. It had also provided the basic materials and done some of the building. But the completion of the edifice was the work of Germans and, for it to stick, could only be effected by Germans. In essence, the West German government eschewed a 'German' solution to Germany's problems and adopted, instead, a 'Western' one. What is more, as much through luck as through political management, by 1953 West Germans accepted this in sufficient numbers for us to see that Adenauer had, indeed, been able to divert the course of German political development. It was a turning point that really had turned.

What was created soon seemed so well-built and solid that people came to forget the difficulties, often extreme, encountered in its construction. It was one thing to reinvent German democracy and uphold the rule of law (which the Germans called the *Rechtsstaat*). It was quite another to establish a West German part-nation whilst at the same time inextricably locking it into the West. Adenauer did this in both a political sense (through treaties and rearmament) and economically (through the Monnet Plan).

As Chancellor in 1949, Konrad Adenauer had a straightforward design. He wanted to persuade the Western Powers to grant the Federal Republic the status of equal partner and to remove the formal barriers to equality as soon as possible. This was the precondition for completing the making of his German state.

On a different and higher level, Adenauer showed that he was determined to provide a definitive solution to the German problem. It was clear-cut and, set against the context of nineteenth and twentieth-century German politics, highly original. West Germany was to renounce the pursuit of any form of dominance. This would lead to the defining of a new interest for this part-nation – one which would, as long it remained a part-nation, ensure that its politics were always Western, more than they were German.

Adenauer's success, then, lay not merely in executing the policies of Western integration but in giving them *form* through treaties, through rearmament and, above all, through economic and political integration with western Europe. We should not forget that this latter aim, integration via Franco-German cooperation, was an idea that Adenauer had himself imagined, many years before Monnet produced his blueprint. The setting-up of the European Community and the precise format of German unity in 1990 were the direct result of Adenauer's statecraft and statesmanship. It was this constraining, this Westernizing of West Germany that proved such an arduous task. As we shall see, Adenauer and his colleagues had to struggle against many opponents, domestic and foreign, in order to be successful. The Western Allies supported Adenauer's ideas in broad outline, but, particularly over German rearmament, contradicted themselves so deeply that policy making became hugely difficult. Within Germany, Adenauer was opposed by the Communists in East Germany (of course), but was also exposed (in respect of both economic and military integration) to fierce, almost lethal, criticism from the SPD and from some of his own ministers.

Adenauer's role as West German leader became central in managing these processes at home and abroad. Before 1951 West German foreign policy was legally the preserve of the Western Allies. Yet thanks to occupation, foreign and domestic policy merged into each other. After 1951 (when the Federal Republic was allowed a foreign policy and a minister with limited powers) Adenauer became his own foreign minister (the only minister he could trust, as he liked to say). Even after sovereignty of a sort was achieved in 1955, Adenauer continued to dominate the foreign policy of the Federal Republic until his retirement. Yet throughout the period from 1949 to 1955 he was obliged to make policy on the basis of a series of utterly bizarre deals with the Western Powers which look even more extraordinary fifty years later than they must have appeared at the time. Meanwhile, Adenauer had a duty to define and articulate the *German* interest and accept what the Western Powers stated was *their* interest in Germany.

In creating a new national interest for a new German state, Adenauer won through by being Western to the core. This meant that he fell in with policies he did not like that could be politically damaging (yielding to French claims on the Saar was a case in point) although, where necessary (increasingly so, he believed, in the late 1950s), also attempt to 'out-west' the West. All too often, the West, and increasingly the USA, seemed confused and inept in its foreign policy management. That Adenauer could manage this situation, however, is attributable not only to his personal skills. He was also greatly helped by the curious position of the entire Bonn Republic; its peculiarities, and the legacy on which it was predicated, greatly assisted him in his task.

In order to test these assertions, we need only ask what the Federal Republic would have looked like had Kurt Schumacher been Chancellor after 1949. There would have been no European Community, no West German membership of NATO and no social market economy. Had German unity been achieved, the price would have probably have been German neutrality, the de-stabilization of Europe, and a tightening of the Communists' stranglehold on eastern Europe.

An early biography by Charles Wighton termed Adenauer a 'democratic dictator'. This was wide of the mark (and a contradiction in terms). But it was not hard to see what it meant. The Chancellor was as authoritarian as he was authoritative. He fought his opponents hard, and often with unsavoury methods. In 1961 he publicly referred to Willy Brandt (his opponent for the chancellorship) as 'Herr Brandt alias Frahm', drawing attention to his illegitimate birth; and he also sneered at his wartime exile in Norway. As Krushchev noted, Adenauer always 'pretended to be the perfect little Christ' whilst pushing his own policy to the utmost.

Building a New Administration

One of the very first tasks of the new Chancellor was to set up an administrative apparatus for himself. By definition, he had no predecessor and there was no office for him to take over. Furthermore, as we have seen, the Basic Law gave the Chancellor a particularly strong position in West German political life on account of his duty to determine the broad thrust of all aspects of government policy. It was thus necessary for him to have a staff large enough to offer him the information and policy advice to enable him to run his government. Thus the Chancellor needed not just a ministry, but a super-ministry which could monitor all the other ministries though this was not realized until the late 1960s.

Establishing a bureaucracy for himself at this level obliged Adenauer to headhunt wildly. This proved difficult. There were no senior Reich civil servants (who would know how to run a federal government) who had not been Nazi Party members. And these the occupiers would simply not accept. One solution was to go for 'outsiders' (they, too, were likely to have Nazi pasts if they were prominent in any way but this could be glossed over more easily). Adenauer took every opportunity to put CDU members in positions of authority.

The key civil servant was Hans Globke who became Adenauer's chief aide. He served the Chancellor from 1949 until 1963, leaving one day after Adenauer (to confirm his master's desk was clear). Globke had helped the Nazis govern. He had been co-author of the official Nazi commentary on the Nuremberg anti-Jewish race laws of 1935. But he had never been a Nazi Party member. After 1945 he joined the CDU. Even so, Globke's true role was, at first, concealed through artful nomenclature. In addition to running Adenauer's office, he dealt with the security and intelligence services.

Other important members of Adenauer's team were Heinrich von Brentano, CDU floor leader and a strong pro-European, Eugen Gerstenmaier (another pro-European), and Walter Hallstein, who became the Chancellor's state secretary in August 1950. Hallstein was an academic without party affiliation. He was given special responsibilities for the Schuman plan, and nominated another academic, the eminent economist Wilhelm Röpke, as expert adviser on this issue. Another academic, Professor Wilhelm Grewe, was asked to take charge of policy connected with the sought-for dissolution of the Occupation Statute. In 1952 Felix von Eckhardt was appointed head of the federal press and information office. Hans von Herwarth was appointed head of protocol. Kurt Georg Kiesinger, himself Chancellor from 1966 to 1969 in the Grand Coalition, was also part of the circle. The Chancellor also turned frequently to his business friends for advice; of these Pferdmenges and Abs were the most prominent.

Adenauer's Public Policy

On 20 September 1949 Adenauer laid down before the Bundestag the broad outline of his government's policies. The main themes of his domestic policy were, he announced, to develop further a social market economy, and to reduce unemployment whilst retaining financial stability. He aimed to give assistance to those who had suffered from the war and to make some restitution to the many millions of expellees and refugees. In foreign policy, he sought to overcome Germany's division and secure the liberty of Berlin, to arrive at a new understanding with France by dismantling their historical rivalry, to solve the Saar problem, to take a part in the measures to promote European integration and to work closely with the United States.

A Westernizing Foreign Policy

Adenauer had his first meeting with the High Commissioners as Chancellor on 21 September 1949, the day on which the Occupation Statute came into force. Adenauer made it clear that his aim was equality. To this end negotiations were started on what was to become known as the Petersberg Agreement of 22 November 1949, under which the allies scaled down *démontage* in return for relatively trivial concessions from the federal government, including its taking up its place on the Ruhr authority (which was, in fact, dissolved on 21 December 1951). Adenauer was also asked to join the OECC and GATT and become an associate member of the Council of Europe.

Real equality of status did not, however, come easily or quickly to the Federal Republic (and in a strictly legal sense it did not come until 15 March 1991, with the final ratification of the treaties uniting Germany). It was to take Adenauer five years from the signing of the Petersberg agreement (which permitted West Germany to have consulates) to gain for the Federal Republic full sovereignty in domestic and foreign affairs (with certain not insignificant exceptions dealing with Allied rights in Germany and Berlin and the issue of German national unity).

Yet in regard to all that had happened since 1933, West Germany's transition from pariah to partner did take a remarkably short time. By 1955 West Germany was obviously not an enemy of the Free World but an important part of it.

The Saar

As it had been for some time, a major obstacle to better relations with France was the Saar question. The French government gave every indication of wanting to have the Saar coal and steel industry for themselves. Adenauer's bottom line was that he would agree to this, even though he knew that West German opinion would be strongly against it. He tried at first to propose (on 7 March 1950) to the French that they form a complete customs union with West Germany, establishing (significantly) a single parliament open also to Britain, Italy and the Benelux states. In return, Adenauer suggested, France might give up its interest in the Saar. Apart from de Gaulle, however, no French politician showed any enthusiasm for this idea. Adenauer pointed out that a customs union had led to German unity in the nineteenth century; it could do so again in respect of Europe. He also insisted that West Germany should be invited to join the Council of Europe and that associate membership should become full membership as quickly as possible. On 2 May 1951 West Germany became a full member.

The Schuman Plan

On 8 May 1950, Adenauer was told of the Schuman Plan (about which the High Commissioners still knew nothing). The details had been worked out by Jean Monnet. He argued that West Germany was already beginning to overtake France as an industrial power (it had asked to expand its steel output from 11 to 14 million tons; the French were only producing 9 million). Economic competition would, he suggested, lead to a conflict in interest between France and West Germany. The antidote, in his view, was to enable French and German industry to compete on an equal footing. Adenauer saw at once that despite being about economic matters, its aim was 'eminently political'. It corresponded to ideas he had held ever since Weimar times, and was, he thought, a step towards his dream of a federal Europe. Yet some of his ministers objected to the idea (Kaiser, in particular, argued that it would delay reunification). But both the Americans and the High Commissioners liked it, as did the Benelux states. Britain wished to be left out.

By March 1951 the draft treaty was ready. The Bundestag then debated it. True to form, Kurt Schumacher for the SPD, declared that it was a 'second capitulation, six years after the end of the war . . . the perpetuation of the occupation statute for fifty years' and added, for good measure, that the term 'European' should not be taken to apply to a relatively small area of north-west Europe, which was the home of capitalism, clericalism and cartels. In June 1950, the SPD voted against joining the Council of Europe.

Defence and Rearmament

Although the Allies did not object to the creation of a foreign affairs office, a West German interest in its own defence (which ultimately implied rearmament) was a far thornier problem. The fact was that the Potsdam Agreement had demilitarized Germany. Rearmament would naturally contravene it. Legally it also contravened the Petersberg Agreement. And a High Commission law of 16 December 1949 provided a penalty of life imprisonment for militarism. Public opinion in France and Britain was opposed to any talk of a new German armed force (and was delighted to see, at long last, a German state without an army). Many West Germans took the same view (not least because it allowed others to pay for their defence). And yet West German security was a burning issue. West Germany was a front-line state when it came to defence against Communism. Its defence was also the defence of the West. Was it right to expect others to defend it?

Adenauer displayed consummate skill in dealing with this fraught matter. He first needed to get the Western Powers to say publicly that they supported rearmament. He then had to come up with a format for this that was acceptable both to them and to the West Germans. Finally, he had to ensure that rearmament strengthened rather than weakened his own grand design of locking West Germany into the West. This last factor was not a foregone conclusion. Hitherto, armies had symbolized national interests and thus the distinctions between states. This reinvention of Germany, however, was required to produce an armed force that would symbolize West Germany's supra-national concerns. Churchill, for example, who supported West German rearmament, nevertheless dismissed the concept of a common European force as a 'sludgy amalgam', preferring instead 'a grand alliance of national armies'.

The Chancellor seems genuinely to have feared an attack from East Germany, but not necessarily one launched by the Red Army (some German historians doubt his sincerity, however). The plan, he believed, would be to take out West Germany in a matter of hours, and then encamp along the Pyrenees. Once there, it was thought, a nuclear attack on the Communists would become redundant since it would merely destroy West Europe. In 1948, the East German government had set up a peoples' police force (but one maintained in garrisons, and thus composed of soldiers to all intents and purposes) estimated at 700,000 men. West Germany, Adenauer reasoned, could quickly establish a similar 'police' force of 150,000. But, mindful of the public opinion of their own people, the High Commissioners vetoed the idea in January 1950. By July, however, they changed their minds and agreed to it, but only on two conditions. First, the force should be restricted to 10,000 men and, second, it should be organized on a *Land* basis, and not commanded by Bonn.

Meanwhile on 11 August at Strasbourg, Churchill spoke out in favour of a European army with a German contribution. On 7 August, Adenauer's military advisers Speidel, Heusinger and Foertsch produced a report on Germany's defence. It argued that Soviet aggression was likely to occur by 1952. Whilst they were prepared to consider a 'police' force, their conclusion was that a federal army, a *Bundeswehr*, should be set up as quickly as possible. The issue assumed a deeply critical importance on the outbreak of the Korean War in the summer of 1950; here another nation was divided between Communism and liberty, and the Communist part had attacked the free half.

On 29 August 1950 Adenauer produced a second memorandum on

the relationship between the Federal Republic and the occupying powers. It represented the refinement of this thinking and a blueprint for his policy for the next five years. In return for making a commitment to Western defence, Adenauer asked for the dissolution of the Occupation Statute. He now offered a German contingent to a European defence force (the point being that it would not be West German 'national' army, but merely the German part of a Western one). He repeated an earlier request that the High Commissioners should become ambassadors, and that West Germany should be permitted to have diplomatic relations with those nations that were most important to it. In addition, there should be a formal ending of the state of war with Germany, and the forces of occupation should become guarantors of West German security instead.

Rearmament now became the central, and highly emotive issue in domestic politics. The SPD opposed it (although Schumacher himself wavered). Even Carlo Schmid, who was seen as being on the right wing, declaimed that it was 'better to be bolshevized than crippled'. The SPD demanded fresh elections on the issue. The FDP was split on it, but the trade union movement under Böckler refused to come out on the SPD's side. The Catholic Church supported Adenauer but the Protestants were far less keen. The Americans did their bit to influence public opinion in favour of the move.

The Creation of a Defence Ministry

In order to realize his plans, Adenauer needed to set up a defence ministry (although it could not be called that). With the covert permission of the occupiers, he gave the secret order to do so in the winter of 1949. By May 1950 the office was ready (led by General von Schwerin), although this was not made public until September 1950; and even then, its real purpose was concealed. It was referred to simply as the 'central office for home service'. The Western Allies had dealings with Schwerin, but only through their secret intelligence services so that in public they could deny any knowledge of him. In October 1950 Blank was appointed putative defence minister (officially he was called 'adviser on questions relating to allied troops'; Schwerin was duly sacked). In 1950 Adenauer also set up a military intelligence unit under Joachim Oster. This office (whose acronym was MAD) was distinct from the security service (the BfV) and the secret intelligence service (the BND). The former was constructed with a British input (its first chief went to East Berlin in 1954, where he attacked Adenauer's defence policies); the second, run by Reinhard Gehlen, was the Americans' preserve.

The European Defence Community (EDC)

The idea of a common European defence force provided the strategy which might take German rearmament forward. It was given concrete form by Jean Monnet, who produced a plan which was put to the French Prime Minister, René Pleven (and which thus became known as the Pleven Plan). It was published on 24 October 1950. The French knew that sooner or later a West German army would come into being; at the same time, they were determined to ensure it should not be a threat to them. Monnet said that there should be a single European army, with its command, organization, equipment and finances under supra-national control. It was to be something more than a joint European army. The French (who assumed they would command the control authority) would thus not only avoid presiding over a reinvented German army, but have real authority over it (in the same way that the Schuman Plan gave them powers over the West German economy). On 27 September 1950, however, the US agreed to accept a 'police' force of 30,000, and two months later, on 18 and 19 December, NATO foreign ministers agreed in principle to construct German units under Allied control in Germany.

These muddles meant the West Germans now had three options to consider: a 'police' force, the EDC, or an associate (and thus subordinate role) inside NATO. Since Adenauer understood that any of these ideas would lock the West German state into the West, he knew they would also effectively block reunification (Stalin, unlike Gorbachev forty years later, would not allow German unity to occur as long as a West German armed force was part of the Western system of alliances). But far from hedging on the issue, he pushed it as hard as he could. He made it clear that unity on Stalin's terms (the only terms on offer) implied a neutral Germany. This, he insisted, was far worse than a divided Germany. Thus, faced with the choice between unity and the West, Adenauer opted for the latter, rather to the amazement of the West.

The Nationalist Attack

Inside the Federal Republic, his stance produced dangerous discord. Schumacher declared the EDC was simply a device to get German soldiers to fight for countries other than Germany. The SPD, he said, opposed rearmament because it made unity impossible to achieve, and he suggested that Adenauer was eschewing national unity in order to create his dream of a Western German state. He was, of course, quite right. But, as so often with Schumacher, being right in an absolute sense could mean he was wrong in a political sense. Schumacher's attack was quickly appropriated by the Conservative Right. Adenauer was accused of selling out on unity. On 5 May 1951 in the Lower Saxony elections a neo-Nazi party, the Socialist Reich Party, led by Otto Remer (who had helped put down the 1944 plotters in Berlin) managed to gain 11 per cent of the vote. A further 27 per cent was won by various other extreme parties; and a few months later the SRP did almost as well in Bremen. These were places with sizeable refugee populations who feared that, without unity, they would never return home. The result showed that the new Republic was genuinely in danger from those who opposed Adenauer's reinvention of Germany.

The success of the SRP raised the spectre of a return to Weimar's extremism and, interestingly, the federal government decided to use Weimar policies to deal with it – namely to seek to dissolve parties that threatened the democratic order of the state. Thus on 19 November 1951 the federal government applied to the constitutional court for an order banning the SRP; and on 23 October 1952 the ban was allowed, and the party was dissolved. A similar, though no less justified measure was taken against the KPD at the same time (attempting to be even-handed by dealing with both Left and Right was another Weimar practice) but the KPD was not banned until 17 August 1956, owing to legal complexities.

Another serious right-wing political threat presented itself in 1952 when some of the leaders of the FDP, in an attempt to increase its support, decided to make a bid for the extremist vote. They published a 'German manifesto' calling for, amongst other things, an end to 'discrimination' against ex-Nazis, and a more independent foreign policy. This group then decided to negotiate with Dr Werner Naumann, a neo-Nazi who had been an aide to Josef Goebbels. The British regarded all of this as a dangerous conspiracy; and because the Western Allies still retained certain security rights decided to act against Naumann. On 14 January 1953 the British High Commissioner Ivone Kirkpatrick ordered the arrest of Naumann and seven others, and seized his files. Adenauer had, of course, been informed of the British intention.

On 18 April 1951 the treaty for the establishment of the European coal and steel community was signed. Adenauer called it the foundation stone for European union, and predicted that other countries would wish to join it one day. Schumacher, on the other hand, said it was an extension of the Occupation Statute for another fifty years. Soon after this, on 30 July 1951, the Americans announced that they now sanctioned the European army idea; they wanted Germany to join NATO at the same time (although the French vetoed this notion at once). Yet the Western Allies wished to retain the right to station troops in West Germany and ensure their safety, to negotiate on German unity, and to sign a peace treaty, on Berlin and on territorial issues. At their meeting in Washington from 10 to 14 September 1951 the Western foreign ministers reiterated their support for the EDC and offered in return to end the Occupation Statute (the German treaty was in fact signed on 26/27 May 1952 in Bonn, to take effect when the EDC gained ratification).

It is sometimes argued that the idea of an EDC was utterly impractical and that mixed divisions were unworkable. Certainly, the French were not ready for the idea; and it was also true that military cooperation signified something quite different from economic cooperation. Yet NATO worked very well and Franco-German co-operation in subsequent years did produce joint Franco-German units with the symbolic value that Adenauer needed so badly.

The Treaties with the West

On 15 September 1951, the GDR Peoples' Chamber called for free all-German elections to form a united and 'peace loving' Germany. This made Adenauer even more determined than before to move quickly to make West Germany sovereign and rearm it; and thus get the Occupation Statute dissolved. The issues involved were extraordinarily complex, not least because occupation had impinged on almost every aspect of West German life. Five areas of negotiation (to produce five agreements or conventions) were identified: a general one, defining the aims of the Western Allies, their rights in Berlin and in dealings with the Soviet Union over Germany. A second one dealt with the rights and duties of the Western armies; the third with unresolved war issues; the fourth with economic and financial contributions to the costs of Western defence forces (a constant source of irritation between the West Germans and the Allies); and the fifth with arbitration on foreign interests in Germany. By the time the talks had been completed, over a hundred alterations had been made to the drafts. Negotiations went on until 17 May 1952.

The Allies were at first not prepared to give way to Adenauer. They rejected full sovereignty, now said 'no' to membership of NATO and 'no' to the removal of restrictions on armaments. This line could be attributed to the strength of their domestic public opinion, and to their knowledge that they had Adenauer over a barrel (since in the end he was bound to go along with them). When he seemed too ready to renounce unity in the short term, they doubted whether the West Germans would support him. When he declared that the lands east of the Oder and Neisse belonged to Germany (and thus saw a united Germany as having the borders of 1937), they feared their own people would not support him. Yet they knew that what Adenauer offered was the very thing they most needed: a West Germany whose aims which ran parallel to those of the West.

At this point, the French decided to compound West German misery. In January 1952 their High Commissioner in the Saar was redesignated 'ambassador', and a Saar diplomatic mission in Paris was opened. In effect, they were claiming independence for the Saar. All Adenauer had to set against these developments was an invitation to a Western foreign ministers' meeting (on 22 November 1951), where he was still not treated as an equal. The next month, he was treated to an official visit to London (where he met the King and visited Oxford) and the Prime Minister. He told Churchill that the Western treaties must precede any attempt at reunification (adding he could not say this in public). Churchill promised that they would never do a deal with the Soviet Union behind Adenauer's back (a promise Churchill thought of breaking: see below pp. 111–3).

Yet Adenauer won through. A treaty ending occupation was signed in Bonn on 17 May 1952. The EDC treaty could finally be signed in Paris on 27 May 1952. But both treaties required ratification by the respective parliaments, and could come into force only thereafter. It was well understood that the French Assembly might not buy the deal, not least when the original idea – that there would be one European defence minister (whom the French assumed would be French) – had been abandoned in favour of a council of nine, a step sure to alienate the French even further.

The Unity Issue

The extent to which the Soviets were unsettled by the progress that Adenauer was now beginning to make can be measured by their sudden interest promoting German unity. There can be little doubt that Stalin and his advisers now believed that the only way in which West Germany could be prevented from locking itself into an anti-Soviet alliance was by robbing Adenauer of popular and parliamentary support with a realistic offer of German unity. Although it must be assumed that in their own terms the Russians' offer was sincere (since they had so much to lose from Adenauer's success), it was precisely because they wished to prevent the integration of West Germany into the West that the offer was made. This means that it was no more than an attempt to secure for themselves a neutral German nation.

On 3 November 1950, Grotewohl had sent a letter to Heuss offering a return to the Potsdam process and a four-power summit on German unity. He also agreed to create a provisional all-German government and hold a plebiscite on its policies. In February 1951, Adenauer told the cabinet it was vital to reassure the Americans that Germany would never wobble between East and West and reject the notion.

The Stalin Notes

Matters became even more complicated following the receipt by the Western Allies of the celebrated Stalin note of 10 March 1952 offering unity via a four-power conference. A reunified Germany would be allowed its own armed forces, he promised; but it must be neutral. Publicly, Adenauer's government stated that the purpose of the note was simply to prevent West Germany's integration into the West and to create a vacuum in Germany into which Russia could move. On 9 April 1952 a second note arrived. This made life still harder for Adenauer. Moscow now accepted the need for free all-German elections *before* an all-German government was established, and said all other details could be solved by a four-power conference. The High Commissioners now decided to put pressure on Adenauer to adopt a more positive line, not least because there was similarity between the line on unity taken by the SPD and the contents of the second note, and they feared the West Germans might vote accordingly. Adenauer reluctantly agreed to declare that the matter should be taken further, to see whether reunification could be achieved.

The 1953 Election

Against this backdrop, Adenauer had to fight his second federal election campaign. The progress he had made so far undoubtedly boosted Adenauer's electoral appeal but his first government was not particularly popular. In the spring of 1950 only 28 per cent of voters supported it. 46 per cent were undecided. 24 per cent favoured rearmament, but 36 per cent opposed it. Although it was (and is) not easy to make predictions about federal politics using *Land* election results as a base, the October 1950 elections in Hesse and Württemberg-Baden produced heavy losses for the CDU. Yet the SPD did not profit from the CDU's decline, the chief beneficiary being the FDP.

Adenauer's government faced other problems. It had to contend with short-term difficulties in the supply of wheat and sugar and, most importantly, with high unemployment, which had reached the 2 million mark in the spring of 1950 and then again in the winter of 1951–2. Adenauer held Erhard personally responsible for this. Erhard was saved only by the economic boom resulting from the Korean War. Investment in industry rose dramatically, the Deutschmark picked up value, and inflation and then unemployment fell. The innate strength of the German economy was beginning to reveal itself yet again. Although this seemed a miracle, it was not really one. The Germans were simply doing what they had been doing well for a hundred years.

Adenauer was himself helped greatly by the so-called 'Wirtschaftswunder' in 1953 and by the prospect of being able to demonstrate to the West Germans that at long last they had gained the status of virtually equal partners of the West, for on 19 March 1953 the Bundestag ratified the two Western treaties, although of four FDP ministers in the government, only one (Blücher) voted for it, an indication of future trouble. In April 1953, with a view to the forthcoming elections, Adenauer travelled to the United States, where he received a very warm reception from the new American president, Eisenhower, and the new secretary of state, John Foster Dulles. He appeared to the West German public both to be a trusted friend of the Americans and to be accepted as a world-class statesman; this was indeed the purpose of the American visit.

Two other interconnected events helped secure Adenauer's reputation as Chancellor. The first was Stalin's death on 5 March 1953. As far as the general public was concerned, this appeared to have put an end to the Soviet initiative on German unity (although away out of the public eye the issue gained a new momentum). It also introduced an element of uncertainty into international affairs that must have militated in Adenauer's favour. Secondly, the East German uprising, which broke out on 17 June 1953, showed that the East German Communist government was disliked by at least some of the very workers it claimed to represent.

Neither the Western Allies nor indeed the West German government believed that there was anything that could be done to assist the rioters, given the presence of some 400,000 Soviet troops in East Germany. The British Prime Minister, Winston Churchill, was at first inclined to be very hostile to the rioters, fearing that they might provoke the new Soviet leadership into a harder line than they might otherwise have wanted to take. This could only help concentrate the West German mind on the many advantages that accrued from their membership of the Western democracies.

Churchill and German Unity

It had been Winston Churchill who had argued that Stalin's death might help rather than hinder the cause of German unity. In a letter to Eisenhower on 12 April 1953 he wrote 'A new hope has been created in the unhappy, bewildered world.' Speaking in Parliament on 11 May

1953 he stated that the 'formidable problem of Germany now presented itself in an entirely different aspect'. Whilst supporting Adenauer generously ('the wisest German statesman since Bismarck') Churchill added 'We have been encouraged by a series of amicable gestures on the part of the new Soviet government.' He then drew up a secret memorandum on the subject that said that, in terms of security against any future German aggression, a West Germany of 55 million inhabitants was no less dangerous than a united Germany of 70 millions. He predicted that the EDC would fail and that with Adenauer or without 'nothing will turn the German people from unity . . .' 'However the election goes, all parties will be ardent for unity. We must face the fact that there will always be a "German problem" and a "Prussian danger".'

He continued: 'But I am of the opinion that a united Germany would not become the ally of the Soviet Union'; his reasons being that the Germans liked liberty, that the GDR was a 'potent object lesson' on the evils of Communism and that Hitler's anti-Bolshevism still influenced German public opinion. Thus, he concluded, any Soviet offer of unity by means of a four-power conference should certainly be taken up.

Adenauer was deeply unsettled by all of this. He knew that he was supported by the British Foreign Office (who thought Churchill was reckless). Frank Roberts reflected correctly that 'the policy of doing everything possible to help Adenauer win the elections is entirely inconsistent with any changeover to a policy of neutralisation as a result, say, of a four-power meeting in the autumn'. He said that the first condition the Soviets would set would be the removal of Adenauer.

As things turned out, Adenauer was quickly able to abandon his fears partly because of the East German uprising, which was put down by Soviet tanks and thus destroyed their political credibility with some emphasis, and partly because Churchill suffered a stroke on 23 June 1953 that rendered him *hors de combat*. Yet the revolt also showed Churchill was justified in not believing that the East Germans, if left to their own devices, would turn to Communism. Furthermore, the window of opportunity presented by Stalin's death (and closed shortly afterwards) showed that in 1953, Churchill sought German unity, and Adenauer rejected it. In so doing, an opportunity for German reunification was clearly missed. On the other hand, this allowed Adenauer to proceed with his Western reinvention of a German state to the benefit of all concerned. The Americans – Eisenhower and Dulles – were far less inclined to do any deals with the Soviets at Adenauer's expense. They shared his hatred of Bolshevism and they knew full well, not least because of the then current success of McCarthyism, that American public opinion would not tolerate any softness towards the Russians.

Like Adenauer, they knew that a Germany unified on Stalin's terms might not go Communist, but would no longer go Western either.

Electoral Success

Adenauer may also have been helped by the change in the leadership of the SPD. Schumacher had died on 20 August 1952 and was replaced by Erich Ollenhauer, an intelligent and decent politician, but outclassed by his more prominent and experienced opponent. His policies were essentially the same as his predecessor's, although his manner was far less antagonistic.

Thus the Bundestag elections of 1953 proved an outstanding success for Adenauer and his party. The CDU/CSU gained 45.2 per cent, almost 15 per cent more than in 1949. The SPD won 28.8 per cent, a little less than in 1949. Its seats in the Bundestag increased, however, on account of the decline in support for smaller parties, in particular the Communists, who lost all their seats. The FDP lost some support, as did the final members of the ruling coalition, the DP. A refugee party, the BHE, formed after the 1949 election, gained 23 per cent of the vote and 27 seats. It and the DP joined the FDP and CDU/CSU in Adenauer's second coalition.

The Failure of the EDC Plan and West Germany's Entry into NATO

The 1953 election set the seal on Adenauer's policy of Westernization. He had achieved virtual majority support for his reinvention of Germany. He had risked a huge amount of political and economic capital, and the risk had paid off. It was now time to finish the job. With his prestige considerably increased, Adenauer first attempted to defuse the Saar issue. He and Strauss had talks with Pierre Mendès-France, the new French prime minister. But the French insisted that the West German wish to enter the Western European Union should be made conditional on the 'Europeanization' of the Saar. Adenauer felt forced to agree to this in October 1954 (and France signed the WEU Treaty on 23 October). Saar public opinion was totally opposed to this move (a referendum on 22 October 1955 produced a 68 per cent vote for the rejection of it).

Then, on 30 August 1954, the French Assembly threw out the EDC treaty, a hundred Communist deputies leading the attack upon it. Their campaign had been assisted by the bizarre apparent defection of Otto John, West Germany's security service chief, to East Berlin on 20 July 1954. Once there John declared that Adenauer was a revanchist.

Adenauer, of course, was mortified. The SPD was delighted at the French vote. Ollenhauer said that the failure of the treaty allowed West Germany to pursue a 'real' European policy, and underwrite the four-power solution to German unity (in fact, the January-February 1954 four-power meeting on Germany in Berlin had produced no tangible results).

A month later, the six EDC states joined with the US, Britain and Canada to produce an alternative at the Lancaster House Conference. The German Treaty was retained, but in place of the EDC treaty the conference produced protocols admitting West Germany to NATO and the Brussels Treaty. The British played a key part in the success of this enterprise. Foreign Secretary Anthony Eden toured the various European capitals in order to get agreement, and Britain gave NATO a guarantee that it would keep four Rhine Army divisions, and the second tactical air force in Germany, for as long as the WEU powers wished this. The SPD, however, continued to oppose the policy. On 5 October 1954 Ollenhauer declared that the energy that had been devoted to rearmament should have been devoted to unity.

On 22 October 1954 in Paris, the Federal Republic was invited to become a member of NATO, on condition only that it undertook not to produce atomic, biological or chemical weapons. At the same time, the Occupation Statute was abolished and the High Commission wound up. West Germany became a sovereign state in almost every regard, the chief exception being its acceptance of the rights of Western Allied forces in West Germany and Berlin and their right to determine the circumstances of German unity.

The treaty (which was finally signed in May 1955) has always been known in Britain as the Relations Convention and in Germany as the *Deutschlandvertrag*. Meanwhile, on 14 May 1955, East Germany was admitted to the Warsaw Pact. In some senses, these events appeared to settle the political division of Germany for all time. The irony of German political development was that without West German integration into the West, unification in 1990, under conditions of peace and genuine liberty, would not have taken place.

Adenauer's Model Germany: 1955–63

The West German Nation

The house called West Germany had been built. It could now be lived in. The years 1955–63 saw the establishment of the essence of West Germany. Internally, the bourgeois values of affluence and respectability became dominant. All West Germans could share in them, provided, of course, that they were prepared to work hard. A strong Deutschmark made this possible: it was worth something, and thus worth working for. West Germany did not become rich overnight; but by 1960 its wealth was tangible. Its political class quickly acquired the values of Rhenish capitalism; owning cars, objects and living well replaced the less savoury norms of earlier German states. Even if they did not always agree with it, opinion formers regularly read *Der Spiegel*, which had been founded by Rudolf Augstein in 1947, and could tell a good story, especially about Bonn political life or contemporary German history. Those believing they needed further education subscribed to *Die Zeit* whose lead writers, Marion Gräfin Dönhoff and Theo Sommer, defined much of what journalists, at any rate, regarded as the German political agenda.

The economy was beginning to deliver. West German consumerism began to take off. Ordinary people began to entertain. They started eating serious amounts of food (this was the so-called 'Fresswelle' which yielded, in due course, to the so-called 'Edelfresswelle' or 'delicatessen-eating' wave, still very much in evidence today). West Germans began to go on holiday in pleasant and reliable, if modest cars. The arts (often critical of the very bourgeois milieu which supported them) started to blossom. Even if this was often the ideal, often the image and not the reality, even if there was poverty and deprivation, the ideal, reinforced by the cinema, television and the media, began to shape reality. To be a West German began to mean something concrete, almost enviable.

There was, however, a desperate, even unnerving, side to the apparently solid life lived by the good burghers of the Federal Republic.

Consensus and consensuality (wanting others to join the consensus) became the values of the day. Unpleasantness was shied away from (particularly in respect of the Nazi legacy, which most West Germans still sought earnestly to forget). The voters disliked serious differences of political opinion (the SPD continued to be punished heavily for its oppositional stance). Politically, the fatherland was rapidly becoming a grandfatherland, led by one. In many ways, this was exactly what both West Germany and its Western neighbours wanted: a reliable, prosperous Western part-Germany, fat and impotent.

This German state in the West was not, of course, a normal nation. But this could not have mattered less. Indeed, the only real indications that West Germany's bourgeois tranquillity was capable of being disturbed emanated from policies pursued by others towards West Germany. However pleasant the Federal Republic was becoming, the hard reality was that it existed, as part of a divided nation, right in the centre of a continent, indeed a world, split between capitalism and Communism. Even if the ordinary West Germans hoped that their life would become increasingly apolitical, external forces still conspired to make this impossible.

Adenauer's model Germany was thus still very much the plaything of the Cold War. It lived in the shadow of the superpowers and their atomic arsenals, and it was still not master of its own fate. Although it was accepted as a fully functioning member of the Western Alliance, it was not considered an equal partner, not by the USA, of course, but not by Britain either and not even, as we shall see, by France, now becoming its closest ally. The Bonn Republic had come very far in its first decade; but it remained different from other states. This was, of course, something that its Allies found proper (since it strongly corresponded to their own national interests). Yet although Adenauer appeared, for the foreseeable future, to have answered both the German problem (which was political), and the problem of Germany (which was geographical), the very idea of a Western pseudo-nation contained the possibility that Adenauer's reinvention might never constitute a final settlement. For West Germans, however, this issue became increasingly remote. They talked about it – but they did not imagine it could happen in a way acceptable to them. The irony was that German unification had become something Germany's victors were far more troubled with than the West German Chancellor. Yet having formed the view that they understood better than the Germans what was good for Germany, the victors ensured that the issue of unity remained alive and the problem persisted. It was easy to argue, as Churchill had done, that the German people would always be 'ardent for unity'. They could, after all, hardly deny this. But, left to their own devices, the matter would have been forgotten by the West Germans. Adenauer had earned his salary several times over and his people were content with his work.

Adenauer's German state had ceased to be restless, at any rate within Central Europe. If it was on the move, it was only to bring about even greater Western integration, most vitally with France. The East, however, was to be in large part (but not wholly) closed to West Germany. These years were none the less turbulent. Adenauer had to confront issues concerned with West German defence, with nuclear weapons, with the Cold War, with Berlin and German unity. The big political questions of this final period of Adenauer's rule, then, were, significantly, not merely all foreign policy issues, but ones injected into West German life as a result of Germany's division. We look at them here as they were seen by the West Germans, it should be added, not as the objects of the diplomacy of the Great Powers.

The Prestige of the Federal Republic

Adenauer reached the zenith of his career in 1957 when the CDU/CSU won an absolute majority. Thereafter, particularly after 1961, his authority waned, and both his political sense and tactical judgement became flawed. His vision, however, even if increasingly out of tune with the times, remained consistent and in its core both right for West Germany and right for its Western partners.

The years up to 1960 were marked by the growth of harmonious relations between the Federal Republic and two nations in particular, France and the United States. As the years went by, the American relationship was retained, and added to. But it was the relationship with France that was to generate most change for Germany and, for a time, seemed likely to catapult the Bonn Republic into a new, post-national era by opening up the possibility of a real merging of the national interests of both countries. This slipped away with Adenauer's loss of power. But so strong was its base that, thirty years on, it remains the core relationship even for a united Germany within Europe.

During this time, West Germany became more independent and also more powerful. The West German government, and in particular its Chancellor, continued to be moved by a strong and not unjustified fear of the Soviet Union. This waned only in 1962 after the peaceful end to the Cuban missile crisis. In 1953 the USSR had exploded its first hydrogen bomb; in October 1957 it launched the world's first man-made satellite, and with it raised the spectre of nuclear weapons being launched from space. This had a deep impact on Western notions of security.

Adenauer left office in 1963, but his legacy endured. 1966 saw the first major political transition in West German politics (although what had been reinvented was fundamentally unaltered by it) leading to significant changes in foreign policy and in domestic affairs. As far as the former was concerned, after the Cuban Crisis in 1962 the Cold War began to diminish in harshness and *détente* began to be actively pursued. It has been suggested that the waning of the Cold War had deep structural effects on West Germany, and especially on its foreign policy because the Bonn Republic had been born from it. There was plainly great truth in this view. Foreign policy changes were made to deal with this. But West Germany continued to be of the West.

Détente implied that the West (and the United States in particular) no longer needed West Germany in the same way as in the past, and was prepared, in the interests of a deal with the Soviet Union, to risk alienating the Federal Republic. Certainly West Germany's political strength began to slip away after 1962, both a function of declining US interest in its policies, and Adenauer's faltering hold on power.

Following Adenauer's success in the 1953 elections, Adenauer introduced new faces into his government. They included Heinrich Lübke, Gerhard Schröder, Franz Josef Strauss and two former Nazis, Waldemar Kraft and Theodor Oberländer, whom even Adenauer called 'brown, dark brown' (brown being the Nazi colour). Yet Adenauer could not as yet bring himself to appoint Heinrich von Brentano (another ex-Nazi) foreign minister, despite his protégé's keenness to take on the post for which he had primed himself. He was to have to wait for a further two years. When this occurred, Kurt Georg Kiesinger became CDU/CSU parliamentary party leader in his place and Theodor Blank was made defence minister (on 8 July 1955).

The German Question Revisited

Stalin's death in 1953, as we have seen, seemed to generate a new sense of initiative on the part of his successors. This may have been the result of their wish to make an impressive profile for themselves on the world stage or the outcome of a genuine desire to improve East-West relations. On 26 March 1955 Soviet Prime Minister Bulganin announced his readiness to have a summit meeting, and on 7 June the USSR invited West Germany to take up diplomatic relations with it.

Eisenhower's apparent interest in doing a deal with the Russians on Germany caused Adenauer almost as much anxiety as had Stalin's note of March 1952. He viewed with ill-concealed disgust the deliberations at Geneva (held from July to October 1955), and attempted to prevent the West from reaching anything they might believe was a satisfactory basis for further discussion. The Soviet position was relatively straight-forward: German unity could be restored if West Germany left NATO.

Yet even here the West had their doubts about the Soviets' good faith, for they could not see how the Russians would be able to ensure that a neutral Germany did not move towards the West unless it were controlled by Communists. Nevertheless, the Soviets accepted that the settlement of the German question was a matter for four-power agreement.

In the middle of the Geneva process, from 9 to 13 September, Adenauer visited Moscow. He took with him representatives of the Bundesrat and also Carlo Schmid for the SPD. As soon as he arrived, he struck a firm note, stating that this was the first time that a representative of the German people had come to negotiate with the Soviets. This was a clear reference to the Federal Republic's claim to the right of sole representation; which the Soviets, having dealt with the GDR for six years, could only regard as provocative. Later he told Khrushchev that although the Germans had attacked Russia and done terrible things there, Russian troops had done terrible things in Germany. The important thing, he said, was to begin again.

It was made clear to the Soviets that the Federal Republic could not have diplomatic relations with them unless those Germans still in Soviet captivity (of whom there were over 9,000) were released. Most of these had been sentenced to 25 years' hard labour. The Russians readily agreed, however, and diplomatic relations ensued, preceded by a peculiar 'letter on German unity' that said that diplomatic relations did not imply acceptance of the existing borders, which were to be determined by a peace treaty. It added that there had been no change in West Germany's view on the issue of the sole representation of all Germans. The idea of a letter on German unity was subsequently taken up by Willy Brandt (see below pXX). For his part, Khrushchev had made it clear that the GDR could not be 'handed back to capitalism'.

The Geneva summit set in motion a further foreign ministers' meeting that lasted from October to November 1955 to take up the themes of the summit. Although there was a general acceptance of the necessity of free elections as part of the package leading to unity, there soon emerged a fundamental disagreement between the Soviets and the West about whether there should be cooperation between the GDR and West Germany as a preliminary step towards unity (which the Soviets wanted and the West did not). The talks thus ended in stalemate.

Domestic Politics

Meanwhile, Adenauer (who had become 80 on 5 January 1956) was beginning to become suspicious about his chief coalition partners, the FDP. He discerned a growing split within it between those who were content to follow his lead and those who took issue with his evident lack of interest in German unity, with his personal style of government and with the very principles of Christian Democracy. There were Liberals who argued that liberalism was a distinctive and secular political force, able to coalesce as easily with a sound SPD as with the CDU. The Chancellor toyed repeatedly with ideas on how the FDP might be brought to heel, even considering asking it to leave his cabinet. He was particularly irked by Thomas Dehler, the chairman of the FDP. The FDP was also proving unpredictable in North Rhine-Westphalia. Here, in February 1956, 'young Turks' in the FDP including Walter Scheel, Walter Döring and Erich Mende (all of whom were to become major figures) had plotted with the SPD to bring down the CDU-led government. This was the first stirring of a movement which in 1969 was to bring the SPD into government with the FDP. Adenauer had tried to bring it to heel (threatening a first-past-the-post-electoral system to squeeze it out of politics altogether); but the FDP decided in February 1956 to leave the government.

As a consequence, Adenauer was obliged to produce a new cabinet in October 1956. He sacked Blank as defence minister; replacing him with Strauss. Blank had been badly embarrassed by the fact that the NATO annual review of 30 October 1956 revealed that the *Bundeswehr* was under strength. Strauss enabled West Germany to become an effective military power. To this end, the constitution was amended for a second time and a start was made to the policy of arming the *Bundeswehr* and *Luftwaffe* with nuclear weapons (under US control).

Nuclear Weapons, the Bundeswehr *and the* Luftwaffe

The nuclear issue provoked antagonism both at home and abroad. It complicated East-West relations and aroused Soviet anger. Indeed, in 1957 the Russians accused Adenauer of having turned West Germany into a NATO atomic base, and thus a legitimate target for their nuclear missiles. West German public opinion would be unsettled by it. Finally, since the nuclear weaponry was the property of the United States, the American role in German affairs seemed set to increase. A debate was initiated which was to last for the next thirty years or so. It would involve both moral and political questions, and questions about strategy and about the proper proportions of conventional forces to nuclear weapons of mass destruction.

Adenauer's and Strauss's position was clear: nuclear weapons were deemed as much of a necessity in order to deter the Soviet Union from an attack in the West, as was a strong conventionally armed force (to prevent the Communists from attempting to make small gains, not worth a nuclear riposte). In addition, they were determined that the

Americans should guarantee that a major Communist attack would always be answered by a full-scale nuclear counter-attack. Until 1960, however, the SPD opposed both nuclear weapons and any increase in the size of West Germany's conventional forces. The Protestant Church took the same line; the Roman Catholic hierarchy, on the other hand, was content to underwrite Adenauer's stance.

Whilst NATO's basic policy was one of massive retaliation in the event of a Soviet attack, it argued the need for conventional forces in order that not every problem should end in a nuclear conflagration. This might allow a decrease in conventional forces. In addition, however, the Americans were anxious to cut the costs of their nuclear arsenal and make the West Germans pay more for their own defence. These thoughts lay behind the plan put forward by Admiral W. Radford, chairman of the US joint chiefs of staff in 1956. Adenauer, a politician and not a strategic expert, believed such a plan would reduce the level of US commitment to West German defence. In fact, NATO planners sought to avoid such a radical move by trying to differentiate between different types of attack, not all of which would require nuclear treatment. This policy was enshrined in NATO document MC-14/1 which naturally, and heavily, affected West Germany.

Franz Josef Strauss

Franz Josef Strauss (1926–88) was one of the most influential figures in the Bonn Republic. Few were hated or supported with as much passion. He was a larger-than-life character, always a democrat but, given the German desire for moderation and consensus, often seen as a para-Fascist on account of his original (and sometimes dangerous) ideas. He became the most important Centre Right figure apart from Adenauer himself, with genuine appeal to many German voters, even if they were – like West Germany's Western partners – often rather afraid of him. He was to prove too unpredictable to lead the Federal Republic (although he was a candidate for the Chancellorship in 1980). Yet he had three qualities, almost to excess: imagination, energy and an ability to combine a strong *Land* identity (based on a huge personal regional support) with a feeling for Germany as a whole.

Strauss had been born in Munich, the son of a butcher. Despite doing well at school, he was at first refused a place at Munich University (possibly because he was not in the Hitler Youth, the SA or the SS) but subsequently received one. He then joined the National Socialist drivers' corps, but was never a Nazi party member. During the war, he became an officer and fought in Russia where he for some months acted as a political propagandist (a fact sometimes used against him). On 28

April 1945 he was taken prisoner by the Americans. In November 1945 he became deputy *Landrat* in Schongau (an indication of the extent to which he was considered acceptable by the American occupation forces) and a founding member of the CSU. Josef Müller, the CSU leader, spotted him, and made him a member of the CSU's executive committee. From here, Strauss was sent in February 1948 to the Economic Council in Frankfurt, entering the Bundestag in 1949.

Strauss said he had accepted the defence portfolio only on condition that after five years, the army would consist of 350,000 men (on 1 April 1957 only 10,000 had been conscripted). He now pointed out that West Germany had promised to produce a 500,000-man army by 1958, set out in twelve divisions. But there was still a shortage of barracks, no uniforms, no weapons and no administration. The shortfall in numbers was to prove a major headache for Strauss and NATO more generally. Some sixty Warsaw Pact divisions faced only fifteen NATO ones. One immediate remedy was to permit the federal border guard to join the *Bundeswehr* and 10,000 did so. He revised the plan for fixing the strength of the *Bundeswehr*. On 7 July 1956 the law bringing in conscription was passed by the Bundestag. The *Bundeswehr* was to have 67,000 men by the end of 1956, and 120,000 in 1957, 172,000 in 1958, and reach 230,000 in 1959. Both Adenauer and Strauss agreed that the period of conscription should be one year (in December 1961 it was increased to eighteen months). They also decided that the *Bundeswehr* should make a bid for nuclear weapons, although the precise details of this were not only to be worked out later but provided many a headache for both Americans and West Germans. The Americans were initially opposed to the idea of giving West Germany nuclear weapons and at the December 1956 NATO Council they said they would never agree to do so.

At the end of 1957 the French defence minister at the time, Jacques Chaban-Delmas, asked Strauss whether the Federal Republic would join with France and Italy in producing nuclear weapons (the costs were to be split 40:40:10). Strauss was enthusiastic, and Adenauer gave his permission (although in the event of any trouble he said he would deny all knowledge of the project). A draft treaty was worked out in January 1958; but de Gaulle vetoed this idea on becoming French leader. He wanted time to think about it.

The Americans then finally agreed that the nuclear warheads which were to be supplied to the *Bundeswehr* and *Luftwaffe* were to remain under US control, although the missiles that carried them were to be West German, thus giving the Americans the say on whether they were to be fired. This was set out in a further NATO document MC-70. The nuclear issue was discussed in the Bundestag on 10 May 1957, and on many subsequent occasions. The SPD did not want the West German forces to have nuclear weapons and, indeed, wanted none on West German territory. Strauss declared that the Federal Republic had never sought to equip the *Bundeswehr* or *Luftwaffe* with nuclear weapons (which was not strictly true) nor had they been offered them or given them (which *was* strictly true since the Americans retained control of them).

There was much opposition to these policies (including a protest from seven nuclear scientists from Göttingen University). In January 1958 the SPD staged another attack on the CDU, led by Helmut Schmidt who fiercely attacked those who had sought to give both German states nuclear weapons. It was not until the Hanover conference of November 1960 that Brandt, Erler and Schmidt finally offered their full support to NATO and thus, by implication, accepted nuclear weapons on German soil.

The creation of a West German defence force was not the only priority. Adenauer was keen to go into the 1957 elections with an impressive record on social policy as well. To this end, on 22 January 1957, a reform of pensions became law. However strong his personal love of foreign policy, Adenauer was aware that pensions were as important, and possibly a more important issue at election time than foreign or defence policy. His government's plan was designed to let pensions rise with incomes, determining the level of pensions by the incomes of those in work. Schäffer, still finance minister, and Ludwig Erhard, the economics minister, saw difficulties with the proposals. But Adenauer insisted on having a measure which allowed the CDU/CSU to enter the 1957 elections as a party that was socially progressive.

Partly to prepare for the elections of May 1957 Adenauer paid the customary visit to the US. Here he managed to get the agreement of the Americans not to pursue the idea of talks on disarmament, at any rate until after the West German elections. These were fought under the slogan of 'safety first – no experiments'. The CDU/CSU did outstandingly well, gaining 50.2 per cent of the votes; the FDP under Reinhold Maier sank to 7.7 per cent, the SPD got 31.8 per cent.

The EEC

Given Adenauer's early keenness on economic and political union with France, his support for the concept of a European economic community could never be in doubt. Hence he decided to go to Rome himself for the signing of the EEC treaties on 25 March 1957. Yet Ludwig Erhard and his adviser, state secretary Alfred Müller-Armack, were extremely anxious about the development, wanting instead a world-wide free trade area. For Adenauer, however, the political implications of a closer community were paramount: on 14 November 1955 he told the Belgian foreign minister Spaak that the European idea offered Germans a way of protecting them from themselves and preventing nationalism. Adenauer was delighted when in December 1957 Hallstein was made President of the Commission, a major step forward for West German prestige. Integration itself was to take twelve years, from 1 January 1958 until the end of 1967. By 1969 a true common market existed amongst the Six.

Each member of the Community was initially to be obliged to trade freely with the other five whilst maintaining its own external tariff. The next stage, a real customs union, would see the removal of tariffs and quotas and a common levy on goods entering the union. The final stage was a common market, with free movement of goods, labour, capital and enterprise, to be gilded by a common monetary and fiscal policy controlled by a central authority. Yet the new institutions – the Commission, the Council of Ministers, the European Parliament and the European Court of Justice proved durable almost at once, and capable of sustaining repeated knocks over the next thirty years, chiefly from the French and the British.

Adenauer himself believed that, as an economic organization, the EEC was of limited use. Further political integration was, he argued, vital: 'We Europeans must make foreign policy jointly to cope with the threat of Communism; but even if it were to disappear as one day it will, advances in technology and [other areas] mean that Europe must unite because no single state can any longer act independently either in economics or politics.' He added, with great significance, that this would not to undermine the idea of the nation: 'That which is national remains; it is simply no longer the most important or the highest thing.'

De Gaulle

De Gaulle's rise to power in France carried with it interesting associations for Adenauer dating back to 1945. At first, Adenauer feared the new French leader would seek an agreement with the Soviets, pull out of NATO, and disrupt European integration. Adenauer asked at once to be received by de Gaulle and was invited to his home at Colombey-les-deux-Églises on 14 September. Adenauer found him reassuring: he was pleased that Franco-German enmity had been overcome for all time and wanted close cooperation in the future as the basis for rebuilding the European Community.

Foreign policy concerns thus once again began to dominate Adenauer's thinking. The West German insistence on the sole representation of Germans by the Federal Republic, enshrined in what was called the Hallstein Doctrine, had been challenged first by the decision to take up diplomatic relations with the USSR, and then by Yugoslavia, which had decided in October 1957 to recognize the GDR. Accordingly, even though dissenting voices could be heard, the Federal Republic broke off its relations with Belgrade. Whilst Adenauer was determined to adhere to the principle of sole representation (and apart from Yugoslavia only Cuba chose to exchange relations with the GDR for those with Bonn), the doctrine made it effectively impossible to have relations with eastern European states.

Nuclear Weapons and the SPD

In April 1957, the Soviets had raised again the issues discussed but not resolved at Geneva. They had pressed for the international recognition of the GDR and of the fact, as they saw it, that Germany now consisted of two independent German states. They were keen to help their German puppet, which by 1958 had lost some 2.3 million of its citizens (some 15 per cent of the population) to the Federal Republic. Basic foodstuffs were still rationed in the GDR and real wages were very low. An East German had to work 65 hours to earn a pair of shoes, a West German 18. Adenauer had been embarrassed by the unity issue. The SPD was doing well in *Land* elections, and pressed its opposition to nuclear weapons and the stalling of unity talks.

From 20 to 24 March 1957 there was a further major Bundestag debate on security and nuclear weapons. It had been inflamed by the announcement that the Americans were proposing to deploy Matador rockets with nuclear warheads. Although Strauss claimed the rockets were merely part of a trial, the SPD, supported by the unions and various Protestant groups, decided on a mass 'anti-atomic death' campaign. Its organizing committee included two leading members of the FDP, Erich Mende and Wolfgang Mischnick. Other supporters included the novelists Heinrich Böll and Erich Kästner, and the leading Protestant theologians Herbert Gollwitzer and Martin Niemoeller.

The campaign made the reasonable point that in any nuclear war between the superpowers, both German states would inevitably be destroyed. As a consequence, the Federal Republic ought not to participate in the nuclear arms race, and support the idea of a European nuclear free zone. But these oppositional ambitions, defined now as policies for Germany, did not bring the SPD the electoral success it had hoped for. In the 1958 North Rhine-Westphalian elections, the CDU (which had been ousted from power by the FDP and the SPD) was now able to gain 50.4 per cent of the vote, and the FDP lost heavily. West

Germans did not believe the Soviets could be trusted and they feared the radicalism of the SPD.

The Berlin Ultimatum

In 1957 a public opinion survey had indicated that 52 per cent of those questioned thought that reunification in the foreseeable future was unlikely. By 1958 this figure had risen to 74 per cent. Increasingly West Germans wondered whether it might not be wisest to accept the existence of two German states and concentrate instead on *détente* and improving life for those in East Germany. The SPD picked up this feeling and began to turn it into policy.

In the autumn of 1958 the Russians decided to increase the pressure on Adenauer to go down this road. Needless to say, their motives were (and are) unclear. They may have wanted to forestall West Germany's becoming a nuclear power. They may, however, have wished to stabilize their western front in order to concentrate on the growing problems with China in the east. There can be little doubt that the impetus behind the more forward Soviet policy was Khrushchev himself. He was an adventurer, and thanks to him, from 1958 until 1962, the Cold War became appreciably hotter and more dangerous. This had a curious effect on the two schools of thought in the West. Those like Adenauer, who had never trusted the Soviets, now believed they had been more than ever right. Other leaders, particularly in the United States, Britain and France, argued that unless the West made a real attempt to negotiate a settlement with the Soviet Union, an unwanted nuclear disaster might follow.

The new tension was carefully stage-managed by the Soviets. First, Khrushchev and his Polish colleague, Gomulka, started to attack Adenauer for his alleged revanchism and demanded that East Berlin should be legally made over to East Germany. The Western powers riposted at once with a somewhat lame declaration that to do so would contravene previous international agreements. Then on 27 November 1958 Khrushchev delivered his famous Berlin ultimatum. He demanded that West Berlin should be made a free city within six months, and that the Western allies should leave.

In mid-December NATO formally rejected the ultimatum, but offered the Soviets a chance to discuss the German question and disarmament. Adenauer feared the Americans might waver, succumbing to the British argument that a refusal to recognize existing realities (that is, the GDR) could easily launch an otherwise unnecessary war. In January Khrushchev raised the stakes by issuing a draft German peace treaty. Its aim, once again, was to gain recognition for the GDR. If the

West refused to comply, the USSR would sign a treaty with the GDR unilaterally ('Khrushchev marrying himself', as Willy Brandt called it).

Further worry struck the Chancellor when, from 21 February to 3 March, Macmillan and Selwyn Lloyd, the foreign secretary, visited Moscow. Adenauer distrusted both of them intensely, believing they were ready to do a deal over his head. In addition, John Foster Dulles, whose anti-Communism was every bit as fierce as Adenauer's, became terminally ill. He died on 24 May; this was a heavy loss for Adenauer. He said he had been closer to Dulles than any other US secretary of state, not least because they shared a common 'ethical concern' – namely fear of the might of Soviet communism. Adenauer was now in deep trouble.

Khrushchev then agreed to withdraw the six-month ultimatum in return for a Geneva conference on the German question, to be held on 11 May 1959. The Social Democrats quickly exploited the situation. Carlo Schmid and Fritz Erler visited the Kremlin in March. Khrushchev told them, untruthfully, that unification was a matter for the Germans, East and West, to resolve by themselves. If it proved impossible to make a peace treaty with both German states, the Soviet Union would sign one with the GDR. It would, he insisted, inevitably lead to the ending of occupation rights in Berlin, which would become part of the GDR. Seeing an obvious gap in German policy, the Social Democrats published their German Plan (*Deutschlandplan*), which called for a European nuclear-free security zone. Helmut Schmidt was one of its authors, although its chief public proponent was Herbert Wehner, a man Adenauer never trusted on account of his pre-1945 Communist past.

Although Adenauer did not believe that a realistic chance of unity existed, he needed to have some concrete policy formulations of his own. Accordingly, he asked Globke to produce a plan on unification (which was made public in 1974, in a feeble attempt to show that there was more to Adenauer's *Ostpolitik* than the Hallstein Doctrine). Part of the plan was old – that there should be a plebiscite on unity, all-German free elections, with the new government to decide between the Warsaw Pact or NATO. What was new was a tentative offer of recognition for the GDR, as a preliminary move to unification (which would have made it redundant).

In reality, that the Soviets were more interested in changing the status quo in West Berlin than in solving the German question emerged clearly from the Geneva talks, which lasted from May to August 1959. The Western position was that there should be staged progress towards unity, beginning with free elections, the uniting of the two parts of Berlin and the creation of an all-German commission to draft an electoral law. This would allow the election of an all-German assembly and an all-German government, which could then sign a peace treaty. The Russians, however, stated that they wanted a demilitarized West Berlin before considering anything else. Agreement was impossible. During a visit to the USA from 15 to 27 September 1959, Khrushchev withdrew his ultimatum and further talks on Berlin were put on ice for the time being.

The German Armed Forces

During this period, arrangements were finally agreed between West Germany and the United States for the transfer of tactical nuclear weapons to the *Bundeswehr*. It was confirmed that the warheads would remain under US control. A further and ongoing debate between the US and West Germany concerned the offsetting of the expense of stationing US troops there. Before 1955 and the gaining of sovereignty by West Germany, the West Germans had been obliged to pay the costs of stationing foreign troops in the Federal Republic. After 1955, the Americans first accepted that they would pay for their own troops in dollars (but not pay anything towards the cost of the *Bundeswehr*); but after 1958 the expense led to a disturbing increase in the US balance-of-payments deficit. The Americans thus became keen that the Federal Republic should make a contribution to the cost of its own security.

Over the years, a variety of two-year 'offset' agreements were signed. In 1959, the US asked for $600 million; the West Germans offered instead an advance payment to cover its post-war debt of precisely this amount and said they were ready to shoulder a larger part of NATO's cost. In November 1961 West Germany accepted the idea of purchasing US military equipment and weapons. This procedure was continued. By November 1964 West Germany said it would purchase $1.3 billion of military goods by June 1967; although it proved reluctant to pay up, not least because of domestic coalition pressures (the FDP was hostile) and the fact that one kind of purchase, the Starfighter jet, was proving something of a liability (from June 1965 to May 1966 56 of them crashed). In 1967 Strauss (by then minister of finance) worked out a deal by which, instead of military equipment, the federal government would purchase $500 million of US government bonds.

Adenauer's unease at the apparent willingness of the Americans to negotiate with the Russians over his head continued unabated. He feared the outcome of the summit between the Americans and Russians planned for 16 May 1960 in Paris. In the event, however, the conference collapsed before it began as a result of the American U2 spy plane incident (shot down ten days earlier over Sverdlovsk). Khrushchev, significantly, had blamed the incident on the 'imperialist lackeys of

Adenauer who failed to appreciate they were defeated at Stalingrad' and the summit collapsed.

Neo-Nazi Activity

The final years of the decade saw an unpleasant and damaging outbreak of neo-Nazi activity in the form of swastika daubing. There is some evidence to suggest that the East German security service, the Stasi, may have played some role in promoting this. That there were West Germans who were fanatics and anti-Semitic was not surprising: most Western states had numbers of Nazi supporters. But West Germany was not like other states and serious damage was done to its reputation. In order to try to contain the problem, in January 1960 Adenauer told West Germans that if they chanced upon any anti-Semites in the process of daubing, they should 'give them a good hiding on the spot'. He added that the Jews had always helped him and that he wanted 'the whole world to know that the Germany of today totally rejects anti-Semitism'.

The Election of John F. Kennedy as US President

On 8 November 1960 Kennedy was elected US President. The fact that Bonn now had to deal both with a younger man (whose elder brother had been shot down over Germany during the war) and with a Democratic administration, bound to have new ideas, introduced a new and potentially difficult element into the vital US-German relationship. The Kennedy era marked what was to prove a decisive change in the way in which the interrelated issues of *détente* with the Soviet Union and German unification were to be handled. It was hardly a coincidence that this new thinking did more than anything to bring about Adenauer's political demise. He had constructed a world in which close alliance with the USA was an absolute imperative. He had always hoped that the anti-Communism of the Americans was fixed and immutable, and that they, like he himself, would always eschew a unified Germany in order to have a West Germany locked into the West.

What Adenauer ignored was the possibility that a new generation of Americans might see this as a false opposition. He seemed unable to understand that policy making had become far more complex, and dangerous, with new developments in nuclear weaponry. His tendency to think in broad terms might come into conflict with a more modern, piecemeal and disaggregated approach to problem solving. It is sometimes suggested that the core issue at stake was German unity; and, in a way, it was. But this is not to say very much for, over the years, the Americans and the West Germans had developed very different lines on unity. The Americans now believed that events since 1950 had shown that unity was not merely a dream, but one that hindered the making of deals on *real* issues. Kennedy himself took this view. Adenauer was, of course, equally realistic, and equally unconcerned with the distant quest of unity. Yet whereas the American concern was to do deals with the Soviets over Germany, Adenauer's concern was that West Germany, and the idea of the West, should not be undermined by such deals. Adenauer seems to have thought that without a Cold War, there might no longer be a West at all. Unity, he continued to hold, in the form of a neutral German nation *between* East and West, was thinkable but not desirable. From this it followed that the West Germans could have no interest in seeing the Cold War end unless it could do so with the defeat of Communism, which seemed totally incredible.

Adenauer was sure he could win the argument at home by claiming that *détente* implied the side-stepping of unity. This does not mean, however, that unity itself had become Adenauer's goal; rather that he felt he could only outsmart the Americans by playing the unity card. This was, of course, a vastly overelaborate high policy (though wholly in keeping with the statesman's style). It proved, however, to be a serious miscalculation, which was to cost him his job.

Whose vision of the future of Europe was the more perceptive? History (and most Germans) would suggest it was Kennedy's. The question was whether real *détente* was possible. Here, initially at any rate, Adenauer's view seemed the right one. The 1961 Berlin Crisis and the 1962 Cuban Missile Crisis showed plainly that the Soviet Union represented a real threat to the West. Yet, once these crises had passed, reality validated the opposite point: that without *détente*, the world could easily be blown apart. This fact supported the need for agreements in areas where agreements were possible.

The Soviets and Berlin

Their differing views on *détente* meant that, with Kennedy in the White House, Adenauer was no longer seen as America's most influential ally in continental Europe, and German unity has no longer considered the central factor in foreign policy making with the Soviets. The Americans showed themselves willing to side-step Bonn. On 11 June 1961 in Vienna the Soviets produced another ultimatum demanding, by the end of the year, a four-power conference leading to a peace treaty with both German states, to be followed within six months by direct talks between the two German states. Were agreement not reached, the Soviets would sign a separate peace with the GDR. In reality, Khrushchev was demanding the recognition of Germany's division. The situation in the

GDR had, indeed, become critical. By 1961 three million East Germans had left the GDR, 20,000 of them in June 1961. There were to be 30,000 in July and at the beginning of August 1,500 a day were crossing the sectoral border into West Berlin. Recognition would allow the East Germans to plug the gap that Potsdam had constructed in Berlin by making it an Allied city. The Western powers were unnerved by the directness of Khrushchev's demands and decided to try to curb them by staging a show of force. The United States reinforced its Berlin garrison.

The Berlin Wall

On 13 August 1961, to the apparent surprise of all the Western states, the East Germans sealed off West Berlin and began to construct a wall around it three days later. The consequences were profound. East Berliners had now become prisoners: the western sector of the city was turned into a ghetto. Yet the West's response scarcely deserved the name not least because Kennedy did not want a war over Berlin.

Berlin's Western Governors protested, but waited 60 hours before doing so. On 19 and 20 August, Vice President Johnson and General Lucius Clay were sent to Berlin to boost morale. Adenauer had wanted to fly in with them but they refused on the grounds that they did not wish to interfere in domestic West German politics by appearing to boost Adenauer's prestige during an election campaign. Adenauer's feelings can easily be imagined at a move which allowed his SPD opponent, Brandt, to be the sole beneficiary of their Berlin trip. Adenauer did not visit until 22 and 23 August.

It may well be queried whether the West was truly as surprised as it subsequently maintained. For one thing, Ulbricht had himself in June issued a gratuitous denial that the GDR would build a wall around West Berlin. For another, each Western state had its own secret intelligence agency, and it is (as both Willy Brandt and Franz Josef Strauss have independently suggested) not possible to believe they were unable to identify the build-up of men and material that was a necessary precondition of the sealing off of West Berlin. The Wall was a gross and totally unacceptable violation of human rights and international agreements. The lack of a harsh response can only have served to encourage the Soviet hardliners, at any rate, that their hold on East Germany and on East Berlin was never going to be called into question by the West.

Adenauer's stance at this very critical phase in German political history was bizarre. On the one hand, he plainly aimed to keep all Germans calm and to try to ensure that a popular protest did not inflame the situation and precipitate armed intervention. He and his defence minister both insisted that the building of the wall was a self-contained event and not a prelude to any further aggressive action. On the other hand, Adenauer failed to respond to the significance of the occasion. He refused to attend the big protest meeting at the Schöneberg town hall and claimed, unwisely, that the Wall had been built to help the SPD in its election campaign. Brandt, however, emerged from the crisis with a reputation considerably enhanced. He, too, did not want to see an escalation of the problem, but saw how to make political capital of the affair: 'I do not wish to attack the Chancellor', he said, 'I wish him nothing more than a peaceful evening of his life. I don't think the old gentleman grasps the situation any more.' But Brandt personally went to pacify a crowd apparently intent on ripping the Wall down and he used his authority wisely to cool down emotions. After the building of the Wall, Kennedy and Khrushchev continued to correspond with each other, to Adenauer's anger, especially on the question of whether West Berlin should become a free city. This led to a serious flare-up in April 1962 when Americans accused the West German media of doing 'incurable harm' to US-German relations by leaking a US document supporting *détente* in Europe.

European Integration

There was plainly a major crisis emerging between Adenauer and Kennedy, the more serious precisely because it had less to do with the aim of German unity, than with what being Western now entailed. This had two consequences: the first was to encourage Adenauer to think of new, and different, ways of defining and articulating the essential Westernness of West Germany; the second was the unwanted weakening of his own position inside the CDU/CSU. Having stressed for so long the importance to West Germany's interests of staying in with the Americans, it was hard for him to justify his policy of falling out with them. This second matter (which was to drive Adenauer from power) is dealt with later on. The former imperative inevitably pushed Adenauer towards the only other option available: France.

In August 1960 de Gaulle and Adenauer had a further meeting at which the French President produced a document on European political union. It proved that de Gaulle had been thinking creatively about how the Paris–Bonn axis could be made to fit in with his plans. His immediate aim was to give the European Community a role in world affairs. The concept of union was to be applied to political, economic, defence and cultural questions, and its first stage should be a Franco-German agreement. De Gaulle also wished to reform the Commission and to make changes to NATO, which he believed should itself become more European and less American. De Gaulle disliked the concept of a supra-national Commission ('there is no other European reality' as he put it 'than our nations and the governments that speak for them') and a supra-national defence force ('France believes its defence should have a national character'). His views on NATO were given added urgency by France's first successful nuclear test in February 1960. De Gaulle wished to make fast progress, although what he meant by European Union was that France, assisted by West Germany, should lead the other four EEC states. He hoped to have a preliminary agreement signed by the six EEC states in the autumn. In fact, it was not until February 1961 that the discussions on union were begun.

Adenauer, ever cautious, sought to ensure that any changes in the EEC and NATO should take place with the agreement of the USA: 'The development of Europe must take place in cooperation with the US.' At the same time, he was quite prepared to explore de Gaulle's propositions. But he did not believe the time was ripe for a European government. As far as the more theoretical aspects of defence and security policy were concerned, the new American administration had unwittingly introduced an element of confusion into the increasingly complex matter which was both politically difficult to manage, and tended to alienate fundamentalists like Adenauer. The US defence minister, MacNamara, argued that NATO should turn away from its policy of massive retaliation towards a policy of flexible response. In order to encourage the West Germans to come round to the American viewpoint, Strauss was warned by the Americans in May 1962 that he was relying too heavily on nuclear weapons and doing too little to build up West Germany's conventional strength. Indeed, the *Bundeswehr* was still unable to sport twelve divisions.

The American answer to this was formulated in Kennedy's speech of 4 July 1962 where he promoted a 'grand design' for greater inter-dependence between the United States and western Europe and the creation of two pillars, an American and a European one, on which NATO might be secured. Underlying these ideas was the American belief that the nuclear threshold needed to be raised rather than lowered.

The 1961 Federal Election

On 17 September 1961 the fourth federal elections took place. The campaign had been fought chiefly on foreign affairs, and the CDU/CSU's main tactic had been to suggest that the SPD could not be relied upon to conduct foreign policy. The result was a good one for the CDU/CSU but one that was seen as not quite good enough. It gained 45.3 per cent, seven seats short of a majority; the FDP got 12.8 per cent, and the SPD with Willy Brandt as its candidate for the Chancellorship boosted its vote from 31.8 per cent to 36.2 per cent.

It was now necessary to construct a coalition and on 25 September, in what appeared a major turning-point in the domestic political development of West Germany, Adenauer invited the SPD chairman, Ollenhauer, as well as Erler and Wehner to a two-hour discussion. Since its Godesberg conference in 1959, the SPD had become – in theory at any rate – a possible coalition partner for the CDU. It had dropped its Marxism and now supported the key elements of Adenauer's foreign and domestic policy. In fact, the Chancellor was merely playing (although the CDU/CSU and the SPD believed, rightly as it turned out, that his power was ebbing). His aim was to pressurize the FDP. Despite the fact that Erich Mende, by now the FDP leader, had said that he would not serve under Adenauer, on 28 September he agreed to his party entering government on condition that Adenauer accepted in writing that he would step down in two years (to give his successor time to prepare for the 1965 elections). This was kept secret, although it was not only the FDP who wanted Adenauer to go. Franz Josef Strauss, now chairman of the CSU, began to negotiate with the FDP to nominate Erhard to replace Adenauer.

On 7 November Adenauer was re-elected Chancellor. The FDP had demanded the resignation of von Brentano, who was replaced by Gerhard Schröder. According to Strauss, this move was meant to appease a far wider desire to bring about the end of the 1955 Hallstein Doctrine. It was now believed by many leading figures that the doctrine had not only made it virtually impossible for the Federal Republic to establish relationships with eastern Europe, but was increasingly antagonizing West Germany's allies.

Adenauer, now 85, was on his last legs. To add to his woes, he learned that Harold Macmillan had tried to get the Americans to force him to accept the Oder-Neisse line, give a high degree of *de facto* recognition to the GDR and loosen the ties between West Berlin and West Germany. Adenauer had hoped to mend broken fences when he visited Kennedy in November, but he fell ill and the meeting was unsuccessful. Back home, on 21 January 1962, he suffered his first heart attack, which was kept a close secret.

The Spiegel Affair

1962 ended with two grave crises, the one over Cuba, the other over the *Spiegel* magazine. The political lesson of the Cuba crisis was less obvious to Adenauer than to others (he wanted Kennedy to press home the advantage he believed the Americans had won). The *Spiegel* affair, on the other hand, made it plain that the time to resign had come. It showed not only how strongly Adenauer still believed his model Germany was still just a construct, that needed to be protected at all costs, but also how tightly he wanted to control affairs of state. In fact, he had achieved rather more than he suspected. West Germany was sufficiently secure to weather a minor scandal.

On 8 October the *Spiegel* had published an article on the *Bundeswehr*, claiming it was in poor order and that Strauss was, in effect, seeking to lower the nuclear threshhold. The article was based on secret material. Later, photos marked secret were found in the *Spiegel*'s safe by the intelligence services. Arrests of the editor and other followed, and a court case was started. Eventually, the charges against the *Spiegel* and its editor, Rudolf Augstein (defended by Horst Ehmke, then professor of law at Freiburg) were dropped, and no convictions followed against any of the others.

What the affair showed was that Adenauer had, indeed, gone 'over the top'. He was not wrong to believe that the Federal Republic was not the necessary and inevitable outcome of German political development, but only the product of particular and fragile inputs. Yet they were far less fragile by 1962 than he could comprehend.

The End of the Adenauer Era

By 1962, Adenauer's foreign policies were causing severe difficulties within his own ranks. His attitude towards de Gaulle was considered too compliant, and his attitude towards the Communist states of eastern Europe and the Soviet Union too hostile. His critics argued that he was turning the Americans away from the Federal Republic and driving it into the hands of the French. Unity was as far off as it had ever been, they alleged, even further away than in 1952 or 1953, and was denying the Federal Republic a voice in the world.

The publication in 1994 of the German foreign office papers for 1963 revealed the true context against which Adenauer's fall from power in this year must be judged. They indicate that Adenauer had clearly lost his grip on policy making, but not because his policies were wrong, or because he had become senile. Rather, he had allowed himself to be outflanked both within his own party and by the foreign policy experts of the SPD, notably Brandt himself. He was without doubt drawing ever closer to de Gaulle, but this was because he had formed the view that the European Community, as an integrated grouping of several European states, had outlived its usefulness. He preferred to return to his old dream of Franco-German union, in which

France together with West Germany would provide the political and economic leadership of Europe for the rest of the century.

The year appointed for Adenauer's departure, 1963, was to prove an eventful and, in many ways a deeply unsettling year, both for Germany and for other Western states. After fourteen years in power, the Federal Chancellor finally stepped down on 16 October; two days later, his British counterpart, Harold Macmillan, found himself pushed out of office; and on 22 November, President John F. Kennedy was assassinated in Dallas. The same year saw the signing of the Franco-German Treaty, and the rejection of Britain's application to joint the EEC by the French President, de Gaulle; but also the Test Ban Treaty with the Soviet Union and a clear sense in the West that, having taken the world to the brink of a nuclear war in 1962, the Russians were ready to embark upon *détente*.

The Berlin Issue

Alongside these high policy issues that confronted what may still be described as the fledgling Republic, there were more mundane but equally complex questions that also raised fundamental questions about the future of Germany. The most pressing was Berlin, both West and East. The policy of non-recognition was making it hard for the West Germans, and in particular the Governing Mayor of West Berlin, Willy Brandt, to come to relatively minor agreements with the East German authorities about sectoral traffic. There was a reluctance even to write officially to the East Germans since, absurdly, any communication tended to throw the whole of the West German foreign policy apparatus into confusion since the official existence of the East German government was still not recognized. Notes from the GDR were answered by notes which had no address, no named intended recipient, and appeared to have been sent by no one.

Franco-German Union Revisited

We now know that by 1963 the relationship between France and Germany had become more important to both Adenauer and de Gaulle than any other. Its essence was neatly expressed by de Gaulle, speaking to Adenauer on 21 September 1963 at Rambouillet. He said (in an significant amendment to his 1960 utterance) that there was 'no European reality other than Germany and France; the others mean nothing, they don't count'. For de Gaulle, the Federal Republic had become a vital springboard to French dominance in continental Europe, and perhaps the world. For Adenauer, Franco-German cooperation not only allowed the Federal Republic to participate (albeit as junior partner) in the development of the European Community, but also gave it a status in Europe which it might otherwise not have had. De Gaulle was able to exact a high price from Adenauer in return for treating him as a partner, however junior. This was seen clearly at their 21 January 1963 meeting in Paris, just after de Gaulle's veto of Britain's application to join the EEC on 14 January. De Gaulle's position, however, was extremely strong: he had held a successful referendum in 1962 and gained an absolute majority for his party in the National Assembly.

Adenauer saw that the Federal Republic had an overriding interest in a close alliance with France. It is hard to deny that this policy made excellent sense for many reasons. It is clear that both men had agreed that France should take the lead. Adenauer wanted equality for Germany but believed the Germans were a 'wounded and sick people' who needed a period of 'convalescence'. In June he told the French ambassador that because of its Nazi past Germany would not be able to play an active foreign policy role 'for the foreseeable future' and France would have to do this for Germany; West Germany could only use its power *through* France. Furthermore, the future of the EEC as a genuinely federated organization looked uncertain, not because of Britain but because he believed the EEC had simply made itself too comfortable, and would not meet difficult challenges such as a common social policy or a common currency. In the final analysis, Adenauer seemed, by 1963, to be losing his faith in European integration, believing instead that the Franco-German relationship would take over from it.

This is why the Franco-German Treaty had assumed an overriding importance for Adenauer. Hans Osterheld, Adenauer's aide, recorded this, emphasizing the spontaneity of the event right down to the kiss that Adenauer sought to place on de Gaulle's cheek in response to de Gaulle's triumphal Gallic embrace (de Gaulle turned to Schröder, shook him by the hand and said in German 'Sie küsse ich noch nicht'). He added to Adenauer – in French – 'Voila le debut de l'integration; et c'est moi qui le dit.'

Adenauer, Israel and the Arabs

Officials in the German Foreign Office, led by Schröder, now attempted to curb and even counter Adenauer's foreign policy making. They not only had sympathy for the aim of British membership but also understood that de Gaulle was supported only by Adenauer and that the Benelux states in particular were outraged by the veto. They were also plainly unhappy about Adenauer's dealings with Israel. There were two main issues in 1963. The first involved the granting of secret credits for Israel (given the unhappy code name 'business partner'). DM 150 million had already been paid in 1963, but the Israelis wanted more. At a meeting with Ben Gurion in New York on 14 March 1960 Adenauer had agreed to this, but the Foreign Office was sorely put out. Then, on 17 August 1963, Adenauer informed his foreign minister (in a very short note) that he had just promised the Israeli ambassador that the Federal Republic would recognize Israel fully before his departure from office. The Reparations Treaty of September 1952, ratified in March 1953, had also recognized the existence of the state of Israel. The Germans had, at that time, offered full diplomatic relations, but the Israelis had refused.

Carstens, a highly intelligent man who was head of the West German Foreign Office, agreed that Adenauer must be restrained from doing anything further without the agreement of the Foreign Office. The fear was that the advantages of recognition were far outweighed by the disadvantages, not least of which was the Arab states' promise to recognize the GDR immediately if Bonn went ahead. The Foreign Office took the view that since the treaty would expire in March 1966, and since the Arab states had threatened to recognize the GDR, it would be best to do nothing for another two years. The Chancellor had therefore bounced them (and they were forced to make special credit arrangements with the Israelis to placate them).

Adenauer and Kennedy

There is no doubt but that Adenauer's commitment to de Gaulle made things even more difficult in respect of relations with the United States. For one thing, the Americans had a very low opinion of de Gaulle. For another, Adenauer's meeting with President Kennedy on 24 June had gone badly. Adenauer had distanced himself too far from the American position, and he had been unwise to allow the Franco-German relationship to assume ascendancy over the US-German one. Yet Adenauer was genuinely convinced that Kennedy and his staff were not taking the fate of western Europe as seriously as they needed to, and that they were gravely underestimating both the desirability of German reunification and the danger of Communism. It can certainly be argued that (once Adenauer had gone) the Atlanticist viewpoint did generate a new beginning in West Germany's dealings with the Soviet Union and eastern Europe (and led, eventually, to *Ostpolitik*). At the same time, as we shall see, the Atlanticist line did very little to promote the chance of German unity, and US aims were not always identical with those of western Europe.

The End

Adenauer had been in power for almost fourteen years. His critics held three things in particular against him. The first was that he had lost his mental agility and no longer understood what was going on – and what West German interests required policy to be. Evidence of this flaw was, it was argued, found in his fawning attitude towards de Gaulle and Israel. The second was a feeling that his fondness for France had been allowed to contradict (and damage) West Germany's policy towards Britain and the United States. And the third was that his German policy, based on the unequivocal demand for unity on West German terms and on Bonn's insistence that it was the sole representative of the German people, had become a dead-end policy which had led nowhere, and most certainly not to unity. In exploring this very question, Adenauer's most brilliant biographer, Hans-Peter Schwarz, cites Blankenhorn, who wrote that history would come to regard this era in German foreign policy as bearing the hallmark of poor performance by a man who was simply too old to formulate policy appropriate to the complex position in which the Federal Republic found itself. Thus, he concluded, what we are dealing with in 1963 is bad foreign policy.

This view is unfounded. The truth is that even in 1963 Adenauer was still able to think with imagination and foresight about West Germany's destiny; he also, as it happened, kept the Six from disintegrating as a political entity (by standing between the Four and de Gaulle) and set West Germany on a course that not only produced a new and uniquely significant relationship with France, but also established values which themselves led, thirty years later, to the unity Adenauer had wanted, and on the only terms that would have been acceptable to him.

The Elysée Treaty institutionalized the Franco-German relationship. It provided for regular meetings between heads of state and government, as frequently as were needed, and at least twice a year. Foreign ministers were made responsible for the execution of the relationship agreements, and obliged to meet at least every three months. An inter-ministerial Commission, established by both governments, was to carry out practical steps. Other ministers (for defence, education, family and youth) were to meet regularly, from every three months, to once every two months. In foreign affairs, the two governments were bound to 'consult before any decision is taken on any important questions of foreign policy, and questions of common interest, with a view to reaching as far as possible parallel positions'. Adenauer visited France twenty-two times as Chancellor – twice as often as his visits to America, four times as often as his visits to the UK.

One Franco-German institute was established for operational army research and another to take concrete steps to increase numbers learning the two languages, and making it possible for the young to meet, and study together. The Franco-German Youth Organisation has arranged 4.6 million exchanges in thirty years. The majority of visits last six weeks. 1240 French and German towns and cities are partners. By 1992, a staggering 150,000 annual visits had taken place. It is obvious that this relationship was not simply conceived as a pragmatic response to awkward times, but as a bold new enterprise. This has often not been understood by other European nations.

Erhard as Chancellor

Despite much celebration, Adenauer left behind him a legacy of sourness. He had possessed great power, but had become too old and too bitter to bid it farewell easily. His final months in office were unedifying, not least because he intrigued heavily against the man his party saw as his natural successor. On 24 April 1963, Adenauer told the parliamentary group that Erhard, whom he had known and worked closely with for fourteen years (and whose achievements had been lauded by the world) was not suited to be Chancellor. Yet Erhard was duly elected to replace him, backed by von Brentano, Schröder and Strauss. On 16 October, he became West Germany's second Chancellor.

Adenauer's departure from the Chancellorship introduced what his critics termed a new 'realism' into West German foreign policy (even if the apparent benefits of it were not reaped until long after Erhard had left office). The new Chancellor, his Foreign Minister Schröder and Defence Minister von Hassel were all seen as 'Atlanticists', determined to break the 'Gaullism' of Adenauer, Strauss and the increasingly influential Baron von und zu Guttenberg. But their wish to fall in with the United States did not mean that the 'special relationship' of the 1950s was revived, but simply that West Germany too was no longer resistant to the more forward policy in Europe that the United States was now adopting. Adenauer's reinvention of a better Germany, made real by the conviction that such a Germany could be made, was not fundamentally changed by his successors. Where improvements were made, either in domestic politics or in foreign policy, they were made on the foundations laid by Adenauer. The real test of the durability of Adenauer's legacy did not occur in the twenty-five years following his fall. It is taking place today.

−6−

The Grand Coalition and the Brandt Chancellorship

Changing Course

Adenauer's state survived its maker's departure. Indeed, it was Adenauer's reinvention of Germany, forged out of defeat and occupation, with only one major modification, that proved powerful enough to absorb the German Democratic Republic in 1990. What was modified, of course, was the Federal Republic's relationship with East Germany and the Soviet empire, its *Ostpolitik*, (which is dealt with in the next chapter). Though it represented a major change, it should nevertheless be regarded as a move designed to stabilize the Bonn state, thus providing the finishing touch to the new Rhenish pseudo-nation.

Westernization, but also the entire system of government, created by Adenauer, the CDU/CSU, and the occupier-allies, were hugely resilient constructs. This was because they were all successful. The federal structure, the popularity of consensus politics, underwritten by a rising standard of living and enviable economic might, as well as improving ways of managing political problems, produced a secure and democratically acceptable corset around German public life. It was not, however, a system that promoted change. In fact, political change was very hard to achieve by what might be regarded as conventional democratic means, that is, through election results, (and was made totally impossible by undemocratic ones). The system of Bonn was thus clearly not the system of Weimar.

Some observers have equated the increase in demand for consensus politics with 'convergence', the notion that the parties of West Germany moved towards each other. This was true only in a very limited sense. For the main part, what the electorate rewarded was not convergence *per se*. Rather, they rewarded the Social Democratic Party for becoming ever more like Christian Democracy.

The SPD, rightly, came to see that in order to achieve power in Bonn − that is, to have a chance of influencing 'national' policy at home and abroad − it had to accept most of the basic tenets of Christian

Figure 4. Ludwig Erhard. ©Presse- und Informationsamt der Bundesreglerung

Democracy. Yet doing so still did not offer the German electors a positive reason for preferring it to the CDU/CSU. To meet this need, the SPD had two strategies. The first was to suggest that their candidate for Chancellor (by now Willy Brandt) would be a more effective leader of West Germany than Adenauer, because he was thirty years younger. John F. Kennedy had won the 1960 election and had shown the electoral appeal of passing 'the torch to a younger generation'. The second idea was to use coalition politics to steal into power *outside* an election. Neither the 1961 nor the 1965 election indicated that the first strategy would work. Bourgeois West Germans were not fans of youth. Even before the 1965 election, the leaders of the SPD, who included Fritz Erler and Herbert Wehner (deputy leader following the 1957 election debacle), together with Brandt, concentrated on the second option. This was a potent triumvirate, said to have the brains (Erler), the glamour (Brandt) and the ruthlessness (Wehner himself), that was required to take power.

They decided to seek power by suggesting a coalition with the Christian Democrats. Significantly, however, their chief purpose was not domestic reform but a new start in foreign policy.

The Making of the Grand Coalition

The unhappy history of Erhard's wretched Chancellorship was compounded by the apparent reason for his overthrow – his alleged economic incompetence. Erhard proved unable to master the peculiarities of West German political life. He was a fat, jovial cigar-smoker (as well as being exceptionally clever), but he quickly fell out with de Gaulle and cut a foolish figure on the national and international stage. Above all, despite winning an election for his party, he failed to lead it (demonstrating, yet again, the importance of parties, as well as personalities, in the politics of the Federal Republic). His cabinet of 1965 had contained the new faces of Gerhard Stoltenberg and Walter Scheel (as minister for economic cooperation). Erich Mende carried on as minister for all-German affairs. On 10 November 1963, Erhard issued a statement of his policy: the post-war era, he declared, was now over, and the time had come to established what he mysteriously termed the 'formierte Gesellschaft' or 'contoured society', whose aim was to be the protection of society as a whole from individual over-strong interest groups.

In foreign affairs, Erhard was immediately taken up with the Middle East. As we have seen, the Federal Republic did not recognize Israel during Adenauer's tenure, but in May 1965 it was decided to bite the bullet. As if by clockwork, the Arab nations broke with Bonn and recognized the GDR. It was common knowledge in 1964 that West Germany had supplied Israel with arms; but this ceased in February 1965. In March the Bonn government decided to try to repair the damage done to its diplomatic standing. It sent a 'peace note' to all the governments of the world (except the GDR) stating West Germany's desire to improve East-West relations. This was a public admission that Bonn now wished to support US-led *détente* wholeheartedly. Coming at the very time when the first big demonstrations against US intervention in Vietnam were taking place, it seemed wise to try to curry favour with Washington even if it meant negotiating with the Soviets. Foreign Minister Schröder believed that such negotiation would, in due course, transform the Communists (an opinion held increasingly amongst American foreign policy experts). He made overtures to Poland, Hungary, Romania and Bulgaria with the hope of establishing diplomatic relations with them. His enterprise was lauded by many in the CDU/CSU and, of course, by the SPD. Indeed, it was the need to further *détente*, which Erhard's apparent incompetence was stalling, that precipitated his fall, rather than the problems facing the economy.

In the middle of 1966 the Federal Republic did indeed find itself in the midst of an economic crisis. Erhard's old colleague, Müller-Armack (now working in industry) spoke out angrily against economic non-intervention and said it was an 'illusion' to believe that 'the market will put everything to rights by itself'. Erhard was the CDU/CSU's most important asset and Erhard's most important asset was his economic know-how, based of course on a faith in market capitalism. Now that this was being called into question, the SPD was able to project itself not so much as different from the CDU/CSU but more efficient. In the *Land* elections in North Rhine-Westphalia, the SPD gained almost 50 per cent of the vote. Unnerved, the government introduced a welfare bill on child support. By the autumn of 1966 it became plain that more cash was required to fund this. Erhard's coalition partners, the FDP, wanted taxes to be lowered and the economy to be stimulated; Erhard believed he had to insist on tax increases. It came as no surprise to anyone (and private relief, one imagines, to Erhard) when on 27 October 1966 the FDP decided the time had come to leave what it regarded as a sinking ship. Erhard's government duly fell.

The 1966–9 Grand Coalition and the Coming of Brandt

It is generally argued that in its forty-year history, the Federal Republic has seen only two changes of political direction. The first of these took place in 1966, with entry of the SPD into the Bonn government, and the second in 1982, when the SPD left it. In reality, neither change was quite what it seemed to be, and both had their bizarre aspects. Each was a significant comment on the nature of the Bonn political system. For one thing, both changes of government were changes in government coalition, and took place within already existing parliaments. They were not, therefore, the immediate consequence of a federal election result. For another, both in 1966 and in 1982, foreign and not domestic policy issues were the *real* motor of change. Finally, the changes that took place in 1966 were not caused by a party (in this case the SPD) pressing a policy which the government (the CDU/CSU) did not support, but by agreement between the parties to develop policy jointly. The changes of 1982 were, in their own way, equally peculiar. Here the oppositional party (the CDU/CSU) continued the policies of the SPD-led government; the window of opportunity arising because the party in government began to doubt its own policy.

Thus the Grand Coalition, which led after three years to an SPD/FDP coalition (only thinkable because it had been preceded by the Grand Coalition), was *not* an American, or British-style move to substitute the 'governing party' with the 'opposition party'. What the West German changes bespeak is the emergence by 1960 of three specific core values in its political life: political management, continuity and a desire for consensus. Whilst there was nothing remotely undemocratic about these values, they did constrain other Western values.

As we have seen, the electoral system dictated the need for coalitions, and 'coalitionability'. Whilst this was not inherently undemocratic (and the coalition changes could all be said to have been validated by subsequent elections), one link between the citizen-voter and his, or her, government – namely choosing it – was undermined. In addition, the bargaining by party bosses, part and parcel of coalition building, inevitably produced a sense of powerlessness in the individual citizen; a feeling that politics was something in which ordinary people were not required to participate. There is such a thing as 'democratic authoritarianism'; it may, indeed, be a better, and more modern way, to run a state, but to many thinking West Germans in the 1960s, it was a danger they wished to avoid.

As to the value of continuity, there was an important element of this linking Adenauer's final, admittedly reluctant, plan to look again at the relationship with the East, and Brandt's readiness to do the same. In 1982 Schmidt's policy on rearmament was taken over in its entirety by Helmut Kohl. In addition, domestic and foreign policy interacted in a curious way. These issues demonstrate, once more, that the Bonn Republic was, politically, a very special, very different sort of Germany. The need for consensus was driven by Germany's past domestic history; the significance of foreign policy was a function of West Germany's life since 1945. Yet most West Germans behaved as if this were all a perfectly normal way for a modern democracy to conduct itself. Even though it was not normal, West Germans had begun to lose sight of the extent to which their pseudo-nation had a provisional, and special, nature.

The Godesberg Conference

At Godesberg in 1959, the SPD had accepted the concept of the social market economy and the pluralistic society that West Germany had become. Marx was retired. *Ostpolitik* was the foreign policy adjunct to these changes in domestic goals. Yet the SPD still had achieve its main aim: to get its hands on 'national' policy making. It had been vital for the Party to demonstrate that it had turned its back on the radical economic and political reform proposals of the first post-war period. This had been done programmatically at the 1959 Godesberg Conference. A coalition with either the CDU/CSU, or the FDP, was unthinkable without this move. Foreign policy, however, represented a particularly appropriate means for Brandt to offer a coalition to the CDU/CSU leadership. He, and his close aides, had used foreign policy as a road to power within the SPD ever since the late 1950s. Indeed, their wresting of control from the old Social Democratic guard relied strongly both on Brandt's own international reputation, and on their realistic approach to the issue of the recognition of the GDR. This reflected the attitudes of a number of leading Christian Democrats.

Of course, West German foreign and domestic policy *were* uniquely and critically interrelated. This is because West Germany had been fashioned by foreign policy (and the foreign policy of Germany's victors rather than German foreign policy) and its security was, and would remain for as long as it was divided, the outcome of the foreign policy of others. Thus in a unique way, Bonn's foreign policy could be exploited for domestic political gain. Adenauer himself had always accepted the primacy of foreign policy for West Germany. Brandt and his friends simply learned the lesson. They could point to the fact that all that Adenauer's *Ostpolitik* had achieved by 1966 was diplomatic relations with the USSR and four trade missions in eastern Europe.

It is true (as is discussed in the next chapter) that there was still an ambiguity in Brandt's declarations on this topic. He did not want to risk seeming unpatriotic, if unification was the ultimate object of patriotism. It was feared the West German electorate would have punished those who did this, particularly if, like Brandt, they had fought against the Third Reich, rather than for it. But it is clear that Brandt believed West Germany needed to drop the demand for something he thought could never be achieved. Thus both he, and his aides, repeated the rhetoric of the desirability of unity for instrumental reasons, but made it clear that *reality* now demanded the acceptance of the existence of an East German state. In this way, they could and would negotiate with the East Germans and with the Soviets. Only thus, they claimed, could there be an improvement in relations between the two states of Germany, which might improve the conditions of the East German people. Indeed, in his acceptance speech as SPD chancellor candidate in 1961, Brandt had declared that he and the SPD spoke as much on behalf of 'the 700,000 Party members in Magdeburg, Leipzig, Halle, Rostock, the Harz, Thüringia, the Elbe and Werra', as for West Germans. This meant, he added, that West German 'foreign policy should achieve practical results, without waiting for miracles' (the miracle in question being reunification).

The SPD and National Unity

Before Brandt and his colleagues took over the party, the SPD (under Schumacher and Ollenhauer) had put the physical achievement of German unity over and above any other foreign policy interest of the Federal Republic. Indeed, SPD opposition to the creation of the Council of Europe, to the Schuman plan, to NATO and the EEC, was justified by the argument that Western integration, both economic and strategic, made unification harder to achieve. At the Hamburg conference of the SPD from 21 to 23 May 1950 Schumacher called the Council of Europe the 'Ersatzeuropa' of Strasbourg, 'ersatz' because the 'real' Europe consisted of East Germany and Eastern Europe as well. On 18 April 1951 he had delivered the SPD's 'No' to the ECSC in a pamphlet entitled 'Unser nein zum Schumanplan'. Close examination of the SPD's internal politics shows how Brandt and Erler singlemindedly pushed out those leaders who would not accept their view that the GDR was not going to disappear, and that the sterile demand for unity should be dropped.

At the 1954 party conference at Berlin, Ollenhauer, as always, called for unity, but Erler and Brandt took a significantly different line. The former argued that it was indeed important that West Germany should be part of the Western security system (implying that the obvious price, German division, might be worth it) whilst the latter suggested that the SPD should seek to exert 'realistic' influence on Adenauer's foreign policy. The implication was that Adenauer's aim of a unified Germany, which would be part of the West, was not realistic. Since no one in their right mind could support any move to undermine the Federal Republic's place in the West, Brandt seemed to suggest the only way forward was to accept the existence of a Communist Germany alongside it; there simply was nothing else on offer. In 1954, when he first made the point, the SPD was not yet ready to hear it. Brandt was strongly put down by Carlo Schmid. Whilst Schmid agreed that unification would have to wait until the Cold War was over (and thus supported Brandt's realism to this extent), he insisted that in the meantime the SPD should ensure Bonn did nothing which might prevent unification (by recognizing the GDR). Indeed, Schmid, like Ollenhauer and Schumacher, used the demand for unity as a reason for opposing Adenauer's policies on Westernization. As late as 1958 Ollenhauer insisted that Germany could be reunited if only NATO and the Warsaw Pact were dissolved. For Brandt, this sort of talk was every bit as unrealistic as Adenauer's statements suggesting that somehow the East Germans would accept unity on Western terms.

Indeed, at the 1959 Godesberg Conference, Brandt himself said that West Germany's chief concern should be to find a way out of what had become a hopeless international situation for their country. Yet he continued to express his wish for unity 'in conditions of secure liberty' and said that division was a threat to peace.

In 1960, Wehner called for 'greater elasticity and a common purpose' in foreign policy. It was necessary to prevent the further deterioration of the position of a divided Germany and Berlin. This, said Wehner, should be the duty of all parties. But, he added, unlike the Kaiser in 1914, who could see 'only Germans and no parties', Adenauer could see 'only parties, and no Germans'. The SPD's suggested that although Adenauer talked about unity, and the interests of the German people, he had done nothing to advance them.

What Brandt, Erler, Wehner and Brandt's most influential foreign policy aide Egon Bahr did was to change the terms of the unity debate. Since Adenauer's policy had plainly not borne fruit, they argued, what was required was an understanding with the East, based on the recognition of the borders that presented themselves. The realistic prize worth having, in Brandt's view, was peace in Europe, and thus peace in the world but not a reunited Germany.

Yet despite the powerful logic of the SPD's position, it still proved unable to generate sufficient electoral support to insist on leading the Bonn government. In the 1965 election, the SPD marginally improved its showing (it gained 3.1 per cent more), but the CDU also increased its vote (by 2.2 per cent). Although the SPD could show that in some *Länder* it was getting stronger (in the Saarland, in North Rhine-Westphalia and the Rhineland Palatinate), its vote was declining in Baden-Württemberg, Lower Saxony and Bremen. There was really only one way forward.

Figure 5. Kurt Georg Kiesinger. ©Presse- und Informationsamt der Bundesreglerung

The Coalition Card

This was to play the coalition card. The FDP's removal of support from Erhard gave the party brokers in the SPD the chance they had been waiting for. Negotiations began with the CDU/CSU. Christian Democrats saw two advantages in what was admittedly a radical step: a chance of ditching Erhard, and perhaps winning more votes with someone else, and an opportunity for a new foreign policy towards the East. In this way, it became possible for the SPD to join a new government, led by a Baden-Württemberger, Kurt Georg Kiesinger, who had been a member of the Nazi party, as Chancellor, gaining for Willy Brandt the post of Foreign Minister of the Federal Republic.

Brandt's main concern was clearly spelt out; but there was a general view that many domestic issues required fresh thinking. Chief amongst these was the restoration of economic health. There was also a widespread feeling that new life should be given to West German democracy and to promote reform (as Ralf Dahrendorf argued so brilliantly at the time). Kiesinger's government statement of December 1966 was, however, most noteworthy for its definition of *foreign* policy aims. It was this that formed the public break with Adenauer's line. The government now recognized Poland's wish to 'at last live in a national territory with secure frontiers'. It accepted that the 1938 Munich agreement could no longer be considered valid. Whilst it was Bonn's aim to gain greater independence in international affairs, it promised this process was to be conducted in concord with the West.

Domestic Issues

Some Social Democrats found it hard to accept that Kiesinger, who had been a Nazi, should have gained the Chancellorship thanks to the SPD. Brandt dismissed this objection. He argued that there was a fundamental symmetry in the prospect of an ex-Nazi cooperating with an anti-Nazi. In fact, there were SPD members of the Bundestag who were ready to 'tolerate' the CDU but not participate in a CDU government for this reason. But Wehner in particular insisted that the SPD now prove itself capable of government. Erler, on his death bed, urged that Wehner be supported. Brandt himself found Kiesinger 'not unpleasant' and described the government (at the November 1967 SPD conference) as 'neither a forced marriage nor a love match but an alliance of two equal partners'.

The SPD took eight cabinet posts and, in addition to Brandt's appointment as foreign minister, five others were given important jobs. Karl Schiller became economics minister, Herbert Wehner minister for all-German affairs, Georg Leber for communications, Gustav Heinemann for justice, and Carlo Schmid the minister for Bundesrat affairs. In its own terms, the Grand Coalition was a rather successful government. It brought stability back to West German political life. But in underwriting the reliability of the system it also damaged it, thanks to the absence of a real opposition. An understandable (if naïve) feeling on the left that the SPD had 'sold out' to the Centre Right, combined with an interest in Marxist and neo-Marxist political thought and a revulsion from US policy in Vietnam, produced a so-called 'extra-parliamentary opposition', and an increase in political unrest outside the Bundestag (rather than within it, where it ought to have been expressed).

Dissent and the Extra-Parliamentary Opposition

The emergence of the notion of 'extra-parliamentary opposition', was based on the proposition that if the Bundestag parties were not prepared to oppose, then opposition to the government would have to be taken out of parliament altogether. There were plainly some German dissidents who were not willing to be 'managed', and who had their own ideas on what West Germany should become. Some of them came from the Socialist (but not Social Democratic) Student organization, the SDS, formed in 1945. The late 1960s were, of course, in any case the time for students to be students, with their 'sit-ins', 'teach-ins' and even 'love-ins'. Partly, these were a not uncharming way of seeking to turn a political break with Adenauer's bourgeois Republic into a social and cultural one as well. During this period the number of students had doubled, but the number of professors, books or rooms had not. Student militancy flourished in circumstances such as these. The SDS became an increasing embarrassment to the SPD and some leading German academics of the left, like Wolfgang Abendroth, Jürgen Habermas, Ossip Flechtheim and Ludwig von Friedeburg, often criticized the Party, and not their students. West Berlin and Frankfurt (home of the Frankfurt School of political science) were particular hotbeds of student protest. In 1961 the SPD decided to disaffiliate the SDS. In June 1967 a student protesting against the visit of the Shah of Persia was shot dead by police in West Berlin. During the Easter of 1968 'Red' Rudi Dutschke, one of the major student leaders, was gravely wounded in an attempted neo-Nazi assassination attempt. The extra-parliamentary opposition, the APO, now began to discuss the use of violence as means of political change.

Brandt took a characteristically ambiguous line on these students which reflected his own humanity and his own early dissent. On the one hand, he was determined that the security of the Bonn republic should not be called into question by this unrest. 'I have seen one German republic come to grief,' he stated; 'we will not repeat that experience.' On the other hand, he admitted to being 'stirred' by youthful protest. The right of the SPD, led by Egon Franke and the conservative Annemarie Renger, but including Georg Leber, Richard Löwenthal (a Berlin professor), and Helmut Schmidt were all opposed to the students. Brandt accepted that the SPD faced internal dissent but it was far less, he claimed, than opposition within the British Labour and Conservative parties of this time.

The Grand Coalition at Work

Nevertheless the Grand Coalition could boast of some solid achievements. Kiesinger (known to his colleagues as King Silver Tongue) was surprisingly good at getting his team to work together. His work was made easier by the formation of a Cabinet management sub-group known as the *Kressbronner Kreis*, which brought together SPD and CDU leaders, including Wehner, Schmidt and Brandt himself for the SPD and Barzel, Strauss and Heck for the CDU. As far as the economy was concerned, the chief problems were inflation, 600,000 jobless and a budget deficit of almost DM 5 billion. Schiller, minister of economics, and something of a genius, worked extremely well with Franz Josef Strauss (the arch bogeyman of the SPD), who was the minister of finance. The government sought to manage the difficulties by stimulating investment, bringing together groups of experts to devise plausible economic plans and reforming the financial relationship between the *Bund* and the *Länder*.

Economic Reform

In May 1969 the Bundestag accepted the government's proposal to amend the constitution in order to redistribute money from the richer to the poorer *Länder*. This also gave the government the ability to direct funding in order to promote particular items of expenditure (for example new universities) that it liked. They managed to enact a stabilizing law which in fact gave them powers to interfere in the economy (something that Erhard would never have countenanced). Taxes were raised, and expenditure cut, so that the budget of January 1967 seemed balanced. In addition, meetings between the government, employers and trade unions were held in accordance with the policy of 'concerted action' (the phrase was Schiller's), a corporatist approach to policy making, well in line with West German thought.

Schiller was also keen on medium-term (four-year) financial planning, which was debated at a three-day cabinet meeting in July 1967. Its chief purpose was to cut spending. Yet there were slight differences in the aims of the coalition partners. The SPD wanted to increase domestic demand and thus stimulate employment, whereas the CDU/CSU wanted to increase exports. Subsidies to farmers and defence expenditure were to be curbed. Both of these proposals caused obvious problems. These measures were not unsuccessful. The economy began to surge forward again, with a growth rate of over 7 per cent and a fall in inflation to 1.5 per cent. Given the pull that economics (and prosperity) exerted on politics, Schiller had done good work for the government as well as West Germans.

Political Reforms

A number of other reform measures were passed, including a law regulating the financing of political parties that gave them federal cash in order to reduce the power of those who made donations to the parties. The coalition also dealt with the statute of limitations on murders and on what was considered manslaughter during the Third Reich, which made 1969 the cut-off date for prosecutions. The junior minister of justice, Horst Ehmke, sought to extend the limit. Kiesinger was less keen, even though the clock was ticking away. He wanted to distinguish between the 'little people' and 'big murderers' (as if there had been 'little' murders). The issue led to one of the most heated arguments in cabinet, with the CDU united in opposition to Ehmke's plans. But he was backed by the SPD, the CDU gave way, and the Bundestag passed a new limit of thirty years. In 1979, this limit was dropped by Schmidt's government and murders were no longer subject to limitation. Other legal reforms were enacted, particularly over family law (where illegitimate children were given rights, and divorce ceased to be regarded as a criminal offence). West German Communists came to see the justice minister Heinemann and asked for a repeal of the 1956 ban: he told them it was not possible, but gave them some free legal advice on how to get round it. Shortly afterwards the DKP (rather than the KPD) made an appearance. The thorny question of how government would function in a state of emergency began to be tackled (it was still the prerogative of the Allies, but needed to be transferred in some way to Bonn). Economic stringency also prompted the government to reduce the strength of the *Bundeswehr* by 60,000 men to 400,000. This aroused US fury, and Bonn quickly backtracked on the plan.

The government also considered changing the electoral law to give West Germany a first-past-the-post system. Kiesinger had demanded this in his government declaration, but the SPD was uncertain whether this would make it easier or harder for it to gain power. The SPD's rank and file did not like it, and the idea was finally killed off in April 1969 by Herbert Wehner. The FDP, of course, were delighted, and, once they joined Brandt's cabinet in that year, the whole thing was quietly forgotten (although the CDU continues to dream hopefully of it to this very day).

A New Foreign Policy

Yet the most enduring impact on German political development made by the Grand Coalition was in foreign policy. Brandt's *Ostpolitik* spans two phases: his period as West German Foreign Minister from 1966 until 1969 and his period as Chancellor from 1969 until 1974 (see Chapter 7).

There was general agreement within the government that the time had come to bury the 1955 Hallstein Doctrine and Bonn's insistence that it alone represented all Germans, whether citizens of the Federal Republic or of the GDR. Brandt started work as Foreign Minister of the Federal Republic on 6 December 1966.

He used four 'directional aids' in his policy making: the safeguarding of peace, the careful defining of West German interests, proving there was not continuity with the Nazi era and, finally, facing up to the consequences of a lost war. At his first NATO meeting in Paris he called for a step-by-step approach to better relations with eastern Europe, particularly with Poland and Czechoslovakia. Defence and *détente* went together. The basis for this was to be an agreement with the Soviet Union and a commitment not to alter the status quo in Europe. It has been claimed that this design was inspired by Egon Bahr (who in 1967 became head of the foreign policy planning staff).

On 31 January 1967 Bonn established diplomatic relations with Romania; meanwhile the GDR signed treaties of friendship with Poland, Czechoslovakia, Hungary and Bulgaria. On the radio on 2 July 1967 Brandt spoke of the need to make the lives of ordinary people more bearable as long as Germany was divided. In August 1967 trade talks were held with the Czechs. In February 1968 a permanent trade mission and diplomatic relations with Yugoslavia were restored. Egon Bahr had started to negotiate with the Soviets in the autumn of 1967, discussing, amongst other things, a declaration on the mutual renunciation of force. The Russians at first dismissed Bonn's aims as revanchist and aggressive. Brandt denied this; but always said (for example to the Soviet Foreign Minister Gromyko, in 1967) that the passage of time would not diminish the Federal Republic's 'peaceful desire' to 'dwell together with the East Germans as a nation in a political community'. Yet the West Germans agreed to supply the Russians with 1.2 million tons of steel tubes in return for DM 4 billion worth of Siberian gas. They also told him that they were ready to discuss a treaty to provide for the mutual renunciation of force. The Soviet intervention in Czechoslovakia put a halt to any progress for most of 1968, until in October Gromyko suggested at the UN that the talks might restart. Interestingly (and unwisely), however, in March 1968 the SPD began to have dealings with the Italian Communist Party, the PCI. Bahr met Enrico Berlinguer, the PCI leader, in Munich. These talks continued over some years: the Italian Communists counted as 'Euro-communists' and were deemed a useful bridge between Western Social Democrats and Eastern 'Socialists'.

Relations with the GDR

What the GDR wanted, as its price for *détente*, was clear: full recognition as a sovereign German state and recognition of the inter-zonal boundary as its state frontier to the West. In addition, it insisted on the abandonment of the Federal Republic's claim to sole representation of the Germans, the complete detachment of West Berlin from West Germany, and seats for both German states in the UN. Yet Ulbricht would not give up East Germany's claim for reunification (under Communist SED leadership) as he told an SED conference in April 1967. There was a basis for negotiation here, since Kiesinger had conceded on 13 December 1966 that agreement on the pursuit of unity was no longer the precondition for talks with the GDR. Brandt added in October 1968 that he was 'enough of a realist to know that the self-determinaton of the German people does not stand on the agenda of practical policies'.

Brandt sympathized with some aspects of the basic Soviet view of Germany: that the (West) Germans were obliged to accept responsibility for what had been done during the war, and that the Federal Republic had been obstructive by refusing to recognize the status quo in Europe. He knew, too, that they wished to change the status of West Berlin. In response, Brandt stated that they would consider the status quo issue, and insisted that he had no desire to incorporate West Berlin into the Federal Republic.

German and East European affairs were not the only object of Brandt's attention. He strongly supported Britain's entry into the European Community, but did nothing to prevent de Gaulle from issuing a second veto in 1968. Brandt recalled with amusement the request made by George Brown, the British foreign secretary, to admit

Britain: 'Willy, you must let us in so that we can take the lead.' At the same time, he repeated his commitment to NATO: 'NATO and a policy of detente are not mutually exclusive; the military deterrent has ensured the peace of Europe.' He understood, as a former governing mayor of West Berlin, the power over Germany that the Red Army's two million soldiers represented; massed in 140 divisions, 75 were based in central Europe and 20 in the GDR.

The Year of Two Elections

The year 1969 was the year of two elections: the Bundestag ones and the presidential ones. There were two candidates in the latter: Schröder, the candidate of the CDU/CSU and Heinemann, a Social Democrat. Heinemann was just able to win. The chief significance of this lay in the fact that Walter Scheel, the FDP leader, had urged his party to support Heinemann. In due course he told Brandt and the SPD leadership that he wished to construct a left-of-centre coalition with them (even though his party was divided on this issue), with 'progressives' in control in Baden-Württemberg, Hamburg and Bavaria, but 'conservatives' in Rhineland and Hessen who favoured the CDU/CSU. The 'conservative' leader, Erich Mende, had been forced to step down in September 1967, joining the CDU in 1970.

The federal election campaign of 1969 was an awkward one since it was difficult for the CDU/CSU and the SPD to attack each other. Brandt was presented as someone primarily concerned with domestic politics as the 'chancellor of internal reforms' and the development of democracy. Two weeks before the election Brandt let it be known that he did not foresee a continuation of the Grand Coalition after the election. The FDP, meanwhile, had generated a new set of leaders alongside Scheel, most notably Hans-Dietrich Genscher and Wolfgang Mischnick. This also marked the demise of the FDP's commitment to solid, old-style German nationalism and the emergence of a more flexible approach to the relationship with the GDR. This new line was strengthened when the FDP's grand old man, Thomas Dehler, expressed his support for this change which was welcomed not merely by bright younger figures like Ralf Dahrendorf, Hildegard Hamm-Brücher and Rudolf Augstein, editor of the *Spiegel*.

The outcome of the election was curious. The CDU/CSU remained the largest single party, suffering only a very small loss in support. It gained 46.1 per cent (compared with 47.6 per cent in 1965); the SPD did less well than the CDU/CSU but extremely well in terms of its own past performance, winning 42.7 per cent (as opposed to 39.3 per cent). But the FDP did badly, dropping from 9.5 per cent to 5.8 per cent. At first, Kiesinger thought that he might still remain Chancellor (Richard Nixon, clearly confused by the mechanics of the West German political system, had already congratulated him on his re-election) but Brandt announced the formation of an SPD/FDP government which would have a majority of only six seats in the Bundestag, declaring emotionally that with this result Hitler had 'finally lost the war'. It was the first SPD-led government in a German democratic state since 1929.

Chancellor Willy Brandt

On 21 October 1969 Brandt was elected Chancellor by only two votes. His cabinet contained several new faces, as well as many old ones. Walter Scheel, the FDP leader and a cheerful Rhinelander, became Foreign Minister. Karl Schiller kept the economics post. Helmut Schmidt, a cabinet minister for the first time, was given the defence portfolio (and became heir apparent); and Horst Ehmke, an increasingly assertive manager, became a minister for special duties, as Minister in Charge of the Chancellor's Office. Egon Bahr became State Secretary (a political civil servant) under him. The Ministry for All-German Affairs was renamed the Ministry for Inner German Relations, with Egon Franke as minister. In his government statement of 28 October 1969, Brandt declared that *Ostpolitik* would continue, but there would be no formal recognition of the GDR in international law. 'Although two German states exist', he declared, 'their relations with each other are special'. Perhaps somewhat disquietingly as far as older West Germans were concerned, he then exhorted all citizens to 'dare to be more democratic. We are not at the end of our democracy, but at its beginning.'

Brandt's Domestic Policies

This exhortation was intended to be seen as the key element in the new administration's platform. Indeed, Brandt maintained that his first concern was to be domestic reform. He had always claimed that it was untrue that he was less interested in domestic policy than in foreign affairs. 'I have always', he wrote later, 'devoted by far the greater part of my time to domestic political issues in the wider sense. This applied even in 1970 with its strong emphasis on foreign policy.' Yet even Brandt accepted that domestic policy did not 'always receive sufficient preparation' and that he himself had 'failed to evaluate new problems as quickly as practical politics required'. His government had also failed to make social and economic policy 'sufficiently intelligible' to the public. The fact was, however, that his real passion was foreign policy.

One of his advisers recalled how during cabinet discussion of domestic issues, Brandt would gaze out of the window, plainly miles away in Moscow or Washington.

At the same time, Brandt undertook a constitutionally legitimate purge of political civil servants who supported the CDU. These were the secretaries of state and the heads of divisions. The most important man to go was Carl Carstens (he later became President). From 1949 to 1963, 51 civil servants had been removed or transferred; from 1969 to 1973, the figure rose to 129 (from 1974 to 1981 the number declined to 50, but in 1982–3 alone, 48 were pushed out). His aim was, of course, to ensure that he could rely on a bureaucracy which sympathized with the SPD's (and the FDP's) policies. Given a system in which political allegiance was a factor, Brandt had no alternative but to act in this way. That it produced more efficient policy making than a neutral civil service might have generated seems doubtful.

Overall, however, both of Brandt's governments were a shambles, 1972–4 more obviously so, perhaps, than the 1969–72 one. They lasted as long as they did only because of Brandt's personal authority and charisma, and because the West German system was resilient, and could manage quite well as long as there was no obvious replacement government. Yet there was another side to Brandt's inability to lead his ministers. As his office minister wrote later, many of the reasons why Brandt came over as lacking personal control over domestic affairs were, paradoxically, sources of strength for him in foreign affairs. His hesitancy, an ability to wait a long time for the 'right' moment, a real dislike of conflict and of decision making, were all important qualities in a diplomat. He was well described as 'a fisherman, not a hunter, waiting for things to happen, and able to use small steps to reinforce larger goals'. The Chancellor's lack of interest in day-to-day domestic decision making was to prove to have fateful consequences. The most damaging was that the men Brandt charged with looking after this side of political affairs were given huge power thanks to the personal authority of their boss. They did not always use this well. Nowhere was this to be more devastating than in the appointment of Günter Guillaume, the Stasi mole, as a personal adviser. In the end, this appointment was to cast a dark shadow over Brandt's entire foreign policy record, and, indeed, his role as Chancellor of the Federal Republic.

Brandt and the USA

It was Nixon's hope that one of the first fruits of *détente* might be the return home of US troops. The reduction of 60,000 men after 1968 (there were now 300,000) had, in fact, caused NATO's European members disquiet. In May 1972, however, Nixon signed the first SALT agreement with the Russians and this was taken by Bonn as proof that *détente* was working. Brandt visited Nixon again in May 1973, although the Watergate affair was already looming. Brandt remained keen to have good relations with the US despite the Vietnam War (a subject which Brandt unconvincingly said he could not understand), and wanted to keep it this way since 'enlightenment would have brought me into conflict with US policy'. Furthermore, and arguably more significantly, the Berlin agreement had been made a precondition by the United States of its acceptance of a Soviet idea for a standing European security conference.

Brandt was particularly interested in developing a personal relationship with the Soviet leader Brezhnev. He visited him in 1970, in 1971 (in Oreanda on the Black Sea) and again in 1975 (when he was told, on the whole implausibly, that the Soviet Union had not known of the spy Guillaume's existence). Yet Brandt was repeatedly pressurized by the Soviets. Brandt claimed (perhaps for his own purposes) that Brezhnev repeatedly tried to get him to agree to full, and final, legal recognition of the GDR. Brandt said he resisted this, but always believed that Brezhnev was quite genuine in his desire to reduce armed forces in central Europe. Brezhnev also encouraged Brandt to believe that political cooperation between Social Democrats and Communists should be undertaken. This was something that Brandt was himself interested in, and he agreed.

'Daring More Democracy'

Brandt's cabinet soon put forward a variety of social measures, such as the increase of widows' pensions and insurance benefits. The notion of industrial co-determination (giving workers a legal right to influence management decisions) was strengthened by a November 1971 law which seemed to underpin the extent to which Social Democracy was now in the saddle. In fact, co-determination had been part of West German industrial life for twenty-five years. Crude market capitalism had always been tempered by a 'social' input which Christian Democrats, particularly on the left of centre, had no difficulty in supporting. The voting age was lowered to 18 (adding over two million voters) and a reform of the education system was promised. Displaying his bright rhetorical skill in allusion to the old Prussian tradition of relying on military training to make Germans German, Brandt said 'The school of the nation is now the school.' There were also reforms of marriage law, including the abolition of the concept of culpability in divorce cases. There were also measures for the environment, first mooted by Brandt in the 1961 elections.

Brandt was obliged to face up to an uncertain economic situation. His reforms were expensive. The educational budget more than doubled from 1969 to 1972; the welfare budget went up from DM 16.9 billion to 21.6, defence from 18.8 to 24.5. This caused early conflicts within the cabinet, demonstrating again that Brandt was not good at keeping his team together and that had the dynamo of his government been domestic rather than foreign policy, he would have fallen very quickly. In November 1970, Genscher, Schmidt and Schiller all discussed the likely effect of a joint resignation and in May 1971 Alex Möller resigned. Brandt let him go. Although there was full employment (two million guest workers were also gainfully employed), prices and wage demands were rising fast.

West Germany's GNP increased by 6 per cent per annum, but there was a 4 per cent increase in the cost of living. Ever since 1952 West Germany had amassed a huge surplus on its foreign trade and many economists argued that the Deutschmark was undervalued. This issue became a theme of the 1969 election, and on a suspicion that the mark would be revalued, half a billion marks were bought by foreign speculators. On winning the election, the SPD first allowed the DM to float and then revalued it by almost 10 per cent in May 1971. In October 1969 the Deutschmark was revalued up by 6.5 per cent and then by a further 8.5 per cent.

In 1972 it emerged that the budget deficit would be twice the expected figure and that inflation would hit almost 6 per cent. On 2 July, Karl Schiller resigned as Minister of Economics and Finances: his colleagues had wanted controls on the large amounts of foreign money pouring into West Germany, whereas Schiller wanted all EEC currencies to join in a free float. Klasen, the head of the Bundesbank, Schmidt, and the head of the economic department in the Chancellor's office, Pöhl, (later a key actor in the unification process) were opposed. Beneath the debates on economic theory, there lay stark personal rivalry between Schiller and Brandt. Schiller was replaced by Helmut Schmidt (at the end of August Schiller announced that he would leave the SPD). For a while he teamed up with Erhard, but later left the CDU to rejoin the SPD.

The 1972 Election

In view of the positive public mood, Brandt and his team decided to dissolve the Bundestag early and call new elections for 19 November (the legal basis for this was provided by a staged passing of a no-confidence vote). The SPD, a trifle oddly, portrayed Brandt as Adenauer's heir: a great German Chancellor and patriot whose foreign policy successes had completed the process by which a new West German state had been established. An additional fillip to the campaign was provided by an agreement in the talks with the GDR reached on 6 November 1972. Turnout was extremely high – 91 per cent. The SPD, for the first time in the Bonn era, became the largest party. Brandt was told by one of friends that 'his exile was now over'. The FDP did well, too, gaining 2.6 per cent. The change of power from Centre Right to Centre Left now seemed complete.

Brandt's Second Administration

The government that had possessed a majority of only twelve in 1969 could now count on one of forty-eight. Brandt's approach to German politics had inspired new voters, but also women, Catholic workers and farmers. It seemed like the beginning of a whole new era in West German political life; but the hard truth was that Brandt had run out of steam and the 1973 oil crisis meant that any thoughts of ambitious reforms (and increased public spending) had to be shelved. Un-employment began to grow and carried on growing; by 1974, 500,000 West Germans were on the dole.

It was more than a little ironic that the federal election of 1972, one of the very few 'national' elections to have generated a real bandwagon effect, huge popular enthusiasm for the SPD leader, and, apparently, for the democratic process itself, produced such a dull and uninspiring Government. Perceptive observers understood that the hopes of the electors were largely misplaced. The Bonn system was not one to promote domestic political change. Foreign policy was a different matter, but here the results were, however important, either finite (an improvement in relations with Eastern Europe and in the living conditions of East Germans) or vague and hazy (the hope that the Communist leopard might lose its spots). The German voters had been invited to legitimate *Ostpolitik* and had done so. The dullness of Brandt's second Government underlined the extent to which the SPD's room for manoeuvre was so constrained as to make the very idea of Social Democracy politically redundant. Electors were happy to reward the SPD, if it could prove it was a more efficient manager of domestic or foreign affairs than the CDU/CSU. This was understood by Helmut Schmidt, the heir apparent, and some colleagues. Others in the Party, however, continued to dream idly of developing *Social Democratic* policies, imagining that distinctiveness might produce electoral success. Beneath the particular instance of Brandt's domestic political decline, it was plain that a far deeper structural crisis of the Left was developing. It involved both questions concerning the values of Social Democracy, and the possibilities for change in any Western, interdependent and market-oriented economy, and not just the Federal Republic.

Brandt himself accepted that something was going very wrong. At first, he defined the problem in personal terms. His old difficulty, of dreaming rather than acting, was to blame. He later admitted that his government had lacked 'vigour' and that he had made unwise appointments to his circle.

Brandt had in fact been left totally exhausted by the campaign. As before, he began to smoke and drink too much. A growth appeared on his vocal cords and he was whisked into hospital (and an ever deeper depression). Meanwhile, the bickering amongst his colleagues turned sour. The FDP demanded the finance ministry, but Schmidt wanted this for himself; in the end the FDP had to yield. Rüdiger von Wechmar, another Free Democrat, became government spokesman in Ahlers's place. The FDP was much strengthened by all of this. On recovering, Brandt raged against both the left and the right in the party; particularly the former, who had established a grouping to oppose the right-wingers who were known as the 'Kanal' or 'trench workers'.

Economic Problems

The economic situation deteriorated gravely. During the autumn of 1973 the oil crisis began to bite. Inflation increased as did unemployment. There were wildcat strikes and a threatened strike in the civil aviation sector. The public services union was demanding a wage increase of 15 per cent (and, after a short strike, got 11 per cent). The inflation rate was 7.2 per cent for the first quarter of 1972 and a 9 per cent rate was considered possible for the year. Brandt seemed even less in control. Over and above personal problems, however, there was a genuine feeling that despite his huge popularity, Brandt had run out of steam. His *Ostpolitik* had, to all intents and purposes, been completed. The next step, possibly full legal recognition of the GDR by West Germany as an independent German nation, was still politically unacceptable. Brandt, whose eye had never been properly on the domestic ball, now took it off altogether. Under these conditions, the government began to unravel.

Schmidt got Brandt's agreement for a statement marking him out as the next Chancellor under the watchword 'Schmidt, first in the SPD team behind Brandt'. Wehner, becoming ever more eccentric, was furious that he had not been consulted about this and intrigued endlessly. Meanwhile, in the CDU, Barzel was relieved of his position and Kohl became party chairman. He appointed the dynamic and highly intelligent Kurt Biedenkopf as general secretary of the CDU. It was quickly reformed into a modern and well-organized members' party.

The Problem of Urban Terrorism: The Baader-Meinhof Gang

Student riots were one, relatively mild, expression of the inability of the Bonn system to promote and sustain deviation from the bourgeois norms laid down by Adenauer. We should not forget that the 1960s and 1970s were genuinely different from later periods, when young and not-so-young citizens became much more content with the ideas of consensus and political management. Today, it would appear that majorities can be won for the view that politics should not be the agent of change but a reaction to it. During Brandt's Chancellorship, however, an increasing number of younger Germans sincerely believed the SPD when it promised political change. Its failure to deliver disenchanted many of them. A few of them, however, went way beyond disenchantment and decided, instead, to become terrorists. Even though the full force of urban terrorism was only felt after 1970 – when West Germany once again had an opposition, albeit a Christian Democratic one – the SPD's participation in the Grand Coalition and its subsequent lack of energy fired a highly dangerous situation.

The emergence of the Baader-Meinhof Gang (sometimes, more favourably, referred to as 'Group') in the early 1970s posed the darkest and most chilling challenge to the legitimacy of the Federal Republic to date. It was precisely because the CDU/CSU and SPD leadership were so convinced that they had brilliantly managed matters for the German voter, so pleased with their own record, that they were totally knocked off balance by the rhetorically gifted band of young political criminals, led by Andreas Baader and Ulrike Meinhof. They were not only different from the previous right-wing and left-wing party challengers, but content to use murder and violence quite blatantly in order to terrify and coerce the legitimate government in Bonn. In the period from 1970 to 1977, the gang's heyday, forty-seven people were killed, of whom seventeen were terrorists, and the rest innocent victims. Given the huge wish for internal peace, prosperity and consensus that existed in West Germany, the possibility of political murder was horrifying.

The gang had, in fact, three and not two main leaders. The third leader was Gudrun Ensslin. Ulrike Meinhof was the 'brains' behind the terrorism. A respected journalist, her first major breakthrough had been a published attack on Franz Josef Strauss in 1961, in which she had compared him to Hitler. He sued her, but she was successfully defended by Gustav Heinemann (later Federal President). Her ideas were not, in fact, original. In almost everything she wrote, she used her journalist's eye for a good news story in order to vent her underlying hostility towards all the untouchable icons of the Federal Republic: the United States of America, Israel, NATO's arsenal of nuclear weapons and consumerism (although this last did not preclude either her or her colleagues from stealing, wherever possible, smart BMWs, quickly renamed 'Baader Meinhof Wagen').

In 1971 she published a manifesto entitled 'The Urban Guerrilla Concept', remarkable chiefly for coining the term 'the Red Army Faction'. (Faction, perhaps, was intended as a reference to 'Fraktion', the word for parliamentary party, drawing attention to the apparent fact that the parties by coalescing were not opposing each other.) Meinhof claimed that the rather pathetic police measures taken against the gang at that time were simply an attempt to destroy socialism in West Germany.

The Munich Olympic Games of 1972 were the scene of an appalling act of terrorism against the Israeli Olympic team, which showed the Bavarian police in an extremely poor light. The West Germans, led by their government, were almost mesmerized by horror: none of these developments fitted into the West German picture of itself. Meinhof quickly published an outrageous polemic on the affair entitled 'The action of Black September in Munich: towards a strategy for the anti-imperialist struggle' (the use of the word 'action' appeared to refer to one of the Nazi words for mass killings of Jews; Black September was the name of the Arab terrorist organization involved). She suggested that the 'German Left' should adopt what she termed Arab tactics of machine-gunning and not waste time with debate.

Her sexy boyfriend, Baader, was less gifted in writing about theory, but did manage a letter to the tabloid *Bild Zeitung* early in 1972 in which he wrote 'We are here to organize armed resistance to the existing property-based order . . . the struggle has only just begun.' In the end, Meinhof appeared to lose faith in the monster she had helped to create, shortly before killing herself whilst in custody. It was Baader and Ensslin (the Lenin and Trotsky to Meinhof's Marx) who provided the violent action which was intended to confirm the correctness of her theories. All of them had abandoned the idea of a 'long march through the institutions', going instead for total violence. Their aim was most probably simply to get the Government to over-react, and thus 'prove' the Federal Republic was a repressive police state, which sought to destroy political freedom.

The 'Berufsverbot'

On 27 January 1972, under the leadership of Genscher, the Interior Minister, the minister presidents of the *Länder* passed an ordinance, known as the *Berufsverbot* (or 'employment ban') in an attempt to prevent a 'long march through the institutions' by radicals less violent than the Baader-Meinhof Gang from taking place. From 1972 to 1976, 500,000 applicants for state posts were examined for their loyalty to the Constitution. Less than 450 were rejected. Whilst it was assumed by all concerned, quite wrongly – as the history of the Green Party proved – that dissidents would never be able to form a political party, the various governments believed there was a real danger of subversion. By entering the professions and the civil service in particular, it was thought terrorists might gain a foothold in the German state.

The measure which demanded a loyalty oath from public servants (who in West Germany included those like postal workers and railway clerks) was deeply resented, particularly by the new cohort of university graduates, who were keen to mark their divergence from what they regarded as old, Adenauerian authoritarianism. Yet it was one thing to oppose the state, but quite another to expect the state to pay those who opposed it pensions and other benefits.

In June 1972 Baader and Meinhof were arrested, but the violence increased. It was soon understood that this now had to become a federal matter since the circumstances had become exceptional. In February 1975 Peter Lorenz, chairman of the West Berlin CDU, was kidnapped. Demonstrating the sort of weakness that was by now expected (and hardly the repression the terrorists claimed), the German government began to negotiate with them. This grave act of folly simply encouraged further outrages.

By 1977 the West German Federal Criminal Agency had a terrorist index with 4.7 million names of suspects and sympathizers, 3,100 different subversive groupings, 2.1 million fingerprints and 1.9 million photos. At one time or another, 6,047 people had been under surveillance.

Baader, Ensslin and Raspe were finally arrested and given life sentences in 1977. Their chief defence counsel was Otto Schily, who was subsequently to become a leader of the new Green Party. In revenge for their conviction, the chief federal prosecutor Siegfried Buback was murdered. In July, the chairman of the Dresdener Bank, Jürgen Ponto, was shot dead, and Hanns Martin Schleyer, President of the Confederation of German Industry was kidnapped. In October, a Lufthansa jet, the *Landshut*, was hijacked and its passengers were taken hostage in the desert airport of Mogadishu in order to secure the release of German and Arab terrorists.

Mogadishu

Although no West German wanted to admit it, a turning point had been reached. Schmidt's government now had only two choices: to continue to try to negotiate the terrorists out of their terrorism, or to strike back, and risk both more revenge attacks, and the inevitable claim that the terrorists' charge of repressiveness was justified. It was a desperately dark moment for the Federal Republic, one which demonstrated how difficult it was to manage those who did not wish to be managed, within the framework of a political system which genuinely sought compromise and consensus. In one sense, the Government's behaviour hitherto had been not unenlightened. Yet it also reminded some observers of the fatal Weimar policy of employing legal means (and sometimes police measures) to try to contain extremism. Above all, however, the reluctance to confront the terrorists head on made re-invented German democracy look weak. The fact was that a new German political system had been created; it was flawed because opposition had been made very difficult, but it was better than earlier systems. If the price that had to be paid to maintain it was firmness, then this could be the only response.

Schmidt decided to fight back and resist the blackmail demands. The special forces known as GSG 9, aided by the British SAS, stormed the *Landshut* and freed the hostages on 18 October. During that night, the chief terrorists (gaoled at Stammheim maximum security prison in Stuttgart) met their deaths. The official version was that they had committed suicide, although it was not easy to see how they had managed to get access to weapons. Others claimed they had, in reality, been shot as a reprisal for holding the jet and its passengers. It was even rumoured that a small quantity of sand had been found next to the corpses, the suggestion being that GSG 9 troops had flown back from Africa and done the shooting themselves, leaving a souvenir of Mogadishu at the same time.

According to a well-respected journalist, Stefan Aust, the evidence was equivocal. Baader had been shot in the neck, but at an angle he himself would have found it virtually impossible to achieve. On balance, however, it was concluded that suicides had been carried out all round. Yet no political leader in German public life came out of this nightmare with credit. Both Brandt and Schmidt had wavered and wobbled for far too long. One of the few heroes was Horst Herold, a counter-intelligence chief who had painstakingly worked to destroy the gang.

What had produced this extraordinary blemish on the face of the Bonn Republic? Herold himself was not sure whether it had been the product of 'a sick brain or sick social situations'. Certainly, police believed that far more members of West Germany's young political class had sympathized with the aims of the gang, if not its methods, than they were prepared to admit in public. In addition, one must ignore the assistance given to the gang by the East Germans and the Stasi (who at various times hid leading members from West German justice), and the Palestinians, who saw in Baader and Meinhof soul brothers, and gave them a convincing training in secret desert camps.

The counter-attack at Mogadishu confirmed the course of Bonn's political development would endure. It showed that this was certainly capable of giving birth to violent extremists. Even if the system was liberal and fair, and even if what the radicals wanted at first was not inherently evil, the system itself could not afford to tolerate them, still less their violence. We should not forget that the gang's arrival in German public life had coincided with the wider clash caused by the modern ideas of the 1960s. The ethic of personal improvement through hard work had yielded to the idea of personal exploration through drugs and sex. Brandt's government permitted the open sale of pornography in the interests of liberalism; Meinhof's own magazine, *Konkret*, juxtaposed pictures of naked men and women and demands for revolution. Certainly, in Baader's case, the sexual revolution had gone hand in hand with the political one. But this was a peculiarly German dimension. In Palestine in 1970 he and his comrades had sunbathed in the nude, upsetting the fedayeen who were their military instructors. In seeking to allay their disquiet, Baader tried to explain to them that 'anti-imperialism and sexual emancipation go hand in hand. Fucking and shooting are the same thing.' Baader had got it wrong, of course, but the terrorism of these years was not insignificant. If their message was that the Western re-invention of Germany required the lid to be kept on violent and extremist dissidence, and if in doing so, the state was obliged to act illiberally (in the widest theoretical sense), then there was simply no alternative for the state to pursue. The implications had to be faced up to. It was certainly unfortunate that the Grand Coalition made parliamentary opposition seem worthless (although the FDP had, in fact, been an opposition of sorts). In reality, old-style opposition had indeed been made redundant, and this would have been obvious in any case, sooner or later. Yet *peaceful* dissidence was perfectly possible; it was just not very effective. If this was what West Germany had become, then this was indeed its nature. The fear of dissidence, an endemic fear in the system, had, in this instance, been allowed to help create the very monster the system was meant to exclude. There were real signals of danger here, not just to do with the past, but with what might happen in the future.

The Emergence of the Greens

In 1972 a Federal Association of Citizen's Initiatives was formed, chiefly concerned with support for ecological policies and opposition to the growth in nuclear power. By 1977 it had about 300,000 members in more than a thousand organizations. In December 1977 a Green Party was formed in Lower Saxony and the following June it gained almost 4 per cent of the vote. In Bremen in 1979 it scored 5.1 per cent, and thus entered the assembly. By 1983 six out of the eleven *Land* parliaments contained Green deputies.

Many politicians and many political observers tended to sneer at the Greens and minimize, or discount, their concern for the environment. The truth, however, was that they had in many ways bravely thought through the consequences of mass industrialization and its impact on the planet Earth. They were the first mass movement to appreciate the immense and deadly damage that was being done to the environment. It was a mark of their success not simply that they survived in West German political life (lending the lie to the view that the system squeezed out small parties), but that, thanks to the old pressure for consensuality, both the Christian Democrats and the Social Democrats could soon be seen busily stealing many of their environmental ideas.

Ostpolitik

West Germany Settled in the West

By the time he left office, Adenauer had virtually completed the process of reinventing a German nation in the west, achieved in large part by locking the Federal Republic into the Western system of politics and alliances. By closing his mind to the possibility of any political settlement with the Soviet Union and East Germany, he had, however, left open the possibility of a revision of Europe's borders. Whilst Adenauer may have wished for a single German state that exhibited all the features of the Federal Republic, he disdained the idea of a single state that might be neutral and unWestern. This was, to his way of thinking, the only realistic political alternative to two Germanies.

This apparent refusal to come to terms with the effects of the Second World War on eastern Europe allowed him to be portrayed as a revisionist (and even a revanchist). It also made Europe and the world more dangerous places, since it was always possible that, one day, a German might attempt to use armed force to alter the status quo of the two German states. This was the very reason why, contrary to the general supposition that the superpower America always supported Adenauer's Cold War stance, by 1960 it had come to oppose it, and sought *détente* with the Soviet Union. The Americans genuinely wanted to reduce the chances of a nuclear holocaust by reaching agreements with the Soviet Union. The Soviets, too, had no desire to see the world blown apart; in addition, their growing fear of a future conflict with Chinese Communism made them receptive to *détente* in Europe.

It was against the needs of the superpowers that Brandt's stewardship of West German affairs needs to be seen. What Willy Brandt did, we may think, was to provide such a settlement for West Germany. Indeed, his name will always be indelibly associated with *Ostpolitik*, the policy of building a relationship with the Communist states of eastern and central Europe, in particular with the Soviet Union and the GDR. The purpose of that policy *in respect of German unity* is, however, unclear. So that we may be able to illuminate this most vital of issues, which will

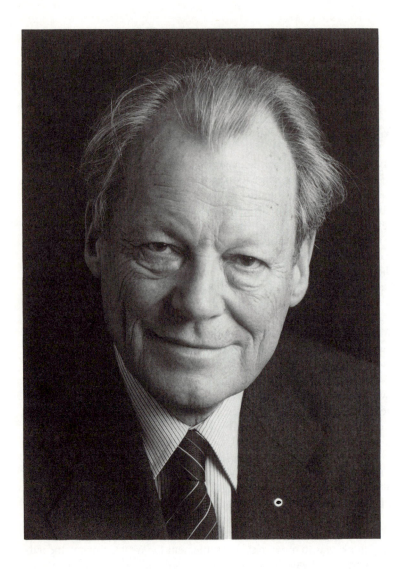

Figure 6. Willy Brandt. ©Presse- und Informationsamt der Bundesregierung

determine the precise meaning of Brandt's policies and their place in German history, we need to examine the policies themselves. We can then interpret *Ostpolitik* in the light of what we know about it today, as well as what was said about it at the time, subsequently paying particular attention to its place in the domestic politics of the Federal Republic and, finally, to the disquieting part played by East German subversion in its construction and execution.

Ostpolitik and German Unity

How we interpret *Ostpolitik* today has been complicated by German unity in 1990. Before unity, *Ostpolitik* was valued both inside and outside the Federal Republic essentially for stabilizing the status quo in Europe. The events of 1989/90, however, showed that the eastern part of Europe had been anything but stabilized. What this means is that any conclusions we may reach today about the real purpose and outcome of *Ostpolitik* must hang on whether we believe it hindered or helped the maintenance of stability in Europe, and thus whether it actually contributed anything at all to German unity. The unrest in eastern Europe was not the result of Germany's division, of course, but of a growing wish on the part of the ordinary people of eastern Europe to escape Soviet domination. The division of Germany, however, was also a consequence of Soviet mastery over eastern Europe.

Without the undermining of the Soviet position, unity was not thinkable. If, therefore, *Ostpolitik* stabilized the situation in Europe, it cannot be said to have furthered German unity; indeed, it may have postponed it. On the other hand, if *Ostpolitik* made German unity seem less threatening, by making it impossible to regard the Federal Republic as the *dominatrix* of Europe, then paradoxically it may have promoted unity, by encouraging the Soviets to believe they would not be harmed by it. Whilst we may be sure that academics, and others, will continue to debate this matter for many years to come, it is clear that evaluations of *Ostpolitik* made before 1989/90 will be different from those made subsequently.

If we argue that the aims of Brandt's *Ostpolitik* were ultimately to unify Germany, it becomes obvious at once that it was in essence a *destabilizing* policy, since it sought to undermine the post-1945 division of Europe, the acceptance of which had become the basis on which European affairs had been conducted since the end of the Second World War. If, on the other hand (as we shall suggest here) its purpose was to offer recognition of the hard and unpleasant truth that Germany had been divided into two separate states, then *Ostpolitik* was indeed a *stabilizing* policy. In this case, it provided the final act in the building of the West German nation. It *confirmed* the map of Europe drafted in 1945, and thus settled the position of the Federal Republic in relation to central and eastern Europe and to the Soviet Union (those states who had most to fear from a restless West Germany).

Moscow and Warsaw

Brandt's assumption of the Chancellorship led to an immediate improvement in relations with the Soviet Union. In 1969 it proved possible to arrange a September meeting with Gromyko at the UN, where Brandt assured him that the Soviet plan for a conference on security and cooperation (first put on the agenda by the USSR in 1954) had West German support and should be actively pursued. On 7 August 1970 (whilst Brandt was in Norway), Scheel returned from Moscow to say that Brandt would soon be invited to the Soviet Union in order to talk to Brezhnev about Berlin. In November, Brandt offered to begin negotiations with Poland; the Poles agreed in December, and the first round of talks was held in Warsaw in February 1970. West German Churches had already engaged in a dialogue with their Polish counterparts. Apart from the moral aspects of relations with Poland and the fact that West Germany had not accepted the cession of the lands east of the Oder-Neisse line (some 25 per cent of Germany as it was in 1935), there were some 60,000–100,000 ethnic Germans in Poland, of whom almost 30,000 were keen to come to West Germany. Dealings with Poland, therefore, demanded the most sensitive treatment, and were intended by the Bonn Government to set the tone on subsequent negotiations with Communist states.

Initially, the Poles demanded the recognition of all existing borders. At first, possibly for tactical reasons, Brandt refused, basing his 'reservations partly on respect for the feelings of the expellees'. In fact, it was plain to the West Germans that any deal with the Soviet Union was bound to involve the recognition of existing borders, not least the Oder-Neisse one. The Poles, presumably, realized this. In any case, after Brandt's speech in Nuremberg, where he offered recognition of the GDR, pending the signing of a peace treaty with Germany, the Poles dropped the demand for the full recognition of the GDR and insisted only on the recognition of the Oder-Neisse line. The negotiations were, however, difficult. On 6 December 1970 Brandt himself went to Warsaw. On 7 December the treaty was signed.

It was during his trip that Brandt visited the monument to the 1943 Jewish Warsaw Ghetto uprising and spontaneously knelt in front of it. It proved one of the most remarkable moments of recognition in West German history: a Federal Chancellor kneeling at a monument to the inhumanity of a previous German regime. Bizarrely, there were still some in West Germany who expressed outrage at his behaviour. Axel Springer, the influential publisher of *Bild* and *Die Welt*, claimed that Brandt had betrayed the 'rights of refugees' by this action. Those with greater sensitivity and perception took the line that 'the man who had no need to kneel, did so on behalf of all those who ought to kneel but don't'.

Relations with the German Democratic Republic

Relations with the GDR were, however, perhaps more awkward to deal with than any others. It demanded full recognition as a sovereign German state, together with an acceptance that the inter-zonal boundary between the two Germanies would be the GDR's state frontier to the west. In addition, it insisted on the abandonment of the West German claim to sole representation at international level, the complete detachment of West Berlin from West Germany, and seats for both German states in the UN. It should be noted that the GDR had consistently pressed for German unity (under Communist leadership, of course) before *Ostpolitik* got underway. *Ostpolitik* was, curiously but also immediately, taken by the East Germans, at any rate, as a sign the West Germans would drop *their* demand for unity. The revised GDR constitution of 1968 (which still carried a commitment to unity) had, it is true, defined the GDR as a 'Socialist state of the German nation'. The 1975 constitution, however, dropped the claim for unity altogether.

As early as December 1969, Brandt's officials produced for him a draft treaty with the GDR. Its object was to 'preserve national unity by deconstricting the relationship between the two parts of Germany'. Neither West Germany nor the GDR were to be 'foreign' to each other, and their relations would always be 'special'. Brandt wrote later that this meant that there could never be any question of the legal recognition of the GDR, even though Bonn had been forced to 'acknowledge the two state reality'. As we shall see later on, the legalistic (but not legal) distinction that Brandt sought to draw between the acceptance of reality (that there were two German states) and formal recognition (that each state should accept the statehood of the other) was more than a little tricky to sustain. States were either recognized or they were not.

Negotiations were pursued through the Soviet Union, and Egon Bahr was given this task. His talks with Gromyko were 'the key to the complex of what came to be known as the Eastern Treaties'. What was agreed by Bonn amounted to three concessions: renunciation of nuclear weapons, agreement to the Conference on European Security and

Cooperation, the CESC, (which Moscow saw as setting the seal on the division of Europe), and economic assistance. On 14 January 1970 Brandt issued a 'Report on the State of the Nation' (the title was significant) and said 'Patriotism must be based on what is attainable. Liberty must be maintained in those parts of Germany where it was already enjoyed and human rights should be nurtured for all Germans.' This was a call to realism, and seen by all observant West Germans as such. They were being asked to accept that there were two German states in existence, even if both of them were populated by Germans who spoke the same language and shared the same historical and cultural heritage. After all, Austrians (even the German Swiss) spoke German and looked to German cultural achievements as their own.

Erfurt and Kassel

Almost immediately (on 11 February 1970), the GDR signified its interest in discussing Brandt's ideas. Willi Stoph invited Brandt to meet him on 12 March in Erfurt in the GDR (in some senses the spiritual home of the pre-Communist, united SPD, since it was at Erfurt in 1891 that the SPD's great manifesto had been sanctioned). It was to be the first official visit by a West German Chancellor to East Germany. Brandt offered a return invitation to Kassel (near the zonal border). Brandt's negotiating position was that one should attempt to distinguish between some kind of limited recognition of the GDR, and the complete and formal recognition of East Germany as an entirely separate German state. The advantage of this would be that West (and perhaps East) German public opinion would not believe the aim of unity had been forgotten, whilst at the same time there could be a new and more realistic relationship between the two German states. Brandt's bottom line, however, was almost certainly a readiness to provide *de facto* but formal recognition of East Germany's statehood, tempered by a statement of intent about the desirability of eventual German unity. Brandt insisted that neither of the formal concepts of legal recognition and non-interference in another country's internal affairs could apply to relations between the GDR and West Germany. But he also agreed that their dealings with each other should be conducted on the basis of 'inter-German' rather than 'internal German' relations, and that the GDR could have an international standing that would not be inferior to that enjoyed by the Federal Republic.

At their Erfurt meeting, Stoph claimed that for twenty years the GDR's peace initiatives had been scorned by Bonn, whose aim was 'restoration and revenge'. He repeated the GDR's standard call for full and normal diplomatic relations and the recognition of all existing borders in Europe. Brandt's somewhat unclear response was that it had been the War that had divided Germany. This could not be unmade, even if its effects could be modified. He said that it was important that nothing should be done by either man to 'make it impossible for the German people to decide in free self-determination how they will live together'. He enunciated six principles that he said should govern inter-German relations: first, that both states must preserve the unity of the German nation. They were not to be foreign to each other. Second, the principles of international law must be upheld. Third, force should not be used to change the structure of either German state; fourth, there should be neighbourly cooperation between them; fifth, four-power rights were to be respected; and sixth, efforts should be made to improve the situation in Berlin.

On 20 March, Brandt reported on the meeting to the Bundestag, concluding that it had been 'right, necessary and worthwhile', even though Stoph had recently declared in East Berlin that West Germany wanted to absorb the GDR. In the wilderness of mirrors that depicted the East-West relationship, it was actually rather helpful to Brandt to be portrayed as a crypto-imperialist, since it made him seem, in West German eyes, tougher on the East Germans than he was. The new CDU/CSU leader Rainer Barzel challenged Brandt by demanding to know whether Brandt was proposing to recognize the Oder-Neisse line, whether he was going to offer some sort of recognition to the GDR and whether and when the two states would join the UN.

The second meeting between Brandt and Stoph took place in Kassel on 21 May amidst hostile demonstrations. Right-wingers chanted the slogan 'Volksverräter Hand in Hand: Willi Stoph und Willy Brandt' ('Traitors to the German people, hand in hand: Stoph and Brandt'). Brandt outlined the principles which he wished to see govern future relations, which now included the improvement of travel, ways of reuniting families as well as seeking membership of the UN by both Germanies, and the abrogation of the principle of sole representation. And the December 1971 transit agreement and the Basic Treaty of December 1972 did underwrite these principles. Yet he insisted that the two German states together would continue to constitute the German nation (which, as we shall see, meant something cultural rather than political). Brandt had, in short, conceded a great deal: the rhetorical, even romantic, attachment to the idea of the nation was retained, but to all intents and purposes Brandt accepted the existence of two sovereign Germanies.

Stoph, however, was strangely even less flexible in Kassel than he had been in Erfurt. He rejected Bonn's principles and accused Brandt's government of revanchism. He continued to demand full legal recognition and full sovereignty. Brandt answered that the issue of legal recognition could be dealt with subsequently. Brandt's readiness to make concessions to this unpleasant Communist was every bit as striking as Stoph's truculent posturing. Yet since Brandt had apparently already given most of what the GDR wanted, his attitude was certainly curious. It is possible that the Communists did not want to give him a deal at once, since that might increase his already substantial popularity in East Germany. Many East Germans regarded him, quite accurately, as someone who would speak up for their human rights. Another explanation, however, was that Stoph knew from a variety of sources how badly Brandt wanted a deal and that he could, with impunity, raise the stakes to assert the power of the GDR. As we explore below, this explanation may be the more plausible of the two, not least because, on the whole, East German public opinion was not a factor the East German Communists believed they needed to pay much attention to (so that Brandt's popularity, though unhelpful, was hardly damaging).

The Soviets and Berlin

In February 1970 Gromyko raised the Berlin issue in conversation with Bahr and pointed out that Bonn plan to make a link between West German ratification of the Moscow treaty (or the Polish treaty) and the Four Power Agreement on Berlin was unacceptable to the Soviets. This was certainly just a negotiating position, because the Soviets in the event agreed to precisely this. It was, however, almost exactly another year before negotiations with the Soviets started properly, with the three Western ambassadors successfully negotiating the Berlin deal (a deal that regulated the Berlin problem rather than solved it). The USSR agreed that West Germany could represent West Berlin internationally and gave West Berliners very important rights of entry into East Germany and East Berlin. West German government offices were also recognized by the Soviets. In return, however, the Western Allies offered a huge reward to East Germany: that its government should be deemed to have similar rights to those granted to the democratic government of West Germany. This was an important step towards the legitimization of the Communist East German regime in the international community of nations, and understood to be this.

The Treaty with the Soviet Union

The Treaty between the Federal Republic of Germany and the Union of Soviet Socialist Republics was signed on 12 April 1970. It was an agreement of the greatest significance, which defined the purpose of

Ostpolitik, and provided the context in which further negotiations with the Communist world could take place. The most important single provision was that the treaty accepted the status quo of a divided Europe (defined as the real, existing situation in Europe). West Germany and the Soviet Union agreed to abide by the existing frontiers in Europe and renounced the use of force. These agreements were, of course, the central concession: the recognition of the existence of two German states and the ending of the definition of German unity as the fundamental imperative of German foreign policy. Brandt insisted that 'the goal of German unity by means of self-determination was not affected by the treaty'. Walter Scheel, the Foreign Minister, presented the Russians with a letter on German unity whose receipt was officially acknowledged, in keeping with the unbending habits of the Soviets, but whose contents (which were, after all, what was important) were bizarrely not acknowledged, still less written into the treaty itself. This letter stated 'This treaty does not conflict with the political objective of the Federal Republic to work for a state of peace in Europe in which the German nation will recover its unity in free self-determination.' In any case, as Bahr had pointed out, as long as the four powers' rights continued to exist, West Germany could not legally recognize frontiers on German soil, even if it wished to do so. Bonn added that it wished to sign treaties with other Warsaw Pact states, in particular to conclude a treaty with the GDR based on equality, non-discrimination and independence, that would have the same binding force as a treaty with any other country. West Germany also sought a treaty with Czechoslovakia to work out issues connected with the invalidation of the Munich Agreement. A treaty with Czechoslovakia was signed on 11 December 1973, when Bonn also exchanged ambassadors with Bulgaria and Hungary.

In his January 1971 report to the German nation, Brandt declared that his government would seek an agreement with the GDR, but that he would uphold the right of self-determination of the German people and would do nothing to undermine the 'reality' of a German nation. It must be pointed out that what this meant, in the *immediate* reality of 1971, was virtually nothing. No Communist regime, supported by the vast power of the Red Army and the massive secret police apparatus that was part and parcel of Communism, had ever expressed the least concern for the right of self-determination, in either any of the satellite states or the Soviet Union itself. If anything, the enunciation of this principle pandered to the propaganda line taken by the Communists that their states were 'people's democracies' and misled those who believed it would truly be upheld. If this was a delusion, it was to cost the SPD dear for the next fifteen years or so when, on the basis of these ideas, the SPD and the SED sought to come to some common agreement on fundamental values and aims.

The Bundestag and the Eastern Treaties

Despite Brandt's believing that he and the SPD/FDP government had scored a famous success, there were clouds on the domestic political front. In Schleswig-Holstein and the Rhineland-Palatinate the CDU won absolute majorities, and it also scored a 9 per cent increase in Baden-Württemberg. It was at this juncture that the CDU decided to oppose *Ostpolitik*. In December 1971 Barzel visited Moscow, and when he returned he declared that the Russians would simply exploit the treaty with West Germany and that Brandt had been duped. He insisted that the USSR be required to recognize the EEC and the right of self-determination for all Germans. The CDU/CSU's opposition was important, because it suggested that the foreign policy alliance on which the Grand Coalition had been built was now in ruins. The Soviets, however, appeared to signal their wish to move forward, as they saw it, when, in May 1971, the old Stalinist Ulbricht was replaced by the younger Erich Honecker.

On 3 September, the agreement was clinched. The Soviets committed themselves to not changing conditions in Berlin unilaterally; visits were made easier. On balance, the deal was good for the West and the East. Each side believed it had been the winner. The West could point to a huge, and humane, improvement in travel to and from Berlin (for Easter 1972 500,000 West Berliners visited their relations in East Berlin) and there was no further talk of turning Berlin into a neutral separate city-state.

The Eastern Treaties had all been initialled and real, if slow, progress was made with the GDR over travel arrangements. Even though Brandt's government had seemed successful in foreign policy terms and had executed ideas implicitly supported by the CDU/CSU (since their origins lay in the Grand Coalition), the CDU leader, Barzel, urged his party to vote against them in a qualified rejection. In December the treaties were sent to the Bundesrat. The first reading was to be in February, the second in May 1972. The government was clear that a rejection in the Bundestag would lead to its dissolution. During the February debate on the first reading, Barzel declaimed that the treaties were 'wrong' and had been presented at the 'wrong time'. The USSR continued to refuse to recognize the EEC, he added, and the Germans' right to self-determination was not expressly guaranteed in the texts. Gerhard Schröder said the treaties would cement the division of Germany and loosen the Western alliance. The Government's case was put by the Chancellor's Office Minister, Ehmke. He accused the CDU of revanchism, and perpetuating views like those of Adenauer's minister, Merkatz, who, he alleged, had talked about the need to 'liberate Germany's occupied territory', rather than negotiating with the GDR regime. According to Ehmke, his speech saved the day. These were rare things: genuine debates in the Bundestag.

On 9 February 1972 the Eastern Treaties failed by one vote to gain a majority in the Bundesrat. The constitution laid down that in order to become law, these treaties would need an absolute majority in the Bundestag. It seemed doubtful whether this would be achieved; Hupka, a leading expellee figure in the SPD, decided to resign from the party in disgust. Other, too, began to waver. The CDU/CSU now decided to force a constructive vote of no confidence in Brandt in order to replace him with Barzel. The debate took place on 26 and 27 April, but there was as much concern over the outcome outside the chamber as inside it. It was significant that the trade union movement staged sympathy strikes for *Ostpolitik*, and there were many other demonstrations of public support for Brandt. The CDU/CSU failed by two votes. It quickly became obvious that some CDU members had voted for Brandt.

Bought Votes

It was rumoured at the time that at least one of them had been bribed by one of the SPD's business managers, Karl Wienand, with DM 50,000 from a 'special purpose fund' held in the Chancellor's Office. This charge is examined below, since we shall see that if it is in fact true that this money came directly from the East German Stasi, it gives one not insignificant clue to the extent to which the East Germans believed they would gain from Brandt's *Ostpolitik*. Since a majority of Germans, and in particular the West German academic class, favoured *Ostpolitik*, and given the pressures on German politics for the creation of consensus, the implications of this serious case of corruption and subversion of due parliamentary process (either by individuals or by collusion between individuals and the Stasi) were never given the academic attention they deserved. There was a half-hearted attempt at the time to get the Chancellor to account for his 'special fund', but it yielded no fruit, a fact itself remarkable in a government committed to greater openness.

The Treaties were passed by the Bundestag on 17 May 1972, with the CDU abstaining. Yet despite the success in this vote, a tie over the budget indicated that new elections were now called for. On 3 June the four-power agreement on Berlin was signed. The Basic Treaty governing relations between West Germany and the GDR was signed in East

Berlin on 21 December 1972. It created the preconditions for further negotiations. The GDR government was also handed a letter on German unity stating that West Germany had the 'political objective of working for a state of peace in Europe in which the German nation could recover its unity in free self- determination'. It was further accepted that neither German state could act in the name of the other, and that each accepted the other's independence. Both states were to seek membership of the United Nations (which was accorded in September 1973). Permanent representative missions (and not embassies) were to be set up in Bonn and East Berlin.

Did *Ostpolitik* Help or Hinder the Cause of German Unity?

As we can see, what is so intriguing about Brandt's *Ostpolitik* is not just that its process was extremely complex, but that the policy itself raises more questions in respect of the pursuit of German unity than it answers. The first of these is whether Brandt intended *Ostpolitik* to promote real unity, or to solemnize Germany's political division. Connected to this, is the further question whether (whatever Brandt may have *intended*) *Ostpolitik* nevertheless produced unity, and thus reached its fruition when unification duly took place in 1990. Finally, we cannot avoid asking what part Communist subversion played in the creation of the policies that formed *Ostpolitik*. That the making of *Ostpolitik* did have at least one subverted aspect (whether or not the Bundestag votes were bought with East German cash) is clear from the simple fact that one of Brandt's most important aides, from December 1969 until May 1974, Günter Guillaume, turned out to be a Stasi officer. It is known that he gave his masters detailed information about Brandt's thoughts on *Ostpolitik*.

Did Brandt's *Ostpolitik* bring unity to Germany? Even if we dismiss the validity of the concept of straightforward causality in politics (that specific policies produce specific outcomes), and accept that politics is a convoluted business, it is still fair to ask whether *Ostpolitik* helped or hindered the actual process of German unification. What Brandt himself said about this is equivocal. His statements on unity seem to contain two mutually incompatible elements: the acceptance that for all foreseeable time there were two German states in existence and the simultaneously held statement of faith that West Germany, representing the German people, would always be desirous of German unity. Both at the time, and indeed until 1989, virtually every observer of German politics believed that unity on terms acceptable to West Germany and its allies was *not* a realistic possibility. Many indeed believed that East Germany was perhaps the most successful Communist state in eastern Europe, with every chance of maintaining and even strengthening its position in the world system.

If Brandt's 'text' contained these two incompatible elements in respect of the pursuit of unity, what did the text actually mean when it spoke of unity? Had unity not occurred in 1990, the answer would have been virtually nothing. Brandt's policy appeared to accept division as a reality, but made it palatable by achieving real improvements for the people affected by the inhumane consequences of division. Yet unity *did* occur. Is it possible that despite the text, the aim of its author was indeed unity, and that it hit its target? Even though we must accept that any policy often produces unimagined consequences (often, indeed, outcomes that are the opposite of those that are wanted), Brandt's reputation hangs, in part, on the answer to this puzzle. Seen one way, he seems a praiseworthy realist, who improved the lives of many Germans in a practical way. Viewed another, however, he becomes one of the most remarkable visionaries of the twentieth century, who sensed how to make his dream a reality and change the entire course of German political development.

One way of resolving the matter is, of course, to test the policy not by analysing Brandt's motives, but by considering those of the Communists. Here, naturally enough, the issue of subversion becomes critical. For one thing, because of their agents, the Soviets and East Germans were able not simply to inject their own aims into West German policy, but also to monitor its progress and test its genuineness. Would the Soviets and East Germans have agreed to what they did agree, if they had not been convinced that Brandt really accepted Germany's political division?

Brandt the Politician

We should not forget that, first and foremost, Brandt was a politician (as well as a brilliant journalist). All politicians like to be proved 'right'; to be seen to have pursued the 'right' policies and foreseen the future accurately. Where they are themselves gifted in the use of words, it is ever easier for them to achieve these aims. Brandt produced a number of autobiographies and helped others to write biographies throughout his career. His statements on reunification, made before unity, in which it does not appear to be the central aim of *Ostpolitik*, often seem more plausible, it has to be said, than his comments on unity after it was achieved.

Careful analysis of the evidence suggests that Brandt strongly preferred the real benefit of *détente* to any spurious goal of unity and knew, in any case, that *détente* and unity were incompatible. But it is impossible to be totally certain: there remains the possibility that, beneath the surface, Brandt was a calculating patriot who chose his words deliberately.

Was Unity the Imperative of West German Policy?

It was not only the West Germans who were equivocal in their attitude towards unity. Germany's 1945 victors did not simply have a formal interest in it; they, too, accepted on the one hand that it was the 'imperative' of West German diplomacy, but on the other not realistically achievable. After 1990, some claimed none the less that the basic aim of *Ostpolitik*, however Brandt expressed himself, was the furthering of unity. Their case was that Brandt was, after all, a German. Calling his patriotism into question, they believed, was to do the work of the Right who had always sought to destroy Brandt. All politicians and diplomats, they insisted, understood only too well that people are often not able to say what they really mean: thus when Brandt spoke of the acceptance of two German states, he meant the opposite and was understood by the West, at any rate, to mean the opposite. *Détente*, they said, was the means by which this could one day be achieved; but unity would be the end. Whilst the internal dynamic of unity may have stemmed from the apparent inner rot in the Soviet Union, they thus conclude that Brandt was the undoubted father of German unity.

Alongside these political interpretations, we must set the views of two leading experts on this subject, Timothy Garton Ash and Richard Davy. For the former, *Ostpolitik* is, on the whole, to be seen as the German version of *détente*, not a specific policy of unification. He suggests that a divided Germany was part of a divided Europe, but that the real meaning of division for the German people was always unclear. *Détente*, he argues, and the overcoming of Europe's and Germany's division are all parts of the same process.

Garton Ash believes that initially, Germany's division was seen by men like Adenauer as 'abnormal', leading, however, to a desire 'to change not the frontiers but the quality of the frontiers'. He concludes that 'the relationship between the [two] questions was extremely complex', and he states it in the form of a question: 'Was *Ostpolitik* a European answer to the European question, a German answer to the European question, a European answer to the German question, or simply a German answer to the German Question?'. Ultimately, Garton Ash states that *Ostpolitik* was 'born as the German version of detente', with Brandt and Scheel as its 'midwives'; *détente*, however, could lead only to reunification.

Davy has put the matter another way. He accepts the reality of ambiguity in Brandt's aims and offers an almost metaphysical model of foreign policy making, where a diplomat succeeds by not succeeding. He describes *Ostpolitik* as a 'paradoxical policy that worked'. He suggests that when the Germans 'eventually allowed themselves to forget' unity, it 'fell into their lap'. Brandt's skill, Davy believes, lay not in '*renouncing unification but pursuing it from the opposite direction* by recognizing East Germany'. Brandt's successors carried on with this policy and 'showered the regime with hard currency, flattered it, drew it into perpetual negotiation, propped it up when it seemed to be tottering and constantly reassured its leaders that destabilization was the last thing they had in mind. The wretched place could not stand all this kindness and obligingly collapsed in 1989.' For Davy, the aim of *Ostpolitik* was unity but as the result of a more complex and differentiated process than straightforward cause and effect. Davy, significantly, speaks of Zen masters of archery who would tell their pupils that they were more likely to hit the target if they stopped trying to hit it.

It is, however, probably unwise to mystify Brandt's *Ostpolitik*, not least because to depict him as a magician is to obscure, rather than reveal, the nature of the political process and the importance of the deal-making that went on, as well as minimize the real thrust of Brandt's policy, which was to improve the quality of life of the German people in a day-to-day context. It is perfectly true that Brandt's rhetoric was unclear, and intended to be unclear. This was because he needed to win the West Germans and the West, as well as the East, for his policy. He knew full well that could be no *détente* without the acceptance of the division of Europe; and no acceptance of the division of Europe without the acceptance of Germany's division. *Ostpolitik*, therefore, as a policy intentionally pursued, was not about reunification.

We must not forget where Brandt had come from on this issue, within the SPD. He had won power from the old guard precisely by differentiating himself from their straightforward demand for unity. It is true that in his famous Harvard speeches, entitled 'The Ordeal of Coexistence', and published as a book in 1963, he not only demanded unity, but also said he supported the sole representation policy. He said he would never accept 'a policy of sly winks and tacit understandings . . . the principles of a peace treaty with Germany must be expounded and upheld'. Germany, he said, was the only country in Europe 'where the boundary separating east and west also divides one single nation'. For this reason, no one should assume that 'the German people are not too intensely interested in re-establishing the unity of the German state'. He added that both the CDU and the SPD had been 'in agreement for years about what constitute the cardinal principles of German foreign policy: the right of self-determination cannot be sacrificed and we must never abandon our fellow countrymen who live today under Communist rule . . . the Federal Republic is the custodian of freedom for all Germans'. Above all, he concluded 'those who advocate recognition and also advocate the existence of two German states are talking nonsense'. This seems clear enough. But it is the opposite of clear.

Brandt the Realist

Against this, however, we must set Brandt's other statements. At the 1966 Dortmund SPD conference, for example, Brandt had called for 'settled coexistence' between the two German states albeit, without legal recognition. He added that the notion of West Germany's sole representation of all Germans was set down in the Federal Constitution, and could thus not be tampered with. But in October 1968 he declared that he was 'enough of a realist to know that the self-determination of the German people does not stand on the agenda of practical policies'. He proposed 'recognition pending the settlement of a peace treaty with Germany', a formulation the SPD accepted. He believed that there was 'no power, still less a political configuration which in the foreseeable future have helped us to restore national unity'. Reunification, he argued, simply did not figure on the current international agenda, and it flowed from this that efforts should now be made to regulate coexistence and cooperation between the two parts of Germany.

What this boiled down to was the view that the West Germans needed to face reality. To encourage them to do so, whilst at the same time appealing to the Soviets, he had, of course, to offer the very 'sly winks and tacit understandings' he had scorned at Harvard. But they were what made *Ostpolitik* possible. Nowhere was this more plain than in the hazy notion of promoting change within the Eastern bloc by seeking to work together with it. It was expounded by Bahr in a celebrated speech at Tutzing, in which he called for 'Wandel durch Annäherung', the goal of 'overcoming the status quo, by first not changing the status quo . . . Thus German reunification would be not a single act but a process with many stops and many steps.' Garton Ash calls this 'brilliant and provocative clarity'. Rather, it was a monumental muddying of the waters in order to dampen even residual longings for unity. Nor is there any evidence that, once the settlement had been reached, Brandt dreamt of altering the status quo that had been accepted, let alone suggest policies to meet this end.

On 20 October 1971 Brandt was awarded the Nobel Peace Prize. In his subsequent acceptance speech, he saluted former fellow resistance members, adding that Germany had finally 'been reconciled to itself'.

He later said that a 'good German cannot be a nationalist . . . he knows he cannot forgo his European destiny [for] it is through Europe that Germany returns home to itself'.

Yet Brandt himself concluded that the treaty with the GDR 'did not directly bring us closer to the goal of German unity'. For East Germany, national unity ceased to be a political goal: it now defined itself as the 'Socialist state of the German nation' and within a few years as the 'Socialist German national state' (although they could never find a substitute for the word 'German'). Brandt by now said he firmly believed that 'there could be no return to a nation state on the nineteenth century pattern. I nevertheless remained convinced that the nation would live on, even under differing political systems because nationhood is a matter of awareness and resolve.' Yet 'in any case', he added, the existence of 'nation and state' in Germany's case had been 'brief'. Germany had existed as a 'cultural nation' and would retain an identity as such 'whatever the chances that in the course of an all-European process, the two states would some day evolve forms of coexistence amounting to more than inter-state relations'. Brandt declared that his aim had always been to keep the 'cultural nationhood' of Germany intact without precluding West Germany's 'search for a wider political home' in the Western community of states.

These words, written in 1978, may be considered special pleading. In the real world of day-to-day politics, Brandt had given the GDR virtually all that it had wanted. Its seat in the United Nations (which confirmed the idea that there were *two* German nations) and the international recognition that this brought, added and did not detract from the Communists' hold on East Germany.

Living with Germany's Division

In this way, *détente* did not promote German unity on Adenauer's terms (the terms Brandt in 1962 insisted were the only acceptable ones) but legitimized, and even prolonged the life, of the Communist regimes in Russia and East Germany. Brandt did not seek to unify Germany but live with Germany's division. His ambiguous statements can therefore be viewed as a means of getting the Germans to face up to this cruel reality. If they were intended to befuddle anyone, it was the West Germans, and not the Soviets or the East Germans.

After he became the grand old man of German politics, Brandt felt able to be quite explicit about this. In November 1984 he called on his fellow countrymen to end, for all time, any discussion of German national unity; on 14 September 1988 he called the aim of unity 'the basic lie in the life of the Federal Republic' ('Lebenslüge'). Egon Bahr said in a speech made on 27 November 1988 in Munich that talk of reunification was 'lying and hypocrisy' and 'political environmental pollution'.

In his memoirs, looking back at the 1960s almost two decades later, Brandt insisted that Adenauer's 'rhetorical demands for reunification created a kind of national living lie for which [his] party paid the penalty after his death by losing control in Bonn'. He described his own *Ostpolitik* as a 'way of facing up to the realities . . . and thus gaining scope for understanding and cooperation . . . with eastern Europe and the other German state'. He elaborated these ideas by suggesting that 'Many citizens of the Federal Republic were being seduced with a belief that the resurgence of the western part of their nation would some day enable partition . . . and the loss of the eastern territories to be abolished by the wave of a wand.' This could not happen, he insisted. What was needed was 'recognition of the altered circumstances bequeathed us by the Second World War fulfilled an international as well as a moral requirement. Anyone who denied this was in effect seeking to persuade the Germans that Hitler had never happened.'

The ambiguity in Brandt's words was deliberately chosen to make this heavy truth palatable. The hard words like 'lie' and 'seduction' demonstrate Brandt's passionate wish to get the Germans to face reality, and learn to live with what he regarded as the permanent damage done to Germany's national status. Brandt, like Adenauer before him, saw that Germany *had* to be different in order to *seem* the same as the other nations of the West.

Communist Subversion

The final piece in the jigsaw of *Ostpolitik*'s interpretation is, perhaps, provided by a brief glance at the role played by Communist subversion. It has three aspects to it. First there was East German cash. This was almost certainly secretly used to buy votes in the Bundestag, and possibly to purchase a favourable picture of the GDR in the West German media; and was a factor in the buying free of so-called political prisoners in the GDR. Second, it has been claimed that one, or more, key actors involved in the making of *Ostpolitik* was a Communist agent. Third, we know that Communist agents were used to inform the Soviet leadership about the real aims and intentions of the West Germans. Here, of course, the role of Günter Guillaume is vital not only as one source of information about Brandt and his entourage (almost certainly not the sole source) but also as the cause of Brandt's resignation.

Garton Ash makes no mention at all of Günter Guillaume and it is virtually impossible to detect any serious attention being paid to the question of subversion. Presumably the reason for this is that he does not think it significant. Other authors have also ignored this matter. Yet, even on a superficial level, this is very surprising. Apart from the fact that Brandt had to resign because of Guillaume – to put it another way, Communist subversion ended up in bringing down a West German Chancellor – everyone, inside and outside of Germany was always aware of the possibility of subversion. Bonn was known as a 'leakey' capital. Diplomats were always wary of passing vital secrets to the West Germans because they suspected they would, within hours, be on the desks of the East Germans. In addition, *Ostpolitik* was in essence about a deal; a deal which could, all too easily, benefit the one side more than the other. As such, it was the object of intense intelligence interest on both sides. This is not to overplay the importance of spying, or subversion. Ironically, the ability of the Communists to truly know what was going on in West German government proved to be to the West's advantage, and to do considerable damage to the East. It meant that the Soviets and the East Germans knew that the Federal Republic was genuinely not seeking to undermine their way of life.

Indeed, in the medium term, this might have encouraged the Communists to feel safer than they ought to have done, thus enabling them to be undermined from within. It is generally accepted that the Russians believed both that they had gained most from *Ostpolitik* and that the West Germans had given up their aim of unity. They had received five huge concessions: acceptance of the status quo, 'national' status for East Germany, West German agreement to eschew nuclear weapons, agreement to the CESC (which Moscow saw as setting the seal on the division of Europe) and economic assistance.

As to the charge of buying votes with East German cash, it has been conceded that DM 50,000 was used to bribe Bundestag members. Ehmke, the minister then responsible for administering the Chancellor's special purpose fund, has refused to say that it was the source of the cash in question (claiming that to do so would create a precedent obliging all future Chancellors to account for how they use their secret funds). Wienand's money, on the other hand, seems likely to have come from the Stasi.

The Communist Interest

What of the allegation that certain key actors in the making of *Ostpolitik* were Russian or East German agents (that is to say, working for the Communists, but not necessarily as spies)? Brandt's widow, a historian and journalist, has recently argued Herbert Wehner was a sort of super-agent. He was not a squalid spy, she alleges, but rather he considered himself the equal of the Communist leadership, entertaining political aims that ran parallel to their own Stalinist ones of establishing a single, 'Socialist' German nation. He did not, she insists, actually take orders from East Berlin; but there was a common purpose that united them. It was this that motivated him to pursue good relations with the East Germans, the reason why he was trusted by them. Many Germans, and not just those on the Left of German politics, were outraged by these remarks. Whilst it seems hard to believe that Wehner acted in the Communist interest, it is perhaps less implausible to believe that in the innermost recesses of his mind, his view of what a Socialist Germany might be, did not contradict the more humane notions held by the East German Communist élite.

Wehner was not just a powerful politician (without doubt he was one of the ten most important figures in the history of the Bonn Republic). He was also its most shadowy and private leader. He had been born in Dresden in 1906, joining the German Communist Party in 1927. Under its Stalinist leadership the KPD was already a deadly enemy of Weimar democracy and of the party most associated with it, the SPD. When the Nazis took power, he was sent first to Prague (where he was soon arrested) and then to Moscow. In Moscow, he was a resident of the Hotel Lux, headquarters of the Communist exiles. He managed to avoid Stalin's camps, it has been alleged, by betraying comrades. In 1942 he was transferred to Sweden (to organize resistance to the Third Reich) and he was arrested, once again.

He subsequently said that it was in prison in Sweden that he came to renounce Communism and espouse Social Democracy. On his release, he married a Communist war widow. After Germany's defeat, they went to Hamburg where he joined the SPD, and was elected to the first Bundestag. As we have seen, Wehner was motivated by an intense desire to see the SPD achieve power in the Bonn Republic, and did all he could to help transform it from being a narrow Marxist-based party of the working class into a broad-based 'party of all the people'. He had argued that it would have to bow to the political realities of the Bonn Republic if it were to win through, and accept many of Adenauer's core policies, even though it had opposed them in the past.

He was quite prepared to be totally ruthless in going for power. He was instrumental in getting the Godesberg Programme passed by the rank and file, and his 1960 speech, supporting NATO, was to prove a key factor in getting the CDU to accept the SPD as a coalition partner in 1966. He became Minister for All-German Affairs in the Grand Coalition, and supported *Ostpolitik* to the hilt. 'The two parts of Germany must speak to each other as equals', he stated, adding enigmatically, 'though neither need accept the other as equal'.

His reputation was as a pragmatist rather than as an ideologue. In an interview given in 1971, rare because it was revealing, he agreed that he had presided over what he believed to have been the death of ideology in German politics. He said that he had been able to do this because he had, at first hand, experienced the 'strait-jacket of Communism'. He was, however, a bitter man, and his readiness to use his elbows to lever out opponents in the party made him many enemies. Without Wehner, Brandt would not have been Chancellor. There was, therefore, a certain logic in the fact that his withdrawal of support for Brandt in 1974 led to the Chancellor's resignation. He quickly transferred allegiance to Schmidt. When Schmidt resigned from his party office in 1983, Wehner went too. He died on 19 January 1990, during the process of German unification.

It is true that Wehner had repeatedly blotted his copy book. In May 1973, for example, without having first got permission from Brandt, he went to East Berlin to speak to Honecker. In September 1973 whilst on a visit to Moscow, Wehner attacked the foreign policy of his government. He suggested that now that the treaties were ratified, the government was going slow; the effect was to weaken Brandt's position. He was very keen in promoting contacts between the SPD and the SED (which tended to weaken the former, and strengthen the latter).

Yet none of this means that Wehner was a 'super-agent'. If there was a sense in which Wehner's plans for West German policy came to mirror East German ambitions, this was perhaps because like those of the East German leadership, Wehner's ideas had been, in part, fashioned by the same realities: the success of Nazism and the power of the Soviet Communists. At the same time, there was undoubtedly something sinister and secretive about him, and archival evidence may one day prove that those who felt uncomfortable about his loyalty were justified in their fears.

The *Spiegel* has also recently suggested that Bahr was also a Communist agent, codenamed David. That Bahr, admittedly a mysterious man (like many of Brandt's advisers), was an agent seems incredible. He is bound to have had a KGB codename – but this does not mean he was a KGB agent.

Were the claims against Wehner ever to be proved, it would certainly necessitate a rewriting of the history of *Ostpolitik* (as Frau Brandt has argued) and it might indeed show that Brandt's *Ostpolitik* (despite the benefits that it brought to the Germans themselves) was, to some extent at least, also Russia's *Westpolitik*. This may sound far more horrifying than it ought to; all it may mean is that the Western policy of *détente* genuinely suited the Soviet Union as well. It does not indicate that the

policy itself was subverted; as we have seen, *détente* was a policy generated by the United States, to serve Western interests.

Günter Guillaume

Guillaume was the archetypal Stasi agent: intelligent, persistent and
wholly plausible. He destroyed one of the most popular of democratic
German Chancellors. There is no doubt that he spied on Brandt and
hoped to use photos of sex sessions held by Brandt to blackmail him.
Yet neither the impact of his spying, nor his part in the policy process,
has ever been properly subjected to scholarly analysis. West Germans
shy away from matters like these. They suggest either that subversion
is of little real consequence or that it is a mutual activity, cancel-
ling itself out. They sometimes argue that the investigation of it is
McCarthyism in disguise.

Yet West German intelligence and security services were not merely
themselves undermined by Communist agents, but often saw each other
as rivals. Until 1968, the foreign intelligence service (the BND) had
been led by Reinhard Gehlen (said somewhat implausibly to be the
illegitimate offspring of Mata Hari and General Ludendorff, the First
World War hero and early supporter of Hitler). He was succeeded by
General Wessel. The domestic security service (the BfV) was run at the
time by Günter Nollau, a friend of Wehner. Adenauer had secretly asked
the BND to undertake domestic intelligence work, since he seems never
to have trusted the BfV, which had been set up by the British (the
Americans had set up the BND): the individual the British had installed
to be its first chief, Otto John, had defected, or been kidnapped
(depending on the interpretation) to East Berlin in 1954. There he had
(whether defector or not) seriously embarrassed Adenauer over his
plans for German rearmament.

Guillaume and his wife came to the West in 1956 and joined the
SPD in 1957. Guillaume was introduced to the new minister in the
Chancellor's office, Ehmke, by Herbert Ehrenberg, the head of the economics department in the Chancery. On 11 November 1969 Guillaume
joined his office and on 1 December he was appointed personal aide to
the Chancellor. Naturally, he enjoyed direct access to him, at any time.
Initially, he was given a liaison role with trade unions and other groups;
but Brandt soon came to rely heavily on him in other areas. He
repeatedly represented Brandt at the SPD executive meetings and
accompanied him when the Chancellor attended. He was also an active
member of the political club of the Friedrich Ebert Stiftung, the SPD's
politico-educational institution.

West German Secret Services

Guillaume's appointment was not a foregone conclusion. The Chancellor's Office civil servants did not believe he possessed the right educational qualifications; and almost immediately, security objections were raised. For a while, it proved impossible to proceed with the appointment. There was evidence against him stemming from before his flight to the West. Nollau's BfV had responsibility for the security of the government in Bonn. But Ehmke, the responsible minister, decided to get a further view on the man from General Wessel, the head of the BND. This was perhaps partly because the BND did its own counter-espionage work but partly, too, because Ehmke was Wessel's superior, whereas the BfV reported to Interior Minister Genscher (subsequently Foreign Minister). Nollau has written that both Genscher and his aide, Klaus Kinkel (later Foreign Minister under Kohl) were convinced Guillaume was clean. This meant that Nollau was not permitted to put the suspicions he said he had always entertained, directly to Brandt. Yet Ehmke tells us that the BfV had found nothing against him. On 26 January 1970 the BfV said Guillaume could be given access to secret material and his appointment was confirmed. Later on it transpired that the BfV had not used evidence it possessed showing that he had been a witness in East German spy trials, and that radio messages to a 'G' and 'Chr' from the GDR had been intercepted.

Nollau claims he subsequently told both Genscher and Kinkel that he distrusted Guillaume. Genscher dismissed this notion and Nollau then advised Brandt to do nothing to arouse Guillaume's suspicions, so that he could be observed by BfV officers. Brandt had asked Guillaume and his wife and son to accompany him on holiday to Norway. Brandt said that he always felt 'safer' when Guillaume was next to him. The spy was finally caught here; but it took until 24 April 1974 to arrest him, eleven months after the first measures against him and four-and-a-half years after the first doubts had been raised. At first, Brandt had not wanted to resign over the matter which was presented as a breach of security. Like all heads of government, he was not responsible for his own security. But Herbert Wehner insisted he resign; and in the end Brandt was forced to conclude that he had been guilty of taking advice (one presumes from Guillaume) that he should not have taken. Brandt resigned on 6 May 1974. Guillaume was sentenced to fifteen years' gaol on 15 December 1975 (in October 1981 he was swapped for two very minor Western spies).

Guillaume had been able to ensure that the Stasi and thus the Soviets were always aware of West Germany's bottom line in any negotiation after 1 December 1969, in other words for the whole of the high noon of *Ostpolitik*. This knowledge undoubtedly allowed the Russians always to exact the maximum concessions from Brandt. Yet, as we have seen, Brandt was in any case perfectly ready to make the maximum concessions because he believed in the importance of *détente*, and Guillaume, acting as a Communist insurance policy, plainly helped rather than hindered its process.

The Impact of Subversion

What appeared to be merely a personal tragedy for Brandt was, on the one hand, far more than this, but on the other, far less. The Guillaume affair was a further indication of the extent to which Brandt had lost control of his own political destiny, and the extent to which the East Germans wanted him watched. By resigning, Brandt was able to keep his settlement with the East intact. Had he stayed, his policy would almost certainly have been scrutinized for signs of subversion. There appears to be no truth in the allegation that the GDR authorities arranged for Guillaume to be uncovered in order to bring Brandt down (because, it was claimed, he had become too popular in East Germany and thus a threat to the regime).

The Communists had clearly got what they wanted. For the first fifteen or so years following the Basic Treaty with the GDR, there seems no doubt but that the West Germans assisted substantially, by political means and by credits, the bolstering of the Communists. Internally, however, the fact that the West Germans had ceased to be adversaries radically altered the way in which East Germans perceived them, generating grass-roots changes amongst the East German population which, in the end, helped overthrow the regime. This was not something the West Germans had wanted or foreseen. If the East Germans understood this, they must have believed that it could always be suppressed with the help of the Stasi.

Documents discovered at the Stasi headquarters in East Berlin provide harsh evidence of the Stasi's continued espionage against the Bonn government long after Guillaume's arrest. One paper, for example, is a private note dictated and signed by Willy Brandt on 24 March 1981, entitled 'concerning "G"' (that is, Guillaume) clearly handed over by someone to the Stasi. In it, Brandt with some bitterness recalls that he consistently refused to get involved in any attempts to exchange Guillaume for Western agents. On 26 February 1981 *Stern* magazine reported that Brandt had vetoed such an exchange. Brandt was subsequently told the source for the story was the West German Secret Intelligence Service. Brandt plainly believed that he was being used in some sinister game to halt further exchanges and further improve relations between the two German states. On 4 March Brandt was approached by Egon Franke, a cabinet minister, and asked whether he would object to any exchange; he said 'no' yet again. The minute, of course, revealed to the East Germans how keen the West Germans were to continue their dealings with them and that even Brandt's bruised feelings over Guillaume would not stand in their way, not to mention evidence of how keen West German intelligence was to participate in this process.

Other documents include a personal note on Honecker's notepaper, initialled by him, sent to Helmut Schmidt in May 1974 (just after Brandt's resignation). Honecker's note claims that the Guillaume affair had not been planned by the East Germans and that it had been a great shame that 'he was not removed before he could do damage'. Honecker adds that his uncovering suited 'those very circles who were determined to bring Brandt down' and thus undermine their treaty. The East German leader can be seen tryng to draw a line under the affair and assure Schmidt of his readiness to continue to negotiate: clear evidence, yet again, of the GDR's strong interest in *Ostpolitik*, its hope that the SPD will win the 1976 election and the GDR's readiness to help. It also shows, by implication, that Schmidt was 'optimistic' about dealings with the GDR. Honecker assured the new Chancellor that the GDR would continue to respect the Federal Republic and promised that no one would be able to deflect it from this course (a rather rich comment, given the GDR's role in Brandt's downfall). He promised to continue to unite families and permit the purchase of prisoners as well as to allow visits by the President of the Bundestag, Annemarie Renger, and Bundestag members to Rostock in the summer of that year.

A third document provides details of a meeting between Schmidt, Wehner and one of Honecker's aides, Michael Kohl, on 16 May 1977 in West Berlin. In over twenty pages, Schmidt gives examples of his total commitment to *Ostpolitik* and to executing detailed aspects of the policy. He promises Honecker that he can be reached, at any time, through Herbert Wehner, plainly a key intermediary between the two heads of government.

Apart from the bribing of deputies in the Bundestag and the provision of information about Brandt's true motives via Guillaume, subversion allegedly played one final role in the process of *Ostpolitik*. This was the shameful purchase of the GDR's political prisoners. This trading in human beings brought the GDR some DM 5 billion from the mid-1970s to the end of the regime in East Germany. In 1968 the Bonn government first agreed to the unsavoury (and unwise) policy of buying the freedom of East German political prisoners. A number of Nazi policies had centred on the exchange of cash for liberty, and in

April 1944 Heinrich Himmler himself had taken charge of attempts to barter Jews for munitions. Hermann Kreutzer, a man who had been gaoled both by the Nazis and the Communists, and had then fled to the West, was charged by Brandt to negotiate with East Berlin with a view to buying East German detainees. The original idea had, in fact, been Axel Springer's. As head of the *Bild Zeitung* which had its office in West Berlin, he agreed in 1964 to pay the first ransoms. The price was originally DM 40,000 per prisoner, the money being given to the Lutheran Church in East Germany, and being used to buy food imports for the citizens of the GDR.

Kreutzer (who personally disliked the process) was sacked in 1975 by the Minister, Egon Franke with the agreement of his deputy, Dieter Spangenberg. Almost at once the price soared to DM 100,000 and payments were now made in cash, direct to the regime in East Berlin. By the end of the 1980s, millions of Deutschmarks had been paid to East Berlin and one billion marks went from West to East in a year. Perhaps even worse, millions of marks could not be accounted for. Franke was investigated and not charged. A Christian Democrat, called Edgar Hirt, another middleman, was given a two-and-a-half year gaol sentence. But the money was neither accounted for, nor returned.

Franke's East German 'business partners' were Wolfgang Vogel, the East German lawyer and Markus Wolf, deputy head of the Stasi and secret intelligence chief. Today, Kreutzer (an eminent and respected man) believes that Hirt may have been rather more than a mere embezzler, and in the pay of the Stasi. He also believes that Franke, too, was gaining personally from the trade in human beings. In effect, he suggests, the Stasi was both asking the price and agreeing to pay it. Furthermore, since the trade hung on political prisoners, the regime had every incentive to imprison dissidents, in order to convert them into cash.

Whilst it is not hard to appreciate the humane motives of the Bonn government in agreeing to this purchase of human beings, two further points about it must be made. The first is that it implies, once again, that *Ostpolitik* was a policy designed to stabilize the division of Germany, and not push reunification since it was predicated on an acceptance that East German political prisoners could not hope to gain their freedom in any foreseeable future. Otherwise there would have been little sense in spending this sort of money on a temporary condition. Second, however, it shows, once again, West Germany's curious position in having to submit to Western demands (and define its own interests in line with this), even where to do so meant that Communism had to be accepted and even appeased. It is worth bearing in mind that if, as is commonly accepted, Soviet Communism collapsed because of the domestic pressures resulting from trying to compete with the West, *détente*, which gave the Soviets a breathing space, might have prolonged its life by a decade or so. To have been harder, however, would have made the position of the German people far worse and might have ended in a nuclear holocaust.

Brandt: The 'Other' German as West German Hero

Brandt was plainly an outstanding representative of the 'other' Germany, which had resisted the Nazis; and his whole political career in the Bonn Republic was evidence of a real concern for human rights (and not just those of Germans, for he actively addressed Third World problems and even tried to help solve the Ulster crisis). His idealism was remarkable and tangible. He was also certainly a German patriot. But for him Germany seemed increasingly a cultural, and not a political concept. The idea that 'Germany' no longer meant anything real in hard political terms was *not* a wicked one; Brandt knew only too well what were the dangers that sprang from a strong German nation seeking to dominate Europe. His aim, to settle West Germany in the East as well as the West, allowed the Federal Republic to thrive, and to add greatly to the states it could count as its friends.

What this suggests is that political reunification was never the goal of *Ostpolitik*; it was *détente*. In this sense, both Adenauer and Brandt in different ways sought to uphold the notion of the reinvention of a German state in the West; the latter completed the settlement initiated by the former. Neither man could have foreseen that a Soviet leader would one day emerge who would no longer try to maintain a Communist regime in East Germany, and that reunification might result from this on the basis of West German political values. Yet the very fact that Brandt was so committed to practical improvements in relations with the East, convinced the Soviets that the Federal Republic was indeed a reliable, liberal and decent German state in a way Adenauer could not do. Had Brandt not been Chancellor of the Federal Republic, the Wall and the regime it protected (which Brandt hated) might well still exist today.

The Two Helmuts – Schmidt and Kohl, 1974–89

Helmut Schmidt

During Helmut Schmidt's Chancellorship the Bonn Republic became, to all intents, the West German nation. Schmidt's Federal Republic won a high reputation for itself, and the Chancellor himself seemed increasingly to assume the guise of the managing director of an impressive business enterprise called West Germany. Indeed, in office Schmidt was more of a manager than a politician. This was beneficial for many reasons: West German politics was increasingly concerned with the rational management of the problems that arose (especially where economic growth was concerned); successful management was viewed much more favourably than skilful party political jockeying, or imaginative theorizing. Economic prosperity was becoming ever more important in making the West German people comfortable in their reinvented pseudo-nation.

Schmidt was born in 1918, the son of a Hamburg schoolteacher. He had served in the *Wehrmacht* (and had been forced to witness the trials of the 1944 plotters). He had originally been on the Left of the SPD, but had come to wider prominence as senator in Hamburg during the 1962 flooding catastrophe, where his decisiveness in directing the emergency services saved many lives. Schmidt himself was a dry man, who found it easier to lecture than to listen. What he had to say was always eminently sensible – but he was often verbose and, alas, tedious.

Managing West Germany to make it ever more profitable was therefore valued; and Schmidt seemed able to deliver. It was thus not without irony that it was a party political matter, one that Schmidt failed to manage, which led to his downfall: he could manage the country (and win huge popularity), but he could not manage his own party. Whilst this indicated that parties still mattered, it did so in a negative sense. Although the SPD rank and file (who brought their Chancellor down) could prove they had sufficient muscle to do so, the West German electors were, on the whole, unimpressed and, in the end, it was the SPD

Figure 7. Helmut Schmidt ©Presse- und Informationsamt der Bundesregierung

that suffered and not the concept of political management. Yet during his period as leader, the Federal Republic reached a high point in terms of its prestige and authority. It was very well regarded in both the West and the East as reliable, utterly democratic, successfully liberal and consensus oriented. Schmidt was, of course, a Social Democrat; but apart from his party label, there was no substantial difference between the policies he pursued and the policies he would have pursued had he been a Christian Democrat.

In seeking to devote himself to what he regarded as the truly important 'national' affairs of the Bonn Republic, he unwisely believed he could disregard what he seems to have found the squalid world of party politics. Bonn was a party democracy as well as being a Chancellor democracy. Without a party, a Chancellor could not exist. Why Schmidt failed to see this remains a matter of conjecture. It is possible to believe that he simply miscalculated the significance of a sound party base, imagining that West German politics would increasingly mirror those in America. He may have believed that party differences had begun to appear at best historical curiosities and at worst redundant distractions.

In September 1973 both German states had become members of the United Nations and in his attitude towards the GDR, and to eastern Europe (as well as towards political issues in general), Schmidt eschewed change. He was a true conservative, in that he sought to conserve all that West Germans had come to want from their country. He was effectively the first citizen of the state, the *Bundesbürger* number one, exemplifying what were, perhaps, all the strengths and weakness of the persona: intelligence, efficiency and arrogance. His period in office saw West German economic strength grow, despite the disaster of the oil price-hike of 1973. His strictures on the importance of sound economic policy were heeded both inside West Germany and beyond. His determination that NATO should not be cowed by the Warsaw Pact led, ultimately, to what many regarded as NATO's victory in the Cold War. Precisely because he was such a competent West German Chancellor, West German political life under him was marked by a prevailing ennui, enlivened only by increasingly ferocious feuding within the ruling party, the SPD.

As we have seen, Schmidt had long been determined to succeed Brandt and tighten up the government. He knew only too well that Brandt had not kept his eye on the ball, and as Defence Minister (allegedly with the best planning staff in Bonn) he had a vision of what might be done. Planning (and then managing what had been planned) was his recipe for political success. Schmidt continued the coalition with the FDP, Genscher becoming Foreign Minister. His cabinet, however, was one 'without stars'. The SPD ministers chiefly came from the right wing, and had trade union links. After the retirement of Erhard Eppler (too left and too visionary for Schmidt, and resentful of his chief's 'military' style to boot), Matthöfer was the only left-of-centre figure. Schmidt encouraged the FDP to develop its more conservative side (which signified a move away from the party of Scheel and the Freiburg theses).

Economic Management

Schmidt wanted West Germany to continue to be reliable and predictable in international terms and economically strong at home. He was convinced these two things went hand in hand. Effective economic management was his nostrum for the latter aim. One of his first steps as Chancellor was to develop an 'economic and political orientation plan' (and it was not coincidental that economics preceded politics in the title). Nine economic summits took place from 1974 to 1982. West Germany had become rich; but the extraordinary shock caused by the first oil crisis of 1973–4, when oil prices quadrupled (followed by the second hike in 1979–82), meant that urgent action was indeed required. Oil, of course, had a crucial role in the production of West Germany's energy needs. Coal production had reached its peak in 1957. Thereafter from providing 90 per cent of the energy requirement, it provided only 30 per cent in 1973 (oil consumption rose in the same period from about 5 to 55 per cent). In 1973 about 4 per cent of energy was nuclear. Schmidt's response to the crisis was characteristically courageous: he forced West German consumers to pay the real price for oil rather than allow hyperinflation to become a temporary expedient. In due course, German industry developed ways of conserving fuel (which soon became the European norms).

In 1975 Schmidt produced an economic stabilization plan that brought the first real cuts in government spending to reduce the budget deficit (and thus further squeeze inflation). It was obvious that these measures would hit the ordinary West German worker most of all; and in order to reduce tension between the government and some of its important supporters, Schmidt introduced his 1976 law on 'codetermination' in industry which gave workers' representatives an important say in the management of the companies for whom they worked. At the same time, he tackled a number of highly complex currency issues. Since March 1973, all European Community (EC) currencies (with the exception of sterling) had been allowed to 'float'. In order to produce some stability within the EC, however, these currencies were linked in what was called the 'snake' (in 1978 this became the European Monetary System). In relative terms, West

Germany coped better with the oil price-hike than any other Western state. For the 1976 election, Schmidt faced a new CDU candidate, Dr Helmut Kohl, then forty-six years old. The SPD gained 42.6 per cent, roughly their 1969 figure. The CDU, however, despite a candidate widely dismissed as provincial, got 48.6 per cent, their second-best ever result.

Foreign Affairs

In foreign affairs Schmidt's desire that West Germany should be a dependable ally was strained by his view that the performance of the American government was poor, that its policy was often too selfish, and after 1976, that then-President Jimmy Carter lacked real grip on policy. Certainly, American politics were in some turmoil following Nixon's resignation in August 1974 as a result of the Watergate break-in. Schmidt liked Nixon's successor, Gerald Ford, a great deal, and unwisely, as it turned out, urged Americans to support him in 1976. When Carter was elected instead, Schmidt dispatched Ehmke to Washington to apologize for this. Yet there remained a coolness between the men, Schmidt believing Carter to be 'not big enough for the game' (as his biographer Jonathan Carr noted), Carter torn between admiration for Schmidt's skills (particularly over economic policy) and dislike for what he regarded as his hectoring manner.

Schmidt at first allowed *Ostpolitik* and *détente* to carry on. In 1975 the Conference on Security and Cooperation in Europe took place in Helsinki (conferring its name on a process even more important than *Ostpolitik* itself). This meeting proved a real breakthrough in East-West relations (Schmidt used the occasion to demonstrate his ability to have amicable talks with Honecker); but its insistence on the inviolability of fundamental human rights and the need for political liberty proved instrumental in the undermining of Communism in eastern Europe more than a decade later. Yet because he believed so strongly in stability, Schmidt refused to do anything to undermine Communism in East Germany or eastern Europe.

The Twin-Track Decision

There is some evidence that Schmidt felt irritated by Carter's insistence on the importance of human rights. He did, however, go along with the strong American response to the Soviet invasion of Afghanistan in 1979. This act of Soviet aggression played an important part in generating a further stage in the arms race. Ultimately it spawned the very issue that was to destroy Schmidt himself. In the 1950s, before they had developed intercontinental ballistic missiles (or ICBMs), the Soviets had installed medium-range rockets for potential use against western Europe. The US response had been to install rockets of similar range in Britain, Italy and Turkey (the latter withdrawn when the Soviets took their rockets out of Cuba). But the Soviet rockets remained in central Europe. Furthermore, and this was the nub of the matter, when they became obsolescent after 1974, the Soviets decided to replace them, much to Western surprise, with their new SS20s. These were highly mobile, had three warheads and were extremely dangerous.

These missiles were, of course, intended for use in Europe (since they could not reach the USA). Because of this NATO leaders agreed that their obvious purpose was to seek to drive a wedge between Europe and the USA, by implying that any attack on Europe would not necessarily be accompanied by an attack on America. At first, the American response was to insist that NATO members should increase their defence budgets, whilst encouraging the generals to think in terms of a limited non-nuclear response to any Warsaw Pact aggression. Schmidt and the British Prime Minister Callaghan (whom he respected) disliked this latter point, since it seemed a move away from the complete deterrence promised by the concept of 'mutually assured destruction', which threatened that any attack on western Europe would be deemed an attack on the USA as well. They therefore preferred to answer like with like. But Schmidt's own party rejected this logic. Social Democrats now declared that the time had come to break out of the arms spiral and create, instead, an environment in which *détente* would lead to disarmament. Schmidt was convinced this would be hazardous and send the wrong signals to Moscow. What was needed was an unequivocal statement that the West would at all times ensure it had adequate nuclear protection. This meant rearmament. At the same time, he proposed formal negotiations on arms reductions to emphasize that NATO was not acting aggressively. The Americans agreed to give the Europeans the neutron bomb, a nuclear device that left buildings intact but would destroy personnel.

These were smaller, more accurate weapons; but for the SPD the danger was that the smaller the weapon, the greater its potential for actual use. At the end of October 1977 Schmidt gave a talk in London in which he urged the West to accept the neutron bomb. But the SPD did not believe that the new Soviet weapons represented a security threat that could not be met by the existing weaponry. In January 1979 Carter, Giscard, Schmidt and Callaghan met on Guadaloupe. They declared their support for the current strategic arms limitations talks, SALT 2, and that they wished for a SALT 3, but meanwhile urged NATO's rearmament. The SPD, however, led here by Herbert Wehner, became increasingly agitated about this: many in the party believed the decision would undermine *détente*. On 12 December 1979 NATO announced its twin-track decision.

Over the next ten years events were to prove that Schmidt and the others had taken entirely the right course of action. To have turned a blind eye to Soviet rearmament would not necessarily have encouraged the Soviet reformers (although, admittedly, it might have). To rearm openly whilst also sincerely negotiating on disarmament, however, made it clear to the Soviets that they could not win the arms race, but might achieve *détente*. It was a conservative policy but wise and less risky than appeasement of the Russians. It certainly brought a new realism to Soviet politics. It was widely known that Brezhnev was no longer master of his own mental processes (at one meeting with the Social Democrats they noted that before he responded to their questions, Gromyko had to write his answers down for him on a piece of paper, which he then read out). Yet within the SPD Schmidt's decision caused uproar, particularly amongst the 'new', or younger left, led by Erhard Eppler, Gerhard Schröder and Oskar Lafontaine, who were being strongly supported by the 'even newer' left of Brandt, Wehner, Bahr and Ehmke, busily rejuvenating themselves in a left-wing mould. Brandt, in particular, was trying to recast himself as a Socialist firebrand. They tried to make Schmidt reject the deployment of any new nuclear weapons. At the end of 1979 Schmidt initially forced the party to accept the twin-track idea. But it was to prove a hollow victory.

However rational (and justified) Schmidt's decision, the fact was that he needed to gain the support of his party for it, or risk leading a divided party and losing political credibility. Certainly, the nuclear issue was complex. The military mind was not always understood by the political one; the ordinary citizen often found it hard to comprehend either. The West was obsessed with overkill. British policy, for example, developed by the new Prime Minister Margaret Thatcher now planned to have sufficient British nuclear weapons to wipe out not just Soviet military centres, but almost every office of state in the Soviet Union. Today we know that many of the nuclear weapons possessed by the Soviets were faulty and might not have worked. On the other hand, the Soviets took every opportunity of threatening the West. The USSR's space exploits showed that when resources were devoted to a particular goal, however complex in technological terms, it could be achieved with breathtaking skill.

Over and above the strategic issues involved, rearmament actually impinged on several equally fundamental political issues. This is why the twin-track decision had such an important impact on German political development. First, as we have seen, the SPD was becoming increasingly pacifist. There were undoubtedly moral reasons for this, and a desire to revisit the pre-Godesberg values of Social Democracy. Party members could feel that their party seemed increasingly out of touch; bizarrely they went back to the past to seek a remedy. Anti-nuclear feeling in the 1950s (which Schmidt himself had supported as a young man) had been a basic plank of SPD policy. The need for fresh thinking was also provoked by the rise of the Greens, who were strongly against rearmament. They were beginning to threaten the SPD's electoral chances by poaching pools of voters the party regarded as its own. Some in the SPD believed the correct course of action was to attack Green ideas (especially those which wanted to put a cap on economic growth and would thus affect the ordinary worker's standard of living); others were convinced the party should try to steal the Greens' clothes. In 1981 Brandt raised the question as to whether the SPD could integrate the ecological movement. In a paper entitled 'Social Democratic Identity' he said the Greens were not enemies of the SPD. This move, of course, was seen as a validation of Green ideas and the beneficiary, not surprisingly, was the Green Party and not the SPD. After their success in the 1980 elections and the first direct elections to the European Parliament, the Federal Green Party was duly founded to reflect this.

Brandt's New Radicalism

Brandt's policy as party chairman was, increasingly, to seek to take on board Green concerns (both in respect of rockets and their other main worry, the environment) and try to cooperate with them and thus enhance the potential to form a coalition with them. His political sense told him that Green issues were real ones. Schmidt, on the other hand, together with other right-wingers and Hans-Jochen Vogel in particular, wanted to draw a clear line between the SPD as a party of government and the Greens as a collection of impractical idealists. They declared that the Greens were unfit for West German political life, since they opposed industrial society and NATO. They attacked younger Party members (who favoured the Greens) and would have liked to expel the Young Socialists from the SPD altogether.

The New Left, however, counterblasted by pointing out that it was not they but the old Left that had been incapable of change, and had tolerated corrupt practices within the party (a charge exaggerated, but not unfounded). This ever-deepening debate, then, was as much about the identity of German Social Democracy in the final third of the twentieth century as about arms. For Schmidt, the logical culmination of the SPD's long march from exile to opposition, from Bad Godesberg to Bonn, was total party acceptance that the SPD should be a de-ideologized party. What should chiefly distinguish it from the CDU was a clearer commitment to higher efficiency and better performance than the CDU/CSU. He never said as much, but all his actions proved that he believed that Socialism within liberal democracy was now effectively dead. For Brandt and the others the SPD was required to rediscover the importance of ideology. Schmidt regarded the view that rearmament might damage the *détente* process as crude appeasement and also idiotic, since his relations with Honecker were extremely cordial. Schmidt knew that the East Germans understood they could always rely on Bonn's desire to do nothing to destabilize the inter-German relationship. This suited Honecker only too well. If anything, the twin-track decision proved that the West still wanted *détente*; its rearmament, however, allowed the Communists to continue to portray it as dangerous and to be resisted.

The 1976 Election

In May 1974 Schmidt had – quite literally – delivered a lecture to the SPD on its future. It must, he said, cease to be like a 'university seminar' and instead grow a 'skin' and not be obsessed with theorizing. Socialism, he claimed, was chiefly about 'solidarity', which he had once compared to comradeship in the army. He demanded discipline but (politics being politics) he got the opposite.

In the 1976 elections, Kohl, assisted by Strauss and Hans Filbinger, marshalled the CDU/CSU behind the slogan 'Freedom or Socialism'; but Schmidt managed to save his skin by stressing his competence as Chancellor. Even so, Helmut Kohl almost gained the Chancellorship. Other SPD members did badly. Scandals abounded. There were allegations of the illegal bugging and Maihofer, Minister of the Interior and FDP member, was forced to resign over his bungling at the time of the terrorist killing of Hanns Martin Schleyer, the head of the German industrialists' association. Schmidt himself, however, as we have seen, came out of the appalling affair with credit.

As far as economic, tax and social policy was concerned, it was said that the SPD was making too many concessions to the FDP. It was a sure sign of Schmidt's desperate plight that, at the end of 1977, Schmidt stopped trying to finance social policy measures through taxation and decided to fund them by borrowing. This meant that by the time the second oil price-hike hit Germany in 1979/80 there was no government money to put into investment or strengthen demand.

The 1980 Election

In 1978 the leading right-wing Social Democrat Georg Leber had decided he had had enough of his party and would seek retirement. This was widely seen as a blow to Schmidt. Meanwhile, Wehner, who was getting older, more irritable and forgetful by the hour, found it increasingly hard to help Schmidt manage the party in the Bundestag. Yet Schmidt was none the less able to win the 1980 election. A major reason for this was that the unpredictable tub-thumping Strauss was the CDU/CSU candidate. Large numbers of anti-Strauss CDU supporters seem to have voted for the FDP rather than the CDU. This win lulled the SPD into a false sense of security, since it appeared that they were not being damaged by their internal disunity, or by their unpopular talks with the SED (which Schmidt did not favour). In reality, what the result proved was that the votes that either party needed to win lay squarely in the centre of the political spectrum. At the start of 1981, Hans Jochen Vogel decided to challenge the moderate Christian Democrat Richard von Weiszäcker as Governing Mayor of West Berlin. This was seen as an implied challenge to Schmidt as well. He did not win, but did unexpectedly well.

In June 1981 the Protestant Church's annual conference, the *Kirchentag*, passed a damaging motion criticizing Schmidt's nuclear policies. A massive peace demonstration was held in October 1981, at which Eppler was to be the main speaker. Schmidt was furious about this, but Brandt refused to support the Chancellor in attacking Eppler. The April 1982 Munich party conference confirmed Schmidt's line for the time being, but agreed to hold a special party conference on the issue of the stationing of the rockets on German soil.

The FDP Changes Sides

The special party conference boded ill for Schmidt. But the final nail in Schmidt's coffin was provided by the FDP. It had begun to do badly in elections. The most obvious explanation was that its prime function in West German politics now seemed to be to shore up a moribund Chancellor. Accordingly, secret talks between Kohl and Genscher took place; later, and in public, the latter indicated his readiness to coalesce with the CDU and leave the SPD-led government. This led to the collapse of the coalition and subsequently Kohl's chancellorship. On 1 October 1982 Schmidt fell in a constructive vote of no confidence. In mid-September 1983, however, Schmidt told the SPD parliamentary party that he still supported the twin-track decision: Brandt said that he never had. Antje Huber, Ehmke and Bahr composed a resolution for the special party meeting in Cologne on 19 November that strongly opposed the stationing of missiles in West Germany. Schmidt put his case there, Brandt spoke against it, and a large majority of the party agreed with Brandt.

The SPD After Schmidt

Schmidt's 'national' popularity was well demonstrated by the fact that his departure marked the beginning of a process of decline for the SPD at the federal level, leading to four consecutive federal election defeats in 1983, 1987, 1990 and 1994. The party saw itself hopelessly torn between the need to stand for something specific, whatever that might be, a wish to continue to offer a distinct Social Democratic identity, and the pressures to converge with CDU/CSU policy to please the West German electorate. Vogel now became the SPD's candidate for the chancellorship for the 1983 elections. The SPD got 38 per cent, a miserable result. The SPD then had to prepare for opposition. It established eight working parties which extended over individual ministries, each to be led by a deputy party floor leader. Yet there was increasingly hostility towards the Right, led by Hans Apel. Ehmke, who had refused to serve in Schmidt's final adminstration, took over the working party for foreign, security, German and European policy. Vogel was a decent man but a hyperactive leader (one Bavarian noted that the only thing about which Vogel would not issue a press release was the weather forecast).

There was a feeling that the SPD needed to have a new programme. Eppler's basic values commission had concentrated on three themes: liberty, justice and solidarity. A manifesto entitled 'Orientation '85' was proposed. At this juncture, Brandt resigned, and Vogel took over the chairmanship of the programme commission. The new programme was accepted in 1989, but made little, if any, impact. The truth was that Social Democracy had run its course. The new ideas were either being produced by the Right (as in Britain and the USA) or by the Greens.

In the spring of 1985 Rau and Lafontaine won absolute majorities in their *Länder*, ostensibly by adopting a hostile attitude towards the Greens (who had gained more than 8 per cent in the European and other elections of 1984). But it proved disastrous to draw simple conclusions from this for the 1987 election. Vogel had wanted to have another go at running, but the SPD Executive would not accept this. Rau was the clear choice, but there was a dispute about who should run the campaign – Rau's own team or the SPD's business manager, Peter Glotz. Brandt, unwisely, decided both should. Rau decided there should not be any talk of cooperation with the Greens. In November 1986 the SPD lost 10 per cent in Hamburg and the Greens gained more than this. In the January 1987 election the SPD lost 1 per cent of its 1983 election result, although Kohl also lost 4.5 per cent. The SPD seemed trapped in its own history, lacking the appropriate skills that the West German political system demanded: a firm party base, good management and an ability to maintain the essential Western-ness of the reinvented German state. The New Left was not able to demonstrate it possessed any of these.

Kohl's First Years

In 1982 Genscher had insisted that Kohl's new government must carry on with *détente*. Delighting in his new power, Kohl was quite happy to agree. In the same year, Brezhnev died. Two more decrepit and moribund leaders, Andropov and Chernenko, followed before Gorbachev became First Secretary in 1985. Kohl's political career, and the whole of West German political life, were to be totally changed by this single event. No one could have foreseen that, without Gorbachev, Kohl's Chancellorship would chiefly have been known as the government that presided over the worst corruption that West Germany had ever experienced.

Corruption in Bonn

On 16 February 1987 (a month after the federal election of that year), verdicts were announced in the so-called Flick trial. There were three defendants, Hans Friedrichs, Otto Graf Lambsdorff (both former Federal Economics Ministers and leading members of the FDP) and Eberhard von Brauchitsch, the former general manager of the vast Flick business empire (and son of Hitler's army chief of staff). The men had faced two extremely grave charges: bribery and corruption (a charge which was dropped) and tax evasion. Although there was circumstantial evidence to back up the first count, it was held to be too weak for prosecution. All three were convicted of tax evasion. Lambsdorff was fined DM 180,000, Friedrichs DM 61,500 and von Brauchitsch DM 550,000; he was also given a two-year suspended gaol sentence.

Yet this trial was about far more than just three men. In fact, virtually all of West Germany's political leaders had been involved in the Flick affair. Franz Josef Strauss, Willy Brandt, Helmut Schmidt, Rainer Barzel, Helmut Kohl, as well as the CDU, the CSU, the SPD and the FDP, all had starring roles. What seemed to have happened was that from 1975 until 1984 government policies, indeed the Bonn Republic itself, had been for sale. Yet it is also true that the state managed to survive this crisis. It proved, once more, that Bonn democracy was resilient; that its political culture in the end allowed the successful management of problems which might have damaged many democracies far older than Bonn's beyond repair. Yet it also demonstrated that consensus could be a two-edged sword and that the Bonn system was capable of corruption. Consensus politics had allowed every democratic party to be targeted by Flick so that it was only the Greens (who were too new to be involved) that were able to criticize their political opponents and exploit the scandal to their own advantage. At the same time, however, had West German politics been more adversarial, Flick's bribery might well have been exposed, and countered, through party political conflict at a much earlier stage. Consensus helped, rather than hindered, the attempted corruption of the state.

The Bonn system was certainly corruptible. For one thing, the parties played the central part in all aspects of public life. They determined the appointment of political civil servants, of higher judges, even at times heads of hospitals, schools and so forth. This seemed democratic (and was widely regarded as being so). But within parties, deals could be done, and people rewarded outside of the public gaze. Parties were thus worth trying to corrupt. Secondly, in some *Länder*, one party could boast very long periods in government. This made bribery doubly worthwhile, because it was so much harder to detect in the absence of oppositional party probing. But, thirdly, even where single-party rule did not apply, the well-managed Bonn system made corruption difficult to spot. If more than one party was implicated, the chances of detection became much reduced since the parties had no incentive to investigate each other. The Flick affair showed clearly how the perfectionism of the West German political system generated the very flaws it was designed to exclude. This was a point that did not escape the West Germans and consideration of this matter was to dominate West German political life until the unforeseen collapse of Communism wiped the slate clean.

Friedrich Karl Flick

One of the Federal Republic's richest men, Friedrich Karl Flick, was the son of the founder of the Flick Industrial Corporation, which had been rebuilt three times (during the Third Reich, in 1950 and in 1972). Flick's father had been made bankrupt by the collapse of the Third Reich, and was sentenced to seven years at Nuremberg (of which he served three) for using slave labour. His company had interests in steel, explosives (it owns Dynamit-Nobel), munitions (it makes the Leopard 2 tank), engineering, paper and chemicals. In 1983 it had a turnover of about DM 6 billion, and is said to have spent DM 14 million buying influence for itself. Flick's case, simply put, was that all he had done was to try to avoid paying tax, not itself illegal. Indeed, Flick himself was not on trial; only his general manager stood accused (itself a peculiar decision, since no one had suggested von Brauchitsch had acted for anyone other than his master Flick). He did not deny making contributions to politicians and political parties, but argued simply that this was never for personal gain but to enhance the constitutional role of the parties in furthering political education and opinion-forming. Yet he was also a generous friend of many of the famous names in German politics. Strauss was presented with a silver horse which cost DM 60,000 on his sixtieth birthday, and Helmut Schmidt received a silver candelabra worth DM 17,000 as an unsolicited gift that embarrassed the recipient.

In 1975 Flick decided to sell his 29 per cent stake in Mercedes Benz to the Deutsche Bank for over DM 2 billion. It was this profit on which he sought to evade tax and for this that he was found guilty. The sale had been conducted at the request of Schmidt to suit the 'national' policy of West Germany at the time (and was thus itself a bribe of sorts). Flick was never found guilty of seeking to bribe parties themselves. Some observers found it hard to believe that Flick and his advisers were truly so naïve as to believe that the presents to parties and their leaders would not be construed as attempts to gain political advantages. Whilst the specific issue of the 1975 tax waiver led to the charges, Flick's actions indicated a return to Weimar practices: Flick's father had made many donations to Weimar parties (but not the Nazis before 1933).

Flick's activities had come to light when a small-town accountant noticed that a local firm was making donations to the CDU via an address in Liechtenstein. In due course, the Bundestag set up a powerful committee of inquiry to investigate the allegations. The most articulate member of the committee was, significantly, none other than the intelligent Otto Schily (who had defended members of the Baader-Meinhof Gang), who was now a Green deputy. The Greens were the only democratic party not to have received money from Flick and Schily could thus pursue the matter to its bitter end. It is doubtful whether the truth would have emerged as clearly as it did without his contributions.

In June 1984 the committee named its first victim: the Friedrich Ebert Foundation, an institution 'close' to the SPD though separate from it in law. Between 1975 and 1981 it had received DM 2.7 million. A leading Social Democrat, Hans Apel, had met Flick in the latter's hunting lodge and agreed to accept a donation. Both men believed that this was not illegal, since the Ebert Foundation was specifically dedicated to political education. Yet it soon transpired that from 1976 until 1980 Flick had given the FDP's analogous institution, the Naumann Stiftung, DM 1.3 million, the Hanns Seidel Stiftung (close to the CSU) DM 280 000 and the Adenauer Stiftung a more modest sum of DM 10,000. On 14 October 1984 the Flick Committee announced that it had evidence that Rainer Barzel, former CDU Chancellor candidate and now Bundestag President, had received DM 1.7 million for extremely scant 'legal advice'. It was claimed that this was a straightforward bribe in order to get Barzel to step down in favour of Helmut Kohl. Barzel had, in fact, stood aside on 9 May 1973 (and been replaced by Kohl) and Professor Kurt Biedenkopf, then General Secretary of the CDU, had allegedly been heard airing the view that if Barzel were to go, he ought not to become an embarrassing 'welfare case' (taken, by some, to mean that cash might encourage him to go quietly).

Worse was to come. At the end of October, it was announced that Kohl himself had personally received at least DM 350,000 from Flick's assistant, von Brauchitsch. Kohl agreed that he had received money, but said that he had no knowledge of the actual sum involved, and that it was money for the CDU and not for him. Furthermore, he stated that he had pointed this out publicly as early as 5 July 1982, a fact that could be confirmed, some two years before it had been 'discovered' by Schily. Yet money had changed hands and Kohl was now invited to appear before the inquiry, which was without precedent and deeply damaging. But before he did so, Genscher, the Foreign Minister, was asked by the committee to account for a note in Brauchitsch's diary which read 'Genscher has promised further support.' This meant, Genscher protested, only that he had given Flick an undertaking not to change his ministerial team. This was, of course, further *prima facie* evidence that Flick had expressed political concerns that had nothing to do with tax issues.

Kohl himself was grilled for seven hours on 7 November 1984. He agreed that he had received DM 50,000, in a plain envelope, and not given a receipt for this on behalf of the CDU. He was also obliged to concede that he had, in 1975, agreed to hold a meeting of CDU and CSU deputies to ensure that the issue of Flick's tax waiver did 'not become emotionalized' as he put it (the meeting did not in the end take place).

It was clear that Kohl was, by now, in serious trouble. Von Brauchitsch's diary showed that on at least five occasions from 1975 to 1979 Kohl's personal secretary, Frau Juliane Weber, had gone to von Brauchitsch's office to collect money for Kohl. There was also a problem about a sum of DM 30,000, which Kohl could not remember receiving, and a further DM 25,000 which appeared to have gone missing altogether. Finally, inadvertently, Kohl had misled the committee. When asked whether he had known money could be donated to the CDU, tax-free, quite legally, he had replied 'no', although in written evidence he had stated that he had certainly known this. A colleague, Heiner Geissler, tried to explain this curious lapse by saying that Kohl had suffered a 'black-out' under fierce questioning.

In March 1986 the Federal Prosecutor announced that he would investigate these allegations of false testimony, and would also examine the charges that Willy Brandt had lied to the committee as well. Brandt had told the committee on 29 November 1984 that the SPD had never received money from Flick. But this contradicted a statement made by Alfred Nau, treasurer of the SPD, that Flick had given him DM 100,000. Brandt declared that the functions of party leader and treasurer were different. It was noted that the donations to the SPD had increased when Flick's tax waiver was being debated in 1975, and when the SPD was in government (e.g. in 1969 DM 60,000, in 1970 and 1971 DM 100,000; in 1973 300,000; in 1973 and 1974 DM 190,000; in 1975 DM 700,000 and in 1976 DM 1.2 million).

Kohl's defence was not just that Brandt and the SPD stood more heavily indicted than he, or the CDU. He also argued, with great justification, that the law in respect of political donations was a mess. Whilst individuals were only able to donate a maximum of DM 1,800 tax-free to a party, big companies could gain tax exemptions in a variety of ways. The problem had stemmed from Adenauer's time.

Party Finance

Kohl's point was a fair one. The fathers of the Basic Law were motivated by a wish to avoid yet another lesson of Weimar: the financing of the extreme Right (including the Nazis) by industrialists. In Article 21 it required parties to be open about their sources of funding. Adenauer (always interested in fund raising) was drawn to the idea of state funding. Yet he was also open to any opportunity to gain private funding for the CDU and, since 1952, he had actively assisted in this. A 1954 law made donations tax-free, but the SPD had appealed to the Federal Constitutional Court and the law was declared unconstitutional because it favoured the Centre Right. Yet funding continued.

In 1961, however, a gift of DM 100,000 towards the building of a CDU federal headquarters from the Industrialists' Association was withdrawn because of its opposition to a CDU plan to revalue the DM; this showed the dangers of the practice. State funding remained a very important source of party cash, however. By 1964 the money paid by the state to parties (DM 50 million) was only slightly less than the DM

60 million received from donations (the amounts varied from year to year). Erhard and then the Grand Coalition both addressed the issue. In 1967 a party law was passed, stating that in addition to putting forward candidates for election and participating in elections, parties had a legal obligation to influence public opinion and form the political will of the citizens. This paved the way for a more generous tax allowance on donations. By 1968 the Constitutional Court determined that funding should be restricted to costs incurred in electioneering, and that there should be a decrease in the unit of funding (from 2.5 per cent of valid votes to 0.5 per cent) to help smaller parties. The 1967 party law stated that each party should receive DM 3.50 for every eligible voter for over 0.5 per cent of votes received. Up to DM 600 could be given as a tax-free donation. But the parties believed this was not enough, and thus sought greater private funding. In 1983 a new law was passed. Parties who polled more than 5 per cent would get their election expenses reimbursed calculated at DM 5 for every voter in relation to the number of second votes received; parties with fewer donations and fewer members were to get an equivalent sum. Tax-free donations of up to DM 100,000 per year, or 0.2 per cent of their turnover, were now to be permitted for both individuals and companies. This desperately complicated legislation made it all too easy, as Kohl correctly said, to fall foul of the law without intending to. Yet it also opened the floodgates to corrupt practice.

In 1984, for example, the CDU/CSU got DM 85.5 million, and the SPD DM 71.7 million from the state. But from 1970 to 1984 the three parties received in all DM 1,024 million in donations (the CDU got DM 451 million, the SPD DM 167 million, the CSU DM 137 million and the FDP DM 118 million). Donations came from some of West Germany's most famous companies: Bosch, Commerzbank, Deutsche Bank, Dresdener Bank, Flick, Henkel, Karstadt, Kaufhof, Melitta, Mercedes Benz, Otto-Versand, Porsche and Siemens. All were investigated and over 1000 charges were laid.

Interestingly, *The Times* of London, in commenting on the affair, argued that the 'captains of industry' and not the West German voter were deciding 'what kind of government' the Federal Republic should have. This was an exaggeration, but it contained a grain of truth. Flick had managed to save DM 850 million, but had also, quite plainly, bought for his own interests a place in the three parties of government. This demonstrated a worrying lack of self-criticism on the part of West Germany's most powerful men and most powerful parties. It would, of course, be wrong to argue that it proved that the Federal Republic was *in essence* corrupt. On the other hand, it showed the potential for corruption, and it highlighted the importance of adversarial politics in destroying parts of the West German consensus which had become too cosy for democratic comfort. Flick also served as an example to German politicians to be more careful (although the subsequent Barschel and Engholm affairs showed they did not heed it). It had resulted in the trial of two very senior political figures, the resignation of the President (or Speaker) of the Bundestag, a thorough investigation of the actions in respect of donations of the fourth, fifth and sixth Chancellors of the Republic, and yet another law on party finance. The Flick affair offered observers a trenchant comment on the current condition of the reinvented West German state and on the perils of corporatism, consensus and managing political affairs as if they were economic decisions. Had Communism not begun to crumble, the Bonn system might have begun to unravel.

The German Democratic Republic

Willy Brandt once said that the GDR was 'neither German, nor democratic nor a Republic'. That is not the whole truth. It was not really a republic, if that form of state implies sovereignty. It was certainly not democratic. But it was a *German* state, which it could never deny, even if it ceased formally to support German unity after 1970. In its governance and its militarism, East Germany was far more obviously the child of Prussian authoritarianism and the Third Reich than West Germany.

The Stasi

Even if in theory the GDR enjoyed majority support, the realities of politics meant that the Communists had to resort to crude means to retain power. On 8 February 1950 the Stasi, the State Security ministry, was founded. By 1952 it had 4,000 officers, 9,000 three years later. At the end of the regime, it numbered about 90,000 officers and a staggering total of about 173,000 'unofficial collaborators' or agents. The Stasi's duties were not only concerned with stamping out opposition to Communism, but also with de-Nazification. In a move analogous to the process in western Germany, on 16 August 1947 the Soviet authorities transferred the purging of Nazis to German security officers.

The first Stasi chief was Wilhelm Zaisser, replaced in 1953 by Ernst Wollweber, who had returned from Russia in 1945. In 1957 he was succeeded by Erich Mielke who saw the regime out. It is noteworthy not merely that so few people held this role, but that they were of the same generation and in the same mould. Mielke's most likely successor would have been Markus Wolf, his deputy from 1967 until 1987 and also secret intelligence chief. Stasi offices operated at every level of East German governance as well as against East Germany's enemies in the West. The Stasi was, until the mid-1950s, closely monitored by its Soviet instructors. Thereafter it was always watched by the KGB, but was better suited, in many ways, to intelligence work against the West.

The real power of the Stasi was seen not only in spectacular coups, like the one which led to the enforced resignation of Willy Brandt in May 1974, but also much more chillingly in the effective liquidation of 'revisionist circles' and the student opposition in 1956–7, the brutal collectivization of farming in the 1960s, or the socialization of all still privately-owned factories before 1972. After the collapse of the GDR and unification, a number of by now ex-Stasi officers formed associations ('Seilschaften'), analogous to the old ex-SS organizations, designed to protect themselves and the massive amounts of money they had managed to salt away (estimated by the Berlin police in 1994 as amounting to DM 26.5 billion).

As intelligence and security service officers, the Stasi had probably known before anyone else that the GDR's days were numbered and begun to plan for this eventuality. The Stasi cash (of which a large part came from West Germany – see below p. 194) was laundered into post-unity Germany by way of investments in new businesses (often dealing in insurance), but also of organized crime. It seems highly likely that the Stasi also provided funding for political activities of those groups, both far Left and far Right, which it saw as appropriate to its interests.

East German Political Life

From 1949 until 1989, the East German regime underwent repeated – and confusing institutional changes. It spoke of 'workers' and peasants' power' but was clearly uncertain how best to express this in reality, or which organs in the state were to have real power. From 23 May until 17 June 1948 a petition was organized in support of a plebiscite to restore German unity which generated 13 million 'yes' votes in eastern Germany. This was intended to demonstrate that the Communists regarded the cause of German national unity as wholly compatible with their other political aims. This was followed almost at once (from 24 to 28 June) by the currency reform in eastern Germany. A 'separation of states' was completed on 7 September 1949 by the formation of a West German government, and on 7 October by the creation of an East German government. A constitution was promulgated, Wilhelm Pieck made President and Otto Grotewohl Minister President. On 15 October, the new state was recognized by the USSR and, over the next weeks, by all the satellites. On 6 July 1950 the GDR government recognized the 'demarcation' of the Oder-Neisse 'friendship border' with Poland, and on 29 September joined Comecon, the Soviet-dominated council for mutual economic aid. On 1 January 1951 the GDR entered into its first Five-Year Plan.

The attempted uprising of 17 June 1953, in which many hundreds were put to death, was glibly dismissed as the 'total defeat of a counter-revolutionary putsch attempt'; in larger 'socialist factories' 'armed fighting groups' were set up – to safeguard the future of Communism. These were overseen by Willi Stoph (who had become Minister of the Interior in May 1952). There had, in fact, been strikes in more than 250 locations, involving some 10 per cent of workers in the most important industrial areas of East Germany (Berlin, Magdeburg, Jena, Gera, Brandenburg and Görlitz).

The establishment of NATO was countered by the setting up, on 14 May 1955, of the Warsaw Pact, signed by eight of the Communist Eastern Bloc states. This had been preceded (in January) by the signing of a treaty between the GDR and the USSR which specifically mentioned the need to counteract the Federal Republic's Western ties. Interestingly, the treaty stated that the Red Army in the GDR would not interfere in domestic politics and that they shared the aim of German reunification. In 1957 Yugoslavia recognized the GDR (and suffered a break in relations with the Federal Republic). Ulbricht, by now East German leader, began a series of official visits in a bid for recognition, most notably Egypt in 1965. In June 1964 a further GDR-USSR treaty was signed, stating, amongst other things, that West Berlin was to be regarded as an independent political entity and that the aim of German unity was still supported.

The GDR, having sought to confirm its position in external terms, then devoted itself fully to the task of building up a Communist German state (the significance of external recognition of its status remained, however, a key concern). In April 1960 all farms were collectivized.

In 1960, following the death of President Pieck, a Council of State was established (the presidency being abolished). It became, in theory, the most powerful institution, with about twenty members, most of whom were from the SED. Real political power was in fact wielded only by the SED, via its Central Committee, itself elected in theory by votes cast at the party conferences, but in reality by the political leadship of the SED. The Central Committee elected the Politburo which met once a week, as a sort of cabinet, shadowing and duplicating the government ministries represented in the Ministerial Council. The Council was mirrored by the Council of Ministers (with which it was often confused) consisting of about forty members, most of whom were also from the SED. A few individuals were members of all three institutions. The Parliament, or People's Chamber, was supposed to reflect the social and political composition of the population of the GDR and had about six hundred members. Alongside this 'parliament' there were a whole host of other political institutions and corporations as well as the non-Communist parties (in reality, of course, Communist front organizations).

Governing East Germany

It is plain that the actual governance of the GDR was in institutional terms fairly chaotic. The power of the SED held things together but nothing could hide the chaos in 1989 when the SED's power disappeared. The reason for this institutional confusion was probably two-fold: on the one hand, the obfuscation was intended to conceal the fact that real power emanated from the Soviet Union via the SED; but also, on the other, the SED sought to disguise the extent to which the GDR was a one-party totalitarian state. At the same time, the regime fiercely attacked any truly democratic viewpoints. It sought to compromise and subvert those who expressed opposition. It railed continuously against Western values and Western music. In 1965 Honecker declared that popular music was a weapon developed in the West to work young people up into frenzy and cause rioting. Yet by 1967 the SED had about 1.7 million members, about ten per cent of the population of the GDR.

The GDR Before 1989

The building of the Berlin wall was described as the outcome of 'measures decided upon by the ministerial council in order to protect the state border of the GDR'. At the same time, much thought was given to ways of keeping East Germans from seeking to flee to the West. In May 1967, for example, a five-day working week was introduced and minimum holiday allowances and minimum wages were increased. The seventh party conference of the SED in June 1971 declared, as its main object, the increasing of the material and cultural standard of living by means of a boost in productivity. At the eighth party conference in April 1972 increases in pensions and a forty-hour week for mothers in full employment were announced, and maternity leave was extended from fourteen to twenty-eight weeks. Each new birth brought the mother 1,000 marks and young couples were now entitled to an interest-free loan of up to 5,000 marks.

In October 1973 the Central Committee of the SED affirmed that up to three million new homes would be built by 1990, thus ending the 'social problem' of poor housing. By 1986, and the eleventh party conference, further economic changes were being put forward to include the development of high-tech goods, in particular micro-electrical ones. The real truth about East Germany's economic position was not established until the regime collapsed. It is certainly clear that East Germany's propaganda about its own economic strength was widely believed in the West (indeed, Kohl gave it as one reason why he underestimated the expense of economic unification). Even the most casual visitor to East Berlin, however, could have reasoned that if the dilapidation, and general air of poverty in respect of consumer goods (although there was always plenty of food in the shops) was as apparent as this in the state capital, then elsewhere in the GDR the position must be horrendous.

It should not be forgotten, however, that the GDR had no Marshall aid to help it. Its only real ally was the USSR which was not only itself greatly impoverished but looked to Germany as a source of economic replenishment, rather than the other way around. In that sense, the GDR's position, however weak in comparison with West Germany, did represent a real achievement in terms of the effort that the ordinary East German had been obliged to put into economic advancement.

In terms of its international position, the GDR welcomed the Berlin four-power agreement of 3 September 1971, since for the first time the Western powers had signed a document accepting the sovereignty of the GDR. The Basic Treaty between the FRG and the GDR of 21 December 1972 was lauded for basing relations on good-neighbourliness and equality, confirmed by the GDR's entry to the United Nations on 18 September 1973 and its recognition by more than seventy states during this period. Recognition (as we have seen elsewhere) was widely supported.

In January 1983 the GDR officially agreed to the establishment of a nuclear-free zone in Europe (Olaf Palme's proposal) and in October 1986 the SED and the SPD jointly produced a document setting out the basis on which a nuclear-free corridor in central Europe might be created. At the same time, the GDR proudly boasted about Honecker's official visit to West Germany in September 1987. In June 1988 the GDR hosted an international conference on nuclear-free zones.

It was from time to time alleged, particularly by the radical West German Left, that the Federal Republic was an American puppet state. The true position was that it was East Germany that was the puppet, to an extent usually not acknowledged in the West and in West Germany in particular. Today, however, there can be no doubt about the extent of Soviet influence over East German life. The German Social Democrats in the 1970s and 1980s (arguably for the best possible motives) were the most culpable when it came to misunderstanding the interests and

–9–

Kohl and Unification in 1990: Germany Resurgent

The Midwives of Unity: Kohl and Gorbachev

The first phase of Kohl's Chancellorship (which lasted until 1986) had indicated that, despite being a first-rate party man, he was, at best, a second-rate Chancellor. The middle phase (which lasted until unity became an issue at the end of 1989) produced an equally unflattering verdict. The third phase, which encompassed his triumph in the 1990 unity elections, and victory once more in 1994, elicits a very different judgement. Here he shines as the modern German Bismarck, arguably the most impressive German leader for over a hundred years. If the chance to reunify Germany had not occurred, and if Kohl had not grasped it, he might well have been ditched by the CDU, without ceremony, before the 1990 elections. Kohl liked to consider himself Adenauer's heir. By this he meant that he was committed to maintaining Adenauer's reinvented Western Republic, with its Western liberal values. In fact, by presiding over unity, Kohl followed Adenauer with a German reinvention of his own. Whilst he may hope that the new Republic of Berlin will simply be the old Republic of Bonn writ large, this cannot possibly be so (for reasons for that are examined in the next chapter). Adenauer's model German state had run its course.

Kohl's central contribution to the creation of a reunited Germany was that he was determined and focused in his pursuit of it, once he saw that it was on offer. His critics argue that the essence of his achievement was purely reactive, that he merely presided over events that had their own historic momentum. We shall not know for another thirty years (when the archival evidence becomes public) whether this is correct; but even today it seems certain that, like Bismarck in his day, Kohl's reputation as the midwife of contemporary German unity must rely on the truth that he saw an opening, created by others, but then pressed home his own policy (and his own advantage). Nor was Kohl, strictly speaking, the chief midwife of reunification. That important title must go to the Soviet leader, Mikhail Gorbachev.

Figure 8. Helmut Kohl ©Presse- und Informationsamt der Bundesregierung

According to his memoirs, Gorbachev originally did not want German unity, if the new Germany was to be a member of NATO. Neither for their own, different reasons did the British leader, Margaret Thatcher, the French President, François Mitterrand or indeed, the Italian foreign minister. At first they all sought to thwart Kohl's nationalist intentions (only President Bush supported the dream unequivocally; the Federal Republic looked a little different when viewed from the USA). Of the Western leaders, Bush alone could have conceivably restrained the Germans from seeking unity (and he favoured it). The Soviet Union, on the other hand, could certainly have prevented it in several ways. Yet the Soviet President decided not to, not least (as he liked to insist) because he had been subjected to great pressure from the German Chancellor. By the autumn of 1989 Gorbachev had given his permission for some sort of union of the two German states, but by the early summer of 1990 he had agreed to Kohl's plan for full reunification. Kohl had said that he could not fund the withdrawal of Soviet troops from the former GDR, unless Gorbachev accepted the new Germany's membership of NATO. Since the Federal Republic was the richest and most generous Western power, Gorbachev believed he could not stand in Kohl's way.

The Soviet President had encouraged the East German people to think about making political and economic changes to their system; he had refused to sanction the use of force to subsequently restrain them; and he had finally allowed reunification to occur. Had Gorbachev not come to power in the Soviet Union, therefore, there would have been no new Germany, and Kohl would probably have been remembered as one of the least distinguished heads of government of the Bonn Republic. Kohl's standing as a national leader began to improve only after Christmas 1989, which seems to have been the moment when he saw that complete German unity might be achievable. Before then, he was hesitant and reluctant to think about formal, or constitutional, unity. He was also, at first, reluctant to accept that Gorbachev was a genuine reformer who might agree to it. Then, transformed by the possibilities, he became insistent and forceful in foreign affairs. Seeing that Gorbachev's position in the Soviet Union was rapidly deteriorating, he pushed the weaker man into agreeing to unity quickly whilst he was still able to deliver it.

Yet neither man would have done anything to forge the new nation had the ordinary East German people not first demanded unity. It was they, and not Kohl or Gorbachev, who caused reunification to take place. The peaceful revolution of 1989/90 was not 'a revolution of the intellectuals' nor of any single party. Even the revolutionaries themselves did not, at first, ask for German unity. Their national revolution was, in the beginning, inspired chiefly by their insistence on their basic human rights, and nurtured by a general sense of dissidence and discontent with East German Communism. Nationalism became a feature of the revolution only when it was already under way.

There can be no doubt that the West German government, and the Germans themselves, had by 1989 forgotten nationalism even if, *in* 1989, they began to rediscover it. Certainly, this creation of the German nation was different from previous ones. No one was frightened by it; the only fear was that the East German authorities might spill blood and use tanks to quell the revolutionaries. West Germans and non-Germans alike were moved by the television pictures of the plight – and the courage – of the vast numbers of East Germans, desperate to escape Communism. In 1989, thankfully, there was no iron, nor any blood; the ideal that inspired the Germans was the wish for Western liberty and the Deutschmark. At the same time, the simple proposition that the Germans of both German states now belonged in the same nation *was* the expression of real nationalism. Kohl alone understood this and achieved political greatness by becoming its master.

Confusions in West German Foreign Policy

Even before the GDR began to smoulder, most of the big themes in West German political life after 1986 were concerned with foreign affairs, and almost all were precipitated by the changes in the Soviet Union. The extent to which the new Soviet leader was not just a reformer but actually himself a revolutionary (even if, depending on one's viewpoint, he was a disastrous one) was something which emerged only slowly. Yet his early readiness to promote what initially seemed to be mere *détente*, had an impact at once on several key German concerns, most notably arms deployment and intra-German relations. The former generated vast amounts of domestic German debate. The arms question was complex, and shrouded in uncertainty about who had what, and how and where they might use it. In a curious way, the question itself contributed to the construction of nationalism, because discussion about alliances and weapons systems, particularly in the medium and short range, defined a German national interest here, one that crossed the frontier between West and East Germany, since these weapons, were they ever to be fired, would be fired from German soil but hit targets in Germany.

Both West and East Germans understood this. There had been a rare fundamental disagreement within the West German state about NATO's rearmament in the early 1980s (which Kohl had strongly supported and exploited to gain power). There were those, like Kohl, who believed that Western toughness had produced the new Soviet line – and was thus a necessary tool for containing the Soviets and exacting new concessions from them. Others, particularly in the SPD, argued that Gorbachev's reforms suggested the exact opposite, namely that rearmament had been wrong and that a cooperation with the Soviet Union would lead to further *détente*.

Kohl's initial reluctance to perceive that Gorbachev was a wholly new sort of Soviet leader was not unjustified. Gorbachev's actions in his first years in power seemed little different from those of his predecessors. In May 1985 (at the VE Day celebrations) he delivered a classic and bitter attack on both the USA and West Germany, accusing them of 'actively reanimating revanchism in West Germany'. He had plainly been reading Kohl's speeches (which many had dismissed) on the desirability of unity. The October 1986 Gorbachev-Reagan summit at Reykjavik ended in abysmal failure when Reagan refused to allow the Soviets to bully him into halting his 'Star Wars' defence system, designed to make the USA immune from ICBM attack.

Kohl and Gorbachev Before 1988

Before 1988, Kohl vacillated between attacking the Soviets (he even likened Gorbachev to Goebbels) and trying to negotiate with them. Gorbachev's ideas on disarmament unsettled him. Whilst they had appeal, they also made Kohl look foolish. Having insisted on the deployment of Cruise and Pershing missiles in Europe, Kohl was loath to pursue the alternative. Ponderously, however, he came to the conclusion that he had little discretion in the matter. Not only was he obliged to fall in with American wishes which favoured a deal on arms, but he began to see that if he could deliver the prize of a better relationship with East Germany as a result of further *détente*, a political volte-face could be worth it.

Yet Kohl was in good company in being suspicious of the Russians. Henry Kissinger, for one, thought the Russians were trying to divide the West Germans and Americans. The West German voters also seemed to agree with Kohl. In October 1986 the SPD (now wholly identified with a soft line towards Russia and antagonism towards Reagan) suffered a crushing defeat in the Bavarian *Land* elections, with a loss of almost five per cent. Rau, the SPD leader, and Brandt, its chairman, were widely seen as appeasers of the Soviets.

Beneath the surface, however, it was plain that although the Iceland summit had collapsed, there had been broad agreement on the reduction of medium-range weapons in Europe. Although some West German commentators pointed out the significance of this fact, Kohl still considered it politically sensible to maintain his stance as a hardline rearmer. He was hard on other questions as well. On 5 November 1986, for example, Bonn sought tougher rules on immigrants. Kohl asked Mrs Thatcher for an EEC declaration to prevent asylum rights being abused as a form of back-door immigration.

Geneva

In March 1987 the Geneva arms negotiations took place. The USSR had 270 intermediate long-range weapons, each with three warheads, in European Russia, 72 SS-12 short-range, 348 Scud, and 390 Frog. NATO had 108 Pershing 2 missiles, 464 Cruise missiles, and, short-range 72 Pershing B, 91 Lance and 44 Plutons. NATO had over 4,000 tactical nuclear weapons. Overall, the Warsaw Pact had 6.2 million men, 46,600 tanks, 5,239 tactical aircraft and 126 warships. NATO had 5 million men, 20,300 tanks, 3,243 aircraft and 308 warships. At Geneva, the Soviet Union once more suggested scrapping all shorter-range missiles in Europe, leaving 100 warheads on each side, to be based in Soviet Asia and the USA. Kohl, yet again, opposed this proposal.

Now, however, the CDU seemed to be losing electoral support because of his stance (the fact that Soviets had stuck by their offer implied it had been sincere). Kohl's party suffered heavy losses in the Rhineland-Palatinate and Hamburg elections. The FDP, not associated with his line, did well and re-entered both parliaments, from which they had been absent for some years. At the Franco-German summit on 22 May 1987, Mitterrand, too, contradicted Kohl on the arms question (although his Prime Minister, Chirac, sided with Kohl). Yet the 1987 federal election results confirmed that a majority of West Germans did not want to take any chances with their security. They still did not trust the SPD, even if they did not particularly like Kohl. The CDU/CSU gained fewer votes than it had done in 1983, but sufficient to renew the coalition with the FDP (who had done well). On 11 March 1987 Kohl was elected Chancellor for the third time.

A New Line

Once reinstated in power, Kohl began to modify his policy. He saw that change was in the air, and that he had four years in which to prepare the West Germans for this. There is some evidence that, secretly, Kohl had decided to offer the East Germans new arms proposals in return for closer intra-German relations. In May 1987 he publicly put forward a new arms policy, urging acceptance of the 'zero option' idea, insisting only that all nuclear weapons be included in it. Four days after this, East

Germany announced that Honecker wished to begin a comprehensive dialogue with Bonn on economic and political issues. He spent ninety minutes in discussion with Franz Josef Strauss, a significant act since hitherto, in public at any rate, Strauss had always been denounced by the East Germans as the unacceptable face of West German revanchism.

Willy Brandt's resignation as party chairman, following the appointment of a new party spokeswoman, who was not a German and not even a member of the SPD, also helped Kohl. Brandt's judgement had been called into question; it undermined faith in other areas as well. Honecker himself then visited Bonn in September 1987. One British newspaper (*The Observer*) wondered, astutely, whether the improving relations between the two German states might not end in unification. There had been the paper explained, a surge in the number of Germans desiring unity (80 per cent of West Germans said this in 1987). Yet the paper concluded 'unification this century is unlikely'. It dismissed as 'fantasy' the idea that Honecker and his Communist colleagues could ever support such a move, since it would spell 'the end of them'. At the same time, there would, the paper concluded, continue to be a question mark over the German future.

Even at the time, however, the links between arms policy, better intra-German relations and German reunification were being made, whilst the Gorbachev factor was still not fully appreciated. In the same month, Kohl's party suffered further losses in Schleswig-Holstein and Bremen (in the former case, an eleventh-hour scandal involving the successful SPD leader, Björn Engholm had added excitement to the result).

In August 1987 the first fruits of Kohl's new line emerged in a public argument between the Chancellor and Mrs Thatcher on the processes of disarmament. She insisted that the West needed to be cautious in dealing with Gorbachev, since, she declared (quite wrongly) that his scope for internal and foreign policy change was only very limited. This meant there should be no piecemeal deals, since that might leave the West at a disadvantage. Hence she argued that the removal of shorter-range weapons, to which Gorbachev would agree, should be accepted only as part of a far more comprehensive agreement to dismantle chemical and other weapons. Kohl, who was not yet a global actor, was quite happy with a piecemeal deal which directly benefited the German people on both sides of the border. This was to prove the first of many major policy disputes between Britain and Germany that demonstrated that both countries could be acting in good faith, and consistently with their perceived national interests but that those interests were dissimilar.

The CDU was divided on the issue. There were those, like Alfred Dregger, who pointed out that the deals being proposed would not remove medium-range weapons, but only eliminate weapons in the 500–1000 km range, still leaving both sides with missiles that could obliterate Germany, East and West, but leave the rest of Europe unscathed. He urged Kohl to reject soft thinking and follow the Thatcher line, which would either leave things as they were, or, if successful, provide everything. He was supported by the ambitious young Volker Rühe (at this time defence spokesman of the CDU and a strong critic of the zero option). Kohl stuck to his position, however, understanding that the US-Soviet INF Treaty signed in December would almost certainly create a new climate.

These were difficult times for the Chancellor. The shooting of two policemen by environmental activists protesting against the extension of Frankfurt airport caused fears that a new wave of urban terrorism might descend upon West Germany. Those responsible were not Green Party members but 'Autonomen', autonomous rebels, of whom there were now some 65,000. Kohl was re-elected party leader in November 1987 with the lowest vote ever registered, and a special celebration planned in Bonn to mark his five years as Chancellor degenerated into a bitter argument about his future. At the same time, the first reports (by Patricia Clough) reached the West that East Germany had the makings of a neo-Nazi problem of its own. Slogans such as 'gas them all' and 'negroes out' (a reference to Third World students in East Berlin) appeared on buildings, and an East German pop concert was broken up by a small group of neo-Nazis shouting 'Sieg Heil' 'Jewish pigs' and 'Communist pigs'. The Churches responded by forming an 'Anti-Nazi league' under Rainer Eppelmann and Wolfgang Schnur, both to play a part in the events of 1989/90.

The Franco-German Axis

Taking a leaf out of Adenauer's book, Kohl tried to strengthen his position by reaffirming the importance of the Franco-German relationship. January 1988 was to see the twenty-fifth anniversary of the Elysée Treaty, and Kohl and Mitterrand agreed to establish a 4,000-man Franco-German Brigade (under French command, but not subject to NATO, from whose military wing the French had withdrawn in 1966, nor armed with nuclear weapons). They also set up a joint defence council to manage this force. Mitterrand said their aim was 'deliberately imprecise', but there was a clear indication that in the event of extensive disarmament in Germany, the French and West Germans would have to boost their own forces as a safeguard. Better relations with France were balanced by worse relations with Britain.

Mrs Thatcher's wish to control the EC budget and reform the

Common Agricultural Policy (CAP) (which many West Germans believed wise) stood in the way of moves towards even greater European integration. At the December 1987 Copenhagen summit she pointed out that the EC budget had increased by 150 per cent in seven years. The EC was virtually bankrupt, as a result, but the net contributors (West Germany, France and Britain) must not, she said, be asked to provide any more cash. Britain's answer was simple: EC costs should be reduced. Indeed, the Federal Republic suffered the largest net loss of all, amounting to almost DM 9 billion in 1987, compared to the UK with a loss of £700 million or DM 2 billion). Yet Kohl was reluctant to side with Mrs Thatcher. He did not want West Germany to appear penny-pinching or un-European, and he regarded Europe as an excellent political and economic investment for West Germany.

In 1986 West Germany had received almost five times its net contribution as its earnings from trade with the rest of the Community (almost DM 45 billion). In addition, for party-political reasons, he believed it was vital to maintain a high level of protection and price support for West German farmers. Not surprisingly, no agreement on the budget was possible.

The Zero Option

Early in 1988 Kohl announced that West Germany now supported the zero option, adding that Bonn would unilaterally give up its own Pershing rockets. It was clear, too, that Kohl had finally decided to drop his earlier reticence towards Gorbachev. Most of West Germany's most important figures had by now already become convinced that the new Russian leader was – as even Mrs Thatcher now conceded – 'a man with whom we can do business'. Franz Josef Strauss and President von Weizsäcker had both been to meet him a few weeks earlier in Moscow and given highly favourable reports upon him. Above all, Foreign Minister Genscher (who had fled from Halle in East Germany as a young man), had recently returned from Prague and Warsaw, and believed a new era was dawning. He urged that Gorbachev be invited to Bonn and Kohl quickly agreed to plan a visit, initially in the summer of 1988, although it was postponed for a year. The Soviet Foreign Minister, Eduard Shevardnadze, visited Bonn at the end of January 1988 with a 'personal message' for Kohl in which an indication was given about likely Soviet reaction to an undefined improvement in the intra-German relationship, whether East Germany wanted this or not.

It was no coincidence that it was then that the East German newspaper *Neues Deutschland* began to run its first stories about the dangers to the GDR presented by East German dissidents, and to claim they were secretly funded by West Germany with the aim of destabilizing the regime. In March more than 80 East German dissidents were arrested as they entered East Berlin's Sophienkirche; similar measures were taken against groups in all the other major East German cities. Given access to the Western media, these dissidents saw that now was a good time to strike their blows for liberty. It was also noteworthy that Honecker suddenly decided to discuss, for the first time ever, compensation by East Germany to Jewish survivors of the Holocaust. This seems to have been a further sign of Honecker's increasing weakness and isolation, since he was beginning to see the need for friends in the West, and not just in Moscow.

Ironically, the arms reductions talks seemed to be assisting the SPD. Having gained two zeros, the SPD now pleaded for the inclusion of the third, and final zero: a nuclear-free Europe and a 'safer' Germany. The SPD hoped to make this their central platform for the 1990 federal elections, and were actively being encouraged to do so by Honecker and Shevardnadze. Not for the first time, Kohl had to face strong demands from within the CDU that he step down. In July the Baden-Württemberg Young CDU called for his resignation, and there was considerable public disquiet when promised tax cuts turned into tax increases (chiefly to fund Europe, the Airbus and the European fighter). A further crisis presented itself on the thirtieth anniversary of the 1938 *Kristallnacht*, when Kohl's close friend Jenninger, the President of the Bundestag, made a mess of his special commemorative speech. He unwisely tried to repeat (in quotation marks that could not be expressed as words) what ordinary Germans may have thought about the Jews in the Third Reich.

It was in this time of great difficulty that Kohl not only regained his reputation as 'Sitzfleisch', as a determined and obstinate leader who would not be moved by criticism, but also developed policies on German affairs that might open up an entirely new way forward. Gorbachev's keynote speech to the Nineteenth Party Conference on 28 June called for 'radical solutions and vigorous and imaginative action'. In foreign policy, he asserted, the Soviets 'had not always made use of opportunities'. 'What is needed', he said, 'is not just a refinement of foreign policy but its determined reshaping'.

At the same time, Gorbachev announced major reforms in the government of the Soviet Union that increased his own power and ability to promote change. On 4 July 1988, in a remarkable interview with Peter Jenkins, the British journalist with expert knowledge of Germany, Hans-Dietrich Genscher spelt out precisely what this speech meant for Germany. He pointed out that Gorbachev had referred to a 'common European house'. This meant 'a house which would have open doors and within which human rights were respected'. He added that the fact should not be ignored that 'Germans belong to a nation which was separated from itself by locked doors . . . I say separation [he said in English] because we are an undivided nation; we are merely a separated nation. Separation did not make two German nations out of one. Nobody is in a position to divide our nation . . . Germany is indivisible.'

NATO was also increasingly challenged by the speed of the change in Soviet policy. The US Defense Secretary, John Tower, said that NATO must not drop its guard. Gorbachev might not succeed, and NATO needed to fight against a 'false sense of security'. Egon Bahr for the SPD, on the other hand, disagreed with the American and British position. He said bluntly that the Soviet Union had given up its ambition to threaten western Europe, and that one should provide economic aid to it in order to bolster its purpose. Kohl's desire to support NATO to the hilt, whilst keeping his options open to the East satisfied few. To add insult to existing injuries, elections in Berlin produced a bad defeat for the CDU (who lost over 8.5 per cent) whilst the extreme right-wing Republicans gained 7.5 per cent and eleven seats in the city parliament. This prompted the East German government to state that the Berlin Wall was needed now more than ever. Franz Schönhuber (a popular television presenter and former Waffen-SS officer), the leader of the Republicans, promised that 'no power on earth' would prevent further right-wing triumphs.

Polls now showed that the Republicans could count on between 4 and 11 per cent of the votes. Whilst Schönhuber insisted his party was not anti-Semitic, he was happy to allow that, to the end of his days, he would not be 'ashamed of having volunteered for the Waffen-SS' and that Germans should 'refuse to allow their history to be permanently reduced to [the word] Auschwitz'.

Vienna

Meanwhile, at Vienna, where the rolling Conference on European Security and Cooperation (CSCE) was now meeting, both the British and the Americans made the somewhat dramatic call for the removal of the Berlin Wall and further reforms in eastern Europe, if relations with Russia were to improve still further. Honecker seemed to be under increasing pressure from the Soviet leader. He announced a 10,000-man cut in the East German army and a reduction of 10 per cent in the defence budget 'so that the National People's Army will have even more of a defensive nature'. The smaller army would consist of about 157,000 men. Honecker clearly wanted to be seen to support

Gorbachev's *détente* policies in order to be free to resist pressure on him to permit Soviet-style domestic changes. He was quoted as saying that the Soviet leader's ideas on this subject were not appropriate for the GDR. In February he expelled a dissident couple for unfurling a banner demanding reform. Indeed, there was now reliable information that popular discontent in the GDR was increasing dramatically (under the ideological protection of the 1975 Helsinki Accord) and that large numbers of men and women were attending meetings in churches to register their opposition to Honecker's hard line.

Behind the scenes, Kohl's government was doing all it could to improve relations not just with the USSR but with Poland in particular. This was because, like the Americans, the British, and the French, the West Germans thought that Polish dissidents were likely to gain most from the Soviets in the immediate future. The Polish Prime Minister, visiting Bonn for Brandt's seventy-fifth birthday banquet, went home with a promise of cash (some of it to fund joint projects, such as the restoration of the large house at Kreisau where some of the 1944 plotters developed their plans). Yet Kohl refused to make any promises about West German recognition of the Oder-Neisse line. He did however tell James Baker, the American Secretary of State, that he would no longer oppose a decision to scrap all remaining missiles with a range of less than 500 km.

In a speech to the Bundestag in April 1989 Genscher made the point that he was talking about short-range nuclear weapons 'which can reach the other part of the Fatherland'. He went on to raise the issue of unity. Every member of the West German government, he reminded his audience, had sworn an oath 'to dedicate their efforts to the well-being of the German people'. This obligation, he said, 'does not stop at the border cutting through Germany, nor exclude the town where I was born, nor the people in the GDR'. He concluded that after two murderous wars, the German people were now ready to play their part as 'the main support in the bridge of trust between East and West'. Genscher's strong verbalization of the desire for unity clearly contributed in its own way to the placing of reunification on the international agenda.

More than Kohl at this point in time, Genscher was now beginning to see that Gorbachev's reforms could be framed in ways that were specifically German and intended to appeal to Germans. He was not wholly sympathetic to the caution demonstrated by the Americans and the British (who sometimes raised doubts about his East German origins). It was, however, not surprising that his popularity with the West German voters flourished (and that CDU/CSU attacks on him started to become serious). Leading Christian Democrats accused him of wanting to leave Germany defenceless. They alleged that he had failed to see that the real aim of Soviet policy was West German neutrality. This attack made little sense, and suggested that they believed that Genscher's line was not only popular but in advance of their own. Only Kohl had the power and the strategic capacity to deliver German unity. Yet it was Genscher rather than Kohl who first saw a tactical means of promoting it (and was rewarded by East Germans in 1990).

The 1989 GDR Elections

In May 1989 local elections took place in the GDR, and there were now signs of major dissent. Hundreds of East Germans took to the streets to protest at what they regarded as the Stalinist management of their country's elections, in which 98.85 per cent of the people appeared to have voted, and the SED and its front organizations appeared to have gained 98.77 per cent of their votes. Dissidents claimed that, in one area of East Berlin, they had counted 11 per cent anti-SED votes although the government had recorded this as a mere 1 per cent. If this were true for the whole of the GDR, then it seemed that as many as 20 per cent of East Germans were voting against their government's official candidates.

Behind the scenes, a thorough re-evaluation of US policy on Europe and Germany was under way. The fortieth anniversary of NATO fell in June, and President Bush used the opportunity to visit West Germany and state his policy towards the changes sweeping through eastern Europe. He said the USA sought 'determination for *all* of Germany and all of eastern Europe . . . the world has waited long enough'. At precisely this time, Gorbachev offered the West a further set of unilateral arms cuts, including the withdrawal of 500 short-range weapons. It seemed clear that he was not only addressing perceived Soviet needs; he was also speaking to European public opinion, in the East as well as the West. On 12 May the Kremlin's chief German expert Valentin Falin explained to reporters that a single German nation would 'not worry Moscow'. It was, he said, the Americans who were blocking movement: their fears of a unified Germany, he said, were merely a way ('part speculation, part remorse') of facing up to 'their mistake in dividing Germany 45 years ago'. He added significantly that there were 'two sovereign German states represented in the UN. If one day they decide to become militarily neutral, that will create a new situation in Europe, and then we'll talk about it.' Whilst this seemed, on the face of it, just the old bait of unity in return for neutrality, Falin pointed out that the recently agreed free movement of people between Hungary and Austria was a 'positive development' which would not 'be the last one'.

Tiananmen Square

Meanwhile, in the other centre of Communism, Peking, the old-style hardliners decided that the forces of change in their own country should be opposed. On 4 June 1989 thousands of dissident students were fired upon in Tiananmen Square and the surrounding streets by more than a hundred tanks and several thousand members of the People's Liberation Army. The precise death toll was never established, but some figures suggested that fifteen hundred people had been murdered. China's leader, the 84-year-old Deng Xiaoping, had given a clear message to those who sought to modernize Chinese Communism. Yet the horror symbolized by Tiananmen Square made the peaceful change in the Soviet Union and in eastern Europe only the more striking: on the same day as the massacre, elections in Poland brought a first-round landslide victory to the anti-Communist Solidarity movement, led by Lech Walesa. Rumours began to circulate immediately to the effect that the Polish Communist party would soon disband, and reform as a new leftist party.

Gorbymania

It was against this background that Gorbachev's dramatic (and moving) visit to the Federal Republic took place, and it was these events that gave the West Germans real confidence that old-style Communism could no longer prosper in Europe. Genscher predicted that, following Walesa's victory, the Iron Curtain and the Berlin Wall would fall; but few listened carefully. The pace of change was now so quick that there was hardly time to reflect on what might happen. German foreign policy pundits virtually ignored the question of German unity, speaking only of a more 'normal' relationship between the two sovereign German states. Whilst they accepted that Kohl would, once again, raise the issue of unity with the Soviet leader, this was thought to be merely for show, and was seen by many as an embarrassing formality that might offend the Russian guest.

Even the most experienced of observers dismissed the idea of the overcoming of the German-German border as totally unrealistic. And Honecker's deputy, Egon Krenz, often viewed as the new hope for East German reform, insisted repeatedly there was 'nothing to unite and nothing to reunite'. On 11 June the West Germans met Gorbachev – and went wild with enthusiasm and admiration. The rest of Europe, at first taken by surprise, suddenly realized that something wholly unique was unfolding, as if by magic. It was symbolic that the only parallel that sprang to mind was Kennedy's visit in 1961. Jubilant chants of 'Gorby,

Gorby', and cheers for the Soviet anthem, signified the extent to which the West Germans supported his reforms. Gorbachev gave them something very concrete in return. Although he underlined the fact that the two German states belonged to 'different military systems', he added that 'time should be allowed to decide' the issue of which one they would prefer.

Seeming the victim of the euphoria he had himself created, Gorbachev went even further. On the last day of his visit, he proclaimed both the end of the Cold War and the imminent end of the division of Germany and Berlin. The Wall, he said, had been constructed during a 'special situation' and 'could disappear once the conditions that generated the need for it disappeared'. He told Ruhr steelworkers that he and Kohl had experienced a 'movement of souls'. On Germany 'everything was possible'.

The European parliamentary elections on 18 June demonstrated that Kohl was still being judged on his past indifferent record rather than on the promise of huge changes in German affairs. Both the Greens and the right-wing Republicans were able to gain over 7 per cent each, whilst the SPD outpolled the CDU for the first time in eighteen years. It was now widely predicted that the 1990 federal elections would be won by the SPD and its energetic new candidate for the Chancellorship, Oskar Lafontaine. The only good news was that Kohl's chief antagonist in Europe, Margaret Thatcher, had also suffered a severe loss of support. At first, it seemed that the effect of this would be to strengthen those in her Cabinet who had opposed her hostile approach to European integration, in particular to Britain's membership of the Exchange Rate Mechanism.

The first fruits of this were seen at the Madrid Summit, on 25 June, when she reluctantly agreed to make the first moves to full membership. The British government said it was 'committed to the goal of economic and monetary union', though not as defined by Delors, President of the European Commission. No one had more strongly wished Britain to adopt a more positive line on Europe than Kohl, and he was delighted at what he regarded a real step forward. Mrs Thatcher also agreed to the proposal that an intergovernmental conference should meet to discuss a further amendment to the Treaty of Rome in order to create a single European banking system and a single European currency, although she argued that it should be 'less rigid' than Delors had proposed.

Ominously, however, Mrs Thatcher decided to take with one hand what she had given with the other. Parliament was told that existing proposals would put some states under the domination of a 'sort of German-French axis'. On 24 July she backed up her new line by sacking the Foreign Secretary, Sir Geoffrey Howe, and replacing him with an affable young right-winger, John Major (who had never before run a government department). Here, once again, were signs of the fault line that was increasingly to place Britain and Germany at opposite ends of the table.

These changes in Britain's attitude towards Europe were obscured, however, by the enormous changes taking place in the east of the continent, precipitated by a new wave of emigration from East Germany. More than 60,000 East Germans were now seeking to cross into the West via Czechoslovakia, Hungary and Austria. These were ordinary working people who were simply fed up with 'real, existing Socialism', as Honecker now described the politics of East Germany, not intellectuals, and precisely the people the GDR could least afford to lose. It was suggested that, if this proved technically possible, up to one million East Germans would leave their country in 1989 alone. The East Germans' first response to this was lame; they spoke darkly of the wickedness of West Germany, and *Neues Deutschland* was crammed with articles about neo-Nazism, Western homelessness and accounts of would-be GDR emigrants cheated by phoney 'couriers' relieving them of their money. Under West German law, all East Germans were legally entitled to travel to West Germany and could automatically claim West German citizenship. East German law, however, did not recognize this right.

The Wall, the zonal death strip and the shoot-to-kill policy of the border guards could easily prevent mass emigration directly to the Federal Republic. The 197 people killed attempting to flee to the West were a potent warning. Escape via another, more lenient Warsaw Pact state was another matter. By the end of September 1989, many hundreds of East Germans awaiting visas had set up camp in the grounds of the West German embassy in Prague, which took on the appearance of a UN refugee camp. The East Germans tried to lure them back with promises of permission to emigrate in six months' time, but the situation was beginning to get wholly out of control, both in Prague and more significantly within East Germany itself, where hundreds of thousands began to think about leaving.

The Soviets and the GDR Rulers

On 1 October, the Soviet Foreign Minister Shevardnadze personally intervened in this dramatic situation. He seems to have made it clear that unless eastern Europe followed the Soviet lead in providing fundamental reforms, there would either be a mass exodus from those states or they would risk being destroyed by the dissidents. He held meetings with Polish, Czech, Hungarian and East German leaders and with Kohl and Genscher. What the Hungarians did with this advice became clear when free elections were called for November. East German leaders, however, made it plain that they intended to remain an island of orthodox Communism. This left Honecker with only two options. The first was to lock the dissidents up and, if necessary, repeat the example of Tiananmen Square. The second was to let his opponents leave (and export his dissidents to West Germany, where they were harmless to the GDR although the economy, of course, would suffer greatly from their loss).

Honecker, and his secret police chief, Mielke, favoured the first policy, but they lacked sufficient collegial support to execute it, and Gorbachev strongly opposed it. Arrests and imprisonment for four Leipzig demonstrators (the city was becoming an important centre of dissidence) were countered by further opposition. In August, the artist Bärbel Bohley (earlier offered secret haven by the Archbishop of Canterbury) founded a dissident group called the New Forum. Interviewed on West German radio, she claimed that the group had 1,500 members, and announced plans for a conference of all dissidents to coincide with the fortieth-anniversary celebrations of the GDR on 7 October, to which hardliners like Ceauşescu and the Czech Communist leader Jakes would be coming. Other cracks in the façade were also appearing.

Against this background of rising turmoil, Kohl had to confront the seemingly endless decline of his party. Local elections in North Rhine-Westphalia showed the CDU had lost almost 5 per cent. Genscher's party seemed to be buoyed by the Foreign Minister's position in the international limelight, and gained a much needed 2 per cent whilst the SPD's vote remained static. Once again, the beneficiaries of Kohl's decline were the right-wing Republicans, who polled up to 7 per cent in some cities. What Kohl needed urgently if he was to survive were policies that could pull in the disaffected Right whilst at the same time reinforcing his position as leader.

It must have been clear to him that the unity issue might prove to be the key. Even Willy Brandt, who had hitherto done all he could to dampen calls for unity, now came out with the phrase 'that which belongs together cannot remain divided indefinitely'. Kohl was not being particularly forward in turning to the unity issue. What made his position special, however, was that he possessed the power to do something with the vast resources of money and goodwill that forty years of Bonn's reliable democratic behaviour had granted him. The window of opportunity for creating unity now existed; what Kohl needed to figure out was how to open it.

By the end of September 1989, Kohl and Genscher were frequently engaged in crisis meetings over the situation in eastern Europe. Genscher was so busy that he was unable to attend an EC Foreign Ministers' meeting to decide on EC aid to eastern Europe. Some 200 million ECU were dispensed, John Major hitting the spot by saying that the situation Kohl and Genscher were having to address was the result of 'a clear expression of the longing of people in East Germany for the kind of changes now taking place in Poland and Hungary'. By now, over a thousand refugees were leaving through Hungary every day; another 300 were camping in the German embassy in Warsaw.

The head of Kohl's office, Rudolf Seiters, who had played a key part in the transfer of 14,000 people from Prague and Warsaw, was now instructed to intervene again. Kohl was actively shaping events, but his policy was not merely extremely cautious, it was still dedicated to maintaining stability. Unification was not on his list of immediate aims. He did not wish to incite the East Germans to revolt, nor, for that matter, did he want them to come to the Federal Republic; rather, he sought ways of keeping them in East Germany. He gave Honecker advice: 'Internal peace cannot be guaranteed by force or denying the people a voice.' An official was quoted as saying 'We don't want to stabilize the existing regime, but we don't want to destabilize it either.' Seiters urged Honecker to regain the trust of his people. Volker Rühe, now General Secretary of the CDU, said West German aid to East Germany should be increased so that its goods became more attractive to its citizens and its environment less polluted.

The Fortieth Anniversary of the GDR

Gorbachev visited East Berlin on 6 October (for the anniversary) and did his best to signal his support for change whilst demonstrating a genuine concern to avoid any bloodshed if at all possible. He told an enthusiastic group of East Berliners 'not to panic, that's the most important thing'. To the press he said 'If states don't react to the impulses of the times, they are in danger. We know the Germans, we've known them for a long time. They look at their problems and they change.'

Gorbachev's own cause (and international standing) were obviously enhanced by the totally unprecedented statements he was now making; Honecker's rage can easily be imagined. In his main speech in the GDR, he spoke only about 'the further development of socialism' adding 'We will solve our problems ourselves, with socialist means.' This seemed to many a cynical warning that dissenters risked being shot – since this, after all, was how Communists had all too often sought to solve their problems. The fortieth anniversary itself was marked by a massive demonstration in East Berlin staged by some seven thousand people, chanting 'Gorby' and defying the police and the Stasi to open fire on them. Whilst the people's police and the Stasi used much violence in constraining the crowds, there were no deaths. Yet, appallingly, Honecker told the Chinese Communist deputy leader that there was a 'fundamental lesson to be learned from the counter-revolutionary unrest in Peking and the present campaign against the GDR'.

The 'China solution' was being publicly discussed, but most ordinary East Germans no longer believed that Honecker, denied Soviet support, would go down this road. Three months later it emerged that the use of force had been very much in the offing. On 7 November, the Politburo had rejected by only one vote a proposal to order the army on to the streets. Honecker had arranged for additional doctors and blood supplies to be sent to Leipzig.

On 9 October 1989, 70,000 citizens of Leipzig took to the streets to demonstrate for freedom and for 'a democratic, more humane Socialism'. Despite Honecker's readiness to fire on the crowds, the demonstration passed off in relative peace. This demonstration was a turning-point. The East Germans had started to jam West Berlin radio, and hundreds of Western tourists were refused entry to East Berlin. Having sacrificed his credibility, Honecker was himself now the sacrifice. His colleagues on the Politburo decided that he should go, and on 18 October he was replaced by the latest heir apparent, Egon Krenz, who was only fifty-two years old.

The East German Revolution

Mass demonstrations were now breaking out everywhere in East Germany. On 23 October, almost a quarter of a million people marched through Leipzig calling for free elections, but also chanting 'we are the people', implying both that they were not satisfied with what was being done in their name, and, perhaps, that they were Germans rather than Communists. In Halle to the south-west of Berlin, ten thousand chanted 'Gorby, Gorby' – a cry which was plainly not in itself anti-regime but whose anti-regime meaning was quite clear. The next day, fifty-two members of the Politburo refused to give support to Krenz, and two days after that, Krenz made the remarkable offer of free travel for East Germans. The new East German leader seems to have believed that this would encourage his people to rest content. But in reality it was merely a desperate gamble, for, despite being a major concession, if carried through literally, it would produce a haemorrhage that could only kill the GDR.

President Bush intervened once again with an interview in the *New*

York Times where he specifically welcomed the notion of a unified Germany. He said he did not 'share the concern of some European countries about a unified Germany because I think Germany's commitment to the Atlantic Alliance is unshakeable'. As to Krenz, Bush said he could not now turn the clock back. A few days later, East German television started carrying objective reports on the situation in the country for the first time ever.

Unity had obviously moved closer to Germany, and yet no German politician, East or West, seemed to understand how very close it had now become (or else they were keeping quiet). Other European states, however, sensed what was in the offing. To the west, the French more than anyone else discussed the possibility of 'slumbering obsessions and the fear of eighty million Germans proclaiming the advent of the Fourth Reich' as *Le Monde* put it. Mitterrand, himself had said, inaccurately, the previous month that France had 'always been amongst those who favoured German reunification, a question which is now more pressing'. But his Foreign Minister, Dumas, stated that 'réunion' was 'legitimate but premature' (and many French people recalled François Mauriac's comment that he loved Germany so much, he preferred two of them).

To the east, similar doubts surfaced. A meeting of the Warsaw Pact states on 27 October rejected 'any attempt to destabilize the situation, to question the post-war border and resume debate of the [German] issue'. But this was whistling in the wind. On 30 October over half a million Leipzigers took to the streets again. A few days later, Krenz spoke again. This time he promised that the head of the Stasi, Erich Mielke, and four others, including Kurt Hager, the leading ideologue and Mayor of Leipzig would all shortly resign with Honecker's wife, Margot, the Education Minister, and Harry Tisch, head of the Free German Trade Union movement. Events were beginning to snowball. On 5 November, Krenz promised all East Germans passports and travel to the West for up to thirty days a year. This massive concession caused panic in Bonn. Officials estimated that up to two million East Germans might now seek to flee to the West.

Vogel, for the SPD, begged East Germans to stay in their own country and help the reform process there, whilst his colleague Rau warned of problems 'which a lot of people in Bonn cannot even imagine'. At the same time, Markus Wolf, Secret Intelligence chief, said the Stasi would be actively involved in the process of change (a slightly ambiguous message but one meant to imply that Wolf was now a reformer). On 6 November the biggest Leipzig demonstration to date took place, led, this time, by Hans Modrow, SED boss in Dresden. It was plain that the new travel regulations had not stemmed the desire for change.

Krenz's government resigned on 7 November. No explanation of this decision was given. East Germans were asked to bear in mind that 'the Socialist Fatherland needs each and every one of you'. The Politburo announced it would choose a new government. Almost nine thousand East Germans were leaving via Czechoslovakia each day. These were days with strong associations in German history, for seventy years earlier, on 8 and 9 November, German Socialist revolutionaries had demonstrated in Berlin, precipitating the birth of the Weimar Republic. This time, the revolutionaries were anti-Socialist, or at least anti-Communist and nationalist, at any rate in a cultural if not a political sense. What the revolutionaries wanted was to have West German political and economic conditions (and values) in East Germany. This implied the destruction of East Germany as a 'Socialist' state.

The European Community understood how close East Germany was to collapse. As a speech made by Sir Leon Brittan (a British EC Commissioner) showed, the EC was already drawing up contingency plans for German unity. It was natural, he said, that West Germany should not want the EC to do anything to make unity 'more difficult to achieve; the EC should neither retard nor accelerate it'. But he warned that to oppose unity would increase what was still 'a small risk: that some in Germany may be tempted to seek reunification on the basis of a unilateral deal with the Soviet Union to set up a new Germany outside the Community'. Sir Leon was raising the old bogey of German neutralism; but there was no evidence that any German was seriously contemplating this. It seems likely that this line of argument came directly from Kohl and Genscher, who, for the first time but not the last, themselves used an implicit fear of Germany (of what it *might* do) to get their own way within the EC. The West Germans wanted EC money to underpin Krenz's reforms. One of their commissioners, Martin Bangemann, specifically said that, without aid, bloody violence might be on the cards.

It was Modrow who became Krenz's successor as head of government (but Krenz remained head of state and head of the SED). Bonn, still desperately cautious, welcomed Modrow's appointment. Seiters called it a 'dramatic new beginning' and Vogel called for free elections to underpin it. Most significantly, however, Kohl, in his state of the nation address to the Bundestag, promised an entirely 'new dimension' to West German assistance to East Germany, on condition that the SED renounce its sole hold on power. He insisted that East Germans would never be satisfied by a mere reshuffle of the Politburo, and also demanded free elections. The former Chancellor Schmidt, however, urged a special tax to help finance East Germany's modernization. His spin appeared to be that West Germany ought to shore up the GDR, as the logic of *Ostpolitik* had required.

Still not Unity

At this critical stage, it was plain that Kohl and Genscher were still being ultra-careful and were too anxious to advance a *practical* plan for German reunification. They spoke about it and thought about it but they still refused to set about actually establishing it. Equally, however, it was this policy that illuminated not just an essential difference between Kohl and Bismarck, but the essential difference between the Republic of Bonn and the old Prussian Germany. When history had presented Bismarck with an analogous turning-point, Bismarck had executed the turn himself. When history presented Kohl with a turning-point, he let history do the turning. On 9 November, the day of the opening of the intra-German border, Kohl declared unequivocally 'Our interest must be that the East Germans stay at home.'

Kohl's policy of reassurance was not confined to the government of the GDR. He was due in Poland on 9 November, and took with him an offer to provide DM 500 million in new loans and DM 2.5 billion in new credits, and to write off debts of DM 1.5 billion. Kohl also promised he would visit Auschwitz and offer a 'final reconciliation' here as well. Whilst he stated that West Germany made no claim on those territories lost after 1945, which had then become part of the Polish state, he refused to pre-empt any final treaty on this for the time being. This was also an act of caution, but one which was misunderstood, not least by Margaret Thatcher.

At 18.55 on 9 November 1989, the Berlin Wall was opened, as Krenz had promised. In effect, Germany's fundamental division had been ended, even if the Communist hold on power continued to linger on. The opening of the Wall – the opening in the Wall – proved that there was no longer any turning back. Communism, as a theory of government, had, it seemed, been overthrown in favour of liberal democracy. The ideals that had established the Bonn Republic had now been accepted by East Germans as well. Kohl broke off his visit to Poland, flying to Berlin, only to face the uncomprehending boos and whistles of a crowd that had earlier cheered Willy Brandt to the rafters when he had said that Germany was growing back together again.

Kohl's caution was harming him. Whatever he had done behind the scenes to expedite this day, the public perception of him was still that of an over-cautious and unimaginative leader. The fact that his motives in being so (to avoid counter-revolution or bloodshed) might have been wholly admirable was simply ignored in the huge surge of emotion that shaped those days.

An East German Social Democratic Party now formed itself, first called, confusingly, the SDP – but the West German SPD eschewed any organizational links with its East German comrades (as it turned out this was a wise move, since many leading East German Social Democrats proved to be Stasi members). It only went to show how fluid the political landscape had now become. Not surprisingly, most Germans, East and West, were in no mood to do anything other than rejoice. Very few German voices could be heard pointing out that change would be far more painful and difficult. Margaret Thatcher did sound what seemed to be a discordant note. She realized that Germany might now reunite, but believed this was something to be avoided, at any rate for the time being. Interviewed on 10 November, she said 'I think to reunify would be going too fast . . . You have to take these things step by step and handle them very wisely. The first thing to do is get a genuine multi-party democracy in East Germany.' She was not only anxious about the change in German affairs, but frightened that Gorbachev's position in the Soviet Union might be undermined. This would, she felt, be fatal, since without Gorbachev none of this would have happened in the first place.

Foreshadowing future doubts on his German policy, Mrs Thatcher wrote to Gorbachev urging him to stick to his 'one step at a time' plan for change. She would later claim that she could not understand why Gorbachev had agreed to German unification taking place so quickly. He should have taken many years over this, she asserted, and demanded annual payments from the Germans for a step-by-step approach (which the Germans would, she believed, have been more than happy to provide). The Americans took a more positive line, but were also doubtful about how far things were likely to move. Secretary of State James Baker welcomed the opening of the intra-German border as the 'most momentous event in East-West relations since the end of the war'. It was, however, 'premature' to talk about reunification and the dismantling of alliances. Baker pointed out that the USA had been taken completely by surprise at the sudden collapse of Communism in the GDR: 'Were we surprised by the speed of it? You bet your life', he declared. The Americans were not the only ones. British Intelligence officers in Berlin first learned of the opening of the Wall from the BBC in London.

It is important to see that although events were to prove that Communism was finished, neither the inevitability of this nor the consequences were always fully realized. The governing Mayor of West Berlin, Walter Momper, spoke for many when he argued that Kohl should stop speaking about unity and instead help the GDR to find a new, *separate*, identity for itself. Jacques Delors, the President of the European Commission, on the other hand, urged the East Germans to join the EC, albeit as a sovereign *second* German state. This line seemed to have the approval of the Soviets: the French Foreign Minister, who was visiting Moscow, was told by Mr Shevardnadze that there should be 'rapprochement between the two sovereign German states', with acceptance of all existing borders and agreements.

At the time, this appeared to dampen any chance of reunification, since there seemed no prospect that the Soviets would ever accept East German membership of NATO. The merging of the GDR into West Germany, however, meant that formally this situation never arose; and it is quite possible that the Soviet phrases were meant to make it obvious that this was, indeed, a way forward.

The GDR's slide into ungovernability could not be stopped for political, economic and social reasons. But the Communists tried. On 17 November, Modrow announced a thorough reform of the GDR. The state was to be 'democratic and socialist'(even though this is what had always claimed; propaganda had made words lose their meaning), the economy was to be opened to market forces, and the Stasi was to be dismantled. East Germany would seek a 'cooperative relationship' with the EC and would aim at the creation of a 'pan-European economic area'. The purpose of these reforms, Modrow insisted, was to 'renew the legitimacy of the German Democratic Republic as a Socialist state and a sovereign German state. This new reality will dispel all unrealistic and dangerous speculation about a reunification.' Yet almost as soon as these words were spoken, new data about the desperate position of the East Germany economy emerged.

Confederation, Union and Unity

It was at this moment, that Kohl's hitherto rather vague plans for union (though still not actual unity itself, since he continued to think in terms of the step-by-step move to a German federation consisting of the two steps) began to take on concrete form. For forty years, West German leaders had always claimed that reunification was their core foreign policy goal – foreign policy, since Germany's division was never the result of domestic wishes, whatever the East Germans said, but the outcome of the foreign policy of others. Now, for the first time, a union of the two Germanies had become a real prospect on terms that the Christian Democrats and their Western allies could accept.

Kohl saw this and understood that now was the moment to start applying all the pressure he possessed – moral, political and economic. He argued that unification must, and could, take place eventually within the existing Western Alliance, and within the EC. To reassure western Europe he pledged to effect what he termed the 'Europeanization' of Germany following on German unity within NATO and the EC.

Speaking later to the European Parliament, Kohl said that the Federal Republic had a constitutional commitment to unity, but emphasized again that any changes would occur under 'a European roof'. 'If Germans again find each other in a spirit of friendship', he said, 'they will never again be a threat but a benefit to the unity of Europe.'

Seiters was sent off once more to negotiate with Krenz and Modrow. He was told that free elections would take place before 1991. Seiters offered a commission to see how the East German economy could be made more viable. But this was conditional upon the abolition of Article One of the East German Constitution (which gave the SED political control of the country). Kohl insisted he would not fund any rescue package for German Communists. The West Germans wanted some sort of financial agreement with the East Germans to bring the black market in Deutschmark exchanges to an end. The Politburo said it would have formal talks with the dissidents, a move welcomed by some of them.

New Forum, for example, which had rejected the idea of re-unification, said it was more than willing to meet SED leaders. As James Fenton pointed out, however, ordinary East Germans did not share New Forum's view of the undesirability of unity. They had now begun to chant 'Deutschland, einig Vaterland' and meant it much as they meant it when they shouted 'Wir sind ein Volk'. The international spotlight then moved away from East Germany to Prague, where under the leadership of the playwright Vaclav Havel, Czech dissidents were seeking an end to Communist rule. On 24 November, the Czech Communist leader Jakes and his entire Politburo resigned.

On 28 November, Kohl announced that he had come up with a first concrete plan for a union of sorts by means of confederation. He told the Bundestag that he had decided to see if East and West Germany could be brought closer to union with a ten-point plan for confederation in three stages. He said he did not believe that unity could occur 'overnight' and thus proposed these 'steps towards confederation'. The first stage of his plan would bring agreement on self-determination through free elections and the abolition of the SED's monopoly on power. Stage two envisaged specific steps towards confederation, with mutual commissions examining issues of mutual concern such as the economy, social policy and pollution.

The final stage would indeed be unity, but this would take a long time and Kohl refused to give a date for it. In East Germany, however, the calls for complete unification became stronger by the hour. Kohl did not say so publicly, but the federal election, fixed for 1990, was bound to demand a clear response from him. Gorbachev and Shevardnadze continued to tell Kohl and Genscher that they would not agree to unification and would reject his plan if full union was its aim. At Downing Street, however, Genscher repeated to Mrs Thatcher his desire to see the two Germanies 'growing together' (a gradual union) in tandem with European integration. Mrs Thatcher was as cool as the East Germans, who rejected the plan outright if it meant, as they believed it might, that East Germany would become economically dependent on the Federal Republic. On 3 December, however, Krenz was surprisingly sacked as SED chief (three days later he was stripped of his position as head of state) in a coup managed by Modrow and Wolf: they seem to have been motivated by the fear that they would be pushed into agreeing to free elections, whether they liked them or not, and that these would lead to a derisory vote for the SED. Meeting in Malta on the same day, Presidents Bush and Gorbachev announced that the Cold War had officially come to an end.

Once again, the crowds turned out in Leipzig. Two hundred thousand people demanded the dissolution of the SED and reunification. They chanted endlessly 'One nation, one fatherland, one state'. Demands for union, few and far between until now, became the order of the day. There were many reasons for this, over and above the obvious one that the East Germans increasingly wished to benefit from the wealth and liberty enjoyed by West Germans.

For one thing, there was growing rage at the disclosures about the activities of the Stasi: more and more East Germans began to understand the extent to which their lives had been controlled by the secret police, and fear the lengths to which the Stasi would still go to retain power. Those Stasi files not destroyed by themselves or the KGB filled 190 km of shelving. A quarter of a million people had been involved in secret police work. West German intelligence services had 6,000 officers and agents, to watch over some 60 million Germans. East Germany used 250,000 people to keep tabs on only 17 million. After unity, Rainer Eppelmann was charged with leading a Commission of Inquiry into the implications of this (the files themselves are being evaluated by the Gauck Commission). In addition, reports of massive corruption began to emerge. East Germans were now seeing their leaders as they had never seen them before. There were shown Honecker's private island in the Baltic, his hunting lodges, his pornographic video collection and evidence of foreign currency accounts obviously held over for a rainy day. The Communists reacted to this disgust by electing a new leader, Gregor Gysi, a forty-one-year-old whose avowed aim was not to dissolve the Communist Party as such but rejuvenate it.

Unity At Last: A Genuine Turning-Point

The Soviets told Genscher, once again, that they would not accept Kohl's Ten-Point Plan, which they said amounted to giving the East Germans orders. But at the EC summit in Paris, European leaders gave a jubilant Kohl the backing on eventual reunification that he sought. Mitterrand said, 'There should be no more barriers between East and West and the people of Germany have a right to realize their deepest aspirations.' They affirmed that Germany should regain its unity through free self-determination. This clear statement added new fire to the East German demands for unity; yet another Leipzig march (on 11 December) took place, with the crowds shouting 'Deutschland, einig Vaterland'.

New Forum tried to plead with the East Germans to hush, saying that they would endanger what had already been won. They warned that unity would bring a resurgence of Nazism (neo-Nazis had turned up to join the demonstration). But they were not heeded, and the decline in their authority followed swiftly. Increasingly, East German groups began to put forward their own proposals for unity. Even Gysi said that a planned referendum on a new East German constitution could be taken as a vote on German unity.

The fact that unity, even as the outcome of a gradual process, was now a real prospect, had a deep impact on domestic West German politics. Kohl's position was becoming clearer. He had decided to visit Modrow in Dresden and to speak to people there. This visit (and the moving and ecstatic welcome he received) proved the real turning-point for him, because what he learned there caused him to drop his plan for confederation and gradual union, and instead demand immediate unity. Kohl himself subsequently confirmed this date as the pivotal one, stating that any 'doubts' he had possessed on the wisdom of urging unity 'were finally brushed aside on December 19 when I stood in front of the ruins of the Frauenkirche in Dresden'.

The SPD lacked a policy. Many observers believed its close contacts with the SED (which were subscribed to, so the SPD said, in order to maintain the momentum of *Ostpolitik*) had consolidated, rather than undermined, the SED. Many East Germans regarded the SPD as traitors, at worst, or too gullible at best. Some in the SPD wanted to move faster than Kohl, although they, too, aimed at confederation rather than actual union. They wanted to fund the East Germans with no strings attached. Others, led by Oskar Lafontaine (who became the SPD's candidate for Chancellor for 1990) wanted to proceed much more slowly, for fear that unity would prove a huge and unacceptable expense. He also demanded that the East Germans be denied free access to the Federal Republic. The Berlin Mayor Momper opposed unity, because he said it would lead to a resurgence of nationalism and he insisted that what East Germans wanted was simply to have the same living standards as the West Germans. Whilst these ideas were successful within the SPD, it was not hard to see that they would prove unpopular not merely with the West Germans, but with the East Germans as well. The SPD (which was also preoccupied with drawing up a sequel to the 1959 Godesberg Programme) found itself marginalized on the most important single issue in German politics in thirty-five years. Politics is not fair, but it was a grave error for the SPD to fail to realize that reunification was *the* major issue in German politics, and that it was a *political* issue, and not an economic one, even if it had important economic implications. This failure damaged the SPD not only in the 1990 unity elections, but a second time in 1994.

On 7 January, tens of thousands of East and West Germans demanding German unity linked their arms to form a human chain across the border near Göttingen. It was a sign of the extent to which German reunification had now ceased to be a matter of high policy and had become an expression of popular will. What made this remarkable was that most non-Germans continued to think that nationalism had ceased to be an effective political force shortly after 1945. Yet it was plain that the pulling power of nationalism wherever it became an issue (and for whatever reason) was almost always irresistible. A man like Jens Reich, Chairman of the New Forum, could declaim against unity, saying that East Germany's special identity would disappear within the confederation that was being talked about (and his prediction was correct). But more and more Germans now thought these arguments had become irrelevant.

Kohl: A Better Bismarck

The obvious beneficiary of this shift in both parts of Germany was Helmut Kohl. He had always put the long-term aim of German reunification at the top of his agenda. Now polls showed the extent to which East Germans and West Germans supported this aim and would vote accordingly. It was already clear that commonly held assumptions that the East Germans were basically left-wing, and natural Social Democrats, would have to be overhauled. In addition, many West Germans now saw that the so-called block parties in East Germany (chiefly the Christian Democrats and the National Liberals) were no more than fronts for the Communists. Thus the CDU rejected early overtures from its Eastern German namesake, led by Lothar de

Maizière, partners in Modrow's government.

The SPD continued to work closely with the Eastern SDP which soon changed its name to 'SPD'. Although the SPD was technically a wholly new party (since the old East German SPD had amalgamated with the KPD to form the SED in 1946), the party landscape was changing so rapidly that no one was wholly certain what the plethora of parties implied other than the growing disintegration of the old system. Polls suggested that the SPD would win the East German elections. But in the months ahead, the CDU's line on unity, and its foresight in being careful whom it regarded as its friends, paid rich dividends. It also helped to alter the political landscape of East Germany at the same time. Meanwhile, the increase in neo-Nazi activity in both parts of Germany began to be noted. There was an obvious, if undefined, link between national pride and nationalist extremism, which Gysi and his colleagues were quick to exploit, implying that unity would lead to the return of the Nazis.

Kohl's attacks on the East German Communists did not deter him from seeking to pressurize Modrow to agree to confederation. The Chancellor was concerned by the continued emigration from East Germany. In the first ten days of 1990 some fifteen thousand East Germans had moved to the West. Kohl began to say 'if the DM does not soon come to Leipzig, Leipzig will come to the DM', implying, accurately, that economic pressures would increasingly drive political change. Modrow, in return, announced he would draft a new electoral law for elections on 6 May. But he appealed strongly for 'national' unity – GDR national unity – and, at first, refused to drop plans to establish a secret police to succeed the Stasi. Although he then had to concede that such a force would only be set up after the elections, his position was severely weakened as a result.

As the days went by, even Modrow had to accept that relations between the two Germanies were bound to grow closer (he now claimed to want confederation or a 'community regulated by treaty'). Popular feeling was amply demonstrated when, on 16 January 1990, thousands of East Germans stormed the former Stasi complex. Meanwhile, some eighty thousand Leipzigers continued their Monday demonstrations in favour of unity (two hundred thousand of them turned out when Douglas Hurd visited their city).

On 30 January, Gorbachev asked Modrow to fly to Moscow, and told him, in public, that his line was untenable. 'Basically', he said, 'no one casts any doubt' on the proposition that Germany should be reunified. Gorbachev added that the transition to unity would be complex; there were 385,000 Red Army troops in East Germany, and any change in Germany's status would require the support of both German states and the Four Powers involved. Germany had never signed a peace treaty (since a German state had gone into abeyance in 1945), and these matters required careful settlement. But Modrow left Moscow in no doubt as to what would follow for him and for East Germany. It was estimated by de Maizière (who hoped to succeed Modrow in May) that one-third of East Germans were now 'sitting on packed suitcases'. Some 350,000 had left in 1989, and 1990 would see an even larger exodus unless Germany were reunified. The country was lurching towards total disintegration; in an attempt to prevent this, Modrow now called new elections for 18 March and proposed, idiotically, a plan for German unity on the basis of neutrality (which meant a Germany outside NATO). Once again, the ordinary people of Leipzig took to the streets, shouting anti-Communist and pro-unity slogans.

Gorbachev's own position on Germany was undoubtedly driven by his personal value-system, but also by the fact that his own power base (the Communist Party of the Soviet Union) was beginning to fall apart. At the beginning of February, mass demonstrations demanded an end to the monopoly on power held by the CPSU, inflamed, in part, by the very policies he had himself pressed so hard. What made Gorbachev very different from other leaders of authoritarian regimes, not least his Chinese comrades, was that he did not seek to stem the tide by repression, but hoped to survive by swimming with it. If this was a miscalculation, it was a deeply humane one, for which, in Germany's case, Gorbachev deserved, and gained, huge credit.

The readiness of the Soviet leader to accept new realities contrasted somewhat with the position of the British Prime Minister and her Foreign Secretary. Speaking in Bonn on 6 February, Hurd declared, patronizingly, that Britain could share the 'excitement' of the German people over unity, but that it would not be in 'their interest to achieve unification in circumstances which aroused anxieties throughout Europe'. Hurd stressed the inherent instability in European affairs, and implied that it would be Britain's aim to dampen down pressure for change. This, of course, was the last thing the Germans wanted to hear. Increasingly, both Kohl and Genscher began to fear for Gorbachev's survival. This meant that German unity, which could at any time have been vetoed by the Soviets, had to be achieved whilst Gorbachev was still in a position to deliver it. For this reason, Kohl and Gorbachev arranged an urgent meeting on 11 February, with East Germany on the verge of total collapse.

Together they agreed a structure for unity. Negotiations were to begin as soon as the March elections had been held between the two Germanies, joined by the Four Powers. Kohl no longer talked of confederation, it should be noted, but union through the use of Article

23 of the Basic Law, which allowed new *Länder* to join the existing Federation. The problem with this course, according to his critics, was not only that it was not strictly constitutional (since the Basic Law made specific provision for unity under a different article that required the dissolution of the Bundestag) but that East Germany, which was a centralized unitary state, would have to be restructured into *Länder* in order to join the Federal Republic. Kohl promised to pay the Soviets for the withdrawal of the Red Army from Germany, and build new homes for the troops. He also offered substantial aid which by 1995 had topped the DM 80 billion mark; today Germany provides 70 per cent of all Western aid to Russia.

Gorbachev's deal with Kohl was the final high-policy decision on unity. On 11 February, Kohl returned from Moscow and told East Germans that they could 'now unpack their suitcases'. The historic deal had been done, and the small print for a whole series of highly complicated and major agreements on every aspect of domestic and international state-making could be embarked upon. The final unity treaty ran to a thousand pages. Modrow insisted that he would oppose the 'Anschluss' of East Germany to the Federal Republic, but he, like everyone else, knew that these words were wasted breath. Kohl's first aim was to promise currency union on what was essentially a 1:1 basis even though the *Ostmark* was as worthless as the *Reichsmark* had been in 1948. Politically, no other course was possible, for this was the only way in which East Germans could be persuaded to stay in the East. But there were many other matters on which agreement was also needed, ranging from pollution control and improved communications to the withdrawal of foreign troops, the recognition of the Oder-Neisse line, and the whole question of the future of NATO and the Conference on European Security and Cooperation. The border with Poland was to prove a particular problem. Kohl, it seems, was forced by Genscher into giving an assurance that recognition would follow unity. Kohl then threw himself into the East German campaign, in which he was usually greeted as 'Helmut, Helmut, Chancellor of the Fatherland'.

Kohlmania

Kohl's hour had come. In a whole series of speeches in East Germany he made emotional appeals to the nationalism of his audience. In Magdeburg, for example, he said, 'Dear friends, the hour of solidarity has come. We are one Germany. We are one people. There must be no question of one country giving and the other taking. We need each other.' To Germany's neighbours in Europe, Kohl added, 'We Germans want the Poles to live in secure borders. There will be no Fourth Reich. This united Germany will be part of a peaceful Europe.' Most of the neighbours, the Americans, and the Soviets seemed to accept this. The elections of 18 March ended forty years of Communist and thirteen of Nazi totalitarianism. The twelve million voters of East Germany were being asked to do what only very few could ever recall having done: vote in a free election. That opportunity had been given to them by two men: Gorbachev, but also Kohl. At the end of the campaign, Kohl spoke, significantly, to the demonstrators of Leipzig. This time two hundred thousand turned up to hear him (it was estimated that almost one million East Germans had attended his rallies). Those parties who supported Kohl won a staggering 48.14 per cent of the vote. Germany was once again to be a nation.

Progress to formal unity six months later was, of course, not straight-forward. Germans had to deal both with external hostility (chiefly expressed by Britain and its Prime Minister Mrs Thatcher) and continued East German upheaval. Mrs Thatcher argued that unity was now a fact, but that it had implications for Germany's neighbours, and they should be listened to. Kohl responded with a new definition of his high policy as unification in tandem with European political union, not least as an antidote to an over-strong Germany. Currency union promised to be far more expensive than Kohl had anticipated. The expectation of huge government loans (and perhaps economic gains in the medium term) drove up the value of the DM, putting pressure on other currencies.

The question of property ownership presented intractable problems. It appeared that various apparently democratic East German political leaders, including the SPD leader Böhme and de Maizière himself, had been Stasi informants; and countless other problems presented themselves. Additional and equally disturbing examples of how Com-munists sought to control East Germany began to emerge, such as the claim that sixty-two political dissidents had been beheaded between July 1952 and January 1960 in Dresden. The more one looked into East German affairs, the greater the challenge was seen to be. It was not merely those East Germans with vested interests who disliked unity and what it might to do to Germany. Günter Grass, the novelist, warned of a 'dream becoming a nightmare'. He disliked the fact that alternatives to unity had been ignored in favour of a 'Greater German Federal Republic'. He believed it was important to allow a different German state to continue to exist. Kohl certainly made promises to the East Germans that were over-generous. In 1990, there was no General Clay to force the Germans to accept the realities of life, as there had been in 1948. But it is hard to blame Kohl. He believed (as did most observers) what the East German Communists had said about their economic strength. Furthermore, he was convinced that West Germany could pay what was required (he liked to point to his own ample girth, and say that if Germans had a problem with their belts, it was how to loosen them, not tighten them). In any case, the die was cast. On 18 May, a financial treaty was signed between the two Germanies, to come into effect on 1 July, bringing West German money but also West German social legislation to East Germany. West Germany also promised a DM 115 billion unity fund to pay for part of the expense of transition.

When, by June, Gorbachev indicated that he was prepared to waive his objection to a united Germany inside NATO (intelligence first received by Mrs Thatcher), the final piece of the jigsaw was ready to be put into place. Kohl and Genscher decided to visit Gorbachev to get his agreement in person. They were taking with them a DM 5 billion EC aid package and a DM 1.7 billion German loan. Their meeting on 15 and 16 July was an outstanding success, which included a visit to Gorbachev's home region of Stavropol in the Caucasus. No other Western leader had ever been taken there. On 17 July the second 'two plus four' meeting took place in Paris, with Poland a party to the talks. There was complete agreement. The Russians said that post-war West Germany had long been a trusted neighbour, and that the final treaty for German unity could be signed on 12 September. Unity itself would follow on 3 October, and then the first all-German elections in more than half a century could be held.

It was not surprising that a number of observers believed that a European Utopia was coming into being. On 22 June, in the presence of various foreign ministers, that odious symbol of the Cold War, man's inhumanity to man, and Germany's division, Checkpoint Charlie, was hoisted off its foundations and taken away from the Friedrichstrasse and into history. James Baker said, 'We meet today to bury the conflict that created it.' Neal Ascherson wrote that suddenly the world had lost its edge, and that what had happened in Germany was 'the best news the German people have heard since 1945'. He added that the border, the Wall, the wires and searchlights, towers and minefields, the sanded death-strips, the dogs, the helmeted men with guns now all belonged to the German past. Echoing the words of Sebastian Haffner, he insisted that 'Hitler's Europe' had finally crashed to destruction.

In fact, this analysis was not correct. In a literal sense, perhaps, the division of Germany could be said to have been the outcome of the war that Hitler lost. But a divided Europe was *not* the Europe that Hitler wanted. His dream was of a racist *united* Europe, from the Atlantic to the Urals. What gave Hitler his chance to build such a Europe was Germany's dominant position in Europe. Germany was thus divided as

–10–

Germany After Unity: German Dominance – German Domination

A European Germany or a German Europe?

In the introduction we noted that the reinvention of Germany that was the Bonn Republic came to be accepted as a normal German state, even though, when set against the context of previous German states, it was very special, and far from normal. Today we may wonder whether this 'abnormal' Western format for a German state will endure, now that Germany is once more a nation. This chapter seeks to provide an answer. It is, of necessity, speculative.

The new Germany is a massive nation with a vast population; because of the collapse of the Soviet Empire, it occupies an entirely new political position in the heart of the European continent. It now has more borders than any other European state. It drives the economic life, and thus the well-being, of an increasing number of its neighbours. For these reasons (but there are many others, too), it is now obliged to engage itself deeply with both eastern and western Europe. It was unified on the basis of the Western political values of the Bonn Republic; the new Germany is still a *Rechtsstaat* belonging to the West. Whilst the lack of a formal systemic change in the *way* Germany is currently being governed indicates few, if any, paper changes for the time being, *what* is being governed *is* plainly different. And if the nature of Germany is changing, its politics will have to adapt accordingly. As we have seen, the old Federal Republic was consciously fashioned to fit into the West; this worked because it was *located* in the western part of the old nation, and the Western powers, particularly the USA, watched over it. Today's reinvented Germany cannot have the same identity because it is not the same country and the world in which it lives has changed.

This means that hard questions must now be asked about the nature of Germany's new national interest; about the health of its domestic political life and about its foreign policy. All three are, of course, connected to each other. We shall see that there is no undue cause for alarm over any of them. Yet all three have their worrying aspects. By virtue of Germany's size and economic strength, pre-1945 political leaders often assumed Germany's national interest required them to be dominant within Europe. This became physical domination *over* Europe when extreme domestic policies and extreme foreign policies inflamed each other. It was so from 1866–71, from 1914–18, and then again from 1933 until 1945. It is true that Germany's neighbours sometimes liked to believe they were fighting against a German foreign and not a domestic policy. We now know, however, that the two policy areas were simply different sides of the same coin.

To make the plausible claim that a united Germany, even one which has the potential to be dominant, could pose a real danger to its European neighbours, we would first have to demonstrate that extremist policies were gaining, or perhaps could gain, wide domestic acceptance in the new Germany *and* that extremist foreign policy views were also being put forward. And even then, one would still have to be prove that foreign and domestic policy were feeding into each other in an alarming way. Then, and only then, could Germany be considered a menace to the rest of the world.

This means that anyone anxious about possible German domination would have to look for signs of danger in domestic German politics *as well as* in German foreign policy (which is where most non-Germans would be inclined to look first). It is actually rather hard to conceive of an extreme foreign policy that would not have been generated by an extreme domestic policy. The fatal flaw in the policy of appeasement in the 1930s (leaving to one side Britain's military weakness) was precisely that it held that Nazi *foreign* policy, and not its domestic extremism, was what was dangerous. It missed the crucial connection between domestic and foreign policy radicalism, and by seeking to address only the latter, helped to fan the flames of the very war it sought to avoid. Yet foreign policy can also drive domestic policy; an unattended, but vital, foreign interest can produce radical or extreme domestic pressure. Here we shall look at problems in both domestic and foreign policy which, if unsuccessfully managed, will pose real problems for Germany and its neighbours.

What was so remarkable about the Bonn Republic was that the liberalization of West German domestic life, and the Westernization of its foreign policy, never generated any real domestic conflict. During the Bonn years, there was never any German 'nationalist militia'; and very few extreme nationalists in politics. It is a point worth dwelling on. The German people had seen a whole variety of regimes come and go in the space of two generations. Now, from 1945 on, in both the west and the east they became compliant. The reasons for this lay in the essential difference between the Federal Republic and other German states.

The Federal Republic was but one part of a divided Germany, and had only one direction in which to move as a polity, namely towards the West. The Berlin Republic, however, can, and must, move in many more directions. This must shape its national interest, which itself may force directional changes in foreign policy that domestic politicians will ignore at their peril. As we explore below, hazardous change is unlikely, but it could occur if there were a major upheaval within the European Union.

The proposition is a simple one. The European Union is about a dynamic relationship between states (the 'ever-closer union' of Rome and Maastricht) which is supposed to produce a concert of national interests amongst its members. On the whole, this has worked well, with states compromising with each other. Germany above all has been content to define its national interest in a European, and thus an anti-national, or un-national way. Indeed, it insists that its national interest lies in the ever-closer integration of Germany into the European Union, the merging of the German interest with the European one. For this to have continued meaning, however, Germany's neighbours must be equally willing to do the same. If they were often reluctant to do so before 1990, the effect on a submissive West Germany was very limited. Now, however, Germany is not only much more powerful, and not only has it new areas of concern to which it must attend, but it is no longer obliged to submit to the wishes of others.

There are those (especially in Germany) who dispute that Germany has any 'national' interest at all, still less that a new one is evolving. If they concede that there is an interest, they suggest it rests either in economic success or in the continuation of Germany's Western alliances and in further integration in the European Union. But all states have interests which can, and do, become detached from old alliances.

What is more, all states are obliged to serve them – especially so if they are democracies. Those interests rely on geopolitical and economic facts. They are not conditioned for any length of time by political likes and dislikes. We should always recall Palmerston's oft-quoted words in respect of Britain, which had, he argued, no permanent friends and no permanent alliances, only 'eternal interests' which the government was obliged to 'follow'. It is considerations like these that drive the current debate about the nature of Germany's *new* national interest.

The Debate on Germany's National Interest

There is a consensus that although the Berlin Republic continues to be 'a political dwarf' in foreign affairs, it is ceasing to be one quite rapidly.

Germany currently holds a temporary seat in the UN Security Council and hopes to have a permanent one, either in its own right, or as a 'European' seat. The German constitution has been amended to give the German Defence Minister the clear right to order Germany's armed forces into battle 'out of area'. Even though neither of these changes is in any way sinister, still less evidence of a new *Weltpolitik*, or demand for a 'place in the sun', they are but two examples of Germany's emerging power. Even those observers who are known for their beliefs in the virtues of the West German political system, and its essential difference from other German systems, now discuss the existence of a new and more frightening set of German possibilities. Peter Katzenstein, for example, speaks of the Federal Republic as a 'Goliath', one which is restrained, it is true, by the shackles of law and constitutionalism. But a Goliath, even a restrained one, is still a Goliath, potentially at any rate. William Paterson's concept of a 'semi-Gulliver' expresses the same idea.

Many German academics now argue that the new Germany *is* different from the Bonn Republic and that its national interest still awaits firm definition. Even those senior German analysts, like Arnulf Baring, who seek to reassure Germany's neighbours (and perhaps themselves) that the new Germany will not dominate Europe, let alone in any menacing way, can nevertheless be seen to accept that change is under way. There is a plethora of German books on the subject and, as Peter Pulzer has recently shown, at least three celebrated German writers, Gregor Schöllgen, Christian Hacke and Hans-Peter Schwarz, have actually berated the Germans for 'being afraid of the concept of power', indicating not merely that German power is a reality, but unhelpfully (and provocatively) goading the German political class into thinking about ways in which it could be exercised. Schwarz insists robustly that Germany is now the 'Central power in Europe' – (*Zentralmacht Europas*), an unfortunate phrase which connotes both a geopolitical shift from the West to the centre of the continent as well as harking back to pre-1918 descriptions of the Reich.

Baring has said in print that it would be good if Germany were 'to play a stabilizing role in Europe', accepting implicitly that Germany is, indeed, in a position to do so but perhaps unaware that what one state may view as 'stabilizing', another state may see as interference. Baring sees 'the Germans', the parties and their supporters, as the real constraint to this new policy. The people, he says, do not want Germany to dominate Europe. The issue for him is not Germany's capacity for dominance, but simply its current inclination against displaying it. He adds that, even if 'Germany today is different from the old Federal Republic and even more different from Bismarck's Reich', in some senses the new Germans are now 'back in the Germany Bismarck created in 1871'. The Germans, he insists, fear the 'new prospects' history has opened up for them. He adds worryingly that 'no German regime of the last two hundred years has lasted long enough to cultivate deep roots in the German mind or to foster lasting traditions; no regime could truly legitimize itself' which implies that radical political change in Germany is always possible. He even muses on the very notion of Germany's continued ability to remain Western, asking whether '*the* West still exists' given the collapse of the threat from the Soviet Union and the failure of the European Union to win the hearts and minds of the people of Europe. The 'most important challenge' for the new Germany, he claims, is not the West but 'the situation in eastern Europe'.

Other commentators, particularly those on the new Right, are even less cautious (and more terrifying) than these liberals. They seek to challenge, and subvert, Germany's Western-ness; they dare its leaders to serve German interests first. What matters is not so much whether they accurately account for current reality (they do not), but that opinions could be formed by them and thus create the very reality they desire.

Even a sober and highly distinguished analyst like Günter Gillessen can, unintentionally, sound disquieting. He insists that 'the Federal Republic has opted for the West and wants to stay there, in spite of a very pressing need to devote attention and resources to the recon-struction of the former East Germany and to assist the states of eastern Europe'. But what, precisely, does 'pressing need' mean? What flows from 'assisting' the new states of eastern Europe? Certainly, it can imply a humane and generous concern to help these nations as Marshall Aid helped West Germany two generations earlier. Yet even Marshall Aid, as we have seen, had political strings attached to it. Whilst this may be a good thing, it is, nevertheless, a form of German interference in the domestic affairs of non-German states. As Gregor Schöllgen has written: 'It is hardly conceivable that any important resolution could be taken [by assisted states] against Germany's wishes and, naturally, this reflects Germany's economic dominance in Europe', adding that Germany must develop 'a culture of legitimate intervention'.

It is perfectly true that these perceptions are in part confused. They are a mixture of imprecise fears of Germany (for some it is too strong, for others too weak) added to precise fears about the future of the Europe Union. What cannot be ignored, however, is that it is plain that there is much evidence, both domestic and foreign, that Germany's needs are perceived by leading Germans to be changing. What Germany's neighbours want of the Federal Republic may indeed be as confused, and contradictory, as these comments are. But this very fact compounds the problem of Germany's future. There has been a tendency for some academics to gloss over emerging conflicts of interest between Germany and its neighbours, and idealize the Federal Republic. Basing their analysis on the peculiarities of the old Bonn Republic, they dismiss the notion that the new Germany could become as selfish as every other state in Europe, but with greater power to press its advantage.

A young American scholar, Bruce Goldberger, has, for example, considered the current debate in the USA as to whether we should once again fear the Germans. He takes the view that we should not, attacking both those who worry about German 'force of arms', and those who believe eastern Europe should be anxious about Germany's economic, cultural and political ambitions in the area. He spins the line that there is a difference between the 'realist' and 'non-realist' views; the former holding that states will always act according to a perception of their national interest, the latter that 'stability arises not from a balance of power . . . but from the widening acceptance of values such as democracy and human rights'. He is certain that Germany is not a state as other states: 'The realist conclusion that Europe should fear the Germans is . . . misguided.' Germany does not see the future through a realist lens, he claims, in which each nation-state continually reinforces its power position *vis-à-vis* its neighbours, but in terms of increasing interdependence, in which nation-states share power with multilateral organizations, businesses and other levels of government. While the European Community faces tough obstacles, he insists its prospects for prosperity – and peace – would be worse without a strong Germany's 'pervasive participation'.

Whilst he agrees that Germany has become less politically coherent since unification, he plays down nationalist sentiment in binding the East and West Germans together, contending, in conclusion, that Germany is in reality the world's first 'post-national state'. Germany, he reflects, has 'long realised that the fruits of cooperation and power-sharing are more fruitful than those of narrow self-interest', a tendency increased by Germany's federal structure which gives the *Länder* important foreign policy-making powers in respect of the EU. Furthermore, he suggests, reunification has not increased Bonn's power; rather the reverse: it has 'reduced its ability to determine the FRG's affairs'. Nor, he insists, is there anything to fear from German militarism: 75 per cent of Germans were against committing German troops to the Gulf War, and the number against committing them to the former Yugoslavia at the time he wrote was even higher. Germany recently reaffirmed its pledge never to possess nuclear, chemical, or biological weapons. Germany both lacks the will and the power, he claims, to have a military impact on Europe or anywhere else. Indeed, this American asserts, with brilliance, that what we might fear is precisely the *lack* of a strong German central government.

Problems in German Domestic Politics

This sounds almost too good to be true. It *is* too good to be true. There is no real evidence that Germany is a 'post-national' state, nor any evidence that such a thing exists or could ever exist. German reunification was a clear expression of German nationalism. No serious German politician could hope to win power by seeking to rubbish nationalism, nor would they be believed, either at home, or abroad, if they did so. Certainly, in the Bonn Republic, it made good sense to play down nationalist feeling (and, as we have seen, Adenauer was no straightforward nationalist). But then the Bonn Republic was not the German nation. Germany may continue to exhibit an element of residual submissiveness towards the international community; its commitment to European integration cannot be questioned. Yet this is hardly 'post-nationalism', but simply a current definition of Germany's national interest, itself, perhaps, a 'pre-national' artefact left over from the Bonn Republic.

The new Germany of today looks quite different from the old Federal Republic in several key respects. It is larger by almost one-third and has increased its population by almost eighteen million. It is the most populous state in Europe, with perhaps the most effective army (even if it does not, at present, possess its own nuclear weapons) and certainly the strongest economy. The significance of the eastern *Länder* for the development of the German nation as a whole is not just that they require massive financial aid if they are to flourish (as they will); nor is it just that they contain their own, specific, complexities which will have an impact upon, and change, Germany in the west. They also have their own traditions of what being German means, their own essential Eastern-ness, reinforced by forty years of Communism, but pre-dating it by hundreds of years. They sprawl towards the eastern and central parts of the continent.

Germany's new capital, Berlin, was chosen as a conscious attempt to pick up on a continuity which the Bonn years appeared to have bypassed. It is being totally rebuilt and will, in its wealth, represent not only Germany itself, but Germany's new position as the economic heart of Europe. Berlin is as far from Bonn, as Bonn is from London, but no more than a stone's throw from the Polish border. Germany has become more heterogeneous since unification; in economic, political and social terms, eastern Germany is still different from the old Federal Republic. The 1994 elections showed the continued existence of a strong neo-Communist party, gaining almost 20 per cent of the vote, *but* only in the eastern part of the nation. In Berlin itself there are still huge political differences between those from the western part, and those from the eastern part. Local voting returns make the point with clarity: for the westerners, the CDU is now the most popular party. For the easterners, however, it is the PDS. In Berlin there are ten newspapers; the six western ones are not read in the east; the four eastern ones are not read in the west. What is more, there are signs that this major political gap between east and west is actually increasing with the passage of time, rather than decreasing. In 1994, in eastern Germany as a whole, the PDS increased its 1990 vote by 78 per cent. Religion has always mattered in German lands even if its significance should, with increasing secularization, not be exaggerated. Yet, for what is worth, even here the new Germany looks different. Whereas the old West Germany was 51 per cent Roman Catholic and 49 per cent Protestant, the new Germany is 55 per cent Protestant and only 38 per cent Roman Catholic.

There are signs that in social terms the gap between the two German societies may be closing, with the two parts of Germany meeting somewhere new for both of them. In family life, for example, the East Germans seem to be delaying marriage, and putting off having children. There has been a rise in the divorce rate. In some respects they seem to be following the 'Western' model of a low birth rate, the toleration of a relatively high incidence of divorce and a proportionate increase in births among unmarried single women. In fact, both divorce and illegitimate births were extremely common in the GDR (and do not thus necessarily signify the adoption of 'Western' values).

What seems to be happening is that eastern German women, used to full employment in the GDR, with cheap and generous crèche provision, are adapting with intelligence to the risks of the market economy (which not only pushed four-fifths of all workers out of jobs but far more women out of employment than men), by seeking to minimize the risks to their own ability to find employment. In the end, this may see the emergence of a new, liberalized family structure. Crime has increased in the new part of Germany, particularly amongst adolescents (many ordinary eastern Germans point to the lack of crime under the old regime). Old-age pensioners, however, have done very well through unification since they now receive the same pensions as in western Germany. By 1997, there will be income parity between east and west. Many eastern German workers complain about the stress of working to western norms. In the GDR they were paid far less, but the cost of living was also far lower (East German workers liked to joke that 'the Government pretends to pay us, and we pretend to work'). Yet many western Germans, led by their Chan-cellor, point out that western working habits are not strenuous (the shortest working week in Europe, the longest holidays and the biggest pensions); if the easterners cannot cope with this, their future must look bleak.

Kohl has told leading journalists in confidence that he made only one real mistake over reunification. It was not an economic, or political error, but a psychological one. He failed to appreciate that the 'wall in people's minds' would be harder to pull down than the wall around West Berlin; and he believes that the 'sensationalism of the media' increases the psychological problems for eastern Germans, who have come to see themselves simply as 'bad news'.

In domestic terms, many of the major political problems currently facing Germany stem from unification. Privately, Kohl's officials have defined a number of problems that they believe will set the agenda of the next four years. They include the quest for sound, inflation-free economic growth, the further integration of Europe, the revitalization of eastern German industry, the crisis in the birth rate (25 per cent of all 25–50-year-olds are childless, whereas only 9 per cent of all 60-year-olds are childless). In addition, Germany faces a labour shortage both to meet the needs of industry, and to pay the benefits of its ageing population. This ought to mean it would be advisable to allow mass immigration into Germany but this is politically unacceptable.

German Economic Problems

At present, Germany's economic performance is not very healthy. German indebtedness is huge: by 1995 Germany had debts of about DM 2,292 billion. This is double the figure for 1990; five times the figure for 1980. Theo Waigel, the current Minister of Finance, has taken out more loans than all his predecessors put together over the previous forty years. They are, of course, designed to address the problems of unification. It is often argued that the generous exchange rate of 1:1 led to many of them. Kohl was, however, right to follow his political instinct here; Helmut Schmidt's prediction that this would lead to 20 per cent inflation has proved wildly off target. The cost of unity is certainly staggering; perhaps DM 1,000 billion every year from 1990 until the millennium. By 1992, the balance sheet looked as follows: DM 180 billion of publicly borrowed money had been spent, representing 6 per cent of GNP. The interest payments on this money are DM 100 billion per annum. Total spending represents about 50 per cent of all Germany's tax revenue. The Central Government deficit is about DM

70 billion. It seems set to double by 1997 to reach about DM 150 billion. By 1995 the East German privatizing agency, the *Treuhand-anstalt*, had amassed DM 200 billion of debt. By 1995 the public sector debt had risen to DM 1.3 trillion.

There is already some indication that privatization in the new *Bundesländer* has achieved some of the goals set out for it. By the middle of 1994, the *Treuhand* agency had put 13,500 former state-owned businesses back into the private sector and secured 1.5 million jobs (out of what had been 12,315 East German companies, of which 3,293 were wound up). Interestingly, in 1994, German industry invested £156 thousand million in Britain – over six times more than Britain invested in Germany. The reason for this is simple: British labour is cheaper. But the capital invested in Britain is German and will return to Germany (even if German jobs will be lost as a result).

Although some of this money for eastern Germany comes from private sources (some DM 200 billion has been privately invested in the new *Länder*) and public borrowing, other cash is gained by a process of redistribution within the *Länder*. In the late 1980s about DM 3 billion flowed from rich *Länder* to the poorer ones. In 1996, DM 12–15 billion will be redistributed, mostly from west to east. There is (and was) no real political alternative to this high policy, and the economic altern-atives were equally hazardous. As is generally known, the disparity between West and East Germany was vast. In 1990 the GDP per capita was DM 38,000 per annum in West Germany, but only DM 13,000 per annum in East Germany. In 1991 the eastern German GDP fell by 15 per cent; industrial output fell by 65 per cent. In 1990–1 three million jobs were lost in eastern Germany. Furthermore, with over four million people out of work at present (half a million more than in 1993) unemployment benefit creates a hefty expense – DM 51.1 billion in 1993. Add to this a growth rate of 2 per cent overall (but 7.5 per cent in the east), and an average hourly manufacturing cost of £16.45, the highest in Europe, and it is not hard to see why the German economy is in some difficulty.

The German tax burden represents 43.7 per cent of GDP. By 1996 every fifth DM gained in tax went on interest repayments; Germany's debt grows by DM 2,200 every second. Germany's debt index is currently about 3.6 per cent, some 0.6 per cent over the Maastricht norm for currency union. It will be difficult to cut this back, particularly as the deficit is now soaring (indeed, the Bundesbank, for one, does not believe monetary union will be achieved by 1997; although the political will could mean that goal will be met). Unity is expensive, but Germany will almost certainly be able to pay the bill.

There are, however, significant problems with German productivity: many industrialists believe Germany cannot afford the thirty-seven-hour week and the forty days' paid holiday per year, plus another fourteen days' public holiday. Unemployment is high, at 9.3 per cent of the workforce (but not as high, for example, as in France or Britain, where it has reached 11.5 per cent – or Spain, where it is 21.8 per cent). Kohl argued in 1994 that the 'greatest challenge in the whole of Germany is unemployment'.

The expense of unity is plainly capable of being used both politically and economically to undermine Kohl's short-term position and generate change in Germany. Furthermore, the lack of new products and a failure to break out of the European export markets (exports to Japan, for example, amount to 15 per cent of Germany's exports, but imports from Japan amount to 38 per cent of Germany's imports) has led to a failure to gain investment. World capital streams chiefly to the USA (48 per cent). Whilst the European Union attracts about 52 per cent of that investment, Germany itself gains only 5.6 per cent of it; Britain gains about 25 per cent of it. Unification has, of course, caused most of this economic uncertainty, but, in the medium and long term, it is bound to prove an excellent investment. By 2010 there will be a handsome return on this, and bring huge additional prosperity to Germany, not least because the new investment has been an important means of modernizing production.

Over the next few years, therefore, there may perhaps be ample opportunities for the opposition Social Democrats under their new chairman, Oskar Lafontaine, to topple Kohl, despite the Chancellor's 1994 election win. Whether they will be able to so is another matter altogether. The SPD is currently in a state of extreme disarray, as even its friends accept. This stems not only from the SPD's inability to formulate convincing economic alternatives but also from the structural peculiarities of the German political system, which generates political change in Bonn through coalition realignment within already elected parliaments, rather than as the immediate outcome of an election. The SPD's potential coalition partners, the Greens or the PDS, may well not be politically acceptable to the German electorate. Were the SPD to force the issue, a major political crisis of Weimar proportions could ensue. Most Germans will probably put up with Kohl's domestic difficulties on the grounds that no one else could manage them better. And if he avoids foreign humiliation, he could be secure for another decade.

In the medium term, however, there are enormous domestic problems springing from economic change that may well defy liberal solutions. The high price of labour will lead either to additional unemployment in Germany or to a 'reform' of the labour market, increasing the number of part-time posts. This must increase general discontent in a high-wage economy where politics is much taken up with economic well-being. But there are also straightforward political problems that unemployment could exacerbate. Many Germans distrust all their parties (even if they tolerate them by voting for them) and feel the parties over-manage them. There are parties, on the Left and on the Right, waiting to exploit any difficulties that might occur. The latter are particularly dangerous, even if the ex-Communists enjoy far greater support, because at the moment the ex-Communists show no inclination to alter the liberal status quo.

The activities of the neo-Nazi racist groupings must thus be taken very seriously, *not* because they could seize power (which they cannot) but because they could help undermine liberal political culture and force policy changes on the big democratic parties. A neo-Nazi government anywhere in Germany is totally inconceivable. Pandering to neo-Nazism, however, is another matter. The big parties might feel obliged to take on board illiberal ideas (even against their better judgement). The 1993 amendment to Germany's liberal asylum laws (which contradicts Germany's economic needs) is evidence that this has already happened. In a German nation now open to diverse ethnic groups, any sense of German national superiority will inevitably nourish the new German Right (as well as the neo-Nazis), although the evidence suggests that neo-Nazism is *not* by any means exclusively, or even chiefly, an *eastern* German problem. Its incidence seems heaviest in the northern, and western parts of the nation.

The New Right claim not to be racists but national conservatives, with the accent on 'national'. Yet they promote the idea of 'Germany first', and propagate the concepts of 'German-ness' and the German *Volk* (and favour, too, the singing of the prohibited first verse of the national anthem). Unity provided inspiration to both the New Right and the neo-Nazis in other ways too, either because (for eastern Germans) what was a once prohibited political activity had now become possible, or because the implicit nationalism contained in the act of unification had its own impact.

The Right-Wing Extremist Threat

According to the German security service, the BfV, there were, in 1995, 81 right-wing extremist or Fascist organizations and groupings (there were 78 in 1993). They had a membership of about 56,600 people (adjusted to take account of the fact that the same person may join several organizations). This is a slight decrease from the 1993 membership figure of 64,700 but an increase on the 1992 figure of 42,700. In 1994 there were 5,400 militant right-wing extremists (including skinhead groups), compared with 5,600 in 1993. Of these, in 1994 some 3,740 were classified as neo-Nazi, an increase of 1,300 on the 1993 figure. In addition, the right-wing extremist parties (excluding the neo-Nazis) could boast a total membership of 45,600 in 1994 (compared with 55,100 in 1993). Of these parties, the DVU, or German People's Union, was the largest with 26,000 members (an increase of 3,000 on 1993); the National Democrats had 5,200 members (an increase of 500 on 1993); and the Republicans had 23,000 members (an increase of 3,000 on their 1993 figure). The DVU gained six per cent of the votes in Bremen (September 1991) and Schleswig-Holstein (March 1992). Despite bans on the National Front (NF), the German Alternative (DA), the National Offensive (NO) by the Federal Minister of the Interior, and the German Comrades Union (DKB) by the Lower Saxon Minister of the Interior, the number of openly neo-Nazi groups could clearly increase.

The BfV has stated that all these groups espouse an ideology of ethnic (*völkisch*) nationalism, driven by racism. They believe that biological descent, rather than a common history, culture or language, defines membership of a people or a nation. Their perceived enemies are those seen as ethnically different from themselves, and they freely express their hatred for foreigners and ethnic minorities.

In the 1994 federal election, the extreme Right did very badly (it gained only 1.9 per cent of the vote, 0.2 per cent less than in 1990), and it did equally badly in the *Land* elections that year. Against this, however, since October 1990, but particularly since the summer of 1992, there has been a chilling evidence of an increase in racist violence in the new Germany. Sometimes this is attributed to 'right-wing extremists', sometimes to 'Fascists'. Since 1992, at least twenty-five people have been murdered – beaten or burned to death – for racial reasons, in both eastern and western Germany. According to official statistics, in 1992, there were 2,584 racially motivated Fascist attacks on individuals, in which seventeen people were murdered (compared with 1,483 in 1991 – an increase of 74 per cent). Two of the worst cases in 1991 included the September attack on an asylum seekers' hostel in Hoyerswerda in which thirty-two people were injured, some seriously, and the October 1991 fire-bombing of a Lebanese family's home in Hünxe where two children suffered appalling burns. Some of the worst cases in 1992 included the riots in Rostock in August, in which several hundred extremists attacked an asylum seekers' hostel, encouraged by a large crowd of spectators. In May 1993, three Turkish women were burned to death in a fire-bomb attack on their home in Solingen in the Ruhr. A further 18,000 incidents of an anti-Semitic or anti-foreigner nature were also listed. In 1992, there were 2,640 acts of extreme right-

Figure 9. 'The Nazi legacy' the photo of the commemoration of Auschwitz, 26 January 1995. The photo shows the entrance to Auschwitz-Birkenau with Lech Walesa; President Herzog is behind him, on his right; Elie Wiesel is on Walesa's left. © Faßbender

Figure 10. 'The ever-present past': 27 January 1995 Herzog, Ignaz Bubis and Michael Friedman place a wreath at Birkenau concentration camp. © Faßbender

Figure 11. 'The Nazi legacy': 27 January 1995 Herzog lays a wreath at Birkenau.
© Faßbender

wing violence; in 1993, the number rose to 2,232 but dropped in 1994 to 1,489. Yet the number of people involved in these incidents (5,600 in 1993 and 5,400 in 1994) were virtually static. Some 70 per cent of such neo-Nazi acts are committed by young Germans.

The BfV's 1993 Report outlined specific pieces of evidence to support the notion that the neo-Nazis are inspired by ethnocentric ideals. In Wuppertal on 13 November 1992, for example, two skinheads aged 18 and 24 beat a 53-year-old man and then poured alcohol over him, lit it, and watched him burn to death, after he had confided in them that his mother was a Jewess. They shouted 'the Jew must burn' and 'Auschwitz should be reopened'. In Mölln, Schleswig-Holstein, news of two fire-bomb attacks on foreigners' homes was phoned through to police by individuals in messages which began with the words 'Heil Hitler'. On 18 March 1992, two men, aged 25 and 18, beat to death an older man who had made negative remarks about the Third Reich and Adolf Hitler. The report also quoted from various skinhead songs verses such as 'let the knife gouge into Jews' bodies; we shit on the liberty of this Jews' Republic; clean the guillotine of Jews' fat'. The leader of the DVU, Dr Frey, who also publishes the *National Zeitung*, was quoted as having made statements attacking gypsies for 'polluting the blood of Germans with their criminal acts'; and denying the Holocaust. The NPD stated that 'the blood of Germans is a very special juice, quite different from the evil-smelling slime of others'. The Viking Youth declares 'Germany is our duty, a Northland our aim; we want to destroy the political system imposed on us by Germany's victors, and fight the mongrelization of the world.' Ninety per cent of German neo-Nazi attacks were directed against non-Germans or 'foreigners'; but in the fiftieth anniversary year of the defeat of Nazism, there were an increasing number of attacks on Jewish graves and synagogues. These cannot be dismissed as pranks but are plainly intended to make a political (and ethnic) point.

By way of comparison, it should be noted that in the UK, the number of racially motivated incidents increased from 4,383 in 1988 to 6,359 in 1990. The figures show that neo-Nazi outrages are not just a German phenomenon. The 1995 Oklahoma City bombing, and the growth of neo-Nazi and right-wing organizations in the USA like the Montana Militia, make the same point. Neither the UK, nor the USA, however, have a history of successful Fascism. In addition, racism in Britain today lacks a secure party political structure or structures.

In an electoral context, the extreme Right may not be a hazard (its 1994 low was a disappointment to it, compared with its 1993 results). Yet these parties' popularity fluctuates. In contrast, the Republicans scored 8–10 per cent in the March 1993 Hessen local elections. In

September in Hamburg, the two extreme right-wing parties, the Republicans and the DVU, the German Peoples' Union, gained 9 per cent between them – twice the number of votes scored by the FDP, the German Liberals. Electoral support plainly ebbs and flows. But in terms of damaging German political culture (not to mention Germany's image abroad) through ethnic violence and murder the capacity of the extreme right to do serious harm is very worrying indeed. The statistics do prove that there is a hard, if small, racist core in Germany, which its liberal institutions can monitor and contain, but cannot suppress.

Public opinion polls have shown that as late as 1977 26 per cent of West Germans agreed with the statement that Nazism was basically a good idea, just poorly carried out. In 1955, 48 per cent said that, if it had not been for the war, Hitler would have been one of the greatest German statesmen. In 1978, there were still 31 per cent who said this. Polls undertaken in 1979 and 1980 indicated that about 13 per cent had fixed right-wing views.

Those who are on the receiving end of Fascist violence are chiefly members of the 5.6 million 'foreigners' or 'guestworkers' and their families, or asylum seekers, or economic refugees from eastern and central Europe. Of these almost one-third are Turkish in origin. Sixty per cent of these people have lived in Germany for ten years or more; their legal status was changed by the 1991 nationality act, which made it somewhat easier for them to become German nationals. The 1993 Asylum Law (which amended the Constitution) reduced the numbers staying in Germany significantly. Yet what is noteworthy about these 'foreigners' is not that they are actually foreign *qua* foreign but that those with a different non-Germanic ethnic origin, such as the Italian 'guestworkers' do not appear to suffer similar attacks, even though they constitute 10 per cent of the total minority population. As such, 'foreigners' have replaced the Jews of pre-war Europe. In ideological terms, however, where 'Jew' means 'ethnically other', the Jews continue to be the 'enemy'.

In 1992 four organizations were banned as offending against Paragraph 3 of the German Constitution. Three of these were national groupings, one confined to Lower Saxony. These were the National Front (banned on 27 November 1992), the German Alternative (banned on 10 December 1992), the National Offensive (banned on 22 December 1992) and the German Comrades Association (banned on 21 December). The Government in Bonn also acted against individual Fascists, citing Article 18 of the German Constitution. On 2 September 1993 the German Interior Minister announced that he was seeking to ban the 'Free German Workers' Party (FAP) and that Bavaria, Hesse and Lower Saxony had announced similar moves. On the same day, the

Land of North Rhine-Westphalia banned another splinter group, the FFD. Legally, a party can only be banned by an application of the Federal Government to the Constitutional Court, although associations can be banned by *Länder* governments.

Certainly, both Richard von Weizsäcker (when he was President) and the current office holder, Roman Herzog, have taken a lead in seeking to call their country to order on this issue. Herzog's speech at Bergen-Belsen in April 1995 was especially moving and powerful. Their efforts, however, were not always matched by Kohl. He certainly condemned the Solingen fire-bombing, but dismissively, by suggesting it was the work of a 'few weak-minded individuals'. It is plain that the huge influx of aliens into Germany after the collapse of Communism (numbering almost one million in 1992) caused very real social pressures and understandable (though inexcusable) resentment.

German Foreign Policy

The European Union

In foreign policy, there are two distinct (if interrelated) issues to consider in seeking to define Germany's changing role in Europe and the emergence of a new German national interest. These relate to the European Union policy (already mentioned) and to the new German role in eastern Europe. There are already clear signs that the former brings Germany into direct conflict with one key European actor, Britain. Even if it can be shown that Franco-German relations continue to flourish under a new President, Chirac, and that France keenly seeks ever closer cooperation with Germany (and defines the French national interest in this way), genuine integration in Europe (as opposed to German dominance over the Union) must depend on whether there is integration with *all* states within the Union. Integration can have no other meaning. The Franco-German alliance is not a substitute for real integration although it is often mistaken for it.

Although there is no inherent reason why Germany and Britain must collide on this matter (indeed there are many reasons why they ought not to do so) the hard political truth is that they have already demonstrated their inability to avoid conflict. What is more, past crises indicate that neither state can manage this conflict successfully. There exists a fundamental divergence of high policy over the future of Europe between the government of John Major and that of Kohl that makes future policy making extremely difficult, if not impossible. The current leadership of Germany is committed to a strong Union, and to what Dr Kohl calls the 'Europeanization of Germany'. He wants full political union in Europe, which he sees as the only valid response to the new problems facing Europe, east and west, and to the aspirations of young Europeans. If Maastricht does not succeed, it will, he says, take more than one generation to return to it. Such a union would not, he says, be a superstate but provide 'unity in diversity'.

European integration has become the cornerstone of German foreign policy thinking, and the unifying theory behind most of its foreign policy actions. Non-Germans ignore this at their peril. Kohl is supported both by his own party, and by the SPD. The German Christian Democrats have produced two recent major policy statements on the future of the European Union, one on ever closer union, led, perhaps, by an inner core of Germany and France; the other urging a fully integrated defence and security policy in the EU, based on qualified majority voting. Karl Lamers, the foreign affairs spokesman of the CDU, and Kohl's colleague, argued that Germany was now the 'économie dominante' in Europe and demanded 'highly developed, reliable supranational institutions'. He added that in the east, 'a fresh creative field [for German foreign policy] presented itself'. The rest of Europe, he says, should not worry about this because the CDU affirms 'our future does not lie in the East; the future of the East lies in the West'.

Eastern Europe

Germany's desire to bring the Union to the East is, of course, not merely motivated by the altruistic wish to bring political stability to the new democracies. Its interests are also economic. In 1994, German trade with eastern Europe, including the Russian Federation, exceeded DM 100 billion in 1994. Goods traffic totalled DM 69 billion, which represented an increase of 21 per cent on the 1993 figure, more than twice the growth rate of last year's German foreign trade (8.5 per cent). Exports were up by 19 per cent to DM 35.9 billion, imports by 23 per cent to DM 33.2 billion. As in 1993, there was a surplus (DM 2.7 billion) of exports over imports. German goods trade with the CIS countries showed an increase of 10 per cent. Imports and exports both reached DM 15 billion so that trade was in balance. Exports increased by 0.5 per cent, but imports increased by 22 per cent.

The overall volume of trade with eastern Europe is now DM 104 billion, which is *more* than the volume of trade done with the USA. The CIS is the biggest single eastern European trading partner, with a volume of DM 23.9 billion, but Poland produced a volume of DM 20.5 billion. Exports to Russia totalled DM 10.8 billion, to Poland, DM 10.4 billion and to the Czech Republic, DM 9.7 billion. In short, Germany's trade interests in eastern Europe (which many scholars played down, using 1993's figures) represent a massive shift of national concern from west to east. What this means is that the political, social and economic problems of its eastern neighbours cannot be a matter of indifference to Germany. The possibility of security threats, either directly, or, more probably, indirectly (say to the Baltic States) would be bound to affect the German state. These are all *new* problems, it should be emphasized, that did not exist in the less complex Cold War era when Germany was divided. What is more, they are specifically German concerns. Whilst France or Britain, say, support the underwriting of eastern European democratic ventures and, like Germany but more modestly, hope to earn some money at the same time, they have no land borders with these states. Furthermore, German investment outstrips theirs by far.

The new Germany's eastern leaders acknowledge this. As Professor Biedenkopf, the dynamic Minister President of Saxony, has recently argued, in addition to the old north-south divide in the Community, there is now an east-west divide. Furthermore – and perhaps critically – the Germans have to have what Biedenkopf calls a 'Mitverantwortung' (co-responsibility) towards eastern Europe. Others, however, might term it a 'sphere of political and economic influence'. It simply has to matter to Germany, he says, what goes on in Poland, or in the Czech and Slovak states. The issue of instability in eastern Europe and its effect on German security has also been raised by Biedenkopf. For him, the danger of the future is not the danger of the past – namely missiles – but rather chaos in eastern Europe, which could adversely affect Germany and the Union. These are matters, of course, which involve the German armed forces.

German Military Power

For a considerable period, Germans of all parties denied that the new Germany would ever find itself using force to underline a national interest. It was pointed out that the 1949 Basic Law forbade the use of German troops except in the defence of NATO and forbade their use 'out of area' in any circumstances. The Constitutional Court ruling in July 1994 changed this. President Clinton, who was in Germany at the time, underscored America's desire to see the new Germany occupy a more authoritative role. In a snub directed towards Britain, Clinton spoke of the 'unique relationship' between Germany and the United States, which was 'more immediate and tangible' than any other relationship.

The role of the Federal armed forces must, in any case, change now that Communism is no longer a threat. After all, these forces were set up as much to protect the West against Communist invasion as to protect

West Germany. A Europe of nation states, where some (in the west) are interdependent and some (in the east) independent will generate new, and extremely complex, tasks for Germany's servicemen. The current chief of staff of the German armed forces, General Naumann, who is also chairman of NATO's military committee, has given a clear interpretation of Germany's security needs.

Together with his hard-line Defence Minister, Volker Rühe, a role for the new, unified 340,000-man German army has been constructed which is a marked change from the one that Kohl, and his Foreign Minister Kinkel, have previously expounded. Kohl had said that German troops would 'never fight where they fought in the Second World War'. This appears, at a stroke, to rule out any German attempt to 'stabilize' any part of eastern or central Europe. In addition, he likes to focus on the 'Euro-brigade'. These may be a motley crew. They held their first common manoeuvre in 1994 and are intended to be ready for action by 1 October 1995. But in Kohl's mind the Euro-brigade (currently commanded by General Helmut Willmann, another German) has importance as a symbolic way of Europeanizing the German armed forces. Rühe and Naumann, however, see a much stronger national role for the German army. Amongst many tasks highlighted are those in the east, where Naumann has said that the 'historic collapse of the Soviet Union has led to "uncertainty" in "Europe's backyard"'. Germany would not stand idly by, it seems, were anarchy to reign on its eastern frontier. Indeed, General Naumann said that many of his Russian colleagues begged him to assist with the stabilization of their country. German and Russian generals have sought close contacts with each other (even when the Russian army was busy fighting the Chechens, killing thousands and destroying their homes).

The Germans are hoping to make friends of the new Russians. But is that in the European interest, given the Russians' behaviour in their own lands, and their attitude towards neighbouring states in eastern and central Europe? Russian politics are dangerous and totally unpredictable; the return of a strong Communist Party is by no means unthinkable and earlier German policies towards Russia carry warnings which must be heeded. The Germans may, once again, become convinced that they have a stabilizing and civilizing role in Europe, but fail to comprehend that in practice this could unnerve their neighbours. Germans may argue that US interference in the Caribbean or Latin America has long been considered quite acceptable by the US's allies. Why should Germany be different? The answer, of course, lies in the history of Germany from 1871 to 1945.

Just as in the nineteenth century, Germany's strength, expressed in technology and manpower, means the *Bundeswehr* is an awesome tool.

Since nuclear weapons could not be used in Europe in any case, Germany's lack of an independent nuclear deterrent is not a relevant matter. It is clear that under a different leadership, Germany would not only have the means to exert considerable pressure on its neighbours, but could find itself sucked into a situation which this became necessary. Pulzer has argued that the only power that Germany possesses, in an interdependent world, is the power of veto; it cannot command anyone. Yet it would be wrong to confuse the lack of a political desire to command, with the lack of the necessary wherewithal to enforce such a command, were the will ever to change.

Viewed in one way, the situation seems to be that with British power gone for ever, with France the ever more junior partner in the Franco-German axis, and with the Americans content to leave Europe increasingly to its own devices, the only Western power with an ability to shape events is Germany. Viewed in another light, however, this is simply 'the German problem' – the problem of German dominance in Europe.

Mrs (now Lady) Thatcher was perhaps the first Western leader to wonder whether a reunified Germany nation might not seek to resurrect the concept of a German-controlled Europe or central eastern Europe (*Mitteleuropa*). Both in her memoirs and in her 1990 Chequers Meeting, she articulated numerous fears about Germany. In 1990, she tried to achieve a 'slowing down' of unification because 'by its very nature, Germany is a destabilizing force in Europe'. Early in 1990, she made several statements signifying her changed attitude to Germany and claiming 'We dared to say the realities and talk the sense which other people are fearful of saying, lest they be misinterpreted.' At Chequers, on 24 March 1990, a famous memorandum on the subject was composed which stated 'Even those most disposed to look on the bright side admitted to some qualms about what unification would do for German behaviour in Europe. We could not expect a united Germany to think and act in exactly the same way as the Federal Republic which we had known for the last forty-five years.'

The meeting declared that the Germans *would* be 'inclined to resurrect the concept of *Mitteleuropa*'; a united Germany would be 'less Western and less politically stable than the Federal Republic'. It was considered 'likely that Germany would indeed dominate Eastern and Central Europe economically'. The meeting concluded that 'the more assertive Germany became, the easier it ought to be to construct alliances against Germany on specific issues in the Community'. The bottom line of Mrs Thatcher's worries, however, was that there was something in the German national character that was fundamentally unsound and disruptive. Her Chequers questions deserve rather more serious attention than they received, although her answers were certainly not wholly satisfactory: she could not have known that Soviet Union would collapse. Her notion of coalition-building against Germany (taken up by her successor, who aimed with little success to create a new Franco-British *Entente Cordiale* to come between France and Germany) was dangerous. Her view of the German 'character' was plainly wrong (though understandable in someone of her generation). What she did do, however, was to foresee that German unity would change both the map of Europe and alter the nature of Germany's national interest. Her antipathy towards European integration, however, robbed her of the only sensible way of ensuring that the new Germany would threaten no one, least of all the West.

Mrs Thatcher did not err in seeing that unification had caused the new Germany to become potentially dominant in Europe, even if no one, least of all the German government and people, wanted this to happen. Indeed, some observers (including some German ones) argue that Germany has *already* started to dominate its neighbours via the European Union, which is seen as a cover, permitting Germany to assume the role of *dominatrix* of Europe, without anyone realizing. This was, for example, the case put by the late Lord Ridley in 1990, when he declared that the idea of a common European money system was just a 'German racket designed to take over all of Europe', adding that to give further power to the European Commission was tantamount to giving it 'to Adolf Hitler'. Even if this somewhat simplistic view can be countered with the assertion that the very purpose of the Union is to make it impossible for any one nation to dominate the others, the political potency of the notion that Germany speaks of Europe, but means Germany, is not necessarily thereby diminished. What is true, and what is thought to be true, are frequently not the same.

A 'Fourth Reich'?

If Germany's new power is not to cause alarm, German political leaders must ensure that in two critical areas at least, they maintain the traditions of the old Bonn Republic. Germany must, obviously, continue to allow its liberal institutions and its constitutional habits to prosper. There is every sign that it will do so. But the new Germany must also produce a statement of its national interest which satisfies both the German people *and* their neighbours. Naturally it must (like all other states) eschew the pursuit of restless economic or political ambitions in Europe.

Whilst it seems highly unlikely that Bonn's domestic political values or rules will be subject to any great alteration in the foreseeable future as the result of unity, the (new) definition of the German national interest must cause more problems. If mistakes are made in executing this, a nightmare scenario, ending in the creation of a 'Fourth Reich', could conceivably develop. Today's German leaders with their commitment to Western values, and their view that Germany's interests demand closer European integration, could soon lose office if they fail to deliver it. Their places might then be taken by a new generation of politicians, willing to use German power more recklessly under the banner of promoting a German national interest, one which would be unashamedly selfish, and take no account of Germany's historical duty to avoid using its strength to dominate others. In this way, the world might once again witness the lethal combination of assertive German foreign and domestic policy. A rich, technologically advanced Germany of the future might choose to interfere actively with the sovereignty of its neighbours. It might use its power to impose its economic and political will (and service its own interests) whether its neighbours wanted this, or not. In due course, this might even provoke conflict with its neighbours.

As we have seen, many responsible Germans are themselves afraid of such a scenario. Today, such fears of a 'Fourth Reich' seem not merely far-fetched and hard to sustain, but a reinvention of Germany that could be avoided with relative ease, if the new Germany and its European neighbours work hard to do so. The difficulty is that they may not be able to do so. The opposition that is being drawn, then, is between a resurgent and selfish Germany and a genuine and effective European community. Indeed, these are not merely opposites; each rules out the other. If Germany dominates Europe, a genuine Community cannot be created, but if a genuine Community can be made to work, Germany cannot dominate Europe.

In the West, a future without German domination will ultimately hang on whether the existing European Union can continue to function in the face of so many adverse pressures upon it. In the East, what will matter will be the attitude of the new democracies to the Union, and also the durability and stability of their own passage to successful liberal democracy (which possible Union membership could as easily complicate, as facilitate). Whilst there is no doubt that the current leadership of the Federal Republic understands this logic fully, it is not clear that Germany's neighbours in Europe, particularly those in the west, believe they can follow Germany down this particular road. It is one thing for Germany to reinvent itself yet again, by taking its newly-won national sovereignty and dissolving it in Europe; it is quite another for its western neighbours to do the same. Although France and the Benelux states may fall in, Italy and the other Mediterranean nations, and, above all, the United Kingdom, may find such change impossible. Britain's position is critical since without British participation, there can be no real European Community.

Germany's European hopes can, of course, only be realized if they are shared by all its European neighbours. If they refuse to do so, Germany will have to think again about where its interest lies. The danger, therefore, is that it is Germany's neighbours, rather than the Germans themselves, who will end up pushing the Federal Republic into that new selfish definition of the German national interest, which we must term German domination. How Germany shapes its national interest thus depends on how its neighbours choose to regard Germany and on how they define *their* interests. Indeed, this is proving to be the burning political issue of our time; it is at the real heart of the debate about the future of the European Union; a debate about the political shape of the continent in the twenty-first century.

If Germany's neighbours come to reject a European definition of their interests, two things must happen. The first is that Germany's idea of European integration will be seen more generally as just that: a *German* idea, not a European one, with all that this implies for the fuelling of antagonism and hostility. Secondly, if full European integration cannot work (and all the signs suggest that it may not do so), then Germany may have no other option but to define German interests in wholly German terms, and perhaps bend to the winds that blew across Germany before 1945.

Kohl himself has stated very recently (in *Deutschland* No. 4, 1995) that 'I have always assured our European friends that the reunited Germany will not go its own way . . . It is in our own best interests [not to do so]. A neutral Germany would isolate itself more and more – to the detriment of itself and its neighbours.' But what can Kohl do if Germany's European neighbours force Germany to 'go its own way'? In Britain, at any rate, many influential voices can be heard preparing the political ground for this to occur. The London *Times* columnist, Lord Rees-Mogg, has already claimed in an article entitled 'A too German Union' that the German plans for Europe cannot suit Britain. 'Britain', he concludes, 'would no doubt choose to leave a German-dominated European Union, and the Germans would be happy to see us go . . . [because] the Germans cannot bully the British.'

The Times does not speak for Britain, in the same sense that Kohl speaks for Germany; yet Rees-Mogg and many others who share his views (whether right or wrong) demonstrate that it cannot be taken for granted that Germany will be able to realize its European plans. His use of the word 'bully' is important, for it must be conceded that Kohl's own formulation carries within it an implied threat (as his phrase 'to the detriment . . . of its neighbours' shows). Kohl himself thus raises the old spectre of German dominance and domination in Europe. Experienced statesman though he is, he must understand that to present the case for further integration in terms of the re-emergence of German might if it is not accepted, can only make his task harder. Indeed, there is some evidence to suggest that he has now realized this, and accepts he may now have to consider a 'flat enlargement' of the Union, with no further integration for the time being; previously he insisted that there could be no 'widening' of the Union without its simultaneous 'deepening'.

The New German Interest

What this adds up to is not a blueprint for domination, nor even the articulation of a specific German nationally-driven policy, but a *potentially* serious conflict between those who would like the German interest to continue to be defined as it was before unity, and those who understand that this may simply no longer be possible. Whilst the Berlin Republic will need watching very carefully (and as much by non-Germans as by Germans themselves), Germany's neighbours must also watch themselves. For Germany's neighbours, the European Union prevents a German-led Europe from becoming a German-dominated one.

The new Germany is obviously going to be the main European power, a state with the potential to dominate – two things which the Bonn Republic never was. In order that the new Germany should *not* be the *dominatrix* of Europe, it is necessary that Bonn's political culture should continue to exist. In this way, but only in this way, Germany's entrenched constitutionalism, its emphasis on legalistic politics, its enlightened federalism and liberalism can all offer a modern reinterpretation of the famous words of Emanuel Geibel (1815–84): 'Es mag am deutschen Wesen, einmal noch die Welt genesen' – 'Germany will one day benefit the world'.

This means the new Germany must, somehow, continue to make itself different, both from previous German nations and from other European powers. This is a tall order. In domestic policy, it must fight back against extremism. In foreign policy, Germany must still practise self-denial. It must not give up its formal dedication to the merging of Germany's national interests with those of an integrated Europe. Its current commitment to human rights, expressed by its UN policy, should be strengthened. But it must never return to old patterns of dominance or domination. The current reinvention of Germany, which began in 1990, must continue to uphold the values of the reinvention that preceded it.

Bibliography

Abelshauser, W. (1983), *Wirtschaftgeschichte der Bundesrepublik Deutschland 1945–1980*, Frankfurt am Main: Suhrkamp.

—— (1979), 'Probleme des Wiederaufbaus der westdeutschen Wirtschaft, 1945–53' in Winkler, H. A. *Politische Weichenstellungen in Nachkriegsdeutschland, 1945–53*, Göttingen: Vandenhoeck und Ruprecht.

Adelson, Alan and Lapides, Robert (1989), *The Lodz Ghetto*, London: Penguin.

Adenauer, Konrad (1965), *Erinnerungen, 1945–53*, Stuttgart: Deutsche Verlags-Anstalt.

—— (1966), *Erinnerungen, 1953–55*, Stuttgart: Deutsche Verlags-Anstalt.

—— (1967), *Erinnerungen, 1955–59*, Stuttgart: Deutsche Verlags-Anstalt.

—— (1968), *Erinnerungen, 1959–63*, Fragmente, Stuttgart: Deutsche Verlags-Anstalt.

—— (1983), *Briefe 1945–47. Rhöndorfer Ausgabe*. Bearbeitet von Hans Peter Mensing, Stuttgart: Siedler Verlag.

—— (1984), *Briefe 1947–49. Rhöndorfer Ausgabe*. Bearbeitet von Hans Peter Mensing, Stuttgart: Siedler Verlag.

Ahlers, Conrad hrsg (1971), *Bundeskanzler Brandt. Reden und Interviews 1969–71*, Hamburg/Reinbek: Rowohlt.

Albrecht, Willy hrsg (1985), *Kurt Schumacher: Reden-Schriften-Korrespondenzen, 1945–52*, Bonn: Dietz.

Allemann, F. R. von (1956) *Bonn ist nicht Weimar!* Cologne: Kiepenhauer und Witsch.

Annan, Noel (1995), *Changing Enemies. The Defeat and Regeneration of Germany*, London: HarperCollins.

Ardagh, John (1987), *Germany and the Germans*, London: Hamish Hamilton.

Aust, Stefan (1987), *The Baader Meinhof Group*, London: The Bodley Head.

Bacque, James (1991), *Other Losses*, London: Futura.

Baker, Kendall L., Dalton, Russell J. and Hildebrandt, Kai (1981), *Germany Transformed. Political Culture and the New Politics*, London:

Harvard University Press.

Balfour, Michael (1992) *Germany. The Tides of Power*, London: Routledge.

Baring, Arnulf (1971) *Aussenpolitik in Adenauer's Kanzlerdemokratie*, Band I, Stuttgart: Deutsche Taschenbuch Verlag.

—— (1982), *Machtwechsel. Die Ära Brandt-Scheel*, 2nd edn, Stuttgart: Deutsche Verlags-Anstalt.

——, ed. (1994) *Germany's New Position in Europe, Problems and Perspectives*, Oxford: Berg.

Bark, Dennis L. and Gress, David (1989), *A History of West Germany* Volume One. *From Shadow to Substance 1945–63* Volume Two. *Democracy and its Discontents 1963–68*, Oxford: Basil Blackwell.

Bartov, Omar (1986), *The Eastern Front, 1941–45. German Troops and the barbarisation of warfare*, London: Macmillan.

Baum, R. C. (1981), *The Holocaust and the German Elite*, New Jersey: Rowman and Littlefield.

Becker, Jillian (1978), *Hitler's Children. The Story of the Baader-Meinhof Gang*, 2nd edn, London: Granada.

Becker, Winfried (1987), *Die Kapitulation von 1945 und der Neubeginn in Deutschland*, Köln und Wien: Böhlau.

Berghahn, Volker (1982), *Modern Germany*, Cambridge: Cambridge University Press.

Bernecker, Walther L. and Dotterweich, Volker hrsg (1982), *Persönlichkeit und Politik in der Bundesrepublik Deutschland*. Two volumes, Göttingen: Vandenhoeck and Rupprecht.

Beschloss, Michael R. and Talbot, Strobe (1993), *At The Highest Levels: The Inside Story of the End of the Cold War*, New York: Little, Brown.

Beyme, Karl von (1986), *The Political System of the Federal Republic*, Aldershot: Gower.

Beyme, Klaus von, hrsg (1979), *Die Grossen Regierungserklärungen der deutschen Bundeskanzler von Adenauer bis Schmidt*, München: Hanser.

Binder, David (1975), *The Other German: Willy Brandt's Life and Times*, Washington DC: New Republic.

Blackbourn, D. and Eley G. (1985), *The Peculiarities of German History*, Oxford: Oxford University Press.

Blasius, Rainer (1984), *Von Adenauer zu Erhard: Studien zur Auswärtigen Politik der Bundesrepublik Deutschlands, 1963*, München: Oldenbourg.

—— (1989), *Dokumente zur Deutschlandpolitik*, Hrsg. vom Bundesministerium für Inner-deutsche Beziehungen, 1. Reihe, Frankfurt.

—— (1994), *Akten zur Auswärtigen Politik der Bundesrepublik Deuts-*

chlands, 1963, München: Oldenbourg.

Bouvier, Beatrix (1990), *Zwischen Godesberg und Grosser Koalition: Der Weg der SPD in die Regierungsverantwortung*, Bonn: Dietz.

Bower, Tom (1995), *Blind Eye to Murder*, London: Granada.

Bracher, Karl Dietrich (1973), *The German Dictatorship: the origins, structure and consequences of National Socialism*, translated from the German by Jean Steinberg, Harmondsworth: Penguin.

Brandt, Brigitte Seebacher (1984), *Ollenhauer. Biedermann und Patriot*, Berlin: Siedler.

—— (1991), *Die Linke und die Einheit*, Berlin: Siedler.

Brandt, Peter and Ammon, Herbert (1981), *Die Linke und die nationale Frage*, Dokumente zur deutschen Einheit seit 1945, Reinbek/Hamburg: Rororo.

Brandt, Willy (1963), *The Ordeal of Coexistence*, Cambridge MA: Harvard University Press.

—— (1971) *Peace. Writings and speeches of the Nobel Prize Winner, 1971*, Bonn: Dietz.

—— (1974) *Über den Tag hinaus. Eine Zwischenbilanz* 2nd edn, Hamburg: Hofmann und Campe.

—— (1990), *Erinnerungen*, 4th edn, Frankfurt: Propyläen.

—— (1990), '. . .*Was Zusammengehört*', Bonn: Ein Sonderdruck der Ebert Stiftung für die demokratische Reformkräfte in der DDR.

—— and Schmidt, Helmut (1976), *Deutschland, 1976. Zwei Sozialdemokraten im Gespräch*, Reinbek/Hamburg: Rowohlt.

Braun, H. J. (1992), *The German Economy in the 20th Century*, London: Routledge.

Braun, Joachim (1972), *Gustav Heinemann: the committed President*, London: Wolff, (tr. by R. W. Last).

Breitman, Richard (1991), *The Architect of Genocide: Himmler and the Final Solution*, London: The Bodley Head.

Browning, Christopher (1985), *Fateful Months; Essays on the Emergence of the Final Solution*, New York: Holmes and Meier.

—— (1993), *Ordinary Men: reserve police batallion 101 and the Final Solution in Poland*, New York: HarperPerennial.

Buchholz, Marlis (1985), *Die Hannoverschen Judenhäuser: Zur Situation der Juden in der Zeit der Ghettoisierung und Verfolgung, 1941–45*, Hildesheim: Lax.

Buchstab, Günter and Gotto, Klaus, hrsg (1990), *Die Gründung der Union*, 2nd edn, Munich: Olzog.

Bulmer, S. and Paterson, W. (1987), *The Federal Republic of Germany and the European Community*, London: Allen and Unwin.

Bundesministerium für Gesamtdeutsche Fragen (1956), *Die Sow-*

jetische Besatzgungszone Deutschlands in den Jahren 1945–1954, Bonn.

Bundesrepublik Deutschland (1992), *Informationen der Bundesregierung zum Thema Ausländer in Deutschland*, Bonn.

Buttlar, W. von (1980), *Ziele und Zielkonflikte der sowjetischen Deutschlandpolitik 1945–47*, Stuttgart: Klett-Cotta.

Burdick, Charles, Jacobsen, Hans-Adolf and Calleo, David (1984), *The German Problem Reconsidered*, Boulder, Colorado: Westview.

——, Jacobsen, Hans-Adolf and Kudzus, Winfried (1984), *Contemporary Germany: Politics and Culture*, Boulder, Colorado: Westview.

Cairncross, Alec (1988), 'Industrial Recovery from War: a Comparison of British and German Experience' in Birke, Adolf and Kettenacker, Lothar (eds), *Wettlauf in die Moderne*, K. G. Saur.

Carr, Jonathan (1985), *Helmut Schmidt, Helmsman of Germany*, London: Weidenfeld and Nicholson.

Childs, David (1969), *East Germany*, London: Benn.

Craig, Gordon (1983), *The Germans*, New York: Scarborough.

Dalton, Russell M. (1989), *Politics in West Germany*, Boston: Scott, Foreseman.

Davy, Richard, ed. (1992), *European Detente. A Reappraisal*, London: Sage.

Deighton, Anne (1990), *The Imposssible Peace*, Oxford: The Clarendon Press.

Dönhoff, Marion Gräfin (1963), *Die Bundesrepublik in der Ära Adenauer. Kritik und Perspektiven*, Reinbek/Hamburg: Rowohlt.

—— (1970), *Deutsche Aussenpolitik von Adenauer bis Brandt. 25 Jahre miterlebt und kommentiert*. Reinbek/Hamburg: Rowohlt.

Dokumentation der Bundesregierung zur Entführung von Hanns Martin Schleyer (1979), Munich: Goldmann.

Edinger, Lewis J. (1965), *Kurt Schumacher. A Study in Personality and Political Behaviour*, Stanford, California: Stanford University Press.

—— (1986), *West German Politics*, New York: Columbia University Press..

Ehmke, Horst (1994), *Mittendrin. Von der Grossen Koalition zur deutschen Einheit*, Berlin: Rowohlt.

Erickson, John (1985), *The Road to Berlin, Stalin's War With Germany* Volume 2, London: Panther.

Erhard, Ludwig (1963), *The Economics of Success*, Princeton, NJ: Princeton University Press.

Evans, Richard J. (1989), *In Hitler's Shadow. West German Historians and the attempt to escape from the Nazi Past*, London: I. B. Tauris.

Evans, Ruth, ed. and tr. (1979), *Mathilde Wolff-Mönckeberg: On the*

Other Side. To my Children: From Germany 1940–45, London: May-flower.

Flick, Jürgen, *Diaries*, privately published in Bremen by Arend Vollers.

Flood, Charles Bracelen (1989), *Hitler, the Path to Power*, London: London.

Foschepoth, Josef and Steininger, Rolf, hrsg (1985), *Die britische Deutschland – und Bestazungspolitik*, Paderborn: Schöningh.

Frederik, Hans (1972), *Gezeichnet vom Zwielicht seiner Zeit*, Munich: Verlag Politisches Archiv.

Fricke, Karl Wilhlem (1988), *Zur Menschen und Grundrechtssituation in der DDR*, 2nd edn, Cologne: Verlag Wissenschaft und Politik.

—— (1988), *Die DDR Staatssicherheit*, 3rd edn, Cologne: Verlag Wissenschaft und Politik.

Friedrich Ebert Stiftung, hrsg (1988), *Kurt Schumacher als deutscher und Europäischer Sozialist*, Bonn: Friedrich Ebert Stiftung.

Garton Ash, Timothy (1993), *In Europe's Name: Germany and the Divided Continent*, London: Jonathan Cape.

Gaskin, Hilary (1990), *Eyewitness at Nuremberg*, London: Arms and Armour.

Gellately, Robert (1990), *The Gestapo and German Society: Enforcing Racial Policy*, Oxford: Clarendon Press.

Genscher, Hans-Dietrich (1976), *Aussenpolitik im Dienste von Sicherheit und Freiheit*, Stuttgart: Verlag Bonn Aktuell.

—— (1991), *Unterwegs zur Einheit. Reden und Dokumente aus bewegter Zeit*, Berlin: Siedler.

Gesamtdeutsches Institut, Bonn (1988), *Deutschland 1945: Vereinbarungen der Siegermächte. 5. Ausgabe, November.*

Gimbel, John (1976), *The Origins of the Marshall Plan*, Stanford California: Stanford University Press.

Glaser, Hermann (1978), *The Cultural Roots of National Socialism*, London: Croom Helm.

Glees, Anthony (1993), 'The Germans and the British: from enemies to partners' in C. Søe and D. Verheyen (eds), *Germany and its Neighbors*, Boulder, Colorado: Westview Press.

Gorbachev, Mikhail (1995), *Erinnerungen*, Berlin: Siedler.

Gosewinkel, Dieter (1991), *Adolf Arndt. Die Wiederbegründung des Rechtsstaats aus dem Geist der Sozialdemokratie*, Bonn: Verlag JHW Dietz Nachf.

Greifenhagen, Martin and Sylvia (1974), *Ein schwieriges Vaterland. Zur politischen Kultur Deutschlands*, Munich: List.

Griffith, William E. (1978), *The Ostpolitik of the Federal Republic of Germany*, Cambridge, Massachusetts: MIT Press.

Grosser, Alfred (1974), *Germany in Our Time*, London: Pelican.

—— (1982), *The Western Alliance: European-American Relations since 1945*, New York: Viking.

—— (1985), *Das Deutschland im Westen. Eine Bilanz nach 40 Jahren*, Muenchen: Hanser

Gurland, A. R. L. (1980), *Die CDU/CSU: Ursprünge und Entwicklung bis 1953*, Frankfurt am Main: Europäische Verlagsanstalt.

Hallett, G. (1991), 'West Germany' (Chapter Five) in *Governments and Economies in the Post-War World*, A. Graham (ed.), London: Routledge.

Hanrieder, Wolfram F. (1989), *Germany, America, Europe: Forty years of German Foreign Policy*, New Haven and London: Yale University Press.

Hardach, Karl (1980), *The Political Economy of Germany in the 20th Century*, Berkeley, California: Berkeley University Press.

Heidenheimer, Arnold J. (1960), *Adenauer and the CDU. The Rise of the Leader and the Integration of the Party*, The Hague: Martinus Nijhoff.

Heidenheimer, Arnold J. (1975), *The Governments of Germany*, 4th edn, New York: Crowell.

Heisenberg, Wolfgang, ed. (1991), *German Unification in European Perspective*, London: Brassey's.

Herz, John H. (1972), *The Government of Germany*, 2nd edn, New York: Harcourt Brace Jovanovich.

Hitler, Adolf (1943), *Mein Kampf*, Münich: Eher.

Jaspers, K. (1967), *The Future of Germany*, (*Wohin treibt die Bundesrepublik*) tr. and ed. by E. B. Ashton, with a foreword by Hannah Arendt, Chicago: University of Chicago Press.

Jeffery, Charlie and Savigear (1991), *German Federalism Today*, Leicester: Leicester University Press.

Katzenstein, Peter (1987), *Policy and Politics in West Germany: the growth of a semi-sovereign state*, Philadelphia: Temple University Press.

Kershaw, Ian (1983), *Popular Opinion and Political Dissent in the Third Reich, Bavaria, 1933–45*, Oxford: The Clarendon Press.

—— (1987), *The Hitler Myth: Image and Reality in the Third Reich*, Oxford: The Clarendon Press.

—— (1992), *Germany's Present, Germany's Past*, London: University of London.

Kettenacker, Lothar (1989), *Krieg zur Friedenssicherung*, Göttingen: Vandehoeck und Ruprecht.

Kielinger, Thomas (1982), *Im Sog der Freiheit*, Bonn: Bouvier.

Klotzbach, Kurt (1982), *Der Weg zur Staatspartei: Programmatik praktische Politik und Organisation der deutschen Sozialdemokratie*

1945 bis 1965, Berlin/Bonn: Dietz.

Koch, H. W. (1989), *In the Name of the Volk*, London: I.B. Tauris.

Kleinmann, Hans-Otto (1993), *Geschichte der CDU*, Stuttgart: Deutsche Verlags-Anstalt.

Kramer, A. (1991), *The West German Economy, 1945–55*, Oxford: Berg.

Krause-Burger, Sibylle (1980), *Helmut Schmidt. Aus der Nähe gesehen*, Düsseldorf: Econ.

Krausnick, H. and Wilhelm, H.-H. (1981), *Die Truppe des Weltanschauungskrieges*, Stuttgart: Deutsche Verlags Anstalt.

Krieger, Wolfgang (1987), *General Lucius D Clay und die amerikanische Deutschlandpolitik, 1945–49*, Stuttgart: Klett-Cotta.

Kuby, Erich, hrsg (1962), *Querschnitt durch den Spiegel*, Hamburg: Spiegel Verlag.

Kuentzel, Mathias (1995), *Bonn and the Bomb*, London: Pluto.

Lohmann, Hans-Martin (1994), *Extremismus der Mitte. Vom rechten Verständnis deutscher Nation*, Frankfurt: Fischer.

Löwenthal, Richard (1974), 'Vom Klatem Krieg zur Ostpolitik' in Löwenthal, Richard and Schwarz, Hans-Peter, (eds), *Die Zweite Republik. 25 Jahre Bundesrepublik Deutschland – eine Bilanz*, Stuttgart: Seewald.

Marsh, David (1989), *The Germans. Rich, bothered and divided*, London: Century.

Marshall, Barbara (1988), *The Origins of Post-War German Politics*, London: Croom Helm

Maser, Werner (1984), *Deutschland Traum oder Trauma. Kein Requiem*, Munich: Droemersche Verlagsanstalt.

Mayer, Hans (1982), *Ein Deutscher auf Widerruf*, Frankfurt: Suhrkamp.

—— (1991), *Der Turm von Babel: Erinnerung an eine deutsche demokratische Republik*, Frankfurt: Suhrkamp.

Merkl, Peter (1974), *German Foreign Policies, West and East on the threshhold of a new era*, California: Santa Barbara University Press.

Merritt, A. J. and R. L. eds (1970), *Public Opinion in Occupied Germany*, Urbana, Illinois: University of Illinois Press.

Miller, Susanne (1975), *Die SPD vor und nach Godesberg*, Bonn: Verlag Neue Gesellschaft.

Milward, Alan S. (1992), *The Reconstruction of Western Europe 1945–51*, London: Routledge.

Mitscherlich, Alexander and Margarete (1977), *Die Unfähigkeit zu Trauern*, 2nd edn, München: Piper.

Moersch, Karl (1978), *Kursrevision. Deutsche Politik nach Adenauer*, Frankfurt: Societäts Verlag.

Mommsen, Hans (1986), 'Anti-Jewish Policies' in Hedley Bull, (ed.), *The Challenge of the Third Reich*, Oxford: The Clarendon Press.

Morgan, Roger (1974), *The United States and West Germany, 1945–1973*, Oxford: Oxford University Press for the Royal Institute of International Affairs.

Nicholls, A. J. (1994), *Freedom with Responsibility. The Social Market Economy in Germany, 1918–1963*, Oxford: The Clarendon Press.

Nolte, Ernst (1969), *The Three Faces of Fascism*, translated by Leila Vennewitz, New York: New American Library.

Oppen, Beate Ruhm von (1955), *Documents on Germany under Occupation, 1945–54*, Oxford: The Clarendon Press.

Osterheld, Horst (1986), *'Ich gehe nicht leichten Herzens. . .' Adenauers letzte Kanzlerjahre*. Ein dokumentarischer Bericht, Mainz: Grünewald.

Ott, Erich (1978), *Die Wirtschaftskonzeption der SPD Nach 1945*, Verlag Arbeiterbewegung und Gesellschaftswissenschaft, Marburg.

Overy, Richard (1994), *War and Economy in the Third Reich*, Oxford: The Clarendon Press.

Padgett, Stephen and Tony Burkitt (1987), *Political Parties and Elections in West Germany: the Search for a new Stability*, London: Hurst.

—— ed. (1994), *Adenauer to Kohl: the Development of the German Chancellorship*, London: Hurst.

Papadakis, E. (1984), *The Green Movement in Germany*, London: Croom Helm.

Peterson, Edward N. (1978), *The American Occupation of Germany*, Detroit, Michigan: Wayne State University Press.

Peukert, Detlev (1993), *Inside the Nazi Germany. Conformity, opposition and racism in everyday life*, translated by Richard Deveson, Harmondsworth: Penguin.

Plfüger, Friedbert (1990), *Richard von Weizsäcker. Ein Porträt aus der Nähe*, Stuttgart: Deutsche Verlags-Anstalt.

Poppinga, Anneliese (1987), *Konrad Adenauer. Eine Chronik in Daten, Zitaten und Bildern*, Bergisch Gladbach: Lübbe.

Posner, Gerald (1992), *Hitler's Children*, London: Mandarin.

Piper, Serie (1987), 'Historikerstreit' *Die Dokumentation der Kontroverse um die Einzigartigkeit der nationalsozialistischen Judenvernichtung*, Band 816, 2 edn, München.

Prittie, Terence (1972), *Adenauer. A Study in Fortitude*, London: Tom Stacey.

—— (1974), *Willy Brandt, Portrait of a Statesman*, London: Weidenfeld and Nicholson.

Radice, Giles (1995), *The New Germans*, London: Michael Joseph.

Reusch, Ulrich (1985), *Deutsches Berufsbeamtentum und Britische Besatzung, 1943–47*, Stuttgart: Klett-Cotta.

Rudolph, Hagen (1979), *Die verpassten Chancen. Die vergessene Geschichte der Bundesrepublik*, Hamburg: Stern Verlag.

Ryan, Cornelius (1966), *The Last Battle*, London: Collins.

Scheel, Walter, hrsg (1979), *Nach Dreissig Jahren*, Stuttgart: Klett-Cotta.

Schmid, Carlo (1979), *Erinnerungen*, Bern/Munich: Scherz.

Schmidt, Helmut (1967), *Beiträge*, Stuttgart: Seewald.

—— (1970), *Strategie des Gleichgewichts. Deutsche Friedenspolitik und die Westmächte*, 5th edn, Stuttgart: Seewald.

—— (1976), *Als Christ in der politischen Entscheidung*, Gütersloh: Gerd Mohn.

—— (1979), *Der Kurs heisst Frieden*, Düsseldorf: Econ.

—— (1987), *Menschen und Mächte*, Berlin: Siedler.

Schneider, Eberhard (1978), *The German Democratic Republic*, translated by H. Andomeit and R. Clark, London: Hurst.

Schwarz, Hans-Peter (1981), *Die Ära Adenauer, 1949–57*, Stuttgart: Deutsche Verlags-Anstalt.

—— (1986), *Adenauer. Der Aufstieg: 1976–1952*, Stuttgart: Deutsche Verlags-Anstalt.

—— (1989), ed. *Akten zur auswärtigen Politik der Bundesrepublik Deutschland*. Hrsg im Auftrag des Auswärtigen Amtes, Vol. 1, *Adenauer und die hohen Kommisare 1949–51*, Munich: Oldenboug.

—— (1991), *Adenauer. Der Staatsmann: 1952–67*, Stuttgart: Deutsche Verlags-Anstalt.

—— (1994), *Die Zentralmacht Europas*, Berlin: Siedler.

Schweitzer, C. C. *et al.*, eds (1984), *Politics and Government in the Federal Republic of Germany*, Basic Documents, Leamington Spa: Berg

Shlaes, Amity (1989), *Germany: The Empire Within*, London: Jonathan Cape.

Silbermann, Alphons (1982), *Sind Wir Antisemiten? Ausmass und Wirkung eines sozialen Vorurteils in der Bundesrepublik Deutsch-land*, Cologne: Verlag Wissenschaft und Politik.

Smith, Gordon and Paterson, William E. (1981), *The West German Model: Per-spectives on a stable state*, London: Frank Cass.

—— and Döring, Herbert (1982), *Party Government and Political Culture in Western Germany*, London: Macmillan.

——, Paterson, William E. and Merkl, Peter H. (1989), *Developments in West German Politics*, London: London.

—— (1990), *Democracy in Western Germany. Parties and Politics in the Federal Republic*, 3rd edn, Aldershot: Gower.

Smyser, W. (1992), *The Economy of United Germany: Colossus at the Crossroads*, London: Hurst.

Speer, Albert (1969), *Erinnerungen*, Frankfurt: Ullstein.

Steele, Jonathan (1977), *Socialism with a Human Face. The state that came in from the cold*, London: Jonathan Cape.

Steininger, Rolf (1983), *Deutsche Geschichte 1945–1961. Darstellung und Dokumente in zwei Bänden*, Frankfurt: Fischer.

Stöss, Richard (1991), *Politics Against Democracy: Right Wing Extremism in West Germany*, New York/Oxford: Berg.

Stöss, Richard (1991), *Politics Against Democracy: Right Wing Extremism in West Germany*, New York/Oxford: Berg.

Stolper, G. (1967), *The Germany Economy, 1870 to the Present*, London.

Strauss, Franz Josef (1989), *Die Erinnerungen*, Berlin: Siedler.

Sturm, Roland (1991), 'Die Zukunft des deutschen Foederalismus' in Liebert, U. and Merkel, W. (eds), *Die Politik zur deutschen Einheit*, Opladen: Leske.

Tauber, Kurt P. (1967), *Beyond Eagle and Swastika. German Nationalism since 1945*, 2 vols Middletown, Connecticut: Wesleyan University Press.

Thatcher, Margaret (1994), *The Downing Street Years*, London: Harper-Collins.

Trevor Roper, H. R., ed. (1953), *Hitler's Table Talk*, London: Weidenfeld and Nicholson.

Tusa, Ann and John (1988), *The Berlin Blockade*, London: Hodder and Stoughton.

Vansittart, Lord (1941), *Black Record*, London: Hamilton.

Verfassungsausschuss der Ministerpräsidenten-Konferenz der westlichen Besatzungszonen, *Verfassungskonvent auf Herrenchiemsee* vom 10. bis 23. 'August 1948. Protokolle der Sitzungen des Unterschusses 1'. Grundsatzfragen.

Voss, Rüdiger von, hrsg (1978), *Von der Legitimation der Gewalt. Widerstand und Terrorismus*, Stuttgart: Rororo.

Wagenfuhr, R. (1963), *Die deutsche Industrie im Kriege 1939–45*, Berlin: Duncker und Humboldt.

Weber, Hermann (1985), *Geschichte der DDR*, Munchen: DTV.

Weidenfeld, Werner and Korte, Karl-Rudolf (1993), *Handbuch zur deutschen Einheit, Bundeszentrale für Politische Bildung*, Bonn.

Weilemann, Peter R. ed. (1985), *Aspects of the German Question*, Sankt Augustin: Konrad Adenauer Foundation Sozialwissenschaftliches Forschungsinstitut.

Weizsäcker, Richard von (1992), *Im Gespräch mit Gunter Hofmann und Werner A Perger*, Frankfurt: Eichborn.

Weizsäcker, Carl Friedrich von (1977), *Wege in der Gefahr. Eine Studie über Wirtschaft, Gesellschaft und Kriegsverhütung*, 5th edn, Münich: Hanser.

Wessels, W. and Regelsberger, E. ed. (1988), *The Federal Republic of Germany and the European Community and Beyond*, Bonn: Europa.

Wighton, Charles (1963), *Adenauer, Democratic Dictator: a critical biography*, London: Muller.

Willis, F. Roy (1962), *The French in Germany, 1945–49*, Stanford: Stanford University Press.

Wolffsohn, Michael (1995), *Verwirrtes Deutschland? Provokative Zwischenrufe eines deutschjüdischen Patrioten*, Frankfurt am Main: Ullstein.

Wurm, Clemens, ed. (1995), *Western Europe and Germany. The Beginnings of European Integration, 1945–1960*, Oxford: Berg.

Zelikov, Philip and Rice, Condolezza (1995), *Germany Unified and Europe Transformed*, London: Harvard University Press.

Ziemke, E. F. (1971), *Stalingrad to Berlin: the German Defeat in the East, 1942–45*, Washington, DC: Office of the Chief of Military History US Army (repr.).

Zitelmann, Rainer, Weissmann, Karlheinz and Grossheim, Michael (1993), *Westbindung. Chancen und Risiken für Deutschland*, Frankfurt am Main, Berlin: Propyläen.

Articles

Baum, Walter, Deuerlein, Ernst, Gimbel, John and Pollock, James, 'Zusammenbruch und Neubeginn. Zum 8. Mai 1945', *Aus Politik und Zeitgeschichte*, B 18/65.

FCO Historical Branch, *Occasional Papers* No. 3, November 1989.

Glees, Anthony 'The Diplomacy of Anglo-German Relations: A Study of the ERM crisis of September 1992' in *German Politics*, Vol. 3, No. 1, April 1994, pp 75–90.

Goldberger, Bruce N., 'Why Europe should not fear the Germans' in *German Politics*, Vol. 2, No. 2 (August 1993), p. 114.

Kohl, Helmut, 'United Germany in a uniting Europe' speech at St Antony's College, Oxford, 11 November 1992, published by the Konrad Adenauer Foundation.

Lamers, Karl, 'Germany's responsibilities and interests in the field of foreign policy', a paper presented to the conference of the Executive Committee of the CDU/CSU parliamentary party in the Bundestag on 23–24 August 1993.

Mearsheimer, John J. 'Back to the Future: Instability in Europe after the cold war' in *International Security*, Vol. 15, No. 1 (1990).

Pond, Elizabeth, 'Germany in the new Europe' *Foreign Affairs*, Vol. 71, No. 2 (1992).

Ridley, Nicholas, quoted in *The Spectator*, 14 July 1990, p. 8.

Spence, David, 'Enlargement without Accession: the EC's Response to German Unification' in London, Royal Institute of International Affairs, Discussion Paper, no. 36.

Stöss, Richard, 'The Problem of Right Wing extremism in West Germany' in *West European Politics*, Vol. 11, No. 2 April 1988.

Veen, H. J., Lepszy, N. and Mnich, P. 'Die Republikaner-Partei zu Beginn der 90er Jahre', *KAS Interne Studien*, Nr 14/1991–1992.

Index

Index

Suggestions for Further Reading

Introduction

Baring, Arnulf, ed. (1994) *Germany's New Position in Europe, Problems and Perspectives*, Oxford: Berg.

Bark, Dennis L. and Gress, David (1989), *A History of West Germany* Volume One. *From Shadow to Substance 1945–63* Volume Two. *Democracy and its Discontents 1963–68*, Oxford: Basil Blackwell.

Blackbourn, D. and Eley G. (1985), *The Peculiarities of German History*, Oxford: Oxford University Press.

Hanrieder, Wolfram F. (1989), *Germany, America, Europe: Forty years of German Foreign Policy*, New Haven and London: Yale University Press.

Chapter 1

Browning, Christopher (1985), *Fateful Months; Essays on the Emergence of the Final Solution*, New York: Holmes and Meier.

Evans, Richard J. (1989), *In Hitler's Shadow. West German Historians and the attempt to escape from the Nazi Past*, London: I. B. Tauris.

Peukert, Detlev (1993), *Inside the Nazi Germany. Conformity, opposition and racism in everyday life*, translated by Richard Deveson, Harmondsworth: Penguin.

Trevor Roper, H. R., ed. (1953), *Hitler's Table Talk*, London: Weiden-feld and Nicholson.

Chapter 2

Annan, Noel (1995), *Changing Enemies. The Defeat and Regeneration of Germany*, London: HarperCollins.

Balfour, Michael (1992) *Germany. The Tides of Power*, London: Routledge.

Deighton, Anne (1990), *The Imposssible Peace*, Oxford: The Clarendon Press.

Marshall, Barbara (1988), *The Origins of Post-War German Politics*, London: Croom Helm

Chapter 3

Adenauer, Konrad (1983), *Briefe 1945–47. Rhöndorfer Ausgabe.* Bearbeitet von Hans Peter Mensing, Stuttgart: Siedler Verlag.

Albrecht, Willy hrsg (1985), *Kurt Schumacher: Reden-Schriften-Korrespondenzen, 1945–52*, Bonn: Dietz.

Edinger, Lewis J. (1965), *Kurt Schumacher. A Study in Personality and Political Behaviour*, Stanford, California: Stanford University Press.

Schwarz, Hans-Peter (1989), ed. *Akten zur auswärtigen Politik der Bundesrepublik Deutschland.* Hrsg im Auftrag des Auswärtigen Amtes, Vol. 1, *Adenauer und die hohen Kommisare 1949–51*, Munich: Oldenboug.

Chapter 4

Dönhoff, Marion Gräfin (1970), *Deutsche Aussenpolitik von Adenauer bis Brandt. 25 Jahre miterlebt und kommentiert.* Reinbek/Hamburg: Rowohlt.

Morgan, Roger (1974), *The United States and West Germany, 1945–1973*, Oxford: Oxford University Press for the Royal Institute of International Affairs.

Schwarz, Hans-Peter (1989), ed. *Akten zur auswärtigen Politik der Bundesrepublik Deutschland.* Hrsg im Auftrag des Auswärtigen Amtes, Vol. 1, *Adenauer und die hohen Kommisare 1949–51*, Munich: Oldenboug.

Schwarz, Hans-Peter (1991), *Adenauer. Der Staatsmann: 1952–67*, Stuttgart: Deutsche Verlags-Anstalt.

Chapter 5

Adenauer, Konrad (1967), *Erinnerungen, 1955–59*, Stuttgart: Deutsche Verlags-Anstalt.
Binder, David (1975), *The Other German: Willy Brandt's Life and Times*, Washington DC: New Republic.
Nicholls, A. J. (1994), *Freedom with Responsibility. The Social Market Economy in Germany, 1918–1963*, Oxford: The Clarendon Press.
Prittie, Terence (1972), *Adenauer. A Study in Fortitude*, London: Tom Stacey.

Chapter 6

Aust, Stefan (1987), *The Baader Meinhof Group*, London: The Bodley Head.
Baker, Kendall L., Dalton, Russell J. and Hildebrandt, Kai (1981), *Germany Transformed. Political Culture and the New Politics*, London: Harvard University Press.
Garton Ash, Timothy (1993), *In Europe's Name: Germany and the Divided Continent*, London: Jonathan Cape.
Prittie, Terence (1974), *Willy Brandt, Portrait of a Statesman*, London: Weidenfeld and Nicholson.

Chapter 7

Brandt, Willy (1971) *Peace. Writings and speeches of the Nobel Prize Winner, 1971*, Bonn: Dietz.
Brandt, Willy (1990), *Erinnerungen*, 4th edn, Frankfurt: Propyläen.
Griffith, William E. (1978), *The Ostpolitik of the Federal Republic of Germany*, Cambridge, Massachusetts: MIT Press.
Hanrieder, Wolfram F. (1989), *Germany, America, Europe: Forty years of German Foreign Policy*, New Haven and London: Yale University Press.

Chapter 8

Carr, Jonathan (1985), *Helmut Schmidt, Helmsman of Germany*, London: Weidenfeld and Nicholson.
Genscher, Hans-Dietrich (1976), *Aussenpolitik im Dienste von Sicherheit und Freiheit*, Stuttgart: Verlag Bonn Aktuell.
Krause-Burger, Sibylle (1980), *Helmut Schmidt. Aus der Nähe gesehen*, Düsseldorf: Econ.
Schmidt, Helmut (1979), *Der Kurs heisst Frieden*, Düsseldorf: Econ.

Chapter 9

Fricke, Karl Wilhlem (1988), *Zur Menschen und Grundrechtssituation in der DDR*, 2nd edn, Cologne: Verlag Wissenschaft und Politik.
Marsh, David (1989), *The Germans. Rich, bothered and divided*, London: Century.
Steele, Jonathan (1977), *Socialism with a Human Face. The state that came in from the cold*, London: Jonathan Cape.
Thatcher, Margaret (1994), *The Downing Street Years*, London: Harper-Collins.

Chapter 10

Glees, Anthony (1993), 'The Germans and the British: from enemies to partners' in C. Søe and D. Verheyen (eds), *Germany and its Neighbors*, Boulder, Colorado: Westview Press.
Gorbachev, Mikhail (1995), *Erinnerungen*, Berlin: Siedler.
Stöss, Richard (1991), *Politics Against Democracy: Right Wing Ex-tremism in West Germany*, New York/Oxford: Berg.
Zelikov, Philip and Rice, Condolezza (1995), *Germany Unified and Europe Transformed*, London: Harvard University Press.